Contributions to Management Science

The series *Contributions to Management Science* contains research publications in all fields of business and management science. These publications are primarily monographs and multiple author works containing new research results, and also feature selected conference-based publications are also considered. The focus of the series lies in presenting the development of latest theoretical and empirical research across different viewpoints.

This book series is indexed in Scopus.

More information about this series at http://www.springer.com/series/1505

Marc Grau Grau • Mireia las Heras Maestro •
Hannah Riley Bowles
Editors

Engaged Fatherhood for Men, Families and Gender Equality

Healthcare, Social Policy, and Work Perspectives

Editors
Marc Grau Grau
Women and Public Policy Program
Harvard Kennedy School
Cambridge, MA, USA

Mireia las Heras Maestro
IESE Business School
University of Navarra
Barcelona, Spain

Joaquim Molins Figueras Childcare
and Family Policies Chair
Universitat Internacional de Catalunya
Barcelona, Spain

Hannah Riley Bowles
HKS Women and Public Policy Program
Harvard Kennedy School (HKS)
Cambridge, Massachusetts, USA

ISSN 1431-1941 ISSN 2197-716X (electronic)
Contributions to Management Science
ISBN 978-3-030-75647-5 ISBN 978-3-030-75645-1 (eBook)
https://doi.org/10.1007/978-3-030-75645-1

© The Editor(s) (if applicable) and The Author(s) 2022. This book is an open access publication.
Open Access This book is licensed under the terms of the Creative Commons Attribution 4.0 International License (http://creativecommons.org/licenses/by/4.0/), which permits use, sharing, adaptation, distribution and reproduction in any medium or format, as long as you give appropriate credit to the original author(s) and the source, provide a link to the Creative Commons license and indicate if changes were made.
The images or other third party material in this book are included in the book's Creative Commons license, unless indicated otherwise in a credit line to the material. If material is not included in the book's Creative Commons license and your intended use is not permitted by statutory regulation or exceeds the permitted use, you will need to obtain permission directly from the copyright holder.
The use of general descriptive names, registered names, trademarks, service marks, etc. in this publication does not imply, even in the absence of a specific statement, that such names are exempt from the relevant protective laws and regulations and therefore free for general use.
The publisher, the authors, and the editors are safe to assume that the advice and information in this book are believed to be true and accurate at the date of publication. Neither the publisher nor the authors or the editors give a warranty, expressed or implied, with respect to the material contained herein or for any errors or omissions that may have been made. The publisher remains neutral with regard to jurisdictional claims in published maps and institutional affiliations.

This Springer imprint is published by the registered company Springer Nature Switzerland AG.
The registered company address is: Gewerbestrasse 11, 6330 Cham, Switzerland

Preface

It is with great excitement that I write this preface, mostly because the topic is of utmost relevance: fatherhood, and how to facilitate it in organizations and countries. This book presents medical evidence of the benefits of responsible, committed fatherhood to children; to fathers; and to families, which means that is of much relevance also for society and organizations.

Family values are the strong base upon which society is based. The industrial revolution installed the breadwinner-homemaker system. Ever since, the role of the father as caring educator and role model has been devaluated. In the breadwinner-homemaker system, men were the sole family wage earners and women were full-time homemakers, with no external or paid jobs. Thus, children and the home were entrusted to women, and men had no responsibility over them. Today, there are few, if any, societies in which the breadwinner-homemaker model is still prevalent. Yet, the role of the father has not yet been restored to its full essence. In practice, fatherhood receives very little recognition. Institutions, organizations, and society do not facilitate men to fully develop in their roles as fathers. In this book, we aim to help in this restoration. We do so taking an interdisciplinary approach.

Social Trends Institute (STI) has made this book possible. STI provided funds, but even more importantly, they provided help and guidance as we were delineating the objectives of, and managing invitations to participate in, the meeting. Our special thanks go to Tracey O'Donnell, who has been, behind the scenes, the power making things happen. Also, our recognition to Carlos Cavallé, the founder of STI, who inspired us to go beyond our own dreams for the project. We would like to extend our gratitude to the Women and Public Policy Program (WAPPP) at the Harvard Kennedy School. They graciously hosted the main meeting in their facilities back in 2018. Within the WAPPP, our recognition to Hannah Riley Bowles, one of the co-editors of the book, who has worked tirelessly to make this a success for all involved: researchers, institutions, and potential audience as well.

I also thank IESE and the research center I have the privilege to direct, the International Center for Work-Family (ICWF). When Marc Grau, a research fellow at WAPPP, offered us the opportunity to contribute to the project it was a no-brainer for many reasons. First, it is always a pleasure working with Marc Grau. He worked for the ICWF for over 5 years and has been on the organizing committee of our biannual International Work Family Conference for the last five editions. Marc has always contributed his best with a laudable attitude and work ethic. Second, the topic is of much relevance for me as a person, and as a researcher and business professor.

Personally, I have had the joy of having had a loving father. He was very much involved in the family and always trusted my capability and supported my desire to study Engineering, do an MBA, and pursue a doctorate in the USA, very far away from home. Having had such experience, I desire that many people share in it. As a researcher, I study how experiences bidirectionally spillover from home to work, and how they crossover from one spouse to another. Thus, I find that fatherhood is one of the understudied topics that urgently calls for attention.

This book contributes to understanding fatherhood, its benefits, and its challenges, offering 17 chapters divided mainly in three parts: Health and Wellbeing, Social Policy, and Work and Organizations. These chapters offer a nice mix of qualitative, quantitative, and reviews methods that help readers to get a nuanced and rich understanding of the topic. These 17 chapters present data that represent many countries in the world. In the Americas: the USA, Argentina, Chile, Colombia, El Salvador, Guatemala, Mexico, and the Dominican Republic; in Asia: Korea; in Europe: France, Norway, Romania, Scotland, and Spain; in Oceania: Australia; and in Africa: South Africa.

It is our firm believe that we should no longer hold to the myth of the separate worlds. Technology has erased barriers between work and non-work. Globalization demands that services are offered 24/7. Labor markets are more and more inclusive of women and people with various competencies and capabilities. The myth of separate worlds has long disappeared.

The terrible pandemic that all countries experienced in 2020 has forced most people around the world to work from home. They have worked from home while the whole family was there: either attending classes, being quarantined, or working. This has only been a clear example of the current reality in which we live in: work and non-work are no longer separate. Also, the ideal worker, a male who had a person at home who would care for the family, long ago died. The new ideal worker has to emerge, and this ideal will be, either male or female, one who has multiple responsibilities, interests, and needs. To achieve a more fair, inclusive world, all those interests, needs, and personal situations should be welcomed and facilitated. And one notable responsibility is fatherhood. It is time to restore it to its original value. This book aims to contribute to it.

Barcelona, Spain   Mireia las Heras Maestro

Contents

Launching a Cross-disciplinary and Cross-national Conversation on Engaged Fatherhood 1
Marc Grau Grau and Hannah Riley Bowles

Part I Health and Wellbeing

The Role of Fathers in Child and Family Health 15
Michael W. Yogman and Amelia M. Eppel

The Impact of Father's Health on Reproductive and Infant Health and Development 31
Milton Kotelchuck

The Impact of Fatherhood on Men's Health and Development 63
Milton Kotelchuck

Steps in Developing a Public Health Surveillance System for Fathers ... 93
Clarissa D. Simon and Craig F. Garfield

Fatherhood and Reproductive Health in the Antenatal Period: From Men's Voices to Clinical Practice 111
Raymond A. Levy and Milton Kotelchuck

Part II Social Policy

Fathers and Family Leave Policies: What Public Policy Can Do to Support Families 141
Alison Koslowski and Margaret O'Brien

Individual Parental Leave for Fathers: Promoting Gender Equality in Norway 153
Elin Kvande

How Do Men Talk about Taking Parental Leave? Evidence from South Korea, Spain, and the U.S. 165
Xiana Bueno and Eunsil Oh

Part III Work & Organizations

Impossible Standards and Unlikely Trade-Offs: Can Fathers be Competent Parents and Professionals? 183
Jamie J. Ladge and Beth K. Humberd

The New Dad: The Career-Caregiving Conundrum 197
Brad Harrington

French Fathers in Work Organizations: Navigating Work-Life Balance Challenges 213
Sabrina Tanquerel

'It Would Be Silly to Stop Now and Go Part-Time': Fathers and Flexible Working Arrangements in Australia 231
Ashlee Borgkvist

Small Changes that Make a Great Difference: Reading, Playing and Eating with your Children and the Facilitating Role of Managers in Latin America 245
María José Bosch and Mireia Las Heras

Fatherhood Among Marginalised Work-Seeking Men in South Africa 265
Mandisa Malinga and Kopano Ratele

The Role of Love and Children's Agency in Improving Fathers' Wellbeing 279
Alexandra Macht

Part IV Conclusion and Principles for Promoting Gender Equity

Reducing Barriers to Engaged Fatherhood: Three Principles for Promoting Gender Equity in Parenting 299
Hannah Riley Bowles, Milton Kotelchuck, and Marc Grau Grau

Contributors

Ashlee Borgkvist Safe Relationships and Communities Research Group, The University of South Australia, Adelaide, SA, Australia

María José Bosch ESE Business School, Universidad de los Andes, Las Condes, Chile

Xiana Bueno Centre d'Estudis Demogràfics, Universitat Autònoma de Barcelona, Barcelona, Spain

Amelia M. Eppel McGill University, Montreal, QC, Canada

Craig F. Garfield Ann & Robert H. Lurie Children's Hospital of Chicago and Northwestern University Feinberg School of Medicine, Chicago, IL, USA

Marc Grau Grau Women and Public Policy Program, Harvard Kennedy School, Cambridge, MA, USA

Joaquim Molins Figueras Childcare and Family Policies Chair, Universitat Internacional de Catalunya, Barcelona, Spain

Brad Harrington Boston College Center for Work and Family and Carroll School of Management, Boston College, Chestnut Hill, MA, USA

Beth K. Humberd University of Massachusetts Lowell, Lowell, MA, USA

Alison Koslowski University of Edinburgh, Edinburgh, UK

Milton Kotelchuck Harvard Medical School and Massachusetts General Hospital Fatherhood Project, Boston, MA, USA

Elin Kvande Norwegian University of Science and Technology, Trondheim, Norway

Jamie J. Ladge Northeastern University, Boston, MA, USA
University of Exeter Business School, Exeter, UK

Mireia las Heras Maestro IESE Business School, University of Navarra, Barcelona, Spain

Raymond A. Levy The Fatherhood Project at Massachusetts General Hospital and Harvard Medical School, Boston, MA, USA

Alexandra Macht Independent Researcher, Bucharest, Romania

Mandisa Malinga University of Cape Town, Cape Town, South Africa

Margaret O'Brien University College London, London, UK

Eunsil Oh University of Wisconsin-Madison, Madison, WI, USA

Kopano Ratele University of South Africa, Pretoria, South Africa
South African Medical Research Council, Cape Town, South Africa

Hannah Riley Bowles Harvard Kennedy School (HKS) and HKS Women and Public Policy Program, Cambridge, MA, USA

Clarissa D. Simon Ann & Robert H. Lurie Children's Hospital of Chicago and Northwestern University Feinberg School of Medicine, Chicago, IL, USA

Sabrina Tanquerel Ecole de Management de Normandie, Campus de Caen, France

Michael W. Yogman Department of Pediatrics, Harvard Medical School, Boston, MA, USA

Launching a Cross-disciplinary and Cross-national Conversation on Engaged Fatherhood

Marc Grau Grau and Hannah Riley Bowles

1 Origins

This edited volume stems from a multi-disciplinary Experts Meeting on Fatherhood Engagement hosted by the Harvard Kennedy School's Women and Public Policy Program, funded by the Social Trends Institute (STI), and organized in collaboration with the International Center for Work and Family at the Instituto de Estudios Superiores de la Empresa (IESE) Business School. We invited experts from the healthcare, social policy, and work and organization fields because those are the professional fields that have done the most to advance scholarship and practice in relation to fatherhood engagement. The participants arrived at the meeting, not only with distinct disciplinary perspectives, but also with complementary motivations for elevating the importance of fatherhood engagement. Some arrived focused primarily on enhancing the welfare of men. Others were drawn by the importance of fatherhood engagement for the health and welfare of families and for child development. Still others joined for a conversation about work-family balance or to promote gender equality. As the meeting progressed, it was inspiring to see scholars and institutions with diverse worldviews come together so enthusiastically to support a common aim: elevating the importance of fatherhood engagement. This book is a reflection of the kaleidoscopic character of these conversations.

M. Grau Grau (✉)
Women and Public Policy Program, Harvard Kennedy School, Cambridge, MA, USA

Joaquim Molins Figueras Childcare and Family Policies Chair, Universitat Internacional de Catalunya, Barcelona, Spain
e-mail: marc_grau-grau@hks.harvard.edu

H. Riley Bowles
Women and Public Policy Program, Harvard Kennedy School, Cambridge, MA, USA

© The Authors(s) 2022
M. Grau Grau et al. (eds.), *Engaged Fatherhood for Men, Families and Gender Equality*, Contributions to Management Science,
https://doi.org/10.1007/978-3-030-75645-1_1

2 Why Focus on Fathers?

What is urgent or important about a conversation on fathers? Men, and especially working fathers, are arguably a privileged group in a world of inequality. Don't they "have it all" at home and at work? We had two driving motivations to pursue this work. First, over the past 30 years, scholars in the medical sciences, child development, and social policy have gathered an accelerating amount of evidence on the value and importance of engaged fatherhood for the health and welfare of children and families, and for men themselves. Numerous contributors to this volume have been at the leading edge of this work and are capturing growing attention. The second motivation was to elevate the importance of fatherhood engagement for the advancement of gender equality, a topic often sidelined by emphasis on increasing women's occupational attainment.

2.1 Mounting Evidence

As elaborated in the leading chapters by Yogman and Eppel and by Kotelchuck in the Health and Wellbeing section of the book, the importance of engaged fatherhood is now undismissable in ways it was not in earlier decades. A growing body of evidence demonstrates the importance of residential and non-residential fathers on families' welfare and economic wellbeing; on mothers' prenatal health and birth outcomes; on children's cognitive, psychosocial, and educational development and gender identity; and on adolescent behavioral risk reduction among other benefits (Alio et al. 2010; Cano et al. 2019; Yogman et al. 2016). Of particular significance to the development of fatherhood research has been the emergence of national and cross-national longitudinal studies on children and families that explore the contributions of fathers (e.g., Huerta et al. 2013; Nepomnyaschy and Waldfogel 2007; Petts et al. 2020). These social scientific studies have blossomed alongside a proliferation of medical scientific studies on the importance engaged parenting (National Academies of Sciences, Engineering and Medicine et al. 2016; Yogman et al. 2016).

Moreover, as discussed in the chapter on "The Impact of Fatherhood on Men's Health and Development" by Kotelchuck, the benefits of fatherhood involvement are not limited to children's and mothers' wellbeing; there is growing evidence documenting the benefits of fatherhood involvement for men themselves (Eggebeen et al. 2010; Eggebeen and Knoester 2001), ranging from better psychological and physical health outcomes to the development of new capacities as employees (Grau-Grau 2017). There are also significant strains of fatherhood for men that need to be addressed for the welfare of men and their families (Cameron et al. 2016).

In sum, it is no longer possible for evidence-based decision makers—clinicians, policy makers, or other family service providers—to responsibly ignore the significance of engaged fatherhood for the welfare of families and children and for men themselves.

2.2 Gender Equality

Another reason to elevate the importance of engaged fatherhood is to give a push forward to the revolution for gender equality—a movement that is widely perceived to have stalled (England 2010; Esping-Andersen 2009; Gerson 2010). As Goldscheider et al. (2015) have argued, the first half of the revolution toward gender equality has been focused on increasing women's participation in the public realm of paid labor. Completing the revolution will require increasing men's participation in the private realm of familial caregiving.

Women's growing participation in paid labor has been a primary factor in transforming social conceptions of fathers as "caregivers" as well as "breadwinners" (Lewis 2001). The leading chapters to the Social Policy section of the book by Koslowski and O'Brien and by Kvande provide a historical perspective on how social policies designed to support women's workforce participation and the economic welfare of families have contributed to rising rates of participation in early fatherhood.

As illustrated in Fig. 1, fathers across the globe have become more engaged in their children's lives as compared to 50 years ago. The chart plots the percentage of fathers spending at least 15 min on childcare each day, as reported by Altintas and

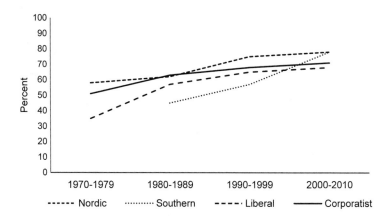

Fig. 1 Percentage of fathers spending at least 15 min on childcare each Day (1970–2010). (Source: Data reported by Altintas and Sullivan (2017; see Table 1, pg. 92) from the Multinational Time Use Study). Note: Fathers are men 20–49 years of age who are married/cohabiting and living with at least one child under the age of 5. Nordic cluster countries are Denmark, Finland, Norway and Sweden. Southern cluster countries are Italy, Spain and Israel. Liberal cluster countries are Canada, the United Kingdom, the United States and Australia. Corporatist cluster countries are France, Germany, the Netherlands and Slovenia

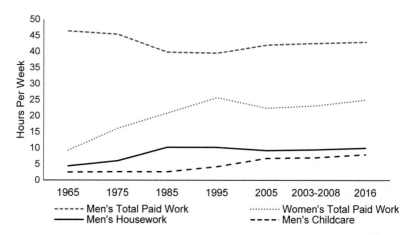

Fig. 2 Time use of mothers and fathers in the United States (hours per week) (1965–2016). (Source: Data for years 1965–2008 were reported by Bianchi [2011; see Tables 1–2, pages 27 and 29, respectively]). Data for 2016 were reported by Livingston and Parker (2019) of the Pew Research Center. Note: Age of sample is 18–64 years

Sullivan (2017) in their analysis of Multinational Time Use Survey data (1971–2010) from 15 countries. As illustrated, the Nordic countries (i.e., Denmark, Finland, Norway, Sweden) started out and surged farther ahead of other regions in the 1990s, but are now simply on par with time-use reports from the Southern region (i.e., Israel, Italy, Spain). The percentage growth in "Liberal" English-speaking (i.e., Australia, Canada, U.K., U.S.) and "Corporatist" European (i.e., France, Germany, Netherlands, Slovenia) has stagnated, but has risen from a minority to a majority of fathers.

The spreading duality of fathers (and mothers) as caregivers and breadwinners has generated new conflicts and tensions for men, especially at work. As discussed in the leading chapter of the section on Work and Organizations by Ladge and Humberd, men are experiencing increasing levels of work-family conflict. One report from United States found that the proportions of working fathers reporting work-family conflict jumped from 35% in 1977 to 60% in 2008, while for mothers the percentage experiencing work-family conflict remained more stable (41% in 1977 and 47% in 2008) (Aumann et al. 2011). Other studies report similar findings that men's sense of work-family conflict is beginning to rival or surpass women's (Eagle et al. 1997; Parasuraman and Simmers 2001), especially among fathers in dual-career couples (Higgins and Duxbury 1992). As discussed by Ladge and Humberd, one explanation for this growing work-family tension for men relative to women is that gender roles around parenting are evolving at a faster pace than employers' masculine stereotypic conception of the "ideal worker" who has no conflicting familial or household obligations (Acker 1990).

While the gendered division of household labor is undoubtedly evolving, there are signs that the rate of change in many places is stalling. Figure 2 is illustrative. It displays 50 years of data from time-use surveys of U.S. mothers and fathers of children under 18 (Bianchi 2011; Livingston and Parker 2019). The marked gains in women's labor-market participation and men's contributions to childcare and household labor between 1965 and 2005 have since largely flattened out. Despite devoting more time to their children than previous generations, fathers are still not typically the primary caregiver "on call" to deal with the vicissitudes of family life (e.g., being available at short notice for the care of sick children), leaving working mothers as the primary consumers of family-friendly social and work policies (Goldin and Mitchell 2017; Kelly et al. 2010; Mandel and Semyonov 2005). The final Work and Organization chapters of the book explore how cultural conceptions of masculinity and of fatherhood, as well as variations in the culture of work, constrain men's capacity to integrate their breadwinning and caregiving roles and identities.

2.3 Increasing Fatherhood Engagement Is a Win-Win Proposition

The participants in the Experts Meeting and contributors to this volume approach the challenge of fatherhood engagement from a "win-win" rather than zero-sum perspective. The larger objective of this volume is not to "win more" for fathers, but rather to reap the mutual gains from engaged fatherhood for families, children, and men themselves and, in the process, to advance the ideals of gender equality. In the concluding chapter, Bowles, Kotelchuck, and Grau Grau propose a set of working principles for reducing the barriers to fatherhood engagement, which were generated from this collaboration to apply across the social policy, work, and healthcare systems.

3 Fostering Cross-disciplinary Learning and Coordination

The Experts Meeting and this volume have enabled an unprecedented flow of ideas across burgeoning, but largely separate, streams of work. At the meeting, top health experts, social policy scholars, and organizational scientists from around the globe presented and discussed research on the antecedents and implications of men's engagement in fatherhood. It was an extraordinary learning opportunity, even for those who had been in the field for decades. It was particularly eye-opening to recognize the differential and common struggles across these three fields and across national cultural contexts. This volume was motivated by our enthusiasm to share our exchange of ideas and insights.

Reflecting the contributions to the Experts Meeting, the book is organized in three sections: Health and Welfare, Social Policy, and Work and Organizations. Across the sections, the chapters review evidence and case examples from more than 20 different countries representing 6 global regions. Each chapter is intentionally crafted to speak to mixed audiences in order to be useful to scholars and practitioners in different fields, as well as to families and loved ones supporting fathers and mothers in parenting roles.

3.1 Health and Wellbeing

The first section of the book is dedicated to voices of medical scholars discussing the implications of early fatherhood involvement for the health and development of children, parenting partners, and men themselves. It offers strategies for healthcare providers to support men more directly and effectively as prospective and current fathers. In spite of the growing evidence, the health community struggles to increase recognition of fathers' roles and contributions in the care of infants and children in a sector traditionally focused on the mothers as parents. Fathers currently interact with healthcare systems, albeit to a lesser extent than mothers, during the antenatal period, the birth of the child, and after the birth. However, fathers commonly feel as if they are "secondary parents" in these healthcare interactions (Steen et al. 2012).

The contributors to the Health and Wellbeing section advocate for engaging fathers preceding infants' conception through reproductive health and birthing services into the pediatricians' offices in order to enhance infant, maternal, and men's own health. They emphasize that failure to do so reinforces traditional cultural expectations of fathers rather than leading the charge for gender role changes. It also fails to recognize that the perinatal period is a demanding developmental period for fathers, who too experience important physical, psychological, and social changes.

In the chapter on "The Role of Fathers in Child and Family Health", Yogman and Eppel present the impact of fatherhood across four stages of childhood: prenatal, infancy, childhood, and adolescence. Their review advocates for policies enhancing father involvement, accessible and more extensive paternity leave, and increased attention to paternal postpartum depression by the medical community. In his chapter on "The Impact of Father's Health on Reproductive and Infant Health and Development", Kotelchuck articulates eight direct and indirect pathways by which fathers' perinatal health and health-related behavior impact reproductive and infant health. His review organizes a heretofore scattered scientific knowledge base and pulls back the developmental time frame for fathers' reproductive health importance into the antenatal pre-birth period. In his second chapter on "The Impact of Fatherhood on Men's Health and Development", which is deeply interrelated with his prior chapter on "The Impact of Father's Health on Reproductive and Infant Health and Development", Kotelchuck explores the bidirectional life-course impact of fatherhood on men's physical, mental, social and developmental health in the perinatal period. This represents a new focus for the Maternal Child Health (MCH) field, especially in the perinatal time period, a time not usually thought of as impacting men's health. In their chapter on "Steps in Developing a Public Health Surveillance System for Fathers", Simon and Garfield describe efforts to establish a new public health surveillance system for fathers in the United States. The ultimate goal of this research is to collect and assess fathers' health and parenting experiences in the perinatal period, in order to support the development of effective perinatal clinical and public health practices, programs, and policies to improve the health and development of infants, mothers, and fathers.

Finally, in their chapter on "Fatherhood and Reproductive Health in the Antenatal Period: From Men's Voices to Clinical Practice", Levy and Kotelchuck present the results of the first Massachusetts General Hospital Fatherhood Prenatal Care Survey. This survey is path breaking as there is very limited literature on the experiences of fathers during Obstetric prenatal care, especially that directly includes fathers' voices. They find that fathers who have responded to the survey are actively and deeply engaged with the impending birth; have substantial physical and health needs including lack of primary care, depressive symptoms, and personal isolation; and have a strong desire for greater involvement in reproductive health care services. In conclusion, they make multiple practical recommendations to create a more father-friendly environment in Obstetric care.

3.2 Social Policy

At the meeting, social policy experts on family leave presented cross-national comparative studies of the implications of social policy, national culture, and socio-economic conditions on men's involvement in infant and childcare. A central struggle they discussed is how to motivate more gender equitable familial caretaking and economic outcomes.

There are multiple ways in which social policies can foster fatherhood involvement (Hearn et al. 2018). Parenting-related leaves, the set of social policies most analyzed in this book, are perhaps the most examined reproductive health policies in the literature. A key finding from this literature is that the initial transition from "mother-specific" to more general "parenting-related" leave policies enabled the inclusion of men, but had little practical effects because mothers continued to be the primary users (Bueno and Grau-Grau 2021; Moran and Koslowski 2019). In order to encourage men's participation in parenting-related leave policies, some countries, especially in Nordic Europe, offered father-specific leaves (e.g., "daddy quotas"). Evidence now shows that father-specific quotas tend to have significantly more positive effects relative to the use of gender-neutral parental leave (Mayer and Le Bourdais 2019), particularly in terms of increased paternal involvement with childcare over time (Bünning 2015) and increased solo parenting time (Wray 2020).

In their chapter on "Fathers and Family Leave Policies: What Public Policy Can Do to Support Families", Koslowski and O'Brien provide an overview of specific design features of family leave policies that tend to influence fathers' utilization, and they discuss documented effects of fathers' leaving taking on families' welfare and gender equality. In her chapter on "Individual Parental Leave for Fathers: Promoting Gender Equality in Norway", Kvande takes as a point of departure the design elements of the Norwegian parental leave system for fathers and examines how it works as a regulatory measure to promote equality in care work. The chapter on "How Do Men Talk About Taking Parental Leave? Evidence from South Korea, Spain, and the U.S." by Bueno and Oh enriches these first two chapters with more cross-national comparative perspectives. They present qualitative data on how men in South Korea, Spain, and the U.S. perceive parental leave, and comparatively analyze the fathers' perspectives as a function of their distinctive national cultural, social policy, and labor market contexts.

3.3 Work and Organizations

The Work and Organizations section provides further cross-national perspectives on fathers' experiences striving to fulfill work roles and family responsibilities. The grand challenge of this sector is how to practically operationalize a father-friendly work environment that is economically viable for both the family and the work organization.

The workplace is the environment where cultural and organizational norms and prejudices most clearly limit or enhance fathers' child-care and in-home family engagement. Many organizational cultures make engaged parenthood difficult. Even when organizations offer policies designed to reduce work-family conflicts, such as paid family leave and flexible work arrangements, they are commonly underutilized, particularly by fathers. Evidence suggests this is largely because being a person with limited family obligations tends to project a better work image than being one with a rich family life but obligations that could distract from the centrality of paid employment (Acker 1990; Tanquerel and Grau-Grau 2020; Williams et al. 2013).

In the chapter on "Impossible Standards and Unlikely Trade-Offs: Can Fathers Be Competent Parents and Professionals?", Ladge and Humberd set the stage for the Work and Organizations chapters by reflecting on contemporary challenges for working fathers and related unanswered questions in work and family research. In the chapter on "The New Dad: The Career-Caregiving Conundrum", Harrington reports on findings from a series of trailblazing studies conducted by the Boston College Center for Work & Families, in which they surveyed working fathers about their transition to fatherhood and about their attitudes toward paternity leave, caregiving, and work-family balance. In the chapter on "French Fathers in Work Organizations: Navigating Work-Life Balance Challenges", Tanquerel presents an insightful comparative perspective on how French professional and working-class fathers address tensions between their work and familial roles. In the chapter on "'It Would Be Silly to Stop Now and Go Part-Time': Fathers and Flexible Working Arrangements in Australia", Borgkvist examines how social constructions of masculinity in Australia sharpen the dissonance between men's identities as fathers and workers and how these incongruities inhibit men from utilizing family-friendly policies. In the chapter on "Small Changes That Make a Great Difference: Reading, Playing and Eating with Your Children and the Facilitating Role of Managers in

Latin America", Bosch and Las Heras delve into a rich sample of data collected from working parents in seven Latin American countries. They analyze how organizations, through their managers, can promote positive fatherhood engagement, as measured by their participation in reading, playing and eating together with their children. In the chapter on "Fatherhood Among Marginalised Work-Seeking Men in South Africa", Malinga and Ratele illuminate ways in which men's precarious employment hinders the fatherhood engagement of day laborers in South Africa. Lacking the ability to provide financially for their families, the fathers are impeded from being physically present and showing their children love. In the final chapter on "The Role of Love and Children's Agency in Improving Fathers' Wellbeing", Macht closes the narrative circle of the contributors' chapters by returning to the theme of father-child wellbeing. Through her inductive exploration of data from interviews with fathers in Scotland and Romania, Macht proposes ways in which fathers are emotionally transformed and uplifted through loving relationships with their children, including by re-energizing them for work and helping them let go of negative health habits.

4 Conclusion

In the concluding chapter of the book, Bowles, Kotelchuck, and Grau Grau integrate insights gained from the Experts Meeting and from editing the chapters to propose a set of working principles for overcoming barriers to engaged fatherhood through social policy, work practices, and healthcare delivery. The motivations for this concluding chapter are twofold: first, to propose a preliminary framework to align efforts across the three sectors to support fatherhood engagement; and, second, to offer a rough conceptual foundation upon which to advance and broaden cross-disciplinary, cross-national collaboration.

Acknowledgements This volume would not have been possible without the collective and concerted efforts of numerous people and multiple institutions. First, we wish to express our absolute thankfulness to the Social Trends Institute (STI), who generously funded the Experts meeting, which was the inception of this book. Without STI, this journey would not have started. We are especially grateful to Carlos Cavallé, the President of STI, and Tracey O'Donnell, the Secretary General of STI, for their guidance and for trusting in this idea from the very beginning. We have enormous gratitude for their support in opening the access of this book to all readers.

We would like to express especial thanks to the Harvard Kennedy School's Women and Public Policy Program (WAPPP) for enabling our partnership, the vision for which Marc Grau Grau crafted as a post-doctoral Research Fellow. As WAPPP's co-director, Hannah Riley Bowles transformed this vision into a vivid event by hosting our Experts Meeting on the Harvard Kennedy School campus and has also co-crafted this volume. Among the warmly supportive and generously helpful WAPPP staff, we owe extra thanks to Nicole Carter Quinn, Lindsey Shepardson, and Ruth Hampton Reyes plus three interns who served as notetakers during the Experts Meeting: Raiya Al-Nsour, Tamar Harrison, and Grace Hoffer Gittell. We would also like to recognize WAPPP Research Fellow Logan Berg's instrumental assistance with our literature reviews, especially her careful eye for clarity and precision. Logan's contributions were made possible by the Lara Warner

Scholars Fund, which supports WAPPP's mission to empower leaders and change makers with evidence-based strategies to advance gender equity.

As we worked to bring our aspirations for a cross-disciplinary dialogue to fruition, Mireia Las Heras was an early and enthusiastic partner and the linchpin in forming our institutional partnerships with IESE's International Center for Work and Family and STI. We are grateful for the cheerful assistance of Gemma Palet, Manager of the International Center for Work and Family, in the planning of the meeting.

Mireia Las Heras also served on our Steering Committee for the Experts Meeting representing the Work and Organizations section, along with Alison Koslowski from the University of Edinburgh and the International Network on Leave Policies and Research representing Social Policy, and Milton Kotelchuck and Raymond Levy from Harvard Medical School and The Fatherhood Project representing Health and Welfare. We are grateful for the Steering Committee's encouragement and intellectual guidance as we pulled together the Experts Meeting and this volume. We owe a special debt of gratitude to Milton Kotelchuck for working hand in hand with us in the final months of production.

We are enormously appreciative of the thought-provoking manuscripts the chapter authors have submitted. We also gratefully acknowledge their additional multi-faceted contributions as presenters at the Experts Meeting, as peer reviewers, and as advisers to the editors.

Finally, we would like to recognize Greg Dorchak's innumerable administrative and substantive contributions. Greg Dorchak led the logistical planning and implementation of the Experts Meeting and the operational production of the book with unerring professionalism and good humor. No chapter in this volume made it to press without his skillful text-editing. As a hardworking and engaged father, his enthusiasm for the subject has buoyed our collective work.

Finally, we thank our families who remind us every day of the joys and significance of loving fatherhood engagement.

References

Acker J (1990) Hierarchies, jobs, bodies: a theory of gendered organizations. Gend Soc 4(2):139–158

Alio AP, Kornosky JL, Mbah AK, Marty PJ, Salihu HM (2010) The impact of paternal involvement on feto-infant morbidity among whites, blacks and Hispanics. Matern Child Health J 14(5):735–741

Altintas E, Sullivan O (2017) Trends in fathers' contribution to housework and childcare under different welfare policy regimes. Soc Politics Int Stud Gend State Soc 24(1):81–108

Aumann K, Galinsky E, Matos K (2011) The new male mystique. Families and Work Institute, National Study of the Changing Workforce, Hillsborough

Bianchi SM (2011) Family change and time allocation in American families. Ann Am Acad Pol Soc Sci 638(1):21–44

Bueno X, Grau-Grau M (2021) Why is part-time unpaid parental leave (still) gendered? Narratives and strategies of couples in Spain. J Fam Issues 42(3):503–526

Bünning M (2015) What happens after the 'daddy months'? Fathers' involvement in paid work, childcare, and housework after taking parental leave in Germany. Eur Sociol Rev 31(6):738–748

Cameron EE, Sedov ID, Tomfohr-Madsen LM (2016) Prevalence of paternal depression in pregnancy and the postpartum: an updated meta-analysis. J Affect Disord 206:189–203

Cano T, Perales F, Baxter J (2019) A matter of time: father involvement and child cognitive outcomes. J Marriage Fam 81(1):164–184

Eagle BW, Miles EW, Icenogle ML (1997) Interrole conflicts and the permeability of work and family domains: are there gender differences? J Vocat Behav 50(2):168–184

Eggebeen DJ, Knoester C (2001) Does fatherhood matter for men? J Marriage Fam 63(2):381–393
Eggebeen DJ, Dew J, Knoester C (2010) Fatherhood and men's lives at middle age. J Fam Issues 31(1):113–130
England P (2010) The gender revolution: uneven and stalled. Gend Soc 24(2):149–166
Esping-Andersen G (2009) The incomplete revolution: adapting to women's new roles. Policy Press, Cambridge
Gerson K (2010) The unfinished revolution: coming of age in a new era of gender, work, and family. Oxford University Press, Oxford
Goldin C, Mitchell J (2017) The new life cycle of women's employment: disappearing humps, sagging middles, expanding tops. J Econ Perspect 31(1):161–182
Goldscheider F, Bernhardt E, Lappegård T (2015) The gender revolution: a framework for understanding changing family and demographic behavior. Popul Dev Rev 41(2):207–239
Grau-Grau M (2017) Work-family enrichment experiences among working fathers: evidence from Catalonia. The University of Edinburgh, Edinburgh
Hearn J, Pringle K, Balkmar D (2018) Men, masculinities and social policy. In: Shaver S (ed) Handbook on gender and social policy. Edward Elgar, Northampton, pp 55–73
Higgins CA, Duxbury LE (1992) Work-family conflict: a comparison of dual-career and traditional-career men. J Organ Behav 13(4):389–411
Huerta MdC, Adema W, Baxter J, Han W-J, Lausten M, Lee RH, Waldfogel J (2013) Fathers' leave, fathers' involvement and child development: are they related? Evidence from four OECD countries. OECD social, employment and migration working paper no. 140. OECD, Paris
Kelly EL, Ammons SK, Chermack K, Moen P (2010) Gendered challenge, gendered response: confronting the ideal worker norm in a white-collar organization. Gend Soc 24(3):281–303
Lewis J (2001) The decline of the male breadwinner model: implications for work and care. Soc Polit Int Stud Gend State Soc 8(2):152–169
Livingston G, Parker K (2019) 8 facts about American dads. Pew Research Center, Fact Tank news in the numbers. https://www.pewresearch.org/fact-tank/2019/06/12/fathers-day-facts/. Accessed 31 Aug 2020
Mandel H, Semyonov M (2005) Family policies, wage structures, and gender gaps: sources of earnings inequality in 20 countries. Am Sociol Rev 70(6):949–967
Mayer M, Le Bourdais C (2019) Sharing parental leave among dual-earner couples in Canada: does reserved paternity leave make a difference? Popul Res Policy Rev 38(2):215–239
Moran J, Koslowski A (2019) Making use of work–family balance entitlements: how to support fathers with combining employment and caregiving. Community Work Fam 22(1):111–128
National Academies of Sciences, Engineering and Medicine, Board on Children, Youth, and Families, Division of Behavioral and Social Sciences and Education, National Academies ofSciences, Engineering, and Medicine (2016) In: Gadsden VL, Ford M, Breiner H (eds) Parenting matters: supporting parents of children ages 0–8. National Academies Press, Washington, DC
Nepomnyaschy L, Waldfogel J (2007) Paternity leave and fathers' involvement with their young children. Community Work Fam 10(4):427–453
Parasuraman S, Simmers CA (2001) Type of employment, work–family conflict and well-being: a comparative study. J Organ Behav 22(5):51–68
Petts RJ, Knoester C, Waldfogel J (2020) Fathers' paternity leave-taking and children's perceptions of father-child relationships in the United States. Sex Roles 82(3):73–88
Steen M, Downe S, Bamford N, Edozien L (2012) Not-patient and not-visitor: a metasynthesis fathers' encounters with pregnancy, birth and maternity care. Midwifery 28(4):422–431

Tanquerel S, Grau-Grau M (2020) Unmasking work-family balance barriers and strategies among working fathers in the workplace. Organization 27(5):680–700. https://doi.org/10.1177/1350508419838692

Williams JC, Blair-Loy M, Berdahl JL (2013) Cultural schemas, social class, and the flexibility stigma. J Soc Issues 69(2):9–34

Wray D (2020) Paternity leave and fathers' responsibility: evidence from a natural experiment in Canada. J Marriage Fam 82(2):534–549

Yogman M, Garfield CF, Committee on Psychosocial Aspects of Child and Family Health (2016) Fathers' roles in the care and development of their children: the role of pediatricians. Pediatrics 138(1):e20161128

Open Access This chapter is licensed under the terms of the Creative Commons Attribution 4.0 International License (http://creativecommons.org/licenses/by/4.0/), which permits use, sharing, adaptation, distribution and reproduction in any medium or format, as long as you give appropriate credit to the original author(s) and the source, provide a link to the Creative Commons license and indicate if changes were made.

The images or other third party material in this chapter are included in the chapter's Creative Commons license, unless indicated otherwise in a credit line to the material. If material is not included in the chapter's Creative Commons license and your intended use is not permitted by statutory regulation or exceeds the permitted use, you will need to obtain permission directly from the copyright holder.

Part I
Health and Wellbeing

The Role of Fathers in Child and Family Health

Michael W. Yogman and Amelia M. Eppel

1 Introduction

The involvement of fathers in their children's health and development has come to the fore of recent research, including several national longitudinal studies on families, such as the *Fragile Families and Child Wellbeing Study*. Academic studies, policy initiatives and socio-economic forces have documented the variety of ways enhanced involvement of fathers influences the health and development of their children. Twenty-First Century fathers are more involved in caretaking of their children and see parenting as central to their identity (Livingston and Parker 2019). Their involvement right from birth is beneficial to their child in many ways, and preparation during pregnancy increases their involvement (Teitler 2001). Challenges remain, however, especially for the 24 million children who live without a father in their home (Jones and Mosher 2013). However, instead of focusing on fathers as the absent figure in children's lives, policies are beginning to reflect the evidence that fathers have significant family involvement. This can be seen especially in the paid family leave laws created by a number of states (Connecticut, New Jersey, Rhode Island, Massachusetts) which have been implemented to support father-infant attachment (National Conference of State Legislature 2015). In spite of this, concerns about career development still discourage many men from taking advantage of family leave (Halverson 2003; see also later chapters in this volume).

M. W. Yogman (✉)
Department of Pediatrics, Harvard Medical School, Boston, MA, USA
e-mail: mwyogman01@gmail.com

A. M. Eppel
Department of Integrated Studies in Education, McGill University, Montreal, QC, Canada
e-mail: amelia.eppel@mail.mcgill.ca

Major socioeconomic and cultural changes have led to more fathers having the opportunity to contribute at home, or to become stay-at-home dads in families where the mother sustains the family's income. These cultural changes include (1) the growth in women's educational achievement and economic power and (2) the great recession of 2008 with its severe impact on paternal employment (Yogman et al. 2016). Fathers are increasingly attendant at their children's births, more involved in their children's education and health care, experience similar work-family conflicts to mothers, and have unique relationships with their children (Yogman et al. 2016). Fathers have a consequential impact on their children's nutrition, exercise, play, and, eventually, their own parenting behavior. In this chapter, particular emphasis will be placed on father involvement across the stages of childhood, and the influence of fathers' physical and mental health on their children and wider family dynamic. The implications of father involvement for child health, and considerations for future research and policy areas will also be discussed.

1.1 Who Is a Father?

Before considering these trends and their implications, we must re-examine the role of "father" as a diverse category that challenges outdated notions of the heterosexual nuclear family. The working definition used in this review is that of male-identified adults who are most involved in the caregiving of a child, regardless of living situation, marital status or biological relation (Yogman et al. 2016). The role of father may be manifest in a multitude of ways: as the primary parent, as one of two primary parents, or as a secondary parent. They may be a biological, foster, or adoptive father, a stepfather, or a grandfather (Gogineni and Fallon 2013). Some children have a single father or two parents who are both fathers. Children may also have both a biological, non-resident father *and* a stepfather. In some families, children have three or four adults in a parenting role, with one or two of them being fathers. Some children do not have a male-identified figure involved in raising them. Within these configurations, fathers may be legal custodians of the child or not, resident or non-resident. In this chapter, fatherhood will be considered from these many perspectives, while maintaining a focus on fathers as part of the heterosexual couple, as the bulk of research lies within this framework.

2 Changing Trends in Parenting

The number of fathers in the United States is estimated at about 72 million at the last census survey, conducted in 2014 (US Census Bureau 2020), increasing from 60.1 million in the year 2000 (US Census Bureau 2013). The number of single fathers raising children in 2019 was two million—a significant increase from that figure in 2000 (Yogman et al. 2016). Single fathers now make up 18% of the single parent population. Although 1 in 6 fathers do not reside in the same home as their children, only 1–2% of them have no contact or participation in their children's lives (Jones and Mosher 2013). Most often this is because they meet a new partner and father a new infant.

Estimated at a total of 98,000 in 2003 (Yogman et al. 2016), there are now around 191,000 fathers who stay home to care for their children (US Census Bureau 2020). Significantly, this increase happened predominantly in the years 2003–2007, during which stay-at-home fathers increased by 60% to 159,000 (US Census Bureau 2013). According to a recent Pew Research Center report, this census data is in fact a gross underestimate; in 2012 there were 2.2 million stay-at-home fathers (Livingston 2014). Eight percent of these men were home because they were unable to find work, another 8% were in school and 11% were retired, while 24% chose to stay home to care for their home or family (an increase from 4% in 1989). A significant 40% were home because of illness or disability (Livingston 2014). Although most stay-at-home parents are mothers, fathers' share of stay-at-home parenting increased from 10% in 1989 to 16% in 2012, caring more than 200,000 children full-time and almost two million preschoolers part-time (Livingston 2013, 2014).

Demographic research from 2016 has shown that parenting is as central to the identities of this generation's fathers as it is to its mothers: 57% of fathers in a 2015 survey reported that parenting was extremely important to their identity, compared with 58% of mothers (Livingston and Parker 2019). Fifty-four percent of fathers also reported that parenting was rewarding all of the time, as did 52% of mothers. This data shows the centrality with which adults identifying as both mothers and fathers value their role as parents. Fathers in 2016 also reported taking care of their children on average 8 h/week, three times as much as fathers reported in 1965. Comparatively, mothers still spend more time taking care of their children: on average 14 h/week in 2016. Sixty-three percent of fathers report not feeling as though they spend enough time with their children, compared with only 35% of mothers. Additionally, only 39% of fathers in 2015 felt that they were doing a "very good job" raising their children, compared with 51% of mothers. This shows a discrepancy in the sense of competence that mothers and fathers on average feel as parents, which also aligns with the amount of time spent caring for their children.

In the Pew study both mothers and fathers cited work obligations as the main reason for spending less time with their children than they would like (Livingston and Parker 2019). Only 27% of heterosexual two-parent families with children under 18 are supported solely by a father's income: 20% less than in 1970. While only 2% of families were solely supported by a mother's income in 1970, this hasn't significantly increased over the past 50 years, rising only to 5% in 2016 (Livingston and Parker 2019). Clearly, this data reflects only one part of the father population, yet it reveals a clear trend toward a more equal share of income and working patterns in heterosexual two-parent families. Despite this, 76% of Americans surveyed in a 2017 study felt that fathers faced "a lot of pressure" to support their family financially (Parker et al. 2017b). Only 40% said the same of mothers, reflecting the data which shows only a limited increase since 1970 (from 2% to 5%) in families supported solely by a mother's income (Livingston and Parker 2019).

Along the same lines, 53% of Americans surveyed in 2017 still buy into the gender stereotype that, breast-feeding aside, mothers are better at caring for infants (Livingston and Parker 2019). Only 1% felt that fathers do a better job, while 45% felt mothers and fathers are equally able to care for children. At the same time, 64% felt that mothers and fathers have different approaches to parenting. Two thirds of fathers felt this had a biological basis, while, conversely, two thirds of mothers felt this was due to socialized gender roles and expectations. 56% of those reporting gender differences in parenting said that these differences were a good thing. Based on this data, it seems that gender stereotyping is more significantly practiced and believed in by fathers, which equally impacts on their parenting. Only 53% of fathers felt it was a good thing to encourage their sons to participate in activities typically associated with girls, compared with 72% of mothers. Interestingly, the data shows that parents saw their daughters participating in typically "boy" activities more positively: 69% of fathers, and 83% of mothers. These data points raise important questions about masculinity and its role in creating and perpetuating stereotyped views of gender. This has clear implications for professionals supporting fathers in their parenting.

3 Father Involvement Across Childhood

Research has found that father involvement in a child's life right from birth is beneficial to children in a myriad of ways but needs to be conceptualized as part of a supportive family system (Cabrera et al. 2017; Pruitt et al. 2017). The Pew Research Center trends reflect an increased engagement in parenting by fathers over the past few decades. As a result, fathers have more involvement in their children's lives than ever before. This involvement, however, looks different than it has in the past. One in six fathers do not live with their children, however only 1–2% of these are not involved with their children to any degree (Jones and Mosher 2013). There is thus a clear need to consider fatherhood from perspectives that value involvement in all its forms. Paternal involvement in a child's life has been linked to positive child outcomes, including reduced obesity and asthma, and improved mental health and cognition (Allport et al. 2018). The nature of these benefits are complex and deserve careful attention in order to ascertain what makes father involvement unique as well as how it can be nurtured. It is important that this be considered without excluding the interplay of other salient factors, such as the overall quality of family relationships and socioeconomic status. In order to reflect on the ways in which fathers play a unique role in their children's lives research findings on father involvement at the prenatal, infant, childhood, and adolescent stages will be summarized.

3.1 Prenatal

Paternal involvement begins prenatally. This is exhibited in practical terms by attendance at health care visits and at the child's birth (Teitler 2001). Father involvement in the prenatal period can also be seen in men's biological responses to a partner's pregnancy, such as in the presentation of Couvade syndrome (or 'sympathetic pregnancy'), where a father may experience insomnia, restlessness, and excess weight gain during their partner's pregnancy (Conner and Denson 1990). The impacts of father involvement during pregnancy are profound: one study found that it correlated with mothers being 1.5 times more likely to receive first-trimester prenatal care (Teitler 2001). Father involvement during pregnancy has also been associated with a 36% reduction in smoking, compared with mothers whose partners were not involved (Martin et al. 2007). In two studies a correlation was also found between a lack of paternal involvement and adverse birth outcomes in certain racial and ethnic populations (Alio et al. 2011a, b). These findings suggest that increased paternal involvement can have a positive impact on birth outcomes, which may be important for decreasing the racial and socioeconomic disparities in infant morbidities. Overall, prenatal paternal involvement in heterosexual couples (as well as residence at birth) was the strongest predictor of continued paternal involvement by the time a child reached 5 years old (Shannon et al. 2009).

3.2 Infancy

Most fathers are now present at the birth of their children, although the median amount of time new fathers take off from work is still much lower at only 1 week, compared with mothers' 11 weeks (Livingston and Parker 2019). Parental leave issues aside, there are numerous benefits to fathers' involvement with their newborn children evidenced by medical, developmental, and sociological research. One such study compared father skin-to-skin care with conventional cot care during the first 2 h after birth (Erlandsson et al. 2007). Newborn infants who were given skin-to-skin care by their father became drowsy more quickly, cried less and exhibited fewer rooting and sucking behaviors than those in cot care These findings imply that fathers can play an important role in this crucial stage after birth, a time where mothers' care is usually prioritized. To enhance paternal involvement at this stage, research has shown that simple interventions such as bathing and changing demonstrations and father support groups increase sustained father-infant connection (Yogman 1982).

During infancy, fathers have been found to have similar psychological experiences as mothers and have equally positive interactions with their infants (Yogman 1982). Interestingly, in one prospective study, children with fathers who were more involved with them in infancy displayed a lower level of mental health symptoms at age 9 than those with minimal paternal input in infancy (Boyce et al. 2006). Of significant import was the finding that this kind of involvement could serve to mediate detrimental effects from maternal depression.

Studies show that fathers are more likely to play with their infants than mothers, and that the play between father and infant tends to be of a higher intensity (Yogman 1982; Yogman et al. 1983). Taking cues from their infant, the fathers studied were able to support and help regulate their child's positive emotional state during social interactions by synchronizing arousal rhythms with their infants just as successfully as mothers (Yogman et al. 1983; Feldman 2003). This research also found that the quality of interactions (especially in play) was different between male-identified parents and their children than female-identified parents and their children. The interactions between fathers and their infants tended toward more intense peaks of positive emotion than with mothers. These high intensity interactions with fathers may encourage children's exploration and independence, while the less intense interactions with mothers may provide safety and balance (Raeburn 2014; Yogman 1982). A particularly notable finding was that same-sex parent-infant pairs were more responsive to each other's affective states, making co-regulation of emotions through social interaction with the father most important for their biologically male children (Feldman 2003). Whether this is based on socialized expectations of similarity with one's own sex, or on actual biological similarities is unclear.

Despite these findings, which reveal the important role a father can play in a newborn child's life, paternity leave legislation allows for a significantly lesser degree of involvement. In the U.S., the Family and Medical Leave Act (FMLA) is the only federal legislation that allows parents to take leave after the birth or adoption of a child, and to care for a sick family member. The FMLA grants 12 weeks of unpaid leave, and only 59.4% of the workforce are actually covered by it, according to 2014 data (Kleeman et al. 2014). Additionally, 46% of people who do have access to FMLA do not take it as they are unable to financially afford to. Some states have begun to address this issue by instituting paid family leave policies. In one 2011 study, 85% of fathers working for Fortune 500 companies took some time off after the birth of a child, but this was predominantly only 1–2 weeks and unpaid (Harrington et al. 2013). Ninety percent of working fathers in this research reported feeling as though their supervisor expected no change to occur in their working patterns as a result of becoming a father. With these expectations being commonplace, the involvement of fathers in their newborn child's life is minimized, a factor which must be taken into serious consideration by policymakers seeking to positively impact families through greater father involvement.

3.3 Childhood

The benefits of paternal involvement persist through childhood, although most studies do not assert a greater benefit to having a male-identified parent than of having two parents, regardless of their gender (Yogman et al. 2016). However, examples abound in which the presence of a father has positive impacts on children's lives. In studies of chronic childhood disease, children from father-absent families had poorer adherence to treatment, psychological adjustment, and health status than those with fathers present (Wysocki and Gavin 2006). While the reasons for this are complex, the data shows that father involvement in the healthcare setting has a positive impact, which must be considered by professionals seeking to support families of children with chronic illnesses.

Father involvement with their children through play has been the focus of most studies of father-child interaction in early and middle childhood. In one study, when fathers were more involved in infancy, children had lower mental health symptoms at age 9 than those whose parents did not play, communicate and care for them in infancy (Boyce et al. 2006). Father-child play in the preschool years has been found to decrease externalizing and internalizing behavior problems, despite, or perhaps because of the tendency of fathers to encourage more "roughhouse" play with their children (Jia et al. 2012). A positive correlation between father involvement and their children's social competencies and pro-social behaviour has also been found (Chang et al. 2007). Furthermore, the influence of maternal depressive symptoms on child problem behaviors varied by the level of the father's positive involvement. This information suggests that the influence of involved fathers may compensate for the negative influence of maternal depression (e.g., reduced responsiveness to a child's socioemotional needs), thereby reducing the risk of problem behaviors in children of families experiencing maternal depression.

Another significant contribution that fathers can make to their child's development is in the realm of language. One study linked fathers' language input to children's early language development, finding that fathers' language input to their children at 2 years old made a unique contribution to children's later expressive language skills at 3 years old, after parent education and quality of childcare was considered (Pancsofar and Vernon-Feagans 2006). Despite this finding, mothers during the first 6 months with their infants used significantly more expressive language with their children than fathers did, yet it was the father's language contributions which correlated with most impactful language development. One suggested explanation is the possibility that fathers are more likely to introduce new words, while mothers may tailor word choice to the child's known vocabulary (Raeburn 2014). The influence of father involvement on children's language development certainly merits further study based on these results.

3.4 Adolescence

Father involvement during their children's adolescence can be significant and formative. Several large-scale studies have shown that father involvement is associated with a decrease in the likelihood of risk behaviors in adolescence, if the quality of the parent-child relationship is strong. In one such study, a positive father-child relationship was shown to predict a reduced engagement in risky behaviors by adolescents (Bronte-Tinkew et al. 2006). This proved to be more significant for male adolescents, suggesting that positive father-son relationships are important for mitigating risk behavior in adolescence. Studies also showed that adolescents whose nonresident fathers were involved in their lives have been shown to be less likely to begin smoking regularly (Menning 2006). These findings suggest that strong father-child relationships can have a significant positive influence on adolescents.

Father engagement has also been correlated with improved cognitive development, a meta-analysis of studies has shown (Sarkadi et al. 2008). In addition, positive relationships with their father was found to be a predictor of lower rates of behavioral problems in adolescent boys, and fewer psychological problems in adolescent girls. As a result, it also predicted a decreased rate of delinquency in children of families with low socioeconomic status (Sarkadi et al. 2008). Involvement of fathers with their daughters has also been associated with a later onset of puberty, fewer early sexual experiences, and a lower risk of teen pregnancy (Ellis et al. 2012). It is speculated that this may be as a result of exposure to fathers' pheromones, which have the potential to slow female pubertal development (Raeburn 2014). Father involvement in early childhood, in the context of other high-quality family relationships, had the greatest impact on pubertal timing in girls (Ellis et al. 1999). Having an involved father has been associated with greater age-appropriate independence, cognitive development and social skills (Yogman 1982).

While father involvement is clearly important across the span of childhood for the reasons cited above, it is important to note that relationships with two parents regardless of their sex or gender identity is the most significant factor in supporting children's healthy development. Studies have in fact found that same-sex parenting gives no disadvantage: adolescents' psychosocial adjustment, school outcomes, and romantic relationships were stable across family type, with the most well-adjusted children reporting closer relationships with parents (Wainright et al. 2004). In essence, father involvement must be considered crucial both for the unique contribution male-identified parents can make, as well as the part a father plays purely as a parent, regardless of sex or gender identity.

4 Father Health and Its Impact on Children

The mental and physical health of fathers has been found to have major impact on the health and development of their children, most saliently in terms of paternal postpartum depression (PPPD). Research on depression in the postpartum period has shown that up to 25% of fathers experience depression in this time; this increases to 50% when mothers are also experiencing postpartum depression (Davis et al. 2011; Goodman 2004; Edmondson et al. 2010; Ramchandani et al. 2011; Paulson and Bazemore 2010; Gawlik et al. 2014). New fatherhood increases the likeliness of depression in men: fathers were 1.38 times more likely to be depressed than same aged men who were not fathers (Giallo et al. 2012). One study found that fathers who do not live with their child reported higher depression symptoms during the transition to fatherhood, while those who do live with their children had a 68% increase in depressive symptoms in the child's first 5 years (Garfield et al. 2014). Because of higher rates of several stressors (e.g., racism, unemployment, poverty, incarceration, and homelessness) which disproportionately affect Black fathers, this population is at a higher risk for depression and other mental health conditions (Anderson et al. 2005; Reinherz et al. 1999; Davis et al. 2009). A prior history of depression, sleep deprivation, or having a sick or premature child are additional risk factors for PPPD.

Paternal postpartum depression is frequently under-identified as it is not often screened for, despite the fact that the Edinburgh Postnatal Depression Scale has been validated for use with fathers as well as mothers (Matthey et al. 2001). When PPPD is identified, treatment is often inadequate, as specific resources targeting fathers rather than mothers are currently scarce. Paternal postpartum depression has a different presentation and symptomatology to maternal postpartum depression, therefore treatment needs also to be different (Yogman et al. 2016). Men are more likely to avoid expressing vulnerability, and seek help for mental health issues at lower rates (Mansfield et al. 2003; Rochlen 2005). Men often experience depression in uncharacteristic ways, psychology research shows. It may show up instead as substance misuse, anger and/or violence, interpersonal issues and compulsive behaviors (Cochran 2001). These types of presentations more often lead to relationship stress and domestic violence and can undermine positive attachment behaviors between mother and child, such as breastfeeding (Yogman et al. 2016). It can also explain the discrepancy in the prevalence of postpartum depression between men and women, as PPD may not be the most obvious diagnosis based on typical presentation in men.

Onset of depression in the postpartum period can also occur later for fathers (i.e., up to a year postpartum) than mothers, who usually experience it in the first 3 months postpartum (Goodman 2004). Screening for PPPD should thus be prioritized by healthcare providers throughout the child's first year of life. Research shows that depressed fathers are four times more likely to physically punish their infants and less likely to engage positively with their infants by reading to them (Fletcher et al. 2011; Davis et al. 2011). One study, which asked fathers to rank different aspects of their lives, found that the emotional experience of parenting along with work-life conflict, were the most negative and tiring activities in their life (Kahneman et al. 2004). Significantly, nearly a quarter of fathers have experienced depression by the time their child is 12 years old (Davé et al. 2010).

Recent research shows that paternal depression has negative effects on child behavior, mood, and development in similar ways to the impact caused by maternal PPD (Yogman et al. 2016). The Avon Longitudinal Study of Parents and Children found correlative evidence that paternal depression in the postpartum period increased the likelihood of child behavioral problems in the preschool years, even when maternal depression and other sociodemographic correlates were controlled (Ramchandani et al. 2005). Furthermore, new findings from this study have revealed that daughters of men who had PPPD when they were infants were at a significantly greater risk of experiencing depression at the age of 18 (Gutierrez-Galve et al. 2018).

Parents' mental health problems have negative impact on their childcare habits, their involvement, and their parenting styles (Yogman et al. 2016). Parents who are depressed are less likely to spend quality time with their young children, provide less nurturing physical contact, and are more likely to express frustration at their children (Davis et al. 2011; Lyons-Ruth et al. 2002). In a study of families enrolled in Head Start programs (a nationwide early childhood education program in the U.S.), depressed fathers were found to be less involved with their infants than fathers who did not report depressive symptoms (Roggman et al. 2002). A reduction in father-child engagement and play, poorer relationships with their partner, and less effective co-parenting, were also associated with depression in fathers who took part in the Fragile Families and Child Wellbeing study (Bronte-Tinkew et al. 2007). It is possible that parental conflict increases the risk of depression in fathers; further research is required to ascertain the most significant influences on paternal mental health and their role in family health and wellbeing (Yogman et al. 2016).

Fathers' physical health also plays a role in their children's health. One example of how a father's physical well-being may affect a child's well-being is in the case of obesity. Current research suggests that when only one member of the parenting couple is in a higher weight status category, it is the father's and not the mother's weight status that is a significant predictor of later child obesity (Brophy et al. 2012; Freeman et al. 2012). This suggests that fathers play an important role in how childhood obesity develops in the family environment.

5 Diversity of Fathers

The roles, social expectations, and support needs of fathers are varied. Military families are one example. Among the 200,000 American military personnel currently serving overseas (Bialik 2017), many are fathers and continuity of their relationships with their children during prolonged absences is an ongoing challenge. Around 15% of military personnel are women (Parker et al. 2017a), meaning that many more mothers serving in the U.S. armed forces are also being deployed, leaving fathers to be single parents, a situation which little support is offered for. Similarly, incarcerated and formerly incarcerated fathers who wish to remain connected to their children are especially important to support, as more than 750,000 U.S. fathers are serving time in prison (Geller et al. 2012). Children growing up without a father face greater risks of homelessness, truancy, school drop-out, and suicide (American Institutes for Research 2013).

According to 2018 census data, there are 485,065 gay male couple households in the U.S., with 9% of these raising children (US Census Bureau 2018). This data does not include gay fathers who share custody after a divorce, or single gay fathers. By comparison, of the 510,355 gay female couple households in the U.S., 23% are raising children. Children with gay parents have been found to be comparable to children with heterosexual parents on key psychosocial and developmental outcomes (American Academy of Pediatrics - COPACFH 2013). There is as yet no conclusive research on the benefits of having two mothers over two fathers, or vice versa, although the evidence currently points to the fact that having two loving parents regardless of sex or gender identity is key in raising healthy successful children. Adequately supporting fathers to play a central parenting role regardless of their partnership status or sexual orientation remains the most important factor to consider.

Significantly, ethnic and racial differences in fathering have also not been well studied. While definitions of masculinity are beginning to transition from an emphasis on toughness to an emphasis on tenderness, racial differences persist in this domain. In one study, white fathers were more demonstrative with children under age 13 than Black fathers: hugging their children more and telling them they loved them (Child Trends Data Bank 2002). This is, however, an understudied area, and there is no adequate research that has been conducted more recently than the one cited above to compare it to. The important role of fathers in the Black community are nonetheless evident; an intervention program with 8- to 12-year-old Black boys that focused on the parenting skills of nonresident fathers was associated with reduced aggressive behavior in the boys (Caldwell et al. 2014). Parenting by Hispanic fathers, who make up a significant portion of the U.S. father population, is currently under-researched, and undocumented immigrant fathers have not yet been studied at all.

Nonresident fathers are a particularly important group of men to support with ongoing engagement with their children. Forty percent of births are to unmarried women (Parker et al. 2015). However, for the remaining 60% of children born within a marriage, one in five children will see the breakup of that marriage by the age of 9. Nonresident father relationships are thus exceptionally common. While the adult couple bond may be fractured, these fathers may continue their involvement with their children if adequately supported. Additionally, racial diversity in nonresident fathering must be considered. Black fathers, while more likely to be nonresident than white fathers (24% versus 8%), are found to be more engaged than white nonresident fathers, giving support with dressing, bathing, and reading to their children in the early months (Jones and Mosher 2013; Edin and Nelson 2013). It has been suggested that, while eager to learn about child rearing, many nonresident fathers prefer information from their community and peers than from professionals (Smith et al. 2015).

Another trend in fatherhood that has increased over the past 20 years is men bearing children with multiple partners. Around 17% of all fathers aged 40–44 have children with 2 or more partners, and more than 22% of fathers with 2 or more children have had them with 2 or more partners (Guzzo 2014). These men are typically more engaged with the children of their most recent partner and often provide diminished resources for each child they have (Cancian et al. 2011; Manning and Smock 2000). The diversity of father's roles and social relationships add a level of complexity to understanding the effect fathers have on family health.

6 Implications for Future Research and Policy

Current research suggests that fathers are more involved in parenting than ever before and see that role as central to their identity. Father involvement from birth is beneficial to children in myriad ways. Preparation increases father involvement, especially engagement during pregnancy. Fathers can play a unique role with infants and children as play partners, a role distinct from that of mothers. Although fathers may not initially feel comfortable parenting young infants, simple interventions that normalize apprehension, provide specific advice and have targeted outreach, can produce long lasting effects. Challenges remain with the increase in nonresident fathers, which effects 24 million children, and for which there are limited effective engagement strategies.

There is also a need for research that considers the diversity of fatherhood from perspectives that look beyond the norms of heterosexual two-parent families. While there is some research on parenting in same-sex families, there is scope for development of research into how family structures differ and align across sex and gender roles. Many of the research conclusions cited co-parenting relationships and the family environment as significant context for many of the outcomes and implications. Further exploration of the contextual elements that shape how father involvement and father health impacts children would also help build a more nuanced picture of how these elements function. Much of the existing research suggests that the most important role a father plays to a child is as one of two parents, yet there are many unique ways in which fathers also contribute. Further research in these areas would perhaps help resolve the contention of these seemingly opposing views.

Finally, the two most significant implications for policy are, identifying and treating PPPD—which is both dangerous and underdiagnosed—and supporting paternity leave. Many of the findings stress the importance of the father-child relationship in infancy, but changes in workplace policies, community services and legislation regarding parental leave are essential to produce sustained improvements that will support both mothers and fathers to successfully raise children.

References

Alio AP, Mbah AK, Kornosky JL, Wathington D, Marty PJ, Salihu HM (2011a) Assessing the impact of paternal involvement on racial/ethnic disparities in infant mortality rates. J Community Health 36(1):63–68

Alio AP, Mbah AK, Grunsten RA, Salihu HM (2011b) Teenage pregnancy and the influence of paternal involvement on fetal outcomes. J Pediatr Adolesc Gynecol 24(6):404–409

Allport BS, Johnson S, Agil A, Labrique AB, Nelson T, Kc A, Carabas Y, Marcell AV (2018) Promoting father involvement for child and family health. Acad Pediatric Assoc 18(7):746–753. https://doi.org/10.1016/j.acap.2018.03.011

American Academy of Pediatrics, Committee on Psychosocial Aspects of Child and Family Health (COPACFH) (2013) Promoting the wellbeing of children whose parents are gay or lesbian. Pediatrics 131(4):827–830

American Institutes for Research (2013) Guide for father involvement in systems of care. https://www.air.org/resource/guide-father-involvement-systems-care. Accessed 14 Jun 2013

Anderson EA, Kohler JK, Letiecq BL (2005) Predictors of depression among low-income, nonresidential fathers. J Fam Issues 26(5):547–567

Bialik K (2017) US active-duty military presence overseas is at its smallest in decades. Pew Research Center Fact Tank, Washington, DC. https://wwwpewresearchorg/fact-tank/2017/08/22/u-s-active-duty-military-presence-overseas-is-at-its-smallest-in-decades/. Accessed 21 Nov 2020

Boyce WT, Essex MJ, Alkon A, Goldsmith HH, Kraemer HC, Kupfer DJ (2006) Early father involvement moderates biobehavioral susceptibility to mental health problems in middle childhood. J Am Acad Child Adolesc Psychiatry 45(12):1510–1520

Bronte-Tinkew J, Moore KA, Carrano J (2006) The father-child relationship, parenting styles, and adolescent risk behaviors in intact families. J Fam Issues 27(6):850–881

Bronte-Tinkew J, Ryan S, Carrano J, Moore KA (2007) Resident fathers' pregnancy intentions, prenatal behaviors, and links to involvement with infants. J Marriage Fam 69(4):977–990

Brophy S, Rees A, Knox G, Baker J, Thomas NE (2012) Child fitness and father's BMI are important factors in childhood obesity: a school based cross-sectional study. PLoS One 8(5): e36597

Cabrera N, Volling BL, Barr R (2017) Fathers are parents, too! Child Dev Perspect 12(3):152–157

Caldwell HC, Antonakos CL, Assari S, Kruger D, De Loney EH, Njai R (2014) Pathways to prevention: improving non-resident African American fathers' parenting skills and behaviors to reduce sons' aggression. J Child Dev 85(1):308–325

Cancian M, Meyer DR, Cook ST (2011) The evolution of family complexity from the perspective of nonmarital children. Demography 48(3):957–982

Chang JJ, Halpern CT, Kaufman JS (2007) Maternal depressive symptoms, father's involvement, and the trajectories of child problem behaviors in a US National Sample. Arch Pediatr Adolesc Med 161(7):697–703

Child Trends Data Bank (2002) Parental warmth and affection. wwwchildtrendsorg/?indicators=parental-warmth-and-affection. Accessed 24 Mar 2015

Cochran SV (2001) Assessing and treating depression in men. In: Brooks GR, Good GE (eds) The new handbook of psychotherapy and counseling with men, vol 1. Jossey-Bass, San Francisco, pp 3–21

Conner GK, Denson V (1990) Expectant fathers' response to pregnancy: review of literature and implications for research in high-risk pregnancy. J Perinatal Neonatal Nurs 4(2):33–42. https://doi.org/10.1097/00005237-199009000-00006

Davé S, Petersen I, Sherr L, Nazareth I (2010) Incidence of maternal and paternal depression in primary care: a cohort study using a primary care database. Arch Pediatr Adolesc Med 164 (11):1038–1044

Davis RN, Caldwell CH, Clark SJ, Davis MM (2009) Depressive symptoms in nonresident African American fathers and involvement with their sons. Pediatrics 124(6):1611–1618

Davis RN, Davis MM, Freed GL, Clark SJ (2011) Fathers' depression related to positive and negative parenting behaviors with 1-year-old children. Pediatrics 127(4):612–618

Edin K, Nelson TJ (2013) Doing the best I can. University of California Press, Berkeley

Edmondson OJ, Psychogiou L, Vlachos H, Netsi E, Ramchandani PG (2010) Depression in fathers in the postnatal period: assessment of the Edinburgh postnatal depression scale as a screening measure. J Aff Disord 125(1–3):365–368

Ellis BJ, McFadyen-Ketchum S, Dodge KA, Pettit GS, Bates JE (1999) Quality of early family relationships and individual differences in the timing of pubertal maturation in girls: a longitudinal test of an evolutionary model. J Pers Soc Psychol 77(2):387–401

Ellis BJ, Schlomer GL, Tilley EH, Butler EA (2012) Impact of fathers on risky sexual behavior in daughters: a genetically and environmentally controlled sibling study. Dev Psychopathol 24 (1):317–332

Erlandsson K, Dslina A, Fagerberg I, Christensson K (2007) Skin-to-skin care with the father after cesarean birth and its effect on newborn crying and prefeeding behavior. Birth 34(2):105–114

Feldman R (2003) Infant-mother and infant-father synchrony: the coregulation of positive arousal. Infant Ment Health J 24(1):1–23. https://doi.org/10.1002/imhj.10041

Fletcher RJ, Feeman E, Garfield C, Vimpani G (2011) The effects of early paternal depression on children's development. Med J Austr 195(11–12):685–689

Freeman E, Fletcher R, Collins C, Morgan PJ, Burrows T, Callister R (2012) Preventing and treating childhood obesity: time to target fathers. Int J Obes 36(1):12–15

Garfield CF, Duncan G, Rutsohn J, McDade TW, Adam EK, Coley RL, Chase-Lansdale L (2014) A longitudinal study of paternal mental health during transition to fatherhood as young adults. Pediatrics 133(5):836–843

Gawlik S, Muller M, Hoffmann L et al (2014) Prevalence of paternal perinatal depressiveness and its link to partnership satisfaction and birth concerns. Arch Womens Ment Health 17(1):49–56

Geller A, Cooper CE, Garfinkel I, Schwartz-Soicher O, Mincy RB (2012) Beyond absenteeism: father incarceration and child development. Demography 49(1):49–76

Giallo R, D'Esposito F, Christensen D, Mensah F, Cooklin A, Wade C, Lucas N, Canterford L, Nicholson JM (2012) Father mental health during the early parenting period: results of an Australian population based longitudinal study. Soc Psychiatry Psychiatr Epidemiol 47(12):1907–1966

Gogineni R, Fallon AE (2013) The adoptive father. In: Brabender VM, Fallon AE (eds) Working with adoptive parents. Wiley, Hoboken, pp 89–104

Goodman JH (2004) Paternal postpartum depression, its relationship to maternal postpartum depression, and implications for family health. J Adv Nurs 45(1):26–35

Gutierrez-Galve L, Stein A, Hanington L, Heron J, Lewis G, O'Farrelly C, Ramchandani PG (2018) Association of maternal and paternal depression in the postnatal period with offspring depression at age 18 years. JAMA Psychiat 76(3):290–296. https://doi.org/10.1001/jamapsychiatry.2018.3667

Guzzo KB (2014) New partners, more kids: multiple-partner fertility in the United States. Ann Am Acad Pol Soc Sci 654(1):66–86. https://doi.org/10.1177/0002716214525571

Halverson C (2003) From here to paternity: why men are not taking paternity leave under the family medical leave act. Wisconsin Womens Law J 18(2):257–259

Harrington B, Van Deusen F, Fraone JS (2013) The new dad: a work (and life) in progress. Boston College Center for Work and Family, Boston

Jia R, Kotila L, Schoppe-Sullivan S (2012) Transactional relations between father involvement and preschoolers' socioemotional adjustment. J Fam Psychol 26(6):848–857

Jones J, Mosher WD (2013) Fathers' involvement with their children: United States, 2006-2010. Natl Health Stat Rep 71:1–21

Kahneman D, Krueger AB, Schkade DA, Schwarz N, Stone AA (2004) A survey method for characterizing daily life experience: the day reconstruction method. Science 306(5702):1776–1780

Kleeman JA, Daley K, Pozniak A (2014) Family and medical leave in 2012: technical report. Abt Associates, Cambridge

Livingston G (2013) Why are dads staying home? Analysis of march current population surveys integrated public use micro data series (IPUMS-CPS). Pew Research Center, Washington, DC. https://www.pewsocialtrends.org/2014/06/05/chapter-2-why-are-dads-staying-home/

Livingston G (2014) Growing number of dads home with the kids. Pew Research Center Social and Demographic Trends Project Blog, Washington, DC. wwwpewsocialtrendsorg/2014/06/05 Accessed 24 Mar 2015

Livingston G, Parker K (2019) 8 facts about American dads. Pew Research Center, Washington, DC. https://www.pewresearch.org/fact-tank/2019/06/12/fathers-day-facts/

Lyons-Ruth K, Wolfe R, Lyubchik A, Steingard R (2002) Depressive symptoms in parents of children under age 3: sociodemographic predictors, current correlates, and associated parenting behaviors. In: Halfon N, McLearn KT (eds) Child rearing in America: challenges facing parents with young children. Cambridge University Press, New York, pp 217–259

Manning WD, Smock PJ (2000) "Swapping" families: serial parenting and economic support for children. J Marriage Fam 62(1):111–122

Mansfield AK, Addis ME, Mahalik JR (2003) 'Why won't he go to the doctor?': the psychology of men's help seeking. Int J Mens Health 2(2):93–109

Martin LT, McNamara MJ, Milot AS, Halle T, Hair EC (2007) The effects of father involvement during pregnancy on receipt of prenatal care and maternal smoking. Matern Child Health J 11 (6):595–602. https://doi.org/10.1007/s10995-007-0209-0

Matthey S, Barnett B, Kavanagh DJ, Howie P (2001) Validation of the Edinburgh postnatal depression scale for men, and comparison of item endorsement with their partners. J Aff Disord 64(2–3):175–184

Menning CL (2006) Nonresident fathers' involvement and adolescents' smoking. J Health Soc Behav 47(1):32–46

National Conference of State Legislatures (2015) Labor and employment. www.ncsl.org/research/labor-and-employment/state-family-and-medical-leave-laws.aspx. Accessed 24 Mar 2015

Pancsofar N, Vernon-Feagans L (2006) Mother and father language input to young children: contributions to later language. J Appl Dev Psychol 27(6):571–587

Parker K, Horowitz JM, Rohal M (2015) Parenting in America: outlook, worries, aspirations are strongly linked to financial situation. Pew Research Center, Washington DC

Parker K, Cilluffo A, Stepler R (2017a) 6 facts about the US military and its changing demographics. Pew Research Center, Washington, DC. https://wwwpewresearchorg/fact-tank/2017/04/13/6-facts-about-the-u-s-military-and-its-changing-demographics/. Retrieved 22 Nov 2020

Parker K, Horowitz JM, Stepler R (2017b) On gender differences, no consensus on nature vs. nurture. Pew Research Center, Washington, DC. https://www.pewsocialtrends.org/2017/12/05/americans-see-different-expectations-for-men-and-women/#public-sees-more-pressure-for-men-on-job-and-career-front

Paulson JF, Bazemore S (2010) Prenatal and postpartum depression in fathers and its association with maternal depression: a meta-analysis. JAMA 303(19):1961–1969

Pruitt MK, Pruitt KD, Cowan CP, Cowan PA, P. (2017) Enhancing paternal engagement in a co-parenting paradigm. Child Dev Perspect 11(4):245–250

Raeburn P (2014) Do fathers matter? Farrar, Straus, Giroux, New York

Ramchandani P, Stein A, Evans J, O'Connor TG, the ALSPAC Study Team (2005) Paternal depression in the postnatal period and child development: a prospective population study. Lancet 365(9478):2201–2205

Ramchandani PG, Psychogiou L, Vlachos H, Iles J, Sethna V, Netsi E, Lodder A (2011) Paternal depression: an examination of its links with father, child and family functioning in the postnatal period. Depress Anxiety 28(6):471–477

Reinherz HZ, Giaconia RM, Hauf AM, Wasserman MS, Silverman AB (1999) Major depression in the transition to adulthood: risks and impairments. J Abnorm Psychol 108(3):500–510

Rochlen AB (2005) Men in (and out of) therapy: central concepts, emerging directions, and remaining challenges. J Clin Psychol 61(6):627–631

Roggman LA, Boyce LK, Cook GA, Cook J (2002) Getting dads involved: predictors of father involvement in early head start and with their children. Infant Ment Health J 23(1):62–78

Sarkadi A, Kristiansson R, Oberklaid F, Bremberg S (2008) Father's involvement and children's developmental outcomes: a systematic review of longitudinal studies. Acta Paediatrica 97 (2):153–158

Shannon JD, Cabrera NJ, Tamis-LeMonda C, Lamb ME (2009) Who stays and who leaves: father accessibility across children's first 5 years. Parent Sci Pract 9(1–2):78–100

Smith TK, Darius Tandon S, Bair-Merritt MH, Hanson JL (2015) Parenting needs of urban African American fathers. Am J Mens Health 9(4):317–331

Teitler JO (2001) Father involvement, child health and maternal behavior. Child Youth Serv Rev 23 (4–5):403–425

US Census Bureau (2013) Facts for features: father's day. June 16, 2013b. wwwcensusgov/newsroom/facts-for-features/2013/cb13-ff13html. Accessed 24 Mar 2015

US Census Bureau (2018) Characteristics of same-sex couple households: 2018 table. https://wwwcensusgov/data/tables/time-series/demo/same-sex-couples/ssc-house-characteristicshtml. Accessed 4 Mar 2020

US Census Bureau (2020) Fun facts: father's day. June 21, 2020. https://www2censusgov/programs-surveys/sis/resources/fathers-day-ffpdf. Accessed 17 Nov 2020

Wainright JL, Russell ST, Patterson CJ (2004) Psychosocial adjustment, school outcomes, and romantic relationships of adolescents with same-sex parents. Child Dev 75(6):1886–1898. https://doi.org/10.1111/j.1467-8624.2004.00823.x

Wysocki T, Gavin L (2006) Paternal involvement in the management of pediatric chronic diseases: associations with adherence, quality of life, and health status. J Pediatr Psychol 31(5):501–511. https://doi.org/10.1093/jpepsy/jsj042

Yogman MW (1982) Development of the father-infant relationship. In: Fitzgerald H, Lester BM, Yogman MW (eds) Theory and research in behavioral pediatrics, vol 1. Plenum Press, New York, pp 221–279

Yogman MW, Lester BM, Hoffman J (1983) Behavioral and cardiac rhythmicity during mother-father-stranger infant social interaction. Pediatric Res 17(11):872–876. https://doi.org/10.1203/00006450-198311000-00007

Yogman MW, Garfield CF, AAP the Committee on Psychosocial Aspects of Child, Family Health (2016) Fathers' roles in the care and development of their children: the role of pediatricians. Pediatrics 138(1):e20161128

Open Access This chapter is licensed under the terms of the Creative Commons Attribution 4.0 International License (http://creativecommons.org/licenses/by/4.0/), which permits use, sharing, adaptation, distribution and reproduction in any medium or format, as long as you give appropriate credit to the original author(s) and the source, provide a link to the Creative Commons license and indicate if changes were made.

The images or other third party material in this chapter are included in the chapter's Creative Commons license, unless indicated otherwise in a credit line to the material. If material is not included in the chapter's Creative Commons license and your intended use is not permitted by statutory regulation or exceeds the permitted use, you will need to obtain permission directly from the copyright holder.

The Impact of Father's Health on Reproductive and Infant Health and Development

Milton Kotelchuck

1 The Importance of Enhancing Father's Health and Engagement During the Perinatal Reproductive Health Period to Improve Maternal and Infant Health and Development and His Own Life Course Health

This, the first of two related chapters, provides a broad overview, and new conceptualization, of the various ways in which father's health impacts reproductive and infant health and development. It is paired with a subsequent chapter that examines the ways in which fatherhood influences the health and development of men (Kotelchuck 2021). These chapters endeavor to bring to light the heretofore underappreciated topic of father's importance and necessary active involvement in reproductive health and health care to enhance infant, maternal, family, and men's own health and development outcomes. Fathers' increased participation in reproductive health care activities, their actions on the ground, are perhaps outstripping the public health research and conceptual theories about their role and importance.

Traditionally, the principal focus of the Maternal and Child Health (MCH) field (and closely aligned Obstetric, Pediatrics and Nursing fields) has been on the mother's health and behavior and its impact on reproductive and infant/child health and development outcomes. Reproductive health and early parenting has been perceived as primarily, if not exclusively, the mothers' responsibility and her cultural domain, and to a significant extent fathers and men have been excluded.

This chapter does not argue to diminish the importance of women's health and reproductive responsibility, but rather seeks to expand upon and complement her

---

M. Kotelchuck (✉)
Harvard Medical School and Massachusetts General Hospital Fatherhood Project, Boston, MA, USA
e-mail: mkotelchuck@mgh.harvard.edu

role with an enhanced paternal and family perspective on reproductive and infant health and development and to encourage greater equity in parental responsibility and engagement in reproductive and infant care. Increased paternal involvement in the perinatal period is not a zero-sum game. This chapter focuses on fathers, by far the largest group of women's partners, but it does not presume that traditional two parent families are the only form of families that can raise healthy children; perhaps some of the lessons learned here will apply to all additional parental partners.

First, there is a large, well-established, and growing literature demonstrating the positive impacts of fathers' involvement on multiple facets of child development and family relationships (e.g., Yogman et al. 2016; Lamb 1975, 2010), which co-authors in this volume further discuss (Yogman and Eppel 2021). Fathers' participation, roles, and potential contributions during the perinatal time period (e.g., preconception, pregnancy, delivery, and very early infant life and family formation) are by comparison a very under-studied topic. This chapter will explore how fathers' multi-faceted perinatal involvement and health improves reproductive and infant health outcomes; and more explicitly expand our understanding of men's life course development and responsibility, as fathers, into an earlier temporal period before delivery.

Second, the limited research on the father's contribution to perinatal health can be found across very scattered sets of MCH literature—with often seemingly random observations and assessments of possible paternal causal mechanisms and associations. Hopefully, this chapter will help to coalesce these many diverse threads of research into a more systematic organized framework—in order to better facilitate further discussion, analysis, and ultimately action around enhancing fathers' contributions to reproductive/perinatal health.

Third, many of the conceptual themes about fathers' health in this chapter build upon similar themes from an earlier preconception health and fatherhood article (Kotelchuck and Lu 2017), but here move beyond its more limited preconception health time frame, explore additional new evolving paternal reproductive health themes, and separate the impacts on infants from impacts on fathers. This chapter adopts a very broad holistic approach to men's health, blending mental, physical, genetic, social health dimensions and some health service utilization themes into a single comprehensive fatherhood framework.

Fourth, this chapter, and the following one, model and build upon the current women's pre-conception health perspective in the MCH field, which simultaneously addresses the impact of the mother's pregnancy on both the infant's and the mother's own lifetime health (Moos 2003)—an intergenerational approach that respects the integrity and health of both mothers and infants simultaneously, without valuing one's life above the other (Wise 2008). These paired chapters adopt this same dual orientation.

Fifth, this chapter does not emerge in an ahistorical vacuum, but is linked to numerous ongoing political and professional movements. In particular, this chapter is partially embedded in (and contributes to) the larger evolving social and gender equity debates over roles and opportunities for women and men in society, especially the role of fathers, given that many aspects of parenthood are socially determined.

This is also a period of substantial economic and cultural transitions, as fatherhood transforms from an older patriarchal model of fathers as distant, controlling economic providers with stay-at-home nurturing mothers to a newer model based on greater parental equity in childcare responsibilities and combined joint family incomes. This chapter also builds upon the U.S. National Academy of Science, Engineering and Medicine's (NASEM) multigenerational lifecourse-inspired movement to foster effective parenting and parenting health, recognizing that the "early caregiving environment is crucial for the long-term development of the child" and that "effective parenting presupposes the caregivers own well-being" (NASEM 2016, 2019a), but now expands upon these parenting themes to more actively include fathers.

Sixth, it is hoped that in articulating the multiple domains of fathers' impact on perinatal health, this chapter will guide more effective and targeted ameliorative interventions and policies that will encourage and enhance father involvement in perinatal health period (i.e., moving from theory to action), as well as provide a better framework to guide further research on this emerging topic. Moreover, beyond fathers' potential contributions to improve reproductive and infant health, the perinatal period may also add opportunities for improved men's health and better targeted primary care and mental health services.

This chapter specifically provides the scientific evidence base for the contribution of fathers' health and greater involvement in the perinatal period to healthier infants, families, and men themselves.

2 The Impact of Father's Health on Reproductive and Infant Health

There are multiple pathways by which the father's health and health behaviors can directly and indirectly impact on the reproductive and early life health and well-being of his children. This manuscript will note and briefly explore the current knowledge base within *eight* distinct domains of potential paternal impact.

1. **Paternal planned and wanted pregnancies (family planning)**
2. **Paternal biologic and genetic contributions**
3. **Paternal epigenetic contributions**
4. **Paternal reproductive health practices that could enhance their partner's health behaviors and self-care practices**
5. **Paternal reproductive biologic and social health that could enhance their partner's reproductive health biology**
6. **Paternal support for maternal delivery and post-partum care**
7. **Paternal mental health influences**
8. **Paternal contributions to the family's social determinants of health**

Three of these eight pathways reflect pre-conception to conception influences (1–3); three reflect father-mother perinatal interactions (4–6); and two reflect systemic influences (7–8).

2.1 Paternal Planned and Wanted Pregnancies (Family Planning)

First, father's preconception health and health behaviors have a direct impact on maternal and infant health through family planning, one of the most traditional reproductive health and health service topic. Men are critical participants in family planning, with an inherently shared partnered responsibility (Grady et al. 1996); although traditionally, most family planning efforts have been directed at women, assuming it is their principle responsibility. Currently, in the U.S., men report between 35 and 40% of the births are unintended, 27% mis-timed, and 9% unwanted. Rates vary substantially, with more unintended pregnancies among young, unmarried, low-income, and minority women, especially those with non-residential partners (Lindberg and Kost 2014; Mosher et al. 2012).

Planned and wanted pregnancies are associated with healthier birth outcomes, especially decreased low birthweight (LBW) and pre-term births (PTB) (Kost and Lindberg 2015; Shah et al. 2011; Tsui et al. 2010). More generally, family planning is associated with improved birth spacing, smaller family size, fewer abortions, especially unsafe abortions, and fewer sexually transmitted infections (STI) (Tsui et al. 2010). Active paternal family planning efforts thereby also further mitigate against adverse maternal health behaviors associated with unwanted pregnancies (including less folic acid consumption, increased smoking, elevated maternal stress, less prenatal care and less subsequent breastfeeding) (Cheng et al. 2009; Kost and Lindberg 2015). Unplanned pregnancies are associated with a wide array of negative health, economic, social, and psychological outcomes for the mother, child, and family—both in the U.S. and throughout the world (Brown and Eisenberg 1995).

Planned and wanted pregnancies are associated with greater paternal engagement during pregnancy, childbirth, and postpartum periods (Bronte-Tinkew et al. 2007; Redshaw and Henderson 2013). By contrast, unplanned pregnancies are associated with lessened willingness of fathers to form and sustain family relationships, to live with the mother and child, to remain involved and support them, or to more positively self-appraise their own fathering quality and identity (Linberg et al. 2016).

Family planning is a reproductive health service that directly offers men the opportunity to improve their own health status: to obtain and use effective contraceptive methods, to prevent and treat STIs, and to address their subfertility issues. Increasingly national and state public health efforts are targeting men to encourage their family planning responsibilities and assure access to needed family planning services. Yet only 12% of men of reproductive age in the United States reported receiving family planning services, birth control, or STD screening services in the prior year (Chabot et al. 2011). "Still, the sexual and reproductive health needs of men in their own right—as individuals and not simply as women's partners—have been largely ignored" (Wulf 2002). The first recommendation in the seminal U.S. report on Preconception Health and Health Care calls for partners separately and together to prepare a reproductive life course plan (Johnson et al. 2006). The Centers for Disease Control and Prevention (CDC) has implemented separate men's and women's preconception and family planning websites to improve the chances of healthy planned, conceptions (CDC 2019a). And the U.S. Office of Population Affairs, Title X Family Planning administrators, have now for the first time explicitly mandated clinical guidelines for quality men's family planning and related preconception health services (Gavin et al. 2014).

Europe, in general, has more effective and equitable family planning educational and contraceptive policies than U.S., which perhaps contributes to their less frequent unintended pregnancies (Sedgh et al. 2014) and healthier reproductive outcomes (MacDormand and Mathews 2010). Men's sexual and reproductive health programs are also important to international development agencies, which focus extensively on men's involvement—and, too often, non-involvement or lack of responsibility—in family planning. These programs cover a broad range of topics including: avoidance of unwanted pregnancy; HIV/STI prevention; promotion of women's reproductive health; gender norms and couple communication; intimate partner violence prevention; and promotion of fatherhood (see, e.g., Sternberg and Hubley 2004), although the effectiveness of such interventions for men has been questioned (Hardie et al. 2017).

Paternal family planning (and preconception health care) services ensure that all pregnancy risks and responsibilities are not held solely by women. They provide a locus to enhance future reproductive outcomes through the practical encouragement of planned and wanted pregnancies and the enhancement of men's own health. Family planning promotion and services, a major area of current public health interventions, address a key pathway by which fathers can enhance reproductive and infant outcomes. Given how many pregnancies are unplanned, there remains much room for family planning enhancements, utilization, and targeting. Disappointingly, the relatively extensive male-oriented family planning services are not built upon during the subsequent fatherhood journey into the antenatal period and beyond.

2.2 Paternal Biologic and Genetic Contributions

Second, father's reproductive health, through his genetic contributions, has a direct biologic impact on his infant's health and development. Father's genes reflect half of the child's genetic inheritance. This pathway—father's genetic contributions, his sperm—is the most traditionally conceptualized domain for father's direct biologic responsibility and contribution to his child's subsequent health and well-being (and his/her appearance, personality, and intelligence among other themes). And this is often viewed as his *only* direct biological means of reproductive influence. Moreover, historically in patri-centric cultures, a father's genetic contributions have provided the legal basis to assert his progenitor control over his offspring and to assure the inheritance of societal property, his social determinants of health (SDOH) status and characteristics.

Three inter-related issues are important to successful procreation of healthy non-genetically compromised children: sperm quantity (getting pregnant), sperm quality (assuring a healthy fetus), and men's preconception health, the precursor to both. Each of these reflects long-standing traditional areas of public health research and practice.

Threats to sperm quantity. First, there are increasing reports of threats to the quantity of men's sperm, and therefore to his biologic capacity to impregnate women (e.g., Carlsen et al. 1992). A meta-analysis by Levine et al. (2017) suggests a 52.4% decline in men's sperm concentration and 59.3% decline in sperm count in Western countries in the last 40 years. And these declines are coinciding with increasing incidence of related cryptorchidism, hypospadias, and male testicular cancer (Carlsen et al. 1992; Levine et al. 2017).

Numerous reports document the extensive range of threats to the quantity (and quality) of men's sperm (e.g., Frey et al. 2008; Levine et al. 2017). Major threats include occupational and environmental influences (e.g., radiation, lead, endocrine disrupting chemicals); lifestyle factors (e.g., smoking, alcohol, high BMI); genetic disorders and chronic diseases (e.g., cystic fibrosis or diabetes); medicines (e.g., anabolic steroids, cancer chemotherapies); and demographic factors (e.g., paternal age).

Male infertility and subfertility represent a substantial direct biologic reproductive health problem. Impaired fecundity effects 13% of U.S. women (CDC 2019b). The decline in male sperm quantity likely contributes to the high rates of the total infertility due to male infertility factors alone (~30–40%) or joint male/female infertility factors (~10–20%) (Kumar and Singh 2015; Argwal et al. 2015). Infertility also can be a reproductive mental health stress for men, women, and families; male infertility is associated with increased family stress, low self-esteem, embarrassment, and depression (Noncent et al. 2017).

Threats to sperm quality. Second, similar to the quantity of men's sperm, the *quality* of men's genetic contributions can also strongly influence reproductive and infant health and development. Sperm quality can be damaged through a variety of mechanisms (e.g., immature sperm cells, DNA fragmentation, single or double strand DNA breaks, abnormalities of semen, testicular damage, sperm motility, etc.) (de Kretser 1997). Almost all of the prior risks for reduced sperm *quantity* have also been associated with sperm *quality* (Frey et al. 2008; Levine et al. 2017), and new risks continue to be established. On a more positive note, some damaged sperm can be replaced, as sperm regenerates every 42–76 days (de Jonge and Barratt 2006), and many of the clinical, environmental, and health behavior risk factors can be prevented or minimized.

There is a trend towards increasing number of births to older fathers in developed countries. Notably, advanced paternal age has been associated with poorer birth outcomes (stillbirths, preterm births); increased congenital anomalies (especially Down syndrome and PDA heart defects); and childhood acute lymphoblastic leukemia, autism, and schizophrenia (Andersen and Urhoj 2017), all of which are linked to increased de novo paternal genetic mutations that increase with age (Kong et al. 2012). Additionally, there is a well-established MCH epidemiologic literature demonstrating stable cross-generational father and infant/child characteristics, including height and weight, birth weight, and prematurity history (e.g., Misra et al. 2010; Shah and the Knowledge Synthesis Group on Determinants of Preterm/Low Birthweight Births 2010), although the causal mechanism for these associations may not operate only through direct genetic pathways.

Men's preconception health. Third, efforts to enhance men's successful fertility, via the quantity and quality his sperm, have infused the growing men's preconception health efforts (Kotelchuck and Lu 2017; Garfield 2018). Men's targeted preconception health sites exist, but they mostly encourage personal responsibility and behaviorally focused preventative approaches. Societal and employment policies, such as environmental toxic exposures regulations or community-wide lifestyle improvements or public awareness campaigns, could also be very influential. Primary care clinical approaches targeted at men's preconception health are just now being developed (Frey et al. 2008; O'Brien et al. 2018), however too few men receive any formal preconception care services, despite evident need (Frey et al. 2012; Choiriyyah et al. 2015). Men's preconception interventions could not only enhance his sperm quantity and quality but could also promote his health more generally over his lifetime.

Men's (sub-) fertility and the potential for impaired genetic quantity and quality of his sperm is the most traditionally conceptualized pathway for men's direct biologic impact on reproductive and infant health and development—plus it is a pathway that influences men's own health and development. While an extensive basic, epidemiologic, and clinical research literature exists addressing men's fertility, including a nascent focus on men's preconception health interventions, this pathway still remains understudied and underappreciated. Given how few births are planned, too many fathers are not optimally prepared for their healthiest conceptions.

2.3 *Paternal Epigenetic Contributions*

Scientifically father's sperm (his genetic germ line) has been, heretofore, viewed as the only *direct* biologic means to influence the infant's health, yet emerging today is another newly discovered and important direct biologic mechanism, *epigenetics*, by which men's sperm continues to differentially influence fetal maturation and child development long after the procreation of that infant. Epigenetics can be viewed as an on/off switch for genes based on a man's lived experiences (technically through gene methylation, histone modification, and mitochondrial RNA expression). It represents an exciting new pathway by which father's own *current* well-being and health experiences, a kind of Lamarckian genetics, influences his gene's expression and amends its original genetic contributions to the health and development of his child—and possibly alters his genetic expression over subsequent generations. More broadly, this pathway derives from our increasing scientific understanding of how environmental influences can alter (epigenetically) parental gene expression and ultimately changes the phenotype and behavior/health trajectories of their offspring. It also reflects new thinking about how our species can more rapidly adapt to changing environments, beyond the long periods needed for the genetic adaptation of the fittest.

While the epigenetic field initially focused on the mothers contributions, given that fathers contribute half of the infant's genetic material, paternal epigenetic contributions to perinatal and child well-being has recently emerged as a rapidly developing, though still small, basic science and clinical research area (Hehar and Mychasiuk 2015; Day et al. 2016; Soubry 2018). Soubry (2018) coined the term "POHaD," Paternal Origins of Health and Disease, to describe this newly emerging conceptual area. To date, most paternal epigenetic research utilizes animal models, though there is some limited literature demonstrating epigenetic transformations and impacts in humans.

Diet. Epigenetic changes in their offspring have been associated with father's diet. A growing epidemiologic literature shows that fathers' weight and BMI status independently influences the birth weight, obesity, and diabetes of their offspring (e.g., Dodd et al. 2017). For example, during Swedish famines, low and high food availability in pre-pubescent adolescents males led to changes in their children's and grandchildren's obesity, diabetes, and cardiovascular health, especially among sons, independent of their mother's health and food exposure; these were epigenetic changes too fast for spontaneous genetic alterations (Brygren et al. 2001; Kaati et al. 2002). A wide range of paternal dietary changes in experimental studies in animal models have led to marked epigenetic metabolism and tissue modifications in their offspring (Soubry 2015). Soubry et al. (2016) have shown epigenetic marker differences between obese and lean men in the cord blood DNA methylation among their offspring. Men's pre-conception physical health characteristics, such as men's diabetes, have been associated with sub-optimal birth outcomes (Moss and Harris 2015).

Alcohol and smoking. Paternal drinking/alcohol consumption is associated with epigenetic changes in their offspring. Heavy paternal alcohol intake has long been known to impact reproductive and child's health and developmental outcomes (Finegersh et al. 2015). Seventy-five percent of children with Fetal Alcohol Syndrome Disorders (FASD) have alcoholic fathers—even in the absence of maternal alcohol consumption (Day et al. 2016). Paternal alcohol exposure in rodent studies alters their sperm's DNA and offspring's epigenetic characteristics, and is associated with a variety of alcohol susceptible features in their offspring, including low birth weight and hyper-responsiveness to stress, also commonly seen in children with FASD (Day et al. 2016). Similarly, paternal pre-pubertal tobacco smoking has been linked epidemiologically to their children's obesity and asthma (Northstone et al. 2014; Svanes et al. 2017); and in animal studies, pre-conception smoke exposures have been associated with epigenetic changes in transcription factors and miRNA (Day et al. 2016).

Other environmental and behavioral factors. Soubry (2018) documents a series of other environmental exposures in fathers that are associated with epigenetic changes in their sperm or offspring, including organophosphate flame-retardants, Vitamin D supplementation, and exercise. In rodent studies, paternal stress prior to conception has been shown to alter methylation patterns and gene expression associated with their offspring's brain (Rodgers et al. 2013), HPA axis blunting (Dietz et al. 2011), and increased depressive and anxiety-like behaviors (Mychasiuk et al. 2013). Men's pre-conception elevated lead blood levels are associated with sub-optimal birth outcomes (Esquinas et al. 2014).

A note of caution however, most epigenetic research studies are based in rodent models; human studies are relatively rare and often not sufficiently rigorous. Furthermore, some of the purported paternal effects may be due to maternal or fetal compensatory behavioral changes adjusting to the father's altered characteristics (Curley et al. 2011). The intergenerational permanence of the environmentally induced epigenetic effects in the paternal germ line also remains under-explored, especially in humans. Epigenetic changes, however, do suggest plausible biologic mechanisms by which some of the previously noted paternal sperm quality risk factors and epidemiologic environmental exposures (including older age) are associated with poorer reproductive and infant health outcomes.

The emergence of paternal epigenetic pathways provides exciting new biological insights into how father's preconception and *ongoing current* health status, health behaviors, and environmental exposures can directly impact fetal, infant, and child's health and development over their lifetime and intergenerationally. Epigenetics, a kind of Lamarckian genetics that compliments Mendelian genetics, provides a richer understanding of how father's social and health experiences, his lived experiences, enters into his body and then influences the quality of his sperm and its genetic and, now, epigenetic contributions to his offspring's health and development. These "lived" gene experiences are still a new area of research, and their practical clinical implications are not yet developed. No longer should only women or only pregnant women be encouraged to be healthy to assure their future infant's health, but now fathers should be too; their own current health status and behaviors may have a direct epigenetic influence on their infant's health.

2.4 *Paternal Reproductive Health Practices That Could Enhance Their Partner's Health Behaviors and Self-Care Practices*

Paternal reproductive practices have an *indirect* impact on the infant's health through their encouragement of enhanced or diminished reproductive health behaviors and self-care practices of their partners. Father's own health care, behaviors, and attitudes offer opportunities to support, model and promote positive women's reproductive health and health care seeking behaviors.

Enhancing maternal health behaviors. Fathers can serve as a role model to foster or discourage maternal preventative health-related behaviors—which can directly influence reproductive outcomes—both before conception and during pregnancy. For a woman to eat nutritiously, quit smoking, exercise, and not use drugs, etc., can be more difficult if her enabling partner continues his reproductively negative health behaviors. There is an extensive literature on the co-occurrence of maternal and paternal negative health behaviors across a wide range of reproductive health promoting behaviors, including alcohol usage (e.g., Leonard and Eiden 1999), smoking (e.g., Gage et al. 2007) and dietary habits (e.g., Saxbe et al. 2018). A woman, for example, is 6.2 times as likely to be obese if her partner is obese compared to normal weight (Edvardsson et al. 2013). Fathers who are more actively engaged and socially supportive during the pregnancy are associated with reduced maternal cigarette consumption (Martin et al. 2007; Elsenbruch et al. 2007; Cheng et al. 2016; Bloch et al. 2010) and drug usage (Bloch et al. 2010). Fathers are an important antenatal and postnatal influence on mother's breastfeeding decisions and success (Bar-Yam and Darby 1997; Wolfberg et al. 2004; Rempel and Rempel 2011), and greater paternal involvement is associated with more breastfeeding (Redshaw and Henderson 2013). Improving father's antenatal reproductive health behaviors also directly benefits the father's lifetime health.

Enhancing maternal reproductive health service utilization. Fathers can play an important role in encouraging or discouraging women's utilization of prenatal care (PNC) and other reproductive and pediatric health services. Fathers who were more actively engaged during their partner's pregnancy were more likely to encourage earlier and more frequent prenatal care (Martin et al. 2007; Teitler 2001; Redshaw and Henderson 2013) and more postnatal care (Redshaw and Henderson 2013). PNC utilization was less adequate among couples with disagreement about the pregnancy wantedness (Hohmann-Marriott 2009) and earlier among fathers desiring the pregnancy in a Hispanic sample (Sangi-Haghpeykar et al. 2005). Recognizing that fathers can also be a controlling gatekeeper in decisions around maternal usage of reproductive health services—a role that varies within different cultural groups—fathers could be more actively targeted to encourage their partner's PNC usage, similar to the messages now routinely directed at them to support their partner's breastfeeding.

Providing maternal emotional and logistical support to influence maternal health behaviors. Fathers can be a major source of emotional, logistical, and financial support or stress for their partners during pregnancy and early parenthood (May and Fletcher 2013; Alio et al. 2013); and in general, increased maternal stress is strongly associated with poorer pregnancy outcomes (Wadhwa et al. 2011; Lu and Halfon 2003). More paternal emotional support and involvement during pregnancy is widely associated with less maternal anxiety, stress, and depression (Elsenbruch et al. 2007; Cheng et al. 2016; Bloch et al. 2010), and with less post-partum maternal psychological stress (Redshaw and Henderson 2013). Elevated maternal stress can lead to the adoption of reproductively unhealthy coping behaviors (Lobel et al. 2008; Hobel et al. 2008; Bloch et al. 2010), a possible causal pathway for poorer pregnancy outcomes. Conceptually, this topic encourages fathers to provide the traditionally ascribed positive "support" for their partners during pregnancy.

Women with more direct paternal emotional support during pregnancy (as well as practical or financial support) are associated with better birth outcomes, in low-income Black urban communities (Bloch et al. 2010), in Latin communities with moderate-high stress levels (Ghosh et al. 2010), and among smokers (Elsenbruch et al. 2007), although such findings are not always strong or consistent across all populations (Cheng et al. 2016). Paternal emotional support, as an isolated variable, may not be sufficient to counteract the stronger, longitudinal maternal reproductive health stresses prevalent in low-income communities. Birth certificate analyses of women in father-absent or single-parent households, who would theoretically have less paternal emotional support (as well as less financial support), have poorer birth outcomes (Gaudino et al. 1999; Alio et al. 2011a; b; Hibbs et al. 2018).

Most fathers want to, and can be encouraged to, help ensure healthier offspring by promoting their partner's positive reproductive health behaviors and self-care practices and by diminishing her need to adopt negative stress-related coping behaviors. This indirect paternal reproductive health pathway encourages the traditional supportive roles for fathers during pregnancy. The importance of these efforts however is often under-appreciated; too many fathers unfortunately do not sufficiently model or promote positive health behaviors, nor provide enough emotional, logistical, or financial support. This pathway also encourages fathers to simultaneously improve their own health and health behaviors during the perinatal period, and possibly to enhance the epigenetic health of their future children.

2.5 Paternal Reproductive Biologic and Social Health That Could Enhance Their Partner's Reproductive Health Biology

Father's health status and health behaviors can have a *direct* positive, neutral, or negative impact on the physical and biological health of the pregnant woman and her developing fetus. Or, stated alternatively, the absence of father's negative health status and negative health behaviors can enhance (and/or not harm) the woman's and fetus's reproductive health status during the pregnancy. Conceptually, there are multiple channels through which the father's influence can be manifested. The negative modalities are the more popularly known.

Intimate partner violence (IPV). Sexual violence and reproductive control, disproportionately targeting women of childbearing age, especially younger and poorer women, is a direct threat to the reproductive health of the mother and fetus. Though the vast majority of fathers do not engage in IPV, 3–9% of women report being abused during pregnancy (Chu et al. 2010; Chen et al. 2017), with slightly lower rates reported in Europe and Asia and higher rates in the Americas and Africa (Devries et al. 2010). IPV is associated with a wide range of maternal reproductive health problems (including unintended and rapid repeat pregnancies, increased STIs); maladaptive coping behaviors; serious mental health problems (including pre- and post-partum depression); and poor infant outcomes (including prematurity and infant mortality) (Alhusen et al. 2015). IPV and injuries are the leading cause of maternal mortality, with IPV associated with ~50% of pregnancy related suicides and homicides (Palladino et al. 2011). But importantly, by implication, this means that lack of IPV by fathers is associated with neutral or better birth outcomes for mothers, infants, and families. A wide variety of men's IPV prevention interventions have been implemented, most heavily focused on addressing the masculinity and gender-related social norms implicated in violence. These have proven only marginally effective, and more community-based ecological approaches are now being advocated (Jewkes et al. 2015). The concerns of women's health care providers about the possibility of IPV, and their ability to inquire about IPV confidentially, have often led to the discouragement of, and even hostility towards, fathers participating in maternal reproductive health services during pregnancy (Davison et al. 2019).

Sexually transmitted infections. Fathers with sexually transmitted infections (STIs), can potentially expose their pregnant partners and through them their fetuses to these infectious diseases. The prevalence of STIs in men is substantial and varies by infection; one in two sexually active men will contract a STI by age 25 (ASHA 2019). Untreated STIs are associated with a wide range of poor birth outcomes (including miscarriages, PTBs, infant mortality, and infant eye, lung, or liver damage); maternal morbidities (including pelvic inflammatory disease and tubule infections, that increase the likelihood of infertility); as well as paternal morbidities (including systemic infections, infertility, penile cancer, sores/flare ups and death) (CDC 2019c). Since most STIs can be prevented or well managed through safe sex and antibiotics, fathers must play a key role in their prevention, treatment, and mitigation—a responsibility towards both the current and future pregnancies. Yet, only 12% of adolescents and young adult men are formally screened for STIs annually (Cuffe et al. 2016). STI treatment of women without simultaneous treatment of their infected male partners is doomed to failure.

Paternal infectious diseases. Beyond STIs, the father's exposures to other infectious diseases can serve as a direct vector for their introduction to their partners (e.g., rubella, chicken pox, tuberculosis, Zika, and coronavirus). Recently, CDC/AAP has begun advising fathers to obtain the Tdap vaccines during the pregnancy to ensure a healthy environment during the infant's early life vulnerability to pertussis; and similarly to obtain annual influenza vaccinations (CDC 2011).

Paternal second-hand smoke and other environmental exposures. In meta-review articles, household second-hand smoke (SHS) exposure among non-smoking pregnant women is associated with a small but significant decrease in infant birth weight (Salmasi et al. 2010; Leonardi-Bee et al. 2011). SHS exposure during pregnancy has been also associated with an increased risk of infertility, stillbirth, and pre-term delivery (Meeker and Benedict 2013). The only SHS intervention specifically directed at fathers showed positive impact on paternal quitting rates (Stanton et al. 2004). Beyond SHS, fathers may potentially expose women to a variety of other teratogenic and mutagenic occupational and environmental toxins (Knishkowy and Baker 1986). Infants born to the partners of U.S. and Australian soldiers in Vietnam who handled Agent Orange/dioxin had increased birth defects (Ngo et al. 2006). Paternal pre-conception and perinatal health care screenings potentially allows for the mitigation of maternal and fetal exposure to environmental toxins (Frey et al. 2008).

Direct paternal influence on maternal and child nutritional status. Beyond the already noted *indirect* pathways by which fathers can encourage positive or negative maternal nutritional health practices, fathers can play an important *direct* role in influencing maternal weight gain, obesity, and nutritional status during pregnancy and beyond. Fathers are not necessarily passive bystanders in the nutritional well-being of their households. They can potentially directly influence food and meal preparation, household food and beverage purchases, formal dining practices, and the availability of needed family income to obtain adequate nutrition. More men cook and spend more time cooking now than over the past 40 years (Smith et al. 2013). There is increasing theoretical recognition that fathers could directly contribute to infant obesity prevention and metabolic health, perhaps starting even prior to birth (Davison et al. 2019), yet few nutrition interventions directly target fathers (Morgan et al. 2017; Davison et al. 2017). Father's own weight is an independent predictor of childhood obesity (Freeman et al. 2012; Dodd et al. 2017).

Stress and its direct impact on maternal reproductive health biology. Paternally induced stress can be harmful to mothers and their developing fetuses through multiple direct and indirect modalities, and may even have lifelong impacts. Previously in this chapter, maternal response to elevated stress through maladaptive health behaviors was viewed as an indirect causal pathway. Here, additionally, elevated maternal stress is viewed as having a *direct* causal effect on women's reproductive biology, impacting her developing maternal-placental-fetal endocrine, immune, vascular, and genetic systems, as well as through the effects of stress on nutrition utilization and stress on infectious disease susceptibility (Wadhwa et al. 2011; DiPietro 2012). Both humans and animal maternal stress models (often paternally induced) have repeatedly documented changes in cortisol and corticotropin-releasing hormone (CRH) levels, hypothalamic-pituitary-adrenal (HPA) axis functioning, vascular changes, hypertension, etc. (Wadhwa et al. 2011; NASEM 2019a), reflecting biologic changes widely hypothesized as the physiologic basis for pre-term births, Black-White infant reproductive disparities, and sub-optimal African-American women's health over their life-course (e.g., the "weathering hypothesis" Geronimus 1992, 1996). Moreover, the direct biologic impact of increased maternal stress may have long-term epigenetic consequences on the infant's brain and behavioral response to stress. Furthermore, if the biological responses to stress interact with increased negative maternal pregnancy behaviors, they may perhaps further foster epigenetic dietary and metabolic disease, alcohol susceptibility, etc. in their offspring (Wadhwa et al. 2011).

Father's health and social health behaviors (both positive and negative) during the perinatal period can have a direct biologic impact on maternal and fetal/infant health and development. Beyond the widely noted concerns over IPV and STIs, father's health operates through multiple other modalities to impact the mother's reproductive health biology. Father's health (after procreation) is not usually thought of as a direct mechanism or pathway to influence reproductive outcomes, but it should be. This is an important new and expanding conceptual pathway for paternal reproductive health impact. Moreover, addressing father's reproduction-linked health issues will directly enhance his own lifetime health, as well as enhance the reproductive health biology of women and their fetuses in the current and future pregnancies.

2.6 Paternal Support for Maternal Delivery and Post-partum Care

Fathers can impact reproductive and infant health through their active and direct provision of clinical support to their partners during the perinatal period, especially around delivery and post-partum care. This is a new emerging conceptual pathway—fathers as direct quasi-health care providers for their partners. For example, in most marriages or stable relationships, partners provide palliative and supportive functional nursing care when their partner is sick. During the perinatal period, fathers can and often do provide some very specific maternal reproductive health services.

Obstetric emergency support: Fathers can potentially prevent maternal and infant mortality and morbidity by recognizing and acting on obstetric emergencies, especially for very premature deliveries, as delays in getting antenatal clinical interventions can have serious maternal or fetal consequences. Thaddeus and Maine (1994) emphasized that fathers should be able to recognize an obstetric emergency, be able to take decisions to seek care (or encourage their partner to seek care), and be able to transport their partners to high quality health services. The European WHO agency sees these as some of father's principle antenatal responsibilities (WHO 2007). Most fathers provide ambulance-like transportation to the delivery hospitals for their partner's premature and normal gestation pregnancies.

Delivery support: Fathers can play an important supportive role for mothers during delivery. Starting in the later part of the twentieth century, fathers have been increasingly present in hospital delivery rooms, providing familial emotional reassurance and practical support to their partner during her birthing experience. Recent figures suggest that up to 90% of fathers in Britain are present at delivery (Redshaw and Heikkilä 2010), with nearly universal participation in most western countries today (Redshaw and Henderson 2013). Historically, the women's reproductive health movement led the fight for their partner's presence in the birthing room

(Leavitt 2010). Many women view their partner's presence as a secondary advocate or advisor on emergent obstetric decisions, independent of the clinician-centric hospital culture. Conceptually, these paternal delivery support roles are analogous to some of the roles of a doula (e.g., Dads as Doulas.) Many fathers themselves also now want to be present at delivery for their own emotional and psychological growth and infant bonding.

There is very limited systematic research on the impact of father's presence in the delivery room to date. These are mostly small case series, some reporting more positive impact for the mothers and the fathers (Kainz et al. 2010), and others reflecting more mixed experiences (Bohren et al. 2019), especially for first time fathers who may be unfamiliar or uncomfortable with obstetrical practices during delivery (Johansson et al. 2015; Jomeen 2017). Moreover, many clinicians are resistant to their presence in the delivery room and do not always treat them favorably, i.e., "not patient, not visitor," and hindering fathers' desires to be more supportive (Steen et al. 2012). However, accommodating the increasing father delivery participation trends, many birthing centers now provide supportive father-friendly post-partum sleeping accommodations for both parents.

Post-partum recovery care and support. Following the birth, many fathers provide instrumental help, social support, and nursing-like health care for the mother during her post-partum recovery, especially for post-operative Cesarean sections care, as well as begin to provide newborn and family care. In situations where the mother's or infant's health is seriously compromised, fathers often must take on more emergency or even full-time care of their newborns and be a resource to help manage the mother's emotional and practical needs (Erlandson and Lindgren 2011). And, if an infant is premature, many Neonatal Intensive Care Units (NICUs) now encourage paternal skin-to-skin kangaroo care to reduce neonatal morbidity and facilitate neuro-behavioral development (Ludington-Hoe et al. 1992).

Paternal leave. Beyond the father's own potential desire for infant bonding, paternal post-partum leave allows the time and space to provide more supportive nursing care for his partner. Paternal leave's impact may operate through the mother's well-being; increased paternal workplace paid-leave flexibility is associated with reduced maternal post-partum physical health complications and improved mental health (Persson and Rossin-Slater 2019). While a large literature documents the health and developmental benefits of paid leave for mothers (Gault et al. 2014), less research exists on the paternal leave benefits. Longer paternal leave is associated with greater subsequent infant and childcare involvement (Boll et al. 2014; Huerta et al. 2013; Nepomnyaschy and Waldfogel 2007).

Maternal post-partum depression observer. Finally and importantly, fathers are the frontline mental health observers of maternal post-partum depression (Garfield and Isacco 2009). They would be the first to notice emerging mental health problems and could act on that knowledge, perhaps even before a clinician's awareness. This responsibility is similar to the initial antenatal paternal responsibility for monitoring obstetric emergencies, only now in the post-partum period.

This emerging domain reflects a new reproductive health pathway for fathers as active and direct quasi-clinical care support for their partner. This

role exists throughout the perinatal period, if not before and after, but is especially important around the delivery and the early post-partum period. This pathway potentially offers fathers the opportunity for more concrete action-oriented roles and contributions. Fathers, like doulas, can be a positive influence on maternal delivery and post-partum health experiences. The increased presence of fathers in the delivery room, and their provision of post-partum care, helps serve as a bridge between the father's antenatal reproductive health experiences and his subsequent post-natal family, parenting, and child health and development activities.

2.7 Paternal Mental Health Influences

Father's mental health status (including stress, depression, and anxiety) has a strong and well-established impact on multiple domains of child health and development (e.g., Yogman et al. 2016; Yogman and Eppel 2021, in this volume); however, there is very limited literature on the consequences of father's antenatal mental health on reproductive health or birth outcomes. By contrast though, there is a much larger literature on the impact of pregnancy on father's mental health (Kotelchuck 2021, in this volume). However, given the early origin implications of MCH life course theory, it is likely that father's antenatal mental health status may play an important role in reproductive and infant outcomes.

Paternal mental health functioning is a substantial health issue during the perinatal period. Perinatal period is associated with elevated rates of paternal depression (10.4%) (Paulson and Bazemore 2010); anxiety (4–16%) (Leach et al. 2016; Philpott et al. 2019); and stress (Philpott et al. 2017). Whether paternal antenatal mental health problems impact reproductive outcomes, or vice versa, may be a chicken-egg problem, but father's mental health status amplified by his pregnancy experiences needs to be addressed starting in the antenatal period.

The epidemiologic literature on paternal mental health status and birth outcomes is a very limited. In a Swedish population, Lui et al. (2016) documented that new onset paternal depression, though not chronic depression, was associated with elevated very preterm births. In animal models, paternal stress exposure in the preconception or antenatal periods has been repeatedly associated epigenetically with behavioral stress markers in their offspring (Dietz et al. 2011; Pang et al. 2017); and LBW has been documented among the offspring of paternally alcohol-exposed rodents (Day et al. 2016). Plus, as noted previously, the epigenetic consequences of paternal alcoholism, often a behavioral manifestation of mental health issues, is associated with FASD in their offspring (Finegersh et al. 2015).

The father's mental health status may be the underlying systemic source for several of the paternal perinatal reproductive health pathways discussed in this essay, especially those associated with increased maternal stress. Fathers who provide their partners with limited emotional and relational support may themselves have underlying mental health problems or limited relational skills. Men compared to women with depressive symptomatology often display higher levels of externalized irritability and anger, which may be particularly stressful for pregnant women (Madsen and Burgess 2010). Fathers with elevated mental health or stress symptoms may be a less reliable source of steady employment, financial security, or consistent practical help, important areas of maternal antenatal stress. Fathers often behaviorally self-medicate (e.g., increased alcohol and substance use) to avoid addressing their own mental health problems, which not only may add to the mother's stress, but further serves as a poor behavioral health role models for her. In the extreme, paternal mental health issues could manifest themselves in IPV or family abandonment. Ultimately, it is likely that all of the paternal reproductive health pathways discussed in this chapter reflect, in part, some paternal mental health components. However, to date, an appreciation of the secondary contribution of father's antenatal mental health to the other paternal reproductive health pathways is limited, a derivative topic at best.

Father's positive mental health status may help compensate for mental health problems of their partners. Engaged, non-depressed fathers have been shown to be developmentally protective for the infants and children with depressed mothers (e.g., Hossain et al. 1994; Mezilius et al. 2004), though this same theme hasn't yet been explored in the antenatal period. Father's positive mental health status may also play an important role in fostering a growing sense of paternal generativity and involvement starting in the antenatal period (Kotelchuck 2021, in this volume).

Finally and critically, paternal mental health issues can potentially be acknowledged, assessed, and treated even during the antenatal period. The men's preconception health literature exhorts them to improve their mental and behavioral health (CDC 2019a), but after conception little further attention is directed at this topic. Moreover, despite a nascent advocacy literature calling for attention to fathers often stressed and depressed mental health status during the perinatal period (e.g., Philpott et al. 2017; Gemayel et al. 2018), there are virtually no intervention programs directed at them during this period (Romanov et al. 2016).

Fathers experience substantial mental health challenges during the antenatal period. These may be underlying systemic contributors to many of the paternal reproductive health and health behaviors pathways, especially those associated with increased maternal stress, which ultimately may lead to poorer reproductive and infant health and development outcomes. This domain has not yet been sufficiently addressed by the larger reproductive health community, though it has been emphasized importantly within the child development and pediatric fields. Given the longitudinal assumptions underlying the MCH life course theory, paternal perinatal mental health is likely to be an important and emergent reproductive health topic in the future, similar to the recent increased focus on maternal antenatal depression. Unfortunately, too limited awareness of fathers' needs and too few mental health interventions are currently directed towards them in the perinatal period.

2.8 Paternal Contributions to the Family's Social Determinants of Health

Finally, father's contributions to their family's social determinants of health, the family's social well-being, can be viewed conceptually as a "new" systemic pathway by which father's health and well-being impacts on reproductive, infant, family and their own health. Fathers are a key, and perhaps the dominant vector, for influencing the SDOH of their families. SDOH, in turn, are critically important factors for reproductive and infant health (Kotelchuck 2018; NASEM 2019a). The MCH public health field believes that differential family SDOH over the life course are the *principle* source of optimal or suboptimal lifetime health, and of social and racial health disparities manifested from birth outcomes onward (Lu and Halfon 2003; Pies and Kotelchuck 2014). Between 50 and 80% of health status is believed to be determined by SDOH, not medical care (Whitehead and Dalgren 1991).

The widely known positive stepwise gradient of better child health and development with higher family income or social class (e.g., NASEM 2016, 2019b) has been similarly demonstrated for reproductive outcomes (O'Campo and Urquia 2011). That more positive reproductive outcomes are associated with increasing father/family income is a fact known and documented repeatedly since the 1920s (Woodbury 1925). More recently, for example, adverse birth outcomes throughout Canada were associated with decreasing father education, even controlling for maternal characteristics (Shapiro et al. 2017). Father-absent families, with their much lower incomes, have poorer reproductive and infant health outcomes than father-present families (Gaudino et al. 1999; Alio et al. 2011a, b; Hibbs et al. 2018). Residential geographic location, especially for poorer and minority families, is also strongly associated with poorer reproductive outcomes (O'Campo et al. 2008). European countries, which provide more extensive social welfare benefits to optimize their citizen's reproductive health and diminish social class disparities, have better infant and child health outcomes than the U.S., especially for prematurity and LBW (WHO 2017). And cross-generationally in Chicago, fathers from lower versus higher lifelong social classes, measured by neighborhood income from their own birth to their current paternity, had more infants with early and overall PTBs (Collins et al. 2019).

Father's social class, race, education, employment, and residence are not paternal "reproductive health choices"; they primarily reflect his birth and historical life circumstances, including exposure to systemic racism. Multiple mechanisms have been posited about how the negative structural aspects of paternal or family SDOH, especially those associated with poverty, get translated into poorer reproductive outcomes—limited access to healthier foods, poorer quality housing, more toxic environmental exposures, inadequate education, and poorer quality medical care, to name but a few (e.g., Braveman and Gottlieb 2014; NASEM 2019a, b). But beyond these more obvious direct structural aspects of SDOH, there are also multiple other paternal-specific SDOH experiences that could influence reproductive outcomes.

First, the father's historic and current SDOH experiences influences his mental and physical health, which in turn further impacts reproductive and infant health outcomes. Fathers' own current health status diminishes as their income decreases or poverty level rises (Williams 2003), and their health is further compounded with their life course exposures to childhood poverty and adverse childhood experiences (ACEs) (Treadwell and Ro 2008). Poor and working-class fathers' health is impacted by their economic marginality, adverse working conditions, and greater work-life psychological stress and inflexibilities. Moreover, poorer men have less access to health insurance for themselves or their families (Cormon et al. 2009). Poor paternal health is thus both a consequence and cause of their poverty.

Second, as previously noted, father's SDOH or social well-being can directly and indirectly influence the mother's health, health behaviors and stress levels, which may impact reproductive and infant health outcomes. Poorer paternal SDOH may increase maternal stress over his reliability as a source of financial security and steady employment, his availability to provide consistent needed instrumental and emotional support, or his adoption of maladaptive coping behaviors to avoid addressing his own enhanced SDOH stresses.

Third, father's current social class or SDOH may limit his ability to participate in reproductive and infant health services. Poorer fathers' work schedules, in general, have less work flexibility (Gerstel and Clawson 2018), less time off to accompany their partners to antenatal, delivery, or pediatric care, and less paid newborn family leave—findings confirmed in our MGH fatherhood prenatal care study (Levy and Kotelchuck 2021, in this volume). These social class limitations can potentially diminish father's involvement with the pregnancy and infancy, reinforce traditional parental gender roles, and allow less attachment bonding time.

And finally, paternal SDOH can be conceptualized as a systemic influence that affects all the reproductive and infant pathways discussed in this chapter. For example, paternal poverty may limit access to contraceptive services and supplies; increase exposure to dangerous occupational or environmental toxins that impact sperm quality and quantity; or increase mental health stress and substance use that perhaps also are sources of paternal epigenetic transformations.

However, despite the discouraging epidemiologic associations between paternal poverty and poorer reproductive and infant outcomes, this paternal SDOH pathway does not simply represent a fixed permanent risk factor. It is amenable to broad integrated multifaceted policy and practice interventions to enhance paternal and family social well-being (Kotelchuck 2021). Kotelchuck and Lu (2017) outlined three broad domains of social interventions that are needed: paternal clinical policy and practice transformations; enhanced paternal social welfare and employment policies; and paternal agency and generativity programs.

Unfortunately, to over-generalize, in the MCH health care communities father's social status and well-being, beyond his presence or absence in the family and his insurance status, is not usually singled out as a special reproductive social determinant of health factor that needs to be formally addressed as a potential causal issue for poor maternal and infant health outcomes, but it should be.

Father's contributions to their family's SDOH can be viewed as a "new" foundational pathway by which father's health and well-being impact on reproductive, infant, family and their own health. Fathers are the key vectors

for the social well-being/SDOH of their families, and SDOH are likely the most powerful direct influence on reproductive and infant health and development and their associated racial and social class disparities. Paternal SDOH operates systemically through multiple direct and indirect pathways, many of which are amenable to public programs and policies. However, given the general lack of interest in fathers in the MCH reproductive health communities, not surprisingly, this topic is rarely considered. One cannot ameliorate the SDOH root causes of poor reproductive health without directly addressing father's contributions to his family's SDOH.

3 Significance of the New Father's Reproductive Health Conceptualization and Findings and Their Implications for Health Service Programs

This chapter articulates eight broad pathways through which father's health, health behaviors and attitudes, and social well-being, directly and indirectly influences reproductive health and infant health. Men's contributions to reproductive outcomes are more than the quantity and quality of his sperm. This emerging conceptual framework covers the entire developmental span from preconception through pregnancy until birth and slightly beyond—a time period not usually thought of as reflecting paternal health influences on reproductive health outcomes (beyond his genetics at contraception), and perhaps beyond what most readers or MCH health professionals might currently think. Hopefully, this chapter will serve as a foundational scientific knowledge base for this evolving area of paternal reproductive health conceptualization and be used to support new and enhanced programs, policies, and research that encourage more active, healthier and earlier involvement of fathers during the perinatal period.

First, this chapter presents a broad systematic exploration of the father's multifaceted (biological, behavioral, and social) perinatal contributions to reproductive and infant health outcomes and a new eight-pathway conceptual framework to organize them. Heretofore, there has been only a very diverse and scattered MCH perinatal health fatherhood literature—focusing on a few specialized fatherhood themes (e.g., family planning or inter-generational birth outcome epidemiology) or targeted disease or intervention topics with a strong fatherhood emphasis (e.g., FASD/alcoholism or IPV initiatives). The proposed new conceptual framework builds upon an earlier and more limited one deriving from a men's preconception health paper (Kotelchuck and Lu 2017)—three of the proposed pathways reflect pre-conception to conception influences; three reflect father-mother perinatal interactions; and two reflect systemic influences. Among the pathways are several important new themes (including epigenetics, fathers as SDOH vectors); expansions of several traditional themes (especially father's direct ongoing health impact on mother's biologic health status); as well as several emerging themes (like father's quasi-clinical support of maternal delivery and post-partum care). Hopefully, others will build upon this initial conceptualization, as further new scientific understandings of paternal antenatal health impact emerge and evolve.

Second, this chapter has endeavored to push back the MCH field's appreciation of the developmental time frame for the father's impact on child development and early family life into the reproductive antenatal health period, if not earlier. This expanded time frame better aligns with the emerging scientific knowledge bases deriving from the MCH life course, Developmental Origins of Health and Disease (DoHAD), and First Thousand Days perspectives (Halfon et al. 2014; Wadwha et al. 2009; Blake-Lamb et al. 2018). These perspectives emphasize that conception, or even earlier epigenetically, not the birth, is the true developmental starting point for the impact of both parent's health and well-being on their infant/child's life course risks and protective factors. This expanded temporal framework places fatherhood better into an intergenerational context—both as the source of his infant's health and well-being and as a bi-directional event for his own life's health and development. In addition, it reinforces the perspective that the earlier the father's involvement the better for the infant, family, and his own health. Historically, father's temporal contributions to child development have steadily moved to earlier and earlier ontogenetic time frames.

Third, this chapter's broad holistic view of father's health allows us to appreciate his impact on multiple reproductive and infant health domains simultaneously rather than focus only on single disease topics. This orientation is consistent with life course theory that early generic or upstream exposures impact multiple downstream disease-specific topics. Moreover, this chapter should expand our understanding that critical reproductive and infant health topics, such as nutritional health and dietary intake, substance use, stress, etc., can be, and are, impacted by several of the distinctive fatherhood conceptual pathways, perhaps at the same time. Indeed, for any critical reproductive health topic, one could examine each of the causative paternal health pathways and conceptualize their unique added contributions, thereby, increasing the number and timing of potential paternal interventions. Moreover, the eight specific pathways are written to try to isolate and better articulate them conceptually, but many of them overlap and are synergistic.

Fourth, as noted earlier, this chapter's themes are linked to numerous ongoing political and professional movements. First and most importantly, this chapter contributes to the evolving larger social and gender equity debates about the roles and opportunities for women and men in society. It contradicts the prevailing view that mothers alone are responsible for positive reproductive and infant outcomes. The infant's biology, beyond genetics, is a more shared responsibility than heretofore generally thought. Second, and not surprisingly, this chapter is being written during a period of major economic, social, and childcare transformations, with more than 70% of women with young children in the U.S. and other industrial countries now employed, and more single- and dual-income family fathers are now providing primary caretaking for their children during at least part of the day (Yogman et al. 2016). Third, this chapter expands upon the NASEM-inspired efforts to foster effective parenting and parenting health (NASEM 2016, 2019a); it explicitly highlights some potential additional and under-appreciated pathways to achieve those parenting goals during the antenatal period, beyond simply calling for parent's generic well-being and positive mental health status. Fourth, by recognizing the importance of father's SDOH contributions to reproductive outcomes, this chapter suggests that interventions focused only on maternal SDOH-related themes without also acknowledging or directly addressing the father's SDOH contributions are likely to fail. Moreover, social class differences in the parent's own health, including the fathers' health and mental health, are themselves a major source of developmental inequalities in reproductive and infant health. And finally, this chapter also emphasizes new reproductive health involvement dimensions to the emerging men's health movement.

Fifth, and importantly, this chapter also opens up a new empirical developmental science policy rationale for the father's increased, earlier, and healthier perinatal involvement. It documents the growing enhanced scientific knowledge base to support the emerging paternal perinatal health movements. Independent of one's ideological or policy rationale for supporting greater paternal antenatal involvement, the reality of his greater involvement (via his health and health behaviors) is objectively associated with better reproductive and infant outcomes.

Finally, the themes of this chapter (the impact of father's health on reproductive and infant health) and the next (the impact of fatherhood on men's health) are intractably bound. Fathers impact their child's health, and the child impacts the father's health, development, and generativity. Both perspectives are needed and critical; they coexist at the same time. The MCH field, which historically hasn't heavily emphasized the importance of fatherhood, must address this topic from the perspectives of both the child and family and the father himself—similar to the dual women's preconception health perspectives. One is not more important than another (Wise 2008).

3.1 *Implications for Health Services Programs and Policies*

This chapter's detailed recitation of the father's reproductive and infant health impacts hopefully should encourage more, and more well targeted, men's health care interventions across the lifespan for his family's and his own health. Antenatal reproductive health services for fathers are not currently a major focus of men's clinical health care. While a full discussion of antenatal reproductive health services or programs for fathers is beyond the scope of this chapter, I will simply note four broad health services transformations that would appear to be warranted: (1) Reorient current reproductive and pediatric health services to be more father or family inclusive; (2) Provide some father or family targeted health services during existing mother-focused reproductive and pediatric health services; (3) Encourage more reproductive health-focused primary health care for men; and (4) Increase mental health care for fathers in the perinatal period. Additional potential father-supportive prenatal care obstetric practices are discussed in the Levy and Kotelchuck (2021) chapter in this volume. New and emerging opportunities to foster more specific father-inclusive public health services or policies were also highlighted within each of the eight paternal pathways, where possible. Ultimately however, paternal health is only marginally impacted by the health or medical care sector; it is also deeply influenced by social welfare and employment policies (SDOH) directed at men, as well as father's own agency and generativity (see Kotelchuck and Lu 2017; Kotelchuck 2021). [Additional details about potential fatherhood enhancing programs and policies are discussed in other sectors of this book, and especially in the concluding chapter.]

4 Conclusion

Enhancing father's health and health behaviors before, during, after pregnancy, and in early parenthood is critical to improve reproductive and infant health and development, and ultimately the health of their families, communities, and the men themselves. This chapter articulates eight direct and indirect pathways by which father's antenatal health and health behavior, broadly construed, impacts reproductive and infant health. It brings together and expands upon the existing scattered fatherhood scientific knowledge base and pushes back the developmental time frame for father's reproductive health importance into the antenatal pre-birth period, if not earlier. Awareness of father's increased importance, involvement, and health during pregnancy and early family life should encourage a rebalancing of the culturally traditional maternal and paternal parental role expectations and practices.

Clearly, the core public health action message of this chapter is that there should be earlier, healthier, and more paternal involvement during the perinatal period, in order to improve reproductive and infant health and development and the father's own health and development—"to empower fathers to be active, informed, and emotionally engaged with their children and families" (Levy et al. 2012) from the onset of the pregnancy, if not before. Healthy men and healthy fathers help insure healthy children, healthy families, healthy workforces, and healthy communities.

References

Alhusen JL, Ray E, Sharps PW, Bullock L (2015) Intimate partner violence during pregnancy: maternal and neonatal outcomes. J Womens Health 24(1):100–106
Alio AP, Mbah AK, Grunsten RA, Salihu HM (2011a) Teenage pregnancy and the influence of paternal involvement on fetal outcomes. J Pediatr Adolesc Gynecol 24(6):404–409
Alio AP, Mbah AK, Kornosky JL, Wathington D, Marty PJ, Salihu HM (2011b) Assessing the impact of paternal involvement on racial/ethnic disparities in infant mortality rates. J Community Health 36(1):63–68
Alio AP, Lewis CA, Scarborough K, Harris K, Fiscella K (2013) A community perspective on the role of fathers during pregnancy: a qualitative study. BMC Pregnancy Childbirth 13(60):13–60

American Sexual Health Association (2019) Statistics STIs. wwwashasexualhealthorg/stdsstis/statistics. Accessed 15 Jan 2020

Andersen A-MN, Urhoj SK (2017) Is advanced paternal age a risk factor for the offspring? Fertil Steril 107(2):312–318

Argwal A, Mulgund A, Hamada A, Chyatte MR (2015) A unique view on male infertility around the globe. Reprod Biol Endocrinol 13:37

Bar-Yam NB, Darby L (1997) Fatherhood and breastfeeding: a review of the literature. J Hum Lact 13(1):45–50

Blake-Lamb T, Boudreau AA, Matathia S, Tiburcio E, Perkins ME, Roche B, Kotelchuck M, Shtasel D, Price SN, Taveras EM (2018) Strengthening integration of clinical and public health systems to prevent maternal-child obesity in the first 1,000 days: a collective impact approach. Contemp Clin Trials 65(2):46–52

Bloch JR, Webb DA, Mathews L, Dennis EF, Bennett IM, Culhane JF (2010) Beyond marital status: the quality of the mother–father relationship and its influence on reproductive health behaviors and outcomes among unmarried low income pregnant women. Matern Child Health J 14:726–734

Bohren MA, Berger BO, Munthe-Kaas H, Tunçalp Ö (2019) Perceptions and experiences of labour companionships: a qualitative evidence synthesis. Cochrane Database Syst Rev 3(3): CD012449. https://doi.org/10.1002/14651858.CD012449.pub2

Boll C, Leppin J, Reich N (2014) Paternal childcare and paternal leave policies: evidence from industrialized countries. Rev Econ Househ 12:129–158

Braveman P, Gottlieb L (2014) The social determinants of health: it's time to consider the causes of the causes. Public Health Rep 129(Suppl 2):19–31

Bronte-Tinkew J, Ryan S, Carrano J, Moore KA (2007) Resident fathers' pregnancy intentions, prenatal behaviors, and links to involvement with infants. J Marriage Fam 69(4):977–990

Brown SS, Eisenberg L (eds) (1995) The best intentions: unintended pregnancy and the well-being of children and families. National Academy Press, Washington, DC

Brygren LO, Kaati G, Edvinsson S (2001) Longevity determined by paternal ancestors' nutrition during the slow growth period. Acta Biotheor 49:53–59

Carlsen E, Giwercman A, Keiding N, Shakkebaek NE (1992) Evidence for the decreasing quality of semen during the past 50 years. Br Med J 305:609. https://doi.org/10.1136/bmj.306.6854.609

Centers for Disease Control and Prevention (CDC) (2011) Updated recommendations for use of tetanus toxoid, reduced diphtheria toxoid and acellular pertussis vaccine (Tdap) in pregnant women and persons who have or anticipate having close contact with an infant aged < 12 months—Advisory Committee on Immunization Practices (ACIP). Morb Mortal Wkly Rep 60(41):1424–1426

Centers for Disease Control and Prevention (CDC) (2019a) Preconception health and health care. https://www.cdc.gov/preconception/index. Accessed 15 Jan 2020

Centers for Disease Control and Prevention (CDC) (2019b) Infertility. https://www.cdc.gov/nchs/fastats/infertility.htm. Accessed 15 Jan 2020

Centers for Disease Control and Prevention (CDC) (2019c) Sexually transmitted diseases (STDs). https://www.cdc.gov/std/healthcomm/fact_sheets. Accessed 15 Jan 2020

Chabot MJ, Lewis C, de Bocangera HT, Darney P (2011) Correlates of receiving reproductive health care services among U.S. men aged 15-44. Am J Mens Health 5(4):358–366

Chen P-H, Rovi S, Vega ML, Barrett T, Pan K-Y, Johnson MS (2017) Birth outcomes in relation to intimate partner violence. J Natl Med Assoc 109(4):238–245

Cheng D, Schwarz EB, Douglas E, Horon I (2009) Unintended pregnancy and associated maternal preconception, prenatal and postpartum behaviors. Contraception 79(3):194–198

Cheng E, Rifas-Shiman S, Perkins M, Rich-Edwards J, Gillman M, Wright R, Taveras E (2016) The influence of antenatal partner support on pregnancy outcomes. J Womens Health 25 (7):672–679. https://doi.org/10.1089/jwh.2015.5462

Choiriyyah I, Sonenstein FL, Astone NM, Pleck JH, Dariotis JK, Marcell AV (2015) Men aged 15–44 in need of preconception care. Matern Child Health J 19(11):2358–2365

Chu SY, Goodwin MM, D'Angelo DV (2010) Physical violence against U.S. women around the time of pregnancy, 2004–2007. Am J Prev Med 38(3):317–322

Collins JW, Rankin KM, Desisto C, David RJ (2019) Early and late preterm birth rates among US-born urban women: the effects of men's lifelong class status. Matern Child Health J 23 (10):1619–1626

Cormon H, Noonan K, Carrol A, Reichman NE (2009) Low-income father's access to health insurance. J Health Care Poor Underserved 20(1):152–164

Cuffe KM, Newton-Levinson A, Gift TL, McFarlane M, Leichliter JS (2016) Sexually transmitted infections testing among adolescents and young adults in the U.S. J Adolesc Health 58 (5):512–519

Curley JP, Mashoodh R, Champagne FA (2011) Epigenetics and the origins of paternal effects. Horm Behav 59(3):306–314

Davison KK, Charles JN, Khandpur N, Nelson TJ (2017) Fathers' perceived reasons for their underrepresentation in child health research and strategies to increase their involvement. Matern Child Health J 21(2):267–274

Davison KK, Gavarkovs A, McBride B, Kotelchuck M, Levy R, Taveras EM (2019) Engaging fathers in early obesity prevention during the first thousand days: policy, systems and environmental change strategies. Obesity 27(4):523–533

Day J, Savani S, Krempley BD, Nguyen M, Kitlinska JB (2016) Influence of paternal preconception exposures on their offspring: through epigenetics to phenotype. Am J Stem Cells 5(1):11–18

de Jonge CJ, Barratt CLR (eds) (2006) The sperm cell: production, maturation, fertilization, regeneration. Cambridge University Press, Cambridge

de Kretser DM (1997) Male infertility. Lancet 349(9054):787–790

Devries KM, Kishor S, Johnson H, Stöckl H, Bacchus LJ, Garcia-Moreno C, Watts C (2010) Intimate partner violence during pregnancy: analysis of prevalence from 19 countries. Reprod Health Matters 18(36):158–171

Dietz DM, LaPlanta Q, Watts EL, Hodes GE, Russo SJ, Feng J, Oosting RS, Vialoua V, Nestler EJ (2011) Paternal transmission of stress-induced pathologies. Biol Psychiatry 70(5):408–411

DiPietro JA (2012) Maternal stress in pregnancy: considerations for fetal development. J Adolesc Health 51(2 Suppl):S3–S8

Dodd JM, Du Plessis LE, Deussen AR, Grivell RM, Yelland LN, Louise J, Mcphee AJ, Robinson JS, Owens JA (2017) Paternal obesity modifies the effect of an antenatal lifestyle intervention in women who are overweight or obese on newborn anthropometry. Sci Rep 7(1):1557. https://doi.org/10.1038/s41598-017-01672-w

Edvardsson K, Lindkvist M, Eurenius E, Mogren I, Small R, Ivarsson A (2013) A population-based study of overweight and obesity in expectant parents: socio-demographic patterns and within-couple associations. BMC Public Health 13(1):923. https://doi.org/10.1186/1471-2458-13-923

Elsenbruch S, Benson S, Rücke M, Rose M, Dudenhausen J, Pincus-Knackstedt MK, Klapp BF, Arck PC (2007) Social support during pregnancy: effects on maternal depressive symptoms, smoking and pregnancy outcome. Hum Reprod 22(3):869–877

Erlandson K, Lindgren H (2011) Being a resource for both mother and child: fathers' experiences following a complicated birth. J Perinat Educ 20(2):91–99

Esquinas G, García-Esquinas E, Aragonés N, Fernández MA, García-Sagredo JM, de León A, de Paz C, Pérez-Meixeira AM, Gil E, Iriso A, Cisneros M, de Santos A, Sanz JC, García JF, Asensio Á, Vioque J, López-Abente G, Astray J, Pollán M, Martínez M, González MJ, Pérez-Gómez B (2014) Newborns and low to moderate prenatal environmental lead exposure: might fathers be the key? Environ Sci Pollut Res 21(13):7886–7898

Finegersh A, Rompal GR, Martin DIK, Homanics GE (2015) Drinking beyond a lifetime: new and emerging insights into paternal alcohol exposure on subsequent generations. Alcohol 49 (5):461–470

Freeman E, Fletcher R, Collins CE, Morgan PJ, Burrows T, Callister R (2012) Preventing and treating childhood obesity: time to include the father. Int J Obes 36(1):12–15

Frey KA, Navarro SM, Kotelchuck M, Michael CL (2008) The clinical content of preconception care: preconception care for men. Am J Obstet Gynecol 199(6 Suppl B):S389–S395

Frey KA, Engle R, Noble B (2012) Preconception healthcare: what do men know and believe? J Men's Health 9(1):25–35

Gage JD, Everett KD, Bullock L (2007) A review of research literature addressing male partners and smoking during pregnancy. J Obstet Gynecol Neonatal Nurs 36(6):574–580

Garfield CF (2018) Toward better understanding of how fathers contribute to their offspring's health. Pediatrics 141(1):e20173461

Garfield CF, Isacco A (2009) Urban fathers' role in maternal postpartum mental health maternal postpartum mental health. Fathering 7(3):286–302

Gaudino JA, Jenkins B, Rochat RW (1999) No father's names: a risk factor for infant mortality in the state of Georgia, USA. Soc Sci Med 48(2):253–265

Gault B, Hartmann H, Hegerwisch A, Milli J, Cruse LR (2014) Paid parental leave in the United States: what data tells us about access, usage, and economic and health benefits. Institute for Women's Policy Research, Washington, DC

Gavin L, Moskosky S, Carter M, Curtis K, Glass E, Godfrey E, Marcell A, Mautone-Smith N, Pazol K, Tepper N, Zapata L (2014) Providing quality family planning services: recommendations of CDC and the U.S. Office of Population Affairs. Morb Mortal Wkly Rep 63 (RR-04):1–54

Gemayel DJ, Wiener KKK, Saliba AJ (2018) Development of a conception framework that identifies factors and challenges impacting perinatal fathers. Heliyon 4(7):e00694

Geronimus AT (1992) The weathering hypothesis and the health of African-American women and infants: evidence and speculation. Ethn Dis 2(3):207–221

Geronimus AT (1996) Black/white differences in the relationship of maternal age to birthweight: a population-based test of the weathering hypothesis. Soc Sci Med 42(4):589–597

Gerstel N, Clawson D (2018) Control over time: employers, workers, families shaping work schedules. Annu Rev Sociol 44:77–97

Ghosh JKC, Wilhelm MH, Dunkel-Schetter C, Lombardi CA, Ritz BR (2010) Paternal support and preterm birth, and the moderation of effects of chronic stress: a study of Los Angeles County mothers. Arch Womens Ment Health 13(4):327–338

Grady WR, Tanfer K, Billy JOG, Lincoln-Hanson J (1996) Men's perceptions of their roles and responsibilities regarding sex, contraception, and childrearing. Fam Plan Perspect 28 (5):221–226

Halfon N, Larson K, Lu M, Tullis E, Russ S (2014) Lifecourse health development: past, present, future. Matern Child Health J 18(2):344–365

Hardie K, Croce-Galis M, Gay J (2017) Are men well served by family planning programs. Reprod Health 14:14. https://doi.org/10.1186/s12978-017-0278-5

Hehar H, Mychasiuk R (2015) Do fathers matter: influencing neural phenotypes through non-genetic transmission of paternal experiences? Non Genet Inherit 2(1):23–31. https://doi.org/10.1515/ngi-2015-004

Hibbs SD, Rankin KM, DeSisto C, Collins JW Jr (2018) The age-related patterns of pre-term birth among urban African-American and non-Latina white mothers: effects of father-involvement. Soc Sci Med 211:16–20

Hobel CJ, Goldstein A, Barrett ES (2008) Psychosocial stress and pregnancy outcomes. Clin Obstset Gynecol 51(2):333–348

Hohmann-Marriott B (2009) The couple context of pregnancy and its effects on prenatal care and birth outcomes. Matern Child Health J 13:745–754

Hossain Z, Field T, Gonzalez J, Malphurs J, Del Valle C, Pickens J (1994) Infants of depressed mothers interact better with non-depressed fathers. Infant Ment Health J 15(4):348–357

Huerta MdC, Adema W, Baxter J, Han W-J, Lausten M, Lee RH, Waldfogel J (2013) Fathers' leave, fathers' involvement and child development: are they related? Evidence from four OECD countries. OECD social, employment and migration working papers, no. 140

Jewkes R, Flood M, Lang J (2015) From work with men and boys to changes in social norms and reduction of inequalities in gender relations: a conceptual shift in prevention of violence against women and girls. Lancet 385:1580–1589

Johansson M, Fenwick J, Premberg A (2015) A meta-synthesis of the father's experiences of their partner's labour and birth. Midwifery 31(1):9–18

Johnson K, Posner SF, Biermann J, Cordero JF, Atrash HK, Parker CS, Boulet S, Curtis MG (2006) Recommendations to improve preconception health and health care—United States. Morb Mortal Wkly Rep (MMWR) 55(RR-6):1–23

Jomeen J (2017) Fathers in the birth room: choice or coercion? Help or hinderance? J Reprod Infant Psychol 35(4):321–323

Kaati G, Brygren LO, Edvinsson S (2002) Cardiovascular and diabetes mortality determined by nutrition during parents' and grandparents' slow growth period. Eur J Hum Genet 10 (11):682–688

Kainz G, Eliasson M, von Post I (2010) The child's father, an important person for mother's wellbeing during childbirth: a hermeneutic study. Health Care Women Int 31(7):621–635

Knishkowy B, Baker EL (1986) Transmission of occupational disease to family contacts. Am J Ind Med 9(6):543–540

Kong A, Frigge ML, Masson G, Besenbacher S, Sulem P, Magnusson G, Gudjonsson SA, Sigurdsson A, Jonasdottir A, Jonasdottir A, Wong WSW, Sigurdsson G, Walters GB, Steinberg S, Helgason H, Thorleifsson G, Gudbjartsson DF, Helgason A, Magnusson OT, Thorsteinsdottir U, Stefansson K (2012) Rate of de novo mutations and importance of father's age to disease risk. Nature 488(7412):471–475

Kost K, Lindberg LD (2015) Pregnancy intentions, maternal behaviors, and infant health: investigating relationships with new measures and propensity score analysis. Demography 52 (1):83–111

Kotelchuck M (2018) Looking back to move forward: a return to our roots, addressing social determinants across MCH history. In: Verbiest S (ed) Moving life course theory into practice: making change happen. APHA Press, Washington, DC, pp 57–78

Kotelchuck M (2021) The impact of fatherhood on men's health and development. In: Grau-Grau M, las Heras, Bowles HR (eds) Engaged fatherhood for men, families and gender equality. Springer, Cham, pp 63–91

Kotelchuck M, Lu MC (2017) Father's role in preconception health. Matern Child Health J 21 (11):2025–2039

Kumar N, Singh AK (2015) Trends of male factor fertility, an important cause of infertility: a review of the literature. J Hum Reprod Sci 8(4):191–196

Lamb ME (1975) Fathers: forgotten contributors to child development. Hum Dev 18(4):245–266

Lamb ME (ed) (2010) The role of the father in child development, 5th edn. Wiley, New York

Leach LS, Poyser C, Cooklin AR, Giallo R (2016) Prevalence and course of anxiety disorders (and symptom levels) in men across the perinatal period: a systematic review. J Affect Disord 190 (15):675–686

Leavitt JW (2010) Make room for daddy: the journey from waiting room to birthing room. University of North Carolina Press, Chapel Hill

Leonard KE, Eiden RD (1999) Husbands and wives drinking: unilateral or bilateral influences among newlyweds in a general population sample. J Stud Alcohol Suppl 13:130–138

Leonardi-Bee J, John Britton J, Venn A (2011) Secondhand smoke and adverse fetal outcomes in nonsmoking pregnant women: a meta-analysis. Pediatrics 127:734–741

Levine H, Jørgensen N, Martino-Andrade A, Mendiola J, Weksler-Derri D, Mindlis I, Pinotti R, Swan SH (2017) Temporal trends in sperm count: a systematic review and meta-regression analysis. Hum Reprod Update 23(6):646–659

Levy RA, Kotelchuck M (2021) Fatherhood and reproductive health in the antenatal period: from men's voices to clinical practice. In: Grau-Grau M, las Heras M, Bowles HR (eds) Engaged fatherhood for men, families and gender equality. Springer, Cham, pp 111–137

Levy RA, Badalament J, Kotelchuck M (2012) The fatherhood project. Massachusetts General Hospital, Boston. www.thefatherhoodproject.org

Lindberg LD, Kost K (2014) Exploring U.S. men's birth intentions. Matern Child Health J 18(3):625–633

Lindberg LD, Kost K, Maddow-Zimet I (2016) The role of men's childbearing intentions in father involvement. J Marriage Fam 79(1):44–59

Lobel M, Hamilton JG, Cannella D (2008) Psychosocial perspectives on pregnancy: prenatal maternal stress and coping. Soc Personal Psychol Compass 2(4):1600–1623

Lu MC, Halfon N (2003) Racial and ethnic disparities in birth outcomes: a life-course perspective. Matern Child Health J 7(1):13–30

Ludington-Hoe SM, Hashemi MS, Argote LA, Medellin G, Rey H (1992) Selected physiologic measures and behaviors during paternal skin contact with Columbian pre-term infants. J Dev Physiol 18:223–232

Lui C, Cnattingus S, Bergstrom M, Östberg V, Hjernand A (2016) Prenatal parental depression and preterm birth: a national cohort study. BJOG 132(12):1973–1982

MacDormand MF, Mathews TJ (2010) Behind international rankings of infant mortality: how the United States compares with Europe. Int J Health Serv 40(4):577–588

Madsen SA, Burgess A (2010) Fatherhood and mental health difficulties in the postnatal period. In: Conrad D, White A (eds) Promoting men's mental health. Radcliffe Publishing, Oxford, pp 74–82

Martin LT, McNamara MJ, Milot AS, Halle T, Hair EC (2007) The effects of father involvement during pregnancy on receipt of prenatal care and maternal smoking. Matern Child Health J 11(6):595–602

May C, Fletcher R (2013) Preparing fathers for the transition to parenthood: recommendations for the content of antenatal education. Midwifery 29(5):474–478

Meeker JD, Benedict MD (2013) Infertility, pregnancy loss and adverse birth outcomes in relation to maternal secondhand tobacco smoke exposure. Curr Womens Health Rev 9(1):41–49

Mezilius AH, Hyde JS, Clark R (2004) Father involvement moderates the effect of maternal depression during a child's infancy on behavior problems in kindergarten. J Fam Psychiatry 18(4):575–588

Misra DP, Caldwell C, Young AA, Abelson S (2010) Do fathers matter? Paternal contributions to birth outcomes and racial disparities. Am J Obstet Gynecol 202(2):99–100

Moos M-K (2003) Preconceptional wellness as a routine objective for women's health care: an integrative strategy. J Obstet Gynecol Neonatal Nurs 32(4):550–556

Morgan PJ, Young MD, Lloyd AB, Wang ML, Eather N, Miller A, Murtagh EM, Barnes AT, Pagoto SL (2017) Involvement of fathers in pediatrics obesity prevention and treatment trials: a systematic review. Pediatrics 139(2):e20162635

Mosher WD, Jones J, Abma JC (2012) Intended and unintended births in the United States: 1982–2010. Natl Health Stat Rep 55(55):1–28

Moss JL, Harris KM (2015) Impact of maternal and paternal preconception health on birth outcomes using prospective couples' data in add health. Arch Gynecol Obstet 291(2):287–298

Mychasiuk R, Harker A, Ilnytskyy S, Gibb R (2013) Paternal stress prior to conception alters DNA methylation and behaviour of developing rat offspring. Neuroscience 241:100–105

National Academies of Sciences, Engineering, and Medicine (NASEM) (2016) Parenting matters: supporting parents of children ages 0–8. The National Academies Press, Washington, DC

National Academies of Sciences, Engineering, and Medicine (NASEM) (2019a) Vibrant and healthy kids: aligning science, practice, and policy to advance health equity. The National Academies Press, Washington, DC

National Academies of Sciences, Engineering, and Medicine (NASEM) (2019b) A roadmap to reducing child poverty. National Academies Press, Washington DC

Nepomnyaschy L, Waldfogel J (2007) Paternity leave and fathers' involvement with their young children: evidence from the American ECLS-B. Community Work Fam 10(4):427–453

Ngo AD, Taylor R, Roberts CL, Nguyen TV (2006) Association between agent orange and birth defects: systematic review and meta-analysis. Int J Epidemiol 35(5):1220–1230

Noncent E, Lawson AK, Mendoza G, Brannigan RE, Marsh EE (2017) Will I ever be a dad? Distress, appraisal and coping in male infertility patients. Fertil Steril 108(3 Suppl):e301–e302

Northstone K, Golding J, Smith GD, Miller LL, Pembrey M (2014) Prepubertal start of father's smoking and increased body fat in his sons: further characterisation of paternal transgenerational responses. Eur J Hum Genet 22(12):1382–1386

O'Brien AP, Hurley J, Linsley P, McNeil KA, Fletcher R, Aitken JR (2018) Men's preconception health: a primary health care viewpoint. Am J Mens Health 12(5):1575–1581

O'Campo P, Urquia M (2011) Aligning method with theory: a comparison of two approaches to modeling the social determinants of health. Matern Child Health J 16(9):1870–1878

O'Campo P, Burke JG, Culhane J, Elo IT, Eyster J, Holzman C, Messer LC, Kaufman JS, Laraia BA (2008) Neighborhood deprivation and pre-term birth among non-Hispanic black and white women in eight geographic areas in the United States. Am J Epidemiol 67(2):155–163

Palladino C, Singh V, Campbell J, Flynn H, Gold K (2011) Homicide and suicide during the perinatal period: findings from the National Violent Death Reporting System. Obstet Gynecol 118(5):1056–1063

Pang TYC, Short AK, Bredy TW, Hannan AJ (2017) Transgenerational paternal transmission of acquired traits: stress-induced modification of the gene regulatory transcriptome and offspring phenotypes. Curr Opin Behav Sci 14(1):140–147

Paulson JF, Bazemore SD (2010) Prenatal and postpartum depression in fathers and its association with maternal depression: a meta-analysis. JAMA 303(19):1961–1969

Persson P, Rossin-Slater M (2019) When dad can stay home: fathers' workplace flexibility and maternal health. IZA Institute of Labor Economics discussion paper no. 12386

Philpott LF, Leahy-Warren P, FitzGerald S, Savage E (2017) Stress in fathers in the perinatal period: a systematic review. Midwifery 55:113–127

Philpott LF, Savage E, FitzGerald S, Leahy-Warren P (2019) Anxiety in fathers in the perinatal period: a systemic review. Midwifery 76:54–101

Pies C, Kotelchuck M (2014) Bringing the MCH life course perspective to life. Matern Child Health J 18(2):335–338

Redshaw M, Heikkilä K (2010.0 Delivered with care. A national survey of women's experience of maternity care 2010. Technical report. National Perinatal Epidemiology Unit, University of Oxford, United Kingdom. https://researchonline.lshtm.ac.uk/id/eprint/2548656

Redshaw M, Henderson J (2013) Father engagement in pregnancy and child health: evidence from a national survey. BMC Pregnancy Childbirth 13:70

Rempel LA, Rempel JK (2011) The breastfeeding team: the role of involved fathers in the breastfeeding family. J Hum Lact 27(2):115–121

Rodgers AB, Morgan CP, Bronson SL, Revello S, Bale TL (2013) Paternal stress exposure alters sperm microRNA content and reprograms offspring HPA stress Axis regulation. J Neurosci 33(21):9003–9012

Romanov H, Pilkington PD, Giallo R, Whelan TA (2016) A systematic review of interventions targeting paternal mental health in the perinatal period. Infant Ment Health J 37(3):289–301

Salmasi G, Grady R, Jones J, McDonald SD (2010) Environmental tobacco smoke exposure and perinatal outcomes: a systematic review and meta-analyses. Acta Obstet Gynecol Scand 89(4):423–441

Sangi-Haghpeykar H, Mehta M, Posner S, Poindexter AN, III (2005) Paternal influences on the timing of prenatal care among Hispanics. Matern Child Health J 9(2):159–163

Saxbe D, Corner G, Khaled M, Horton K, Wu B, Khoddam H (2018) The weight of fatherhood: identifying mechanisms to explain paternal perinatal weight gain. Health Psychol Rev 12(3):1–38

Sedgh G, Singh S, Hussain R (2014) Intended and unintended pregnancies worldwide 2012 and recent trends. Stud Fam Plan 45(3):301–314

Shah PS, the Knowledge Synthesis Group on Determinants of Preterm/Low Birthweight Births (2010) Paternal factors and low birth weight preterm, and small for gestational age births: a systematic review. Am J Obstet Gynecol 202(2):103–123

Shah PS, Balkhair T, Ohlsson A, Beyene J, Scott F, Frick C (2011) Intention to become pregnant and low birth weight and preterm birth: systemic review. Matern Child Health J 15(2):205–216

Shapiro GD, Bushnik T, Sheppard AJ, Kramer MS, Kaufman JS, Yang S (2017) Paternal education and adverse birth outcomes in Canada. J Epidemiol Community Health 71(1):67–72

Smith LP, Ng SW, Popkin B (2013) Trends in US home food preparation and consumption: analysis of national nutrition surveys and time use studies from 1965–1966 to 2007–2008. Nutr J 12:45. https://doi.org/10.1186/1475-2891-12-45

Soubry A (2015) Epigenetic inheritance and evolution: a paternal perspective on dietary influences. Prog Biophys Mol Biol 11(1–2):79–85

Soubry A (2018) Epigenetics as a driver of developmental origins of health and disease: did we forget the fathers? BioEssays 40(1). https://doi.org/10.1002/bies.201700113

Soubry A, Guo L, Huang Z, Hoyo C, Romanus S, Price T, Murphy SK (2016) Obesity-related DNA methylation at imprinted genes in human sperm: results from the TIEGER study. Clin Epigenetics 8:51. https://doi.org/10.1186/s13148-016-0217-2

Stanton WR, Lowe JB, Moffatt J, Del CB (2004) Randomised control trial of a smoking cessation intervention directed at men whose partners are pregnant. Prev Med 38(1):6–9

Steen M, Downe S, Bamford N, Edozien L (2012) Not-patient and not-visitor: a metasynthesis father's encounters with pregnancy, birth, and maternity care. Midwifery 28(4):362–371

Sternberg P, Hubley J (2004) Evaluating men's involvement as a strategy in sexual and reproductive health promotion. Health Promot Int 19(3):389–396

Svanes C, Koplin J, Skulstad SM et al (2017) Father's environment before conception and asthma risk in his children: a multi-generational analysis of the respiratory health in northern Europe study. Int J Epidemiol 46(1):235–245

Teitler JO (2001) Father involvement, child, health, and maternal health behavior. Child Youth Serv Rev 23(4–5):403–425

Thaddeus S, Maine D (1994) Too far to walk: maternal mortality in context. Soc Sci Med 38(8):1091–1110

Treadwell H, Ro M (2008) Poverty, race, and the invisible men. Am J Public Health 98(Suppl 1):S142–S144

Tsui AO, McDonald-Mosley R, Burke AE (2010) Family planning and the burden of unintended pregnancy. Epidemiol Rev 32(1):152–174

Wadhwa PD, Entringer S, Buss C, Michael CL (2011) The contribution of maternal stress to preterm birth: issues and considerations. Clin Perinatol 38(3):351–384

Wadwha PD, Buss C, Entringer S, Swanson JM (2009) Developmental origins of health and disease: brief history of the approach and current focus on epigenetic mechanisms. Semin Reprod Med 27(5):358–368

Whitehead M, Dalgren G (1991) What can be done about inequalities in health? Lancet 338(8774):1059–1063

Williams DR (2003) The health of men: structured inequalities and opportunities. Am J Public Health 93(5):724–731

Wise PH (2008) Transforming preconceptional, prenatal, and interconceptional care into a comprehensive commitment to women's health. Womens Health Issues 18(6 Suppl):S13–S18

Wolfberg AJ, Michels KB, Shields W, O'Campo P, Bronner Y, Bienstock J (2004) Dads as breastfeeding advocates: results from a randomized controlled trial of an educational intervention. Am J Obstet Gynecol 191(3):708–712

Woodbury RM (1925) Causal factors in infant mortality: a statistical study based on investigations in eight cities. Children's bureau publication no. 142. Government Printing Office, Washington, DC

World Health Organization (WHO) (2007) Fatherhood and heath outcomes in Europe. World Health Organization Regional Office for Europe, Copenhagen

World Health Organization (WHO) (2017) World health statistics. www.who.int/gho/publications/world_health_statistics/2017/en/

Wulf D (2002) In their own right: addressing the sexual and reproductive health needs of American men. Alan Guttmacher Institute, New York

Yogman MW, Eppel AM (2021) The role fathers in child and family health. In: Grau-Grau M, las Heras M, Bowles HR (eds) Engaged fatherhood for men, families and gender equality. Springer, Cham, pp 15–30

Yogman MW, Garfield CF, the Committee on Psychosocial Aspects of Child and Family Health (2016) Fathers' roles in the care and development of their children: the role of pediatricians. Pediatrics 138(1):e20161128

Open Access This chapter is licensed under the terms of the Creative Commons Attribution 4.0 International License (http://creativecommons.org/licenses/by/4.0/), which permits use, sharing, adaptation, distribution and reproduction in any medium or format, as long as you give appropriate credit to the original author(s) and the source, provide a link to the Creative Commons license and indicate if changes were made.

The images or other third party material in this chapter are included in the chapter's Creative Commons license, unless indicated otherwise in a credit line to the material. If material is not included in the chapter's Creative Commons license and your intended use is not permitted by statutory regulation or exceeds the permitted use, you will need to obtain permission directly from the copyright holder.

The Impact of Fatherhood on Men's Health and Development

Milton Kotelchuck

1 The Importance of Fatherhood for Men's Health and Development over the Life Course

This chapter, the second of a pair of related chapters in this volume, provides a broad overview, and new conceptualization, about the various ways in which fatherhood influences the health and development of men. The first, chapter "The Impact of Father's Health on Reproductive and Infant Health and Development", explores the impact of father's health on reproductive and infant health and development (Kotelchuck 2021). Together these two deeply inter-related chapters endeavor to illuminate the here-to-fore under-appreciated topic of the father's importance and necessary active involvement in the perinatal health period, including for his own health and development. [For purposes of discussion in this chapter, the term "perinatal period" will encompass the period from conception into the first few months of life (i.e., pregnancy and early parenthood)].

As noted in the previous chapter, the traditional focus of the U.S.-based Maternal and Child Health (MCH) field (and the closely aligned Obstetric, Pediatrics and Nursing fields) has been on the mother's health and behaviors and their impact on reproductive and infant health and development outcomes. Reproductive health and early parenting has been perceived as primarily, if not exclusively, the mother's responsibility and her cultural domain; and to a significant extent, fathers and men have been excluded. Not surprisingly, as a result, the impact of fatherhood on men's health and mental health, especially in the perinatal period, has not been the subject of much inquiry.

M. Kotelchuck (✉)
Harvard Medical School and Massachusetts General Hospital Fatherhood Project, Boston, MA, USA
e-mail: mkotelchuck@mgh.harvard.edu

First, these two chapters on father's health are modeled after and build upon the dual orientation of the current women's preconception health movement in the MCH field, which simultaneously addresses the impact of the mother's health during pregnancy on both infant's health outcomes and on mother's own lifetime health. This intergenerational approach respects the integrity and health of both mothers and infants simultaneously, without valuing one's life above the other (Wise 2008). This chapter, like chapter "The Impact of Father's Health on Reproductive and Infant Health and Development", shares this same perspective; together they explore both the father's health contributions to infant health (in the previous chapter; Kotelchuck 2021) and the impact of fatherhood on men's own health (in this chapter)—a virtually new topic in the MCH literature.

Second, this chapter attempts to create a new conceptual framework that can organize and document the multiple pathways by which the perinatal experiences of fatherhood impact on men's own health and development. By comparison to the previous chapter, there is an even more limited and scattered set of research on this under-explored topic. Several of this chapter's conceptual themes build upon similar themes first expressed in an earlier article on preconception health and fatherhood (Kotelchuck and Lu 2017). This chapter however moves beyond its more limited reproductive health time frame, explores additional, newly evolving paternal reproductive health themes, and separates the reproductive health impacts on infants from those on fathers. This chapter adopts a very broad holistic approach to men's health—blending physical, mental, social and generative health dimensions into a single comprehensive longitudinal fatherhood health framework.

Third, this chapter, like the prior one, also explores the perinatal roots of the impact of fatherhood on men's health and development. Here-to-fore, fatherhood research has been supported primarily by the large, well-established developmental psychology literature that has repeatedly demonstrated positive impacts of father's involvement on multiple facets of child development and family relationships (Lamb 1975, 2010; Yogman et al. 2016; Yogman and Eppel 2021). This chapter aims to more explicitly expand the understanding of men's full life course development as fathers into earlier pre-delivery temporal periods.

Fourth, as noted in the initial associated chapter, this chapter's focus on fatherhood and men's health does not emerge in an ahistorical vacuum, but is linked to, and hopefully contributes to, numerous ongoing political and professional movements. In particular, this chapter is partially embedded in the larger evolving social and gender equity debates over roles and opportunities for women and men in society—especially given that many aspects of parenthood are socially determined and that fatherhood is transitioning from an older, traditional, distant economic-provider, patriarchy model to a newer one based on greater parental equity and paternal engagement. The increasingly large numbers of women who have now entered into the paid labor market, with its associated economic, social, and childcare workplace transformations, is undoubtedly hastening these conversations. This chapter also builds upon the National Academy of Science, Engineering, and Medicine (NASEM) inspired multigenerational child-development efforts to foster effective parenting and parenting health, but now expanded to explicitly include fathers (NASEM 2016, 2019). And finally, this chapter derives in part from the emerging men's health movement, with new added emphasis on fatherhood health dimensions.

Fifth, and finally, it is hoped that in articulating the multiple domains of fatherhood's impact on men's health and development, this chapter, along with its companion chapter, will encourage more paternal perinatal health research (both basic and translational), will help guide more effective and targeted father-oriented programs and policies, and will help generate further political will and advocacy for their implementation. These, in turn should further encourage fathers' earlier, more active and healthier involvement in the perinatal health period, strengthen what they bring to, and take from, their fatherhood experiences, and improve their subsequent health and development throughout their life course.

2 Pathways Through Which Fatherhood Impacts on Men's Health and Development

There are multiple potential pathways through which the experiences of fatherhood could have an impact on men's health and development during the perinatal pregnancy and early parenting period and over their life course. This chapter will note and briefly explore the scientific evidence base for *six* distinct pathways. These fatherhood health pathways, in turn, also directly and indirectly influence the current and intergenerational health and well-being of their infants, partners, families, and communities. Specifically,

1. **Men's physical health status during the perinatal period (pregnancy and early parenthood)**
2. **Changes in father's physical health during the perinatal period: Impact of Fatherhood on Men's Physical Health**
3. **Changes in father's mental health during the perinatal period: Impact of Fatherhood on Men's Mental Health**
4. **Changes in father's social health and well-being during the perinatal period: Impact of Fatherhood on Men's Social Well-being**
5. **Men's psychological maturation of paternal generativity: Men's Improved Capacity for Parenthood and Fatherhood**
6. **Men's life course development of fatherhood.**

2.1 Men's Physical Health Status During the Perinatal Period

Men's physical health during the pregnancy and early parenthood period has a much more important and direct impact on reproductive and infant health than perhaps most MCH professionals and parents have here-to-fore understood (Kotelchuck 2021). Given the traditional cultural focus on mothers and their well-being, the topic of father's health has not drawn much attention. However, and perhaps not surprisingly, given men's generally sub-optimal health status and health care utilization, men's *physical health status* during perinatal period reveals substantial health problems and potential opportunities for its improvement.

Ascertaining men's health status on a population-basis during their prime reproductive years has been methodologically challenging, and possibly here-to-fore of limited reproductive health interest. Although some broad longitudinal epidemiologic data sets exists for men of childbearing ages, they are not usually stratified by parenting status; the NHANES survey, for example, appears to have no publications describing father's health. Yet health status may differ for men between pre- and post-fatherhood years. In general, though, matched-age fathers initially should be healthier than non-fathers, as men with a wide variety of health issues are less likely to achieve successful fertility (CDC 2019; Frey et al. 2008).

Choiriyyah et al. (2015) examined the 2006–2010 US National Survey of Family Growth, which suggested that 60% of men aged 15–44 were in need of preconception healthcare; 56% were overweight or obese; 58% binge drank in the last year; and 21% had high sexually transmitted infection (STI) risk. Pre-pregnancy overweight and obesity is a more pervasive problem for men than for women (53% vs. 29%) (Edvardsson et al. 2013), a fact which takes on added importance since men's obesity is an independent predictor of childhood obesity (Freeman et al. 2012). One might assume that fathers in the pregnancy and early parenthood period would continue to still have a similar set of broad health risks. The MGH Obstetrics Prenatal Fatherhood studies (Levy and Kotelchuck 2021) noted nearly 75% of antenatal fathers are overweight (including 25% obese), reflecting their self-reported low physical activity, high sedentariness and extensive media usage; plus 14% of fathers revealed signs of infertility or delayed fertility. Smoking rates are highest among men during childbearing years. For example, almost 30% of men aged 20–24, and 25% of men aged 25–34 smoked in Canada (Canadian Tobacco Use Monitoring Survey 2006).

Men are well known for their lesser use of health services than women, even adjusting for women's reproductive health services usage (Bertakis et al. 2000; Smith et al. 2006). Perhaps due to their own social construction of masculinity, men differentially ignore screening and preventive health care and delay help seeking for symptoms (Smith et al. 2006; Addis and Mahalik 2003). Yet the opportunity for care exists, as most men (~70%) in the US would appear to receive primary health care annually (Choiriyyah et al. 2015; Levy and Kotelchuck 2021). However, too many receive no preconception health care at those visits; Choiriyyah et al. (2015) reported very limited receipt of STI testing (<20%) or counseling (<11%) services.

Perhaps similar to women, the pregnancy and early parenthood period could be an opportune time to address men's health needs overall. Limited, one-time, self-reported assessments of father's health status during the preconception and antenatal periods suggest that there is much room for improvement in men's

own physical health and health care utilization. There remains however great need for more creative epidemiological studies of men's overall health during his prime reproductive years, specifically stratified by fatherhood status.

2.2 Changes in Father's Physical Health During the Perinatal Period

Pregnancy and early parenthood are associated with four broad sets of *changes* in father's physical health status: paternal weight gain; sympathetic pregnancy (couvade) symptoms; brain and hormonal transformations; and increased longevity.

2.2.1 Paternal Weight Gain

Fatherhood, on a population basis, is associated with increased weight and elevated Body Mass Index compared to comparable aged men who are not fathers. Using the American Changing Lives panel data, Umberson et al. (2011), showed that fathers have more accelerated weight gain throughout their life course and weigh ~14 lb more than non-parental males. Garfield et al. (2016), using the National Longitudinal Study of Adolescent to Adult Health (ADD Health) data base, documented that the transition to fatherhood was associated with an additional weight gain of 3.5–4.5 lb more for residential fathers than for non-residential fathers or non-fathers.

Moreover, the popular literature has noted and commented extensively on the "Dad Bod" or "preg-MAN-cy weight." One widely cited informal British study estimates that new fathers gain 11 lb over the course of the pregnancy, speculating that they partake in their partner's binge eating, finish up the left over foods, eat out more in restaurants, and increase eating to respond to their own stress (BBC News 2009). Saxbe et al. (2018) more formally assessed seven possible behavioral, hormonal, psychological, and partner mechanisms for the increased weight gain in fathers; they concluded the likely sources included decreased sleep, less exercise, less testosterone, more stress, and partner effects (shared diets).

Specifically, the transition to fatherhood is associated with significant sleep disturbance and disruption (e.g., partnered men with young children sleep approximately 80 fewer hours per year than single, childless men (Burgard and Ailshire 2013)) and reduced time available for men's own leisure and exercise (e.g., 5 h/week decrease in physical activity with the first child and a further 3.5 h/week decrease with a subsequent child (Hull et al. 2010)). Parenting-associated physical activity declines are more pronounced for men than for women. Fatherhood was not associated with changes in men's diet (Saxbe et al. 2018). Paternal pregnancy weight gains set the stage for men's greater obesity morbidity throughout their lives (Umberson et al. 2011; Saxbe et al. 2018).

2.2.2 Couvade Syndrome

In many cultures, fathers experience "Couvade syndrome" or "Sympathetic pregnancy"; that is, physical and psychological symptoms and behaviors that mimic the expectant mother's during her pregnancy and post-partum period (Kazmierczak et al. 2013), including insomnia, nausea, headaches, toothaches, abdominal pain, as well as increased stress and weight gain. Couvade is not a recognized (DSM-5) mental illness or (ICD-10) disease. Thus, the extent of couvade syndrome's prevalence has been difficult to ascertain, and estimates vary widely, from 11% to 65%, depending on the symptoms and populations being assessed (Masoni et al. 1994). Symptoms seem most common in the first and third trimesters, and most subside after the baby is born (Brennan et al. 2007). The sources of couvade in men remain elusive, drawing extensive psychological and psychosomatic theorizing (e.g., empathetic responses to pregnancy; compensatory or even competitive symptoms; or shared hormonal changes) (Kazmierczak et al. 2013). So called "primitive couvade," is associated anthropologically with male pregnancy rituals, in which men refrained from, or partook in special antenatal or birthing rituals thought to impact the spirit of the developing child. Couvade symptoms are associated with increased paternal health service utilization, though they are often unrecognized or associated with their partner's pregnancy status (Lipkin and Lamb 1982).

2.2.3 Biologic Adaptions: Hormonal and Brain Structure Transformations

While it has long been noted that women's hormones change or adapt as a function of motherhood (Fleming et al. 1997; Edelstein et al. 2015), there is also now growing evidence of men's biologic adaptation to fatherhood (Edelstein et al. 2015; Gettler et al. 2011; Grebe et al. 2019). Testosterone, which is important to male sexuality, mating and aggression, declines notably as men prepare to assume enhanced parental roles. Testosterone levels are lower among fathers than non-fathers (Grebe et al. 2019), decline over the course of pregnancy (Edelstein et al. 2015), and further decrease among fathers who more actively provide infant care compared to men who provide little or no care (Grebe et al. 2019). The synchronous decline in paternal and partner's testosterone levels during pregnancy is associated with stronger post-partum relationship investment (Saxbe et al. 2017). Among the ~6% of animal species where males participate in parenting activities, the post-conception internal regulation of testosterone levels increases the Darwinian survival of their children (Grebe et al. 2019). Other paternal hormones: estradiol (Edelstein et al. 2015); oxytocin (Gordon et al. 2010); and prolactin (Hashemian et al. 2016) increase in men over the course of pregnancy and early post-partum period; and all are associated with increased child care, nurturing behaviors, and engagement in both men and women.

The term "Dad Brain" has also gained some prominence in the popular literature, perhaps inadvertently reflecting the new beginning exploration and documentation of the plasticity of men's brain structure associated with parenting. There is growing evidence that both fathers and mothers neurally process infant stimuli in similar manner (e.g., the global parent caregiving neural network) (Abraham et al. 2014). Paternal brain plasticity is associated with greater paternal caretaking involvement, especially in the social–cognitive pathway network (e.g., the amygdala-superior temporal sulcus brain connectivity), which in part allows men to better infer infant mental states from their behavior (Abraham et al. 2014). Fathers, like most mothers, can recognize and pick out their own infant's crying, but only if they spend extensive time daily with them (Gustafsson et al. 2013). Moreover, within the first 4 months postpartum, there are changes in the volume of gray matter in the regions of the paternal brain involved in motivation and decision-making (Kim et al. 2014), further suggesting plasticity in father's brain after becoming a parent. Additionally, there is an extensive and growing animal research literature showing paternal brain structure changes with active fatherhood, especially among prairie voles (Rolling and Mascaro 2017).

2.2.4 Paternal Longevity

And finally and positively, fathers live longer than men without children, even controlling for marital status (Modig et al. 2017; Grundy and Kravdal 2008; Keizer et al. 2011), similar to that reported for mothers. The longevity impact of parenthood is stronger for men than women (e.g., 2.0 vs. 1.5 years greater life expectancy gap at 60 years of age (Modig et al. 2017)), and for fathers with 2 or 3 children versus none (Grundy and Kravdal 2008; Keizer et al. 2011). As men age, fatherhood could be a source of deep emotional satisfaction, as well as companionship and non-isolation. Alternatively, these longevity findings may also reflect a confounding of healthier men being more likely to wed and have children, which then play out over their life course.

Father's physical health is much more profoundly affected by the onset of early fatherhood than perhaps most of the existing popular and professional literature here-to-fore would have assumed. During the perinatal period and likely beyond, father's minds and bodies, like the mother's, adapt biologically to their new parenting roles—perhaps preparing them for the physical and mental stresses, joys, and requirements of parenthood. The changes in men's physical health associated with fatherhood should encourage both greater attention to paternal health promotion activities and increased utilization of reproductive and primary health care services during the perinatal time period and beyond. Basic research on this topic is now just beginning, with the emerging interest in father's perinatal health.

2.3 Changes in Father's Mental Health During the Perinatal Period

Pregnancy and the onset of parenthood is a time of substantial mental health transition for men—as it is for women (Singley and Edwards 2015). There is greater awareness and recognition of fatherhood's impact on men's mental health than on his physical health. Perhaps the greater awareness of perinatal mental health issues is due to the growing appreciation of perinatal depression on maternal and infant health and the increasing calls to similarly address paternal mental health needs by the family sociology, clinical psychology, and nurse-midwifery communities (May and Fletcher 2013; Baldwin and Bick 2018). Men's mental health responses to fatherhood are very salient during pregnancy and early parenthood—both as sources of stress and of growth and love. And in turn, father's mental health status profoundly influences maternal reproductive and parenting health and infant health and development (Kotelchuck 2021; NASEM 2016, 2019).

Parenthood, especially for first time fathers, is an unknown and unfamiliar event, out of his normal control (Baldwin et al. 2018); multiple potential sources of perinatal stress emerge, including the changing relationship with the mother, added financial obligations, and concerns over the ability to be a competent parent (Coleman and Karraker 1998; Singley and Edwards 2015). Moreover, given limitations in parenting- and sex-education in schools and in gender role experiences developmentally, most men have limited or no understanding about pregnancy biology, perinatal health services, or practical parenting skills. They often feel helpless about what to do or expect as they enter into fatherhood. Postnatally, fathers confront additional new concerns about work-family balance, childcare logistics, all while sleep deprived, and often with limited social or peer support to help them adjust to their new fatherhood roles. Moreover, today, men, especially first-time fathers, are further challenged to create a new internal fatherhood identity for themselves (Baldwin et al. 2018), and often with deep conflicting fatherhood gender role expectations at play (Singley and Edwards 2015). Most men today were raised in an era with more traditional male gender roles and now are being confronted with expectations for more engagement and equity in childcare, roles that some men may perceive as more feminine or weak; i.e., something of a fatherhood generation gap exists today. Overall, these and many other factors contribute to a potent brew of men's mental health challenges in the pregnancy and early parenting period.

2.3.1 Paternal Stress, Anxiety and Depression

Paternal stress. Given the formidable parental role transformations associated with fatherhood, not surprisingly, there are numerous reports of elevated paternal stress associated with pregnancy and early parenthood. A review article by Philpott et al. (2017) located 18 quantitative studies on paternal perinatal stress, 11 with elevated stress levels. Paternal stress increases continuously throughout the antenatal period, peaks at birth and then declines afterwards. The principle factors identified that contribute to paternal stress included negative feelings about the pregnancy, role restrictions related to becoming a father, fear of childbirth, and feelings of incompetence related to infant care. Higher stress levels negatively impact father's health and mental health, contributing to increased anxiety, depression, psychological distress, and fatigue (Philpott et al. 2017).

The MGH Obstetric Prenatal Fatherhood studies (Levy and Kotelchuck 2021) reinforce these observations antenatally; ~56% men endorsed the observation that pregnancy is associated with high levels of paternal stress; with concerns focused on financial issues (44%), ability to care for the baby (29%), less time for self (20%), changing relationship with mother (15%), and not repeating their father's mistakes (14%). Further, 35% of men reported not having any place or person to go to for fatherhood support, which likely further added to their stress symptoms.

Paternal anxiety. Substantial levels of clinical anxiety disorders are found among men during the perinatal period. A recent systematic review by Leach et al. (2016) reported the prevalence rates of anxiety disorders in men ranged between 4.1% and 16.0% during the prenatal period and 2.4–18.0% during the postnatal period. [As compared to a 13.0% rate in general population of men (McLean et al. 2011).] Anxiety disorders increase steadily throughout antenatal period and then decline after birth (Philpott et al. 2019). Factors contributing to anxiety disorders included lower income levels, less co-parent support, fewer social supports, work-family conflict, partner's anxiety and depression, and paternal anxiety history during a previous birth. Higher anxiety levels increase paternal stress, depression, fatigue, and lower self-efficacy (Philpott et al. 2019). The few behavioral or education trials to reduce paternal anxiety, to date, have all been successful (Philpott et al. 2019).

Paternal depression. There are numerous reports of elevated levels of depression associated with fatherhood. A meta-analysis of the prevalence of men's depression in the perinatal period (Paulson and Bazemore 2010) showed higher rates of paternal depression (10.4%) than in similar aged men in the general population (4.8% over a 12-month period) (Kessler et al. 2003). Garfield et al. (2014), using the ADD Health data, documented that new fathers were 1.68 times more likely to be depressed compared to comparable aged men without children, and that resident father's depression symptoms increased from before pregnancy through the pregnancy and beyond. The Paulson and Bazemore (2010) analysis documented substantial rates of paternal depression throughout the pregnancy: 11% in first and second trimester and 12% in third trimester; and then varied rates throughout the first year post-partum: 8% at 1–3 months, peaking at 26% at 3–6 months, and then 9% from 6 to 12 months.

When stratified by country, paternal depression rates are higher in the U.S. (14.1%) than in the rest of the developed world (Paulson and Bazemore 2010), perhaps associated with the lack of childcare support and paid parental leave in the U.S. (Glass et al. 2016). Paternal depression is strongly correlated ($r = \sim.30$) with maternal depression (Ramchandani et al. 2008; Paulson and Bazemore 2010), though prevalence rates are consistently higher for mothers. In the MGH Obstetric Prenatal Fatherhood studies, 26% of the antenatal fatherhood sample endorsed at least one of the two PHQ-2 depression screener symptoms, with

8% reporting more severe or frequent symptoms (Levy and Kotelchuck 2021). A wide variety of risk factors have been linked to paternal depression; including prior mental health depression experiences, changing paternal hormones, lack of social supports, maternal depression, and poor relationship satisfaction (Singley and Edwards 2015; Gemayel et al. 2018).

Paternal post-partum depression. Increasingly, there has been a heightened awareness that post-partum depression (PPD) is not restricted to only women, and that men also experience PPD (Kim and Swain 2007; Ramchandani et al. 2008; Singley and Edwards 2015). Paternal PPD is increasingly recognized as a chronic condition, with the 10% prevalence rate from the Paulson and Bazemore (2010) meta-analysis widely quoted. Ramchandani et al. (2008), using the Avon Longitudinal study (ALSPAC) found the highest predictors of paternal PPD to be high prenatal anxiety, high prenatal depression, and a history of severe depression; findings consistent with a more recent meta-analysis (Gemayel et al. 2018).

2.3.2 Behavioral and Externalizing Mental Health Impacts

The mental health consequences of fatherhood aren't only manifested internally, but also through externalizing behaviors. Men often express their depression, stress, or anxiety through "self-medicating" drinking, over-eating, interpersonal anger, or physical absence. Intimate partner violence (IPV), for example, is known to be markedly elevated after conception and again after delivery (Nannini et al. 2008). Many new fathers retreat to over-working at their employment (the traditional model of fathers as providers) to partially withdraw from their infant care and family involvement and associated stresses (Singley and Edwards 2015; Baldwin et al. 2018). Research on this topic is limited, although theoretically, many negative paternal perinatal health behaviors can be interpreted as mental health linked.

2.3.3 Positive Mental Health Impacts

While fatherhood is a time of much negative emotional stress, it is also a time of deep joy, happiness, and satisfaction for most men. While most qualitative studies of men's mental health during the perinatal period acknowledge positive emotional responses, few have explored them in detail. Baldwin et al.'s (2018) systematic review of this topic noted that paternal satisfaction resulted from achieving mastery, confidence, and pleasure over the reality of dealing with a newborn, becoming a competent father, and doing it in a constructive way with one's partner. Moreover, some men's negative health behaviors change for the better as they move into their new parental roles, similar to many women. In the Fragile Families and Child Well Being Study, for example, among low-income urban fathers, fatherhood was associated with more healthy behaviors and decreased substance use (Garfield et al. 2010). In this chapter's subsequent fifth section (Sect. 2.5), the positive impact of fatherhood on men's psychological development and generativity is further explored.

2.3.4 Perinatal/Infant Specific Sources of Paternal Depression

The post-partum mental health impact of fatherhood has bi-directional roots; it can be influenced by the infant's health and behavior characteristics, not just by men's own psychological responses to the pregnancy and his new paternal and family roles.

Fatherhood and pregnancy loss. While there is a robust literature on the impact of fetal loss on mothers' mental health, the equivalent literature for fathers is very limited. A summary review by Due et al. (2017) identified only 29 articles on paternal responses to fetal loss versus 3868 articles on maternal responses. They concluded that fathers primarily feel the need to be supporters of their partners, but that they also feel overlooked and marginalized about their own responses to the loss. Fathers, like mothers, experience a loss of parental identity and of parental hopes and dreams for their deceased infant, though these negative emotions appear less enduring for fathers. There is a striking absence of informational brochures or clinical materials specifically directed towards fathers to help them deal with the emotional trauma of fetal loss.

Fatherhood and prematurity. Fathers of premature or low birth weight (LBW) infants are more likely than mothers to experience post-partum depressive symptoms (Cheng et al. 2016). This takes on added significance since paternal depression is also an independent predictor of subsequent child development (Cheng et al. 2016). Interventions to address the mental health needs (including depression) of parents of infants in NICUs are increasing, but only some are directed at both parents (Garfield et al. 2014).

In sum, the perinatal period is a time of significant mental health transition for fathers, especially first-time fathers, as they address the multiple new challenges of fatherhood. Fatherhood is associated with both substantially elevated levels of stress, anxiety, and depression, as well as joy, pride, and emotional maturation. Interest in men's perinatal mental health derives heavily from the increasing appreciation of maternal depression and its impact on reproductive and child outcomes. Paternal mental health has been the main initial area of focus for the exploration of the impact of fatherhood on men's health. Moreover, men's perinatal mental health necessarily engages with important cultural crosscutting themes such as contemporary masculinity, family gender roles, and work-life balance. Only recently has there begun to be any, even slight, professional recognition of men's own mental health needs in the perinatal period, and virtually no mental health services are directed towards them.

2.4 Changes in Father's Social Health and Well-Being During the Perinatal Period: The Impact of Fatherhood on Men's Social Health and Well-Being

Fatherhood doesn't only influence men's physical and mental health, but also his social health and well-being. Fathers differ from non-fathers in their social connections, family relationships, and work behavior (Eggebeen and Knoester 2001). Each of these can directly impact maternal, infant, and men's health and development. While the MCH reproductive health community (and popular culture) widely acknowledges and embraces the women's changing social roles (and prestige) as new mothers, the same is *not* true for the social transformative impact of men becoming fathers. By contrast, many other professional communities, in business, social welfare, governmental policy, and economics, have grappled more with men's social well-being and how it is impacted (positively and negatively) by fatherhood, especially as it relates to gender role equity at home and work (Bowles et al. 2021). Indeed, most of this larger book focuses on father's social well-being in society. This topic also reflects, in part, the emerging social determinant of health (SDOH) perspectives in the MCH community, recognizing that fathers are often the main vector for family's SDOH (Kotelchuck 2021). However, importantly here is a new recognition that the father's social well-being (and SDOH characteristics) are not static but are malleable during the perinatal period.

2.4.1 Fathers as Employees

Fatherhood has the potential to profoundly challenge men's relationship to his employment and his traditional employee social roles. Fathers now face new, competing, and deeply-valued societal pressures: to be engaged nurturing fathers and to continue to be economically productive employees (Hobson and Fahlen 2009). New fathers experience substantial added social role conflicts over work versus family life (Baldwin et al. 2018; Harrington 2021; Ladge and Humberd 2021). These may further heighten men's own conflicting internal cultural views about the nature of work and the newer involved fatherhood concepts of this era—especially since most men's identity and sense of masculinity is heavily influenced by his employment/career and its associated income (Humberd et al. 2015; Ladge and Humberd 2021). Men, in general, increase work hours post-delivery, perhaps in part to meet the growing family economic needs and to further assume men's traditional breadwinner social roles (Hodges and Budig 2010). Men's post-delivery work experiences as a father can become a critical arena for impacting his health, mental health, and sense of responsibility for his family's well-being. [Many of the subsequent chapters in this book examine the social health and well-being challenges that new working fathers experience in trying to achieve a healthier work-life balance, and the employment and social welfare policies and practices that could help alleviate them.]

Second, on a more positive note, for some fathers, employee-based paid paternal newborn leave provides a special opportunity for their psychological and practical growth as parents (i.e., paternal generativity). Fathers who take 2 or more weeks of leave are more involved in direct childcare at 9 months (Nepomnyaschy and Waldfogel 2007), are more likely to remain in their marital relationship (Petts et al. 2019), and to enhance their partner's health and wealth (Persson and Ross-Slater 2019); though the direct benefits for fathers of paid paternal leave have been less well researched. Short or no paternal newborn leaves, in general, are associated with difficulties establishing a sense of paternal identity, paternal confidence, and competence in caregiving, and more work-family stress (Harrington et al. 2014).

Third, fatherhood, like for motherhood, can contribute to men's capacities to be a better employee. Father's psychological development and maturity, and the skills of parenthood, often carry over into the workplace, including better self-managerial skills, enhanced time management, focus, patience, responsibility, and leadership (Ladge and Humberd 2021). Fathers at work are perceived as more kind, compassionate, and mature (Humberd et al. 2015), and builders of social connections and bonds (Ladge and Humberd 2021). Among men with similar skill levels and CV's, fathers are more likely to be offered a position (Correl et al. 2007). There is a growing recognition within business communities, especially their human resources professionals, that more family- (and father-) friendly workplaces are associated with higher productivity and profits than traditional workplaces—possibly through more motivated, loyal, and skilled employees, with less work-family conflict, staff turnover, and burn out (Ladge et al. 2015; Ladge and Humberd 2021; Harrington 2021).

2.4.2 Fathers as Family and Community Members

It is widely believed that fatherhood, for most men, draws them ever more tightly into their family and community; and, in general, men do adapt to society's fatherhood expectations and family social welfare responsibilities, no matter what their personal perspectives are on the nature of fatherhood. The MCH reproductive and child development communities acknowledge this important paternal social role transformation, but mostly from a negative or deficit perspective, focusing heavily on father-absent or "deadbeat dad" families. Rarely, does the MCH community discuss paternal family commitment and community involvement from a majoritarian perspective that focuses on father's positive transformative social well-being. [The impact of the non-residential father-absence on children and men's development is discussed, in part, by others in this book (Yogman and Eppel 2021).]

First, the vast majority of fathers readily acknowledge their paternity. Historically, acknowledgement of paternity was related to infant legitimacy and inheritance, and was closely tied to the marital status of the father and mother. Despite increases in births to unmarried parents (~40% of U.S. births) (Martin et al. 2019), the rate that men embrace and acknowledge their paternity is increasing (Almond and Rossin-Slater 2013); perhaps a reflection the increased legal mandates to establish an "Acknowledgement of Paternity" (AOP) for each birth to an unmarried mother in the U.S. Birth outcomes among unmarried women with partners who sign an AOP were significantly better than among unmarried women without an AOP, though still not as positive as among married women (Almond and Rossin-Slater 2013.)

Second, though obviously a partnered decision, the vast majority of fathers reside with and support their families financially, practically, and emotionally during the perinatal period and beyond (whether married or not). Clearly, over time the extent of this involvement does decline, especially among poorer and unmarried families. In the U.S., among Fragile Families Study participants, only 50% of unmarried couples cohabitating at birth are still living together at the child's first birthday, and just 37% are by the child's fifth birthday (Carlson et al. 2008). But even among the non-residential fathers studied, fatherhood serves as a source of engagement and social well-being for themselves and their children; the majority saw their children at 1 year of age and provided informal and in-kind support (Carlson et al. 2008); fatherhood gave meaning to their lives (Garfield et al. 2010). Married marital status increasingly is a marker of higher social classes, conveying social and developmental benefits for the father and his children (McLanahan et al. 2013). Moreover, fatherhood is not restricted solely to biologic fathers, many other men assume parental roles, nearly 4% of U.S. children under age 6 live with a mother and a step-father (Census 2018). The father's continued involvement and presence in his family can be viewed, in part, as a bi-directional impact of fatherhood on men's social well-being—a positive behavioral response to stresses and joys of parenthood and his relationship with the child's mother.

Third, positive perinatal cultural and institutional support for men's social transition to fatherhood is quite limited. Many community and professional organizations and cultural practices are prepared to honor women's new maternal social role and to welcome her and her infant into their communities (e.g., baby showers, prenatal yoga classes, maternity stores, etc.). There are no similar equivalent positive cultural acknowledgements for men's changing social roles. With the exception of limited father-inclusive child-birth education classes, most maternal reproductive health services do not actively encourage father's involvement or acknowledge his new emerging fatherhood status (Steen et al. 2012). Moreover, fatherhood, like the experiences for some women, can also sometimes reveal or increase men's social isolation from their communities. In the MGH Obstetric Prenatal Fatherhood studies, 35% of fathers reported that they had no place to go for fatherhood support or information (Levy and Kotelchuck 2021). Fatherhood and men's family and community involvement needs greater and earlier perinatal social affirmation. If it takes a village to raise a child, that village needs to include the fathers.

2.4.3 Fathers as Economic Providers: Fathers Own Lived SDOH Transformations

Most father's and family's economic realities are transformed as a result of parenthood. Families, almost by definition, have decreased per capita income and substantial new direct childcare expenses, though some potential new financial resources. The impact of fatherhood on the transformation of men's own social and economic welfare, his own lived social determinants of health (SDOH) characteristics, has yet to emerge as a topic in the MCH reproductive health community.

First, fathers are eligible for some societal benefits that favor families relative to single or married men without children. The latter are often restricted from social welfare benefits, such as paid paternity leave or family allowances, or are the last to receive access to public housing, food-assistance, or medical care programs—a positive discrimination in favor of fathers. Tax benefits in the U.S., including direct child, child and dependent care, and earned income tax credits (EITC), in general, also favor working families, and therefore fathers with children.

Second, economists have documented a "fatherhood wage bonus," and women's income "motherhood penalty." In adjusted analyses, fathers earn 6% more salary than non-fathers (Budig and Hodges 2014). Additionally, the wage gaps between employed men and women increases substantially for parenthood; non-parent women earn 93% of non-parent men's salary, whereas, working mothers earn only 76% of father's wages (Budig and Hodges 2014); plus, this wage gap is even greater for low-income fathers and mothers, further reinforcing social disparities. In some employment situations, fatherhood is associated with a "fatherhood premium," increased wages to be able to support their families (Correl et al. 2007).

Third, fatherhood can, however, also limit or harm men's social health and financial status, especially for non-residential, low income, and minority fathers, whose social welfare benefits are heavily influenced by federal and state government programs and policies. U.S. policies often both encourage and discourage paternal involvement with their families—perhaps reflecting the current political ambivalence towards such fathers and their partners (Edin and Nelson 2013). Many social welfare programs are structured to penalize or limit benefits for non-residential, non-married fathers. Traditional U.S. family welfare and Medicaid eligibility was explicitly restricted to mothers without residential male partners. Aggressive federal and state child support enforcement agency efforts, while potentially enhancing mother's income, often inadvertently decrease father's family involvement, by further burdening the poorest men with high arrears penalty interest rates, asset seizures, and possible incarceration (Tollestrup 2018; Boggess et al. 2014). And the U.S. "War on Drugs" disproportionately ensnared poor men (and often fathers) of color. The major U.S. federal Healthy Marriage and Responsible Fatherhood Initiative (ACF 2019) primarily emphasizes the father's traditional social and financial family roles; it provides low income men with relational skills and marriage motivational training, though not direct income or social welfare supports. Its initial program evaluations were mixed (Knox et al. 2011); perhaps its limited, politically-influenced, individual responsibility training model may be insufficient to overcome the structural realities for poor fathers in the U.S. Other countries, especially in Europe, provide more positive supports for father's social well-being as part of their more universal family social welfare policies—including father-specific paid family leave and family allowances (see, e.g., Kvande 2021, in this volume).

Overall, men's own social health and well-being is impacted by their experiences of fatherhood—in employment, family, community involvement, and economic resource provisions. Each of these social experiences of fatherhood are important influences on men's physical health, mental health, and paternal generativity, which in turn can directly impact reproductive and infant health and development. While the social transformation of women into mothers is widely acknowledged and celebrated, a similar recognition of the social health transformation of men becoming fathers is lacking—especially in the MCH reproductive health community. Fatherhood can change men's own SDOH characteristics, though the extent may depend on the unique employment and social welfare policies and practices within each country. The United States, in particular, has weak and often punitive social welfare policies that substantially impact on low income and non-residential fathers. Further reproductive health research on the social impact of fatherhood is needed.

2.5 Men's Psychological Maturation of Paternal Generativity: Men's Improved Capacity for Parenthood and Fatherhood

Fatherhood can be a major influence on men's own adult psychological development and maturation, especially during his first pregnancy and early parenthood experience. This transformation represents one of most important health impacts of fatherhood. Virtually all men can biologically procreate children, but it takes more than just sperm to become a father. Having children is a powerful biologic urge that can profoundly affect men and women's psychological maturation. Many fathers, similar to most mothers, go through substantial psychological transformations and growth during the perinatal period. Fatherhood can be viewed as an adult psychological developmental stage of life.

Psychological transition to fatherhood. In reviews of men's psychological transition to fatherhood studies, Genesoni and Tallandini (2009) found pregnancy to be the most demanding period for the father's psychological reorganization of self, and labor and birth to be the most emotional moments. Baldwin et al. (2018) characterized some of the most salient features of men's positive psychological transition into their new fatherhood identity: "Becoming a father gave men a new identity, which made them feel like they were fulfilling their role as men, with a recognition of changed priorities and responsibility and expanded vision; however they worried about being a good father and getting it right.... Fathers who were involved with their child and bonded with them over time found the experience to be rewarding. Those who recognized the need for change, adjusted better to the new role, especially when they worked together with their partners." Beyond the limited and predominantly qualitative professional literature, this developmental transition is perhaps best noted in the popular media through movies and television shows that capture the profound paternal psychological transformation of men as a result of parenthood (e.g., *Kramer vs. Kramer*; *Mrs. Doubtfire*; *Three Men and a Baby*; and, more recently, *Marriage Story*).

There are numerous different terms used to describe this developmental transformation in men from biological procreation to responsible fatherhood. For many, it is commonly and best discussed in terms of life fulfillment, or even of religious or spiritual goals (e.g., "Fatherhood as the highest calling in life"). I prefer to use the psychological term of "generativity" to describe this transformation; it is a term coined by Dr. Erik Erikson (1950) and defined as "establishing and guiding the next generation, with a capacity for love and sense of optimism about humanity" (i.e., successfully nurturing the next generation). Hawkins and Dollahite (1997); Dollahite et al. (1997), and Hawkins and David (1997) have expanded on this concept and coined the term "generative fathering," a perspective on fathering rooted in the ethical obligations for fathers to meet the needs of the next generation. They conceptualize fathering as generative work, rather than as a social role, embedded in a changing socio-historical context from which both fathers and children benefit and grow. Singley and Edwards (2015) interpret the term generative fathering to describe the type of parenting used by fathers who respond readily and consistently to their child's development needs over time, a key element of Erik Erikson's adult development theory, rooted in broadening the sense of self to include the next generation. The generative fathering perspective highlights a clear way that men can focus their instinct to protect and to provide for their children in a strengths-based way—by being involved and responsive to their children's needs even from their earliest (antenatal) age. Moreover, the concept of generativity, or generative fathering, adds an internal motivational and a moral dimension to men's ongoing psychological transformation in becoming fathers, a sense of paternal agency. Men themselves are, and must be, the agents of their own psychological transformation.

Even for the most marginalized fathers, creating and nurturing life is perceived as one of the most meaningful statements about one's presence on earth and contribution to life (Edin and Nelson 2013). In the Fragile Families and Child Well Being Study, fatherhood was associated with being present for their child's future (Garfield et al. 2010). From a parallel perspective, Roubinov et al. (2016) describe "familism" in Latino (specifically, Mexican-origin) communities as a father's deep ethical and cultural commitment to nurturing his children and family, even if also deeply imbued with a "machismo" social-roles perspective. Additionally, the Black women's reproductive justice movement is now also beginning to recognize the importance of reproductive and economic justice for their impoverished Black male partners as well (e.g., Edwards et al. 2020).

As fathers are increasingly present with their partners in the delivery room, there is now a growing literature on its transformative effects on men's psychological development (Genesoni and Tallandini 2009; Darwin et al. 2017; Baldwin et al. 2018; Johansson et al. 2015). Fathers can share the joy and miracle of birth, be supportive of their partners, and further crystalize their own paternal role transition. However, many men report very mixed experiences in the delivery rooms, with clinical staff not always supportive of their presence (Steen et al. 2012; Jomeen

2017). Only recently have a few birthing services intentionally tried to enhance the father's contributions and engagement, both to foster a more positive family-forming health event and to support men's own psychological development as fathers (Pol et al. 2014; Johansson et al. 2015).

Programmatic support for men's psychological transition to fatherhood. Fatherhood psychological transition is not universal. Generative or responsible fathers don't just magically appear, but they emerge from a gradual transformative process, and they can be helped along in this transformation. Going beyond the previously noted politically constrained U.S. federal Healthy Marriage and Responsible Fatherhood Initiative (ACF 2019), non-governmental community-based, parenting, social service, advocacy, and religious organizations, especially in the Black community, have taken the initiative to develop local fatherhood programs (e.g., Concerned Black Men of America, Omega Psi Phi Fraternity, etc.). These programs generally emphasize men's own social and psychological transformation and healing; paternal responsibility and generativity; and moral, spiritual, and psychological engagement with their children; as well as financial and social support of their families. They are backed up by national fatherhood resource and training organizations (e.g., The MGH Fatherhood Project, the National Fatherhood Initiative, Mr. Dad, etc.). These organizations explicitly counter the debilitating myths of Black men's non-involvement with their children.

The Healthy Start Initiative was the first and is currently the principal U.S. national MCH perinatal program to actively incorporate a positive mandate to address Fatherhood and Male Engagement (Healthy Start 2019). Its "Dads Matter Initiative," with its "Dads and Diamonds are Forever" curriculum, and an annual fatherhood conference, emphasizes father's "inclusion, involvement, investment and integration" across the life course, enhancing men's sense of value to himself, his children, the mothers of his children, and his community (i.e., generative fathering) (Harris and Brott 2018). Several other MCH programs, serving low-income communities in the U.S., such as home visiting, Head Start academic enrichment, and the WIC nutrition supplementation programs, also have begun to target and address father's needs, though not yet as systematically as Healthy Start (Davison et al. 2019).

The perinatal period for many men, as for women, is also a period of marked openness for behavioral, socio-emotional, and health changes (Addis and Mahalik 2003), wherein fatherhood imperatives can trump masculine stereotypes. Mental health, relational, and fathering skills can be taught (Knox et al. 2011; Levy et al. 2012; Tollestrup 2018). The transition from a more traditional distant fatherhood role to a more equitable child caretaking partnership may also free up men from other gendered sex role stereotypes that diminish their psychological capacities to experience and express emotions, acknowledge health needs, or treat their partners more respectfully. Father's psychological developmental transitions during the perinatal period however are not generally recognized or appreciated by most reproductive and primary health care professionals, nor are there programmatic services or support for men's growth as generative fathers (Pol et al. 2014; Johansson et al.

2015). Much more research is needed to understand what facilitates the growth of men's paternal generativity, or even how best to measure it.

Similar to women, men's adult psychological developmental as a more generative parent is one of most important positive mental health impacts of pregnancy and early fatherhood, especially for the first time fathers. Paternal generativity doesn't just happen. While the momentum for paternal generativity must ultimately come from, and be empowered by, each man himself, all MCH and father-involving programs should consciously engage with and support his developmental maturation. We must go beyond the limited federal emphasis in the U.S. on men's financial and marital responsibilities only; and we must create, culturally and professionally, the paternal expectations and opportunities for men to celebrate the joys and deep satisfactions of fatherhood. Most fathers make the successful adult psychological transition to being a more generative parent and are happy to have done so.

2.6 *Men's Life Course Development as Fathers*

The development of generative responsible fathers reflects a gradual longitudinal process that has its roots long prior to the pregnancy conception and continues long after the delivery; and it can be helped and hindered all along the way. Paternal generativity is both personal and intergenerational. The perinatal period, the focus of this essay, is one of its principle sensitive periods of accelerated growth.

Kotelchuck and Lu (2017) in their publication on men and preconception health graphically highlight several key conceptual features about the growth of men's paternal generativity over the life course. To quote from that article:

"First, as with women's reproductive life course (Lu and Halfon 2003), it [Fig. 1, as reproduced here] encourages us to view men's health and development longitudinally, recognizing that the impact of his health and generativity transcends the moment of pregnancy conception, and appreciate the intergenerational continuity and the bi-directionality of men's health. Father's reproductive health and generativity is not fixed; each stage of life and health builds on both prior and current life and health experiences and evolves over the life course (Fine and Kotelchuck 2010). This new MCH fatherhood life course graphic acknowledges that some men have more negative or positive life experiences; that the root causes of men's reproductive health and paternal generativity reflects both the negative and positive social determinants influencing his past and current health – including his adverse childhood and adolescent experiences, sexual health education and socialization, current and past poverty, employment, and environmental and occupational exposures, etc. The paternal MCH life course model thus reflects both a resiliency and a deficit perspective. One's reproductive potential is not immutable. We can and must help build boys' and men's resiliency to achieve both the biology and paternal generativity of fatherhood, and thereby optimize both their own and their children's health and development. The men's reproductive health life course graphic also reminds us that there are multiple times and places to intervene to enhance (or diminish) men's health and paternal generativity."

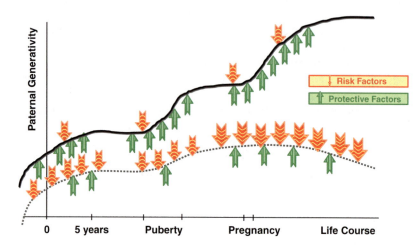

Fig. 1 How differential exposure to risk factors (downward arrows) and protective factors (upward arrows) over the life course affect developmental trajectories in father involvement/generativity. Lower involvement (dashed curve) results from cumulative exposure to more risk factors and less protective factors across the life span, particularly at sensitive periods of development. (Source: Kotelchuck and Lu 2017)

And although this graph focuses on men's individual generativity, efforts to encourage his shared responsibility for healthy parenthood and for equitable parental childcare and involvement must start earlier than conception with his shared responsibility for sexuality and family planning. Further, men's development as generative fathers must also necessarily address his pre-fatherhood adolescent social and gender norms, perhaps beginning in schools with their parenting, sexuality, and gender-based education programs. The preconception time period for paternal generativity must be pushed backwards in developmental ontological time.

Additionally, men's paternal generativity is not a simple linear age trend but is embedded within our larger human biologic development. The roots of men's intergenerational and epigenetic generativity starts before birth, and has at least two special sensitive periods of growth: puberty and the initial antenatal and early postnatal transition to fatherhood. The latter is perhaps the most sensitive transformational life course period for men's psychosocial development and maturation as a father (Genesoni and Tallandini 2009); it may perhaps also reflect a new paternal biological sensitive period due to his changing perinatal hormones and brain structure. The experiences and health consequences of fatherhood are further filtered through and modified by the men's pre-existing life course health and well-being that he brings into the perinatal period, similar to that of pregnant women.

Indeed, the differential risk and protective factors (the conceptual arrows in Fig. 1) influencing the growth of men's generativity over the life course can be viewed as reflecting the many contributors to the fatherhood health pathways already discussed throughout this chapter—including, for example, family income, work-family stress, substance use, social connectedness, etc. These factors, in turn, are strongly modulated (positively or negatively) by national and state health, economic, and social welfare policies and programs—including both those operating in the immediate perinatal period (e.g., paid leave, living wages, health insurance access), as well as those operating long before (e.g., childhood health and education, masculinity gender role socialization and childhood SDOH).

Moreover, fathers are not homogeneous; different subgroups of fathers are likely to experience the life-course health and developmental challenges of fatherhood and fatherhood generativity differently, based on both their personal and socio-historical life course experiences. Potentially important fatherhood subgroups to consider might be based on socio-economic status, race/ethnicity, first-time or experienced fatherhood, teen or older paternal age, planned or unplanned pregnancy, residential status, disability status, incarceration, or military service. In the U.S., the experiences of poor fathers, especially those of color, are particularly challenging given historical structural racism and its ongoing negative health, social welfare, and employment biases. Too little is known about the life course sources of more positive father generativity.

The developmental roots of paternal generativity are not restricted only to the critical and sensitive perinatal period, but build off of men's prior life course health and developmental experiences. Paternal generativity should be viewed as an intergenerational and epigenetic phenomenon, building off of prior generations and towards future generations. Paternal generativity is not fixed but malleable. The momentum for paternal generativity, for fatherhood, with all its satisfactions and stresses, must be empowered by each man himself; but it is embedded in the larger developmental world in which his full reproductive potential is either encouraged and grows or is stunted and underachieved. The fatherhood life course perspective suggests that there are multiple places and times in which both positive and negative program and policy interventions and life experiences can influence men's paternal generativity. Paternal generativity, the essence of fatherhood, is shaped over his life course.

3 Enhancing Fatherhood to Foster Men's Health and Development During the Perinatal Period: Implications for Research, Practice, and Policy

Fatherhood profoundly impacts men's health and development. It impacts his physical, mental, and social health, and his sense of paternal generativity, both immediately and over his life course. These, in turn, impact his infant's, partner's, and family's health. Indeed, fatherhood can be viewed as a risk or resiliency factor for men's subsequent health across his life course. The focus on men's changing health as a consequence of fatherhood is an important new perspective for the MCH reproductive health field, which has historically focused on the mother and her health.

This chapter is one of a pair of inter-related chapters on father's health in the perinatal period that parallels the dual approach of the current women's preconception health movement, which simultaneously addresses the impact of the mother's perinatal health both on the infant's health outcomes and on the mother's own subsequent lifetime health. Both topics for men also are critical and intractably bound. Father's health, like mother's health, is thus similarly a bi-directional and inter-generational topic.

This chapter pulls together and articulates six broad pathways through which fatherhood could potentially positively or negatively impact men's health and development—men's pre-existing health, his perinatal changed physical, mental, and social health, his generativity, and his life-course experiences. This emerging conceptual framework encompasses the father's entire life course, but focuses here on the perinatal time period, a time frame not usually thought of as impacting on men's health. These six specific pathways are written to try to isolate and better articulate them, though many of them likely overlap and are synergistic. Several emerging themes merit further discussion.

First, going beyond the impact of fatherhood on men's physical and mental health, this chapter, in particular, emphasized and explored two new health topics: men's psychological maturation of paternal generativity, and men's social health and well-being. The first topic, men's psychological maturation into more generative fathers, is not a well articulated fatherhood topic, especially antenatally. It has not been the focus of virtually any formal MCH or prenatal health services to date, although a large popular "Advice for New Dads" social media literature exists, which may at times touch on this theme. The psychological empowerment of fathers requires, in part, that our current health service systems (and men themselves) overcome their traditional sexist assumptions about men's supposedly limited roles and needs, his marginality, during the pregnancy and early childhood period.

Second, men's social health and well-being may be a difficult pathway for the MCH reproductive health community to appreciate, as this topic links more broadly to men's larger social roles within the family home and employment. The transformative impact of fatherhood on men's social health, and therefore ultimately on reproductive health, is heavily influenced by social welfare and employment programs and policies, many of which are also closely linked to women's gender equity issues. This emerging pathway has the potential to bring the MCH community productively together with other business and human service professions that are grappling with similar paternal (and maternal) social health and well-being issues to create multi-sector transformative change (Bowles et al. 2021).

Third, this chapter further builds upon the growing recognition that fathers are a key vector for the SDOH and well-being of their families (Kotelchuck 2018, 2021), and begins to add a more nuanced understanding of this theme. As noted previously, this chapter emphasizes that men's own social well-being, his SDOH characteristics, are not fixed, but can change due to his experiences of fatherhood. Moreover, the father's historical and current compromised SDOH can diminish his positive health responses to fatherhood and limit his fullest and healthiest participation in the perinatal period and beyond. And, while paternal generativity is not principally determined by social class, poverty does make it harder for some men.

Fourth, the positive or negative impact of fatherhood on men's physical, mental, social, or generative health and development is not pre-ordained. This chapter, reflecting the limited existing literature, predominantly notes the negative paternal physical and especially mental health impacts of fatherhood. There is much less balanced research on the more positive health experiences of fatherhood, and how to foster them.

Fifth, this chapter documents that the impact of fatherhood on men's health begins before delivery (i.e., the perinatal roots of father's own health). It strongly reinforces the initial chapter's parallel efforts to expand the time frame for the impact of men's health on reproductive and infant health into the antenatal period. This essay however emphasizes not merely the perinatal impact of fatherhood on men's health, but an even longer ontological life course perspective on father's health. The health of men and their paternal generative characteristics start early, epigenetically, long before conception; although like for women, the experiences during the perinatal and early parenthood period seem to be an especially biologically sensitive period of impact. Fatherhood is not simply a sperm and post-partum parenting; paternal generativity must be conceptualized across the life course.

Sixth, this chapter and the prior one dispute the prevailing view that mothers and their health and well-being alone are solely responsible for positive reproductive and infant outcomes and that women are the only or primary gender affected by parenthood. If men actively assume or are encouraged to participate in the joys and responsibilities of reproductive and infant care, they will likely become more generative fathers, and in turn that could help free up women and men from overly prescribed gendered parental behavioral and economic roles. This chapter, while a self-contained MCH theme, has been inspired by, and hopefully contributes to, the larger social gender equity movement, as well as the growing parenting health and men's health movements.

Seventh, hopefully, this chapter and the prior one have demonstrated that a focus on father's health and well-being should be a more formal and important MCH perinatal health research, practice, and policy topic. These chapters provide an ever-stronger, positive, empirical and theoretical developmental science rationale to support more extensive, earlier, and healthier paternal perinatal involvement. The six pathways noted in this chapter summarize our current scientific knowledge base to date (Knowledge Base), which can now provide the basis to develop more effective targeted fatherhood programmatic and policy interventions (Social Strategies) and to support more effective and scientifically justified fatherhood advocacy efforts (Political Will) for their implementations (Richmond and Kotelchuck 1983).

Clearly the core public health action message of this chapter (and the prior one) is that there should be more active, earlier, and healthier paternal involvement in the perinatal period. Many of this chapter's six pathways call out for readily implementable ameliorative actions and interventions to address the added challenges of fatherhood on men's health. The fatherhood life course perspective further suggests that there are multiple places and times for potential synergetic interventions to enhance men's and father's health throughout his life course. Hopefully, this essay will add to the momentum for more targeted and effective father-oriented perinatal health interventions and policies—in order to ensure both more optimal reproductive and infant health and development and more optimal men's health, development, and paternal generativity.

This book highlights three key sectors for paternal program and policy interventions—social policy, work/organizational practices, and health care. No single sector alone can solely enhance the impact of fatherhood on men's health and development or assure greater parental gender equity for men and women; all sectors are needed and must be synergetically involved. Sadly, however, there is relatively little professional recognition of father's own unique perinatal health needs—and even less formal services directed towards him. This Conference and edited book reflect an effort to enhance fatherhood activities within each of three sectors and importantly across sectors (Bowles et al. 2021).

Fatherhood is a life course developmental achievement. Fatherhood is not a singular point in the life course, but a profoundly human experience that occurs over time and across generations. The developmental trajectory of fatherhood starts long before conception and impacts fathers and their children and family throughout their lives, long after conception and inter-generationally. Healthy and engaged fathers help insure healthy children, healthy families, healthy workforces, and healthy communities.

References

Abraham E, Hendler T, Shapira-Lichter I, Kanat-Maymon Y, Zagoory-Sharon O, Feldman R (2014) Father's brain is sensitive to childcare experiences. Proc Natl Acad Sci U S A 111 (27):9792–9797

Addis ME, Mahalik JR (2003) Men, masculinity and the contexts of help seeking. Am Psychol 58 (1):5–14

Administration for Children and Family (2019) Healthy marriage and responsible fatherhood. Office of Family Assistance. U.S. Department of Health and Human Services. www.acf.hhs.gov/ofa/programs/healthy-marriage

Almond D, Rossin-Slater M (2013) Paternity acknowledgement in two million birth records in Michigan. PLoS One 8(7):e70042. https://doi.org/10.1371/journal.pone.0070042

Baldwin S, Bick D (2018) Mental health of first time fathers—it's time to put evidence into practice. JBI Database Syst Rev Implement Rep 16(11):2064–2065

Baldwin S, Malone M, Sandall J, Bick D (2018) Mental health and well-being during the transition to fatherhood: a systematic review of first time fathers' experiences. JBI Database Syst Rev Implement Rep 16(11):2118–2219

Bertakis KD, Rahman A, Jay Helms L, Callahan EJ, Robbins JA (2000) Gender differences in the utilization of health care services. J Fam Pract 49(2):147–152

Boggess J, Price A, Rodriguez N (2014) What we want to give our children: how child support debt can diminish wealth-building opportunities for struggling black fathers and their family. Center for Family Policy and Practice, Madison. https://cffpp.org/wp-content/uploads/whatwewanttogiveourkids.pdf

Bowles HR, Kotelchuck M, Grau-Grau M (2021) Reducing barriers to engaged fatherhood: three principles for promoting gender equity in parenting. In: Grau-Grau M, las Heras M, Bowles HR (eds) Engaged fatherhood for men, families and gender equality. Springer, Cham, pp 299–325

Brennan A, Ayers S, Ahmed H, Marshall-Lucette S (2007) A critical review of the couvade syndrome: the pregnant male. J Reprod Infant Psychol 25(3):173–189

British Broadcasting Corporation News (2009) Fathers-to-be 'gain extra weight'. https://news.bbc.co.uk/2/hi/health/8063004.stm

Budig M, Hodges MJ (2014) Statistical models and empirical evidence for differences in the motherhood wage penalty across the earnings distribution: a reply to Killewald and Bearek. Am Sociol Rev 79(20):358–364

Burgard SA, Ailshire JA (2013) Gender and time for sleep among US adults. Am Sociol Rev 78 (1):51–69

Canadian Tobacco Use Monitoring Survey (2006) Via Health Canada Website. https://www.Hc-Sc.Gc.Ca

Carlson MJ, Mclanahan SS, Brooks-Gunn J (2008) Coparenting and non-residential involvement with young children after non-marital birth. Demography 45(2):461–488

Centers for Disease Control and Prevention (CDC) (2019) Preconception health and health care. https://www.cdc.gov/preconception/index. Accessed 15 Jan 2019

Cheng ER, Kotelchuck M, Gerstein ED, Taveras EM, Poehlmann-Tynan J (2016) Postnatal depressive symptoms among mothers and fathers of infants born preterm: prevalence and impacts on children's early cognitive function. J Dev Behav Pediatr 37(1):33–42

Choiriyyah I, Sonenstein FL, Astone NM, Pleck JH, Dariotis JK, Marcell AV (2015) Men aged 15–44 in need of preconception care. Matern Child Health J 19(11):2358–2365

Coleman PK, Karraker KH (1998) Self-efficacy and parenting quality: findings and future applications. Dev Rev 18(1):47–85

Correl SJ, Benard S, Paik I (2007) Getting a job: is there a motherhood penalty? Am J Sociol 112 (5):1297–1339

Darwin Z, Galdas P, Hinchliff S, Littlewood E, McMillan D, McGowan L, Gilbody S, on behalf of the Born and Bred in Yorkshire (BaBY) Team (2017) Fathers' views and experiences of their own mental health during pregnancy and the first postnatal year: a qualitative interview study of men participating in the UK Born and Bred in Yorkshire (BaBY) cohort. BMC Pregnancy Childbirth 17(1):45. https://doi.org/10.1186/s12884-017-1229-4

Davison KK, Gavarkovs A, McBride B, Kotelchuck M, Levy R, Taveras EM (2019) Engaging fathers in early obesity prevention during the first thousand days: policy, systems and environmental change strategies. Obesity 27(4):523–533

Dollahite DC, Hawkins AJ, Brotherson SE (1997) Fatherwork: a conceptual ethic of fathering as generative work. In: Hawkins AJ, Dollahite DC (eds) Generative fathering: beyond deficit perspectives. Sage, Thousand Oaks, pp 17–35

Due C, Chiarolli S, Riggs DW (2017) The impact of pregnancy loss on men's health and wellbeing: a systemic review. BMC Pregnancy Childbirth 17:380. https://doi.org/10.1186/s12884-017-1560-9

Edelstein RS, Wardecker BM, Chopik WJ, Moors AC, Shipman EL, Lin NJ (2015) Prenatal hormones in first-time expectant parents: longitudinal changes and within couple correlations. Am J Hum Biol 27(3):317–325

Edin K, Nelson TJ (2013) Doing the best I can: fatherhood in the Inner City. University Of California Press, Berkeley

Edvardsson K, Lindkvist M, Eurenius E, Mogren I, Small R, Ivarsson A (2013) A population-based study of overweight and obesity in expectant parents: socio-demographic patterns and within-couple associations. BMC Public Health 13(1):923. https://doi.org/10.1186/1471-2458-13-923

Edwards BN, McLemore MR, Baltzell K, Hodgkin A, Nunez O, Franck LS (2020) What about the men? Perinatal experiences of men of color whose partners were at risk for preterm birth, a qualitative study. BMC Pregnancy Childbirth 20:91. https://doi.org/10.1186/s12884-020-2785-6

Eggebeen DJ, Knoester C (2001) Does fatherhood matter for men? J Marriage Fam 63(2):381–393

Erikson EH (1950) Childhood and society. Norton, New York

Fine A, Kotelchuck M (2010) Rethinking MCH: the life course model as an organizing framework: concept paper. U.S. Department of Health and Human Services, Health Resources and Services Administration, Maternal and Child Health Bureau, Rockville

Fleming AS, Ruble D, Howard K, Wong PY (1997) Hormonal and experiential correlates of maternal responsiveness during pregnancy and the puerperium in human mothers. Horm Behav 31:145–158

Freeman E, Fletcher R, Collins CE, Morgan PJ, Burrows T, Callister R (2012) Preventing and treating childhood obesity: time to include the father. Int J Obes 36(1):12–15

Frey KA, Navarro SM, Kotelchuck M, Michael CL (2008) The clinical content of preconception care: preconception care for men. Am J Obstet Gynecol 199(6 Suppl B):S389–S395

Garfield CF, Isacco A, Bartlo WD (2010) Men's health and fatherhood in urban Midwestern United States. Int J Mens Health 9(3):161–174

Garfield CF, Duncan G, Rutsohn J, McDade TW, Adam EK, Coley RL, Lindsay Chase-Lansdale P (2014) A longitudinal study of paternal mental health during transition to fatherhood as young adults. Pediatrics 133(5):836–843

Garfield CF, Duncan G, Gutina A, Rutsohn J, McDade TW, Adam EK, Coley RL, Lindsay Chase-Lansdale P (2016) Longitudinal study of body mass index in young males and the transition to fatherhood. Am J Mens Health 10(6):NP158–NP167

Gemayel DJ, Wiener KKK, Saliba AJ (2018) Development of a conception framework that identifies factors and challenges impacting perinatal fathers. Heliyon 4(7):e00694

Genesoni L, Tallandini MA (2009) Men's psychological transition to fatherhood: an analysis of the literature, 1989-2008. Birth 36(4):305–318

Gettler LT, McDade TW, Feranil AB, Kuzawa CW (2011) Longitudinal evidence that fatherhood decreases testosterone in human males. Proc Natl Acad Sci U S A 108(39):16194–16199

Glass JL, Simon RW, Andersson MA (2016) Parenthood and happiness: effects of work-family reconciliation policies in 22 OECD countries. Am J Sociol 122(3):886–929

Gordon I, Zagoory-Sharon O, Leckman JF, Feldman R (2010) Prolactin, oxytocin and the development of paternal behavior across the first six months of fatherhood. Horm Behav 58(3):513–518

Grebe NM, Sarafin RE, Strenth CR, Zilioli S (2019) Pair-bonding, fatherhood, and the role of testosterone: a meta-analytic review. Neurosci Biobehav Rev 98:221–233

Grundy E, Kravdal Ø (2008) Reproductive history and mortality in late middle age among Norwegian men and women. Am J Epidemiol 167(3):271–279

Gustafsson E, Levréro F, Reby D, Mathevon N (2013) Fathers are just as good as mothers at recognizing the cries of their baby. Nat Commun 4:1698

Harrington B (2021) The new dad: the career-caregiving conundrum. In: Grau-Grau M, las Heras M, Bowles HR (eds) Engaged fatherhood for men, families and gender equality. Springer, Cham, pp 197–212

Harrington B, Van Deusen F, Fraone J (2014) The new dad: take your leave. Boston College Center for Work & Family, Chestnut Hill

Harris K, Brott A (2018) NHSA healthy start fathers-real life, real dads. National Healthy Start Association, Washington, DC. https://www.nationalhealthystart.org/what_we_do/male_involvement/nhsa_healthy_start_fathers_real_life_real_dads

Hashemian F, Shafigh F, Roohi E (2016) Regulatory role of prolactin in paternal behavior in male parents: a narrative review. J Postgrad Med 62(3):182–187

Hawkins AJ, David C (1997) Beyond the role-inadequacy perspective. In: Hawkins AJ, Dollahite DC (eds) Generative fathering: beyond deficit perspectives. Sage, Thousand Oaks, pp 3–16

Hawkins AJ, Dollahite DC (eds) (1997) Generative fathering: beyond deficit perspectives. Sage, Thousand Oaks

Healthy Start (2019) Health resources and service administration—maternal and child health. https://mchb.hrsa.gov/maternal-child-health-initiatives/healthy-start

Hobson B, Fahlen S (2009) Competing scenarios for European fathers: applying Sen's capabilities and agency framework to work-family balance. Ann Am Acad Pol Soc Sci 624(1):214–233

Hodges MJ, Budig MJ (2010) Who gets the daddy Bonus? Markers of hegemonic masculinity and impact of first-time fatherhood on men's earnings. Gend Soc 24(6):715–745

Hull EE, Rofey DL, Robertson RJ, Nagle EF, Otto AD, Aaron DJ (2010) Influence of marriage and parenthood on physical activity: a 2-year prospective analysis. J Phys Act Health 7(5):577–583

Humberd B, Ladge J, Harrington B (2015) The 'new' dad: navigating father identity within organizational contexts. J Bus Psychol 30(2):249–266

Johansson M, Fenwick J, Premberg A (2015) A meta-synthesis of the father's experiences of their partner's labour and birth. Midwifery 31(1):9–18

Jomeen J (2017) Fathers in the birth room: choice or coercion? Help or hinderance? J Reproduct Infant Psychol 35(4):321–323

Kazmierczak M, Kielbratowska B, Pastwa-Wojciechowska B (2013) Couvade syndrome among polish expectant fathers. Med Sci Monit 21(19):132–138

Keizer R, Dykstra PA, van Lenthe FJ (2011) Parity and men's mortality risks. Eur J Pub Health 22(3):343–347

Kessler RC, Berglund P, Demler O, Jin R, Koretz D, Merikangas KR, John Rush A, Walters EE, Wang PS (2003) The epidemiology of major depressive disorder: results from the National Comorbidity Survey Replication (NCS-R). JAMA 289(35):3095–3105

Kim P, Swain JE (2007) Sad dads: paternal post-partum depression. Psychiatry (Edgmont) 4(2):35–47

Kim P, Rigo P, Mayes LC, Feldman R, Leckman JF, Swain JE (2014) Neural plasticity in fathers of human infants. Soc Neurosci 9(5):522–535

Knox V, Cowan PA, Cowan CP, Bildne E (2011) Policies that strengthen fatherhood and family relationships: what do we know and what do we need to know? Ann Am Acad Pol Soc Sci 635(1):216–239

Kotelchuck M (2018) Looking back to move forward: a return to our roots, addressing social determinants across MCH history. In: Verbiest S (ed) Moving life course theory into practice: making change happen. APHA Press, Washington, DC, pp 57–78. https://ajph.aphapublications.org/doi/10.2105/9780875532967ch03

Kotelchuck M (2021) The impact of father's health on reproductive and infant health and development. In: Grau-Grau M, las Heras M, Bowles HR (eds) Engaged fatherhood for men, families and gender equality. Springer, Cham, pp 31–61

Kotelchuck M, Lu M (2017) Father's role in preconception health. Matern Child Health J 21(11):2025–2039

Kvande E (2021) Individual parental leave for fathers—promoting gender equality in Norway. In: Grau-Grau M, las Heras M, Bowles HR (eds) Engaged fatherhood for men, families and gender equality. Springer, Cham, pp 153–162

Ladge JJ, Humberd BK (2021) Impossible standards and unlikely trade-offs: can fathers be competent parents and professionals? In: Grau-Grau M, las Heras M, Bowles HR (eds) Engaged fatherhood for men, families and gender equality. Springer, Cham, pp 183–196

Ladge JJ, Humberd BK, Baskerville M, Harrington B (2015) Updating the organizational man: fathers in the workplace. Acad Manag Perspect 29(1):152–171

Lamb ME (1975) Fathers: forgotten contributors to child development. Hum Dev 18(4):245–266

Lamb ME (ed) (2010) The role of the father in child development, 5th edn. Wiley, New York

Leach LS, Poyser C, Cooklin AR, Giallo R (2016) Prevalence and course of anxiety disorders (and symptom levels) in men across the perinatal period: a systematic review. J Affect Disord 190(15):675–686

Levy RA, Kotelchuck M (2021) Fatherhood and reproductive health in the antenatal period: from men's voices to clinical practice. In: Grau-Grau M, las Heras M, Bowles HR (eds) Engaged fatherhood for men, families and gender equality. Springer, Cham, pp 111–137

Levy RA, Badalament J, Kotelchuck M (2012) The Fatherhood Project. Massachusetts General Hospital, Boston. www.thefatherhoodproject.org

Lipkin M, Lamb GS (1982) The couvade syndrome: an epidemiological study. Ann Intern Med 96(4):509–511

Lu MC, Halfon N (2003) Racial and ethnic disparities in birth outcomes: a life-course perspective. Matern Child Health J 7(1):13–30

Martin JA, Hamilton BE, Osterman MJK, Driscoll AK (2019) Births: final data for 2018. Natl Vital Stat Rep 68(13):1–47

Masoni S, Maio A, Trimarchi G, de Punzio C, Fioretti P (1994) The couvade syndrome. J Psychosom Obstet Gynecol 15(3):125–131

May C, Fletcher R (2013) Preparing fathers for the transition to parenthood: recommendations for the content of antenatal education. Midwifery 29(5):474–478

McLanahan S, Tach L, Schneider D (2013) The causal effects of father absence. Annu Rev Sociol 399(1):399–427

McLean CP, Asnaani A, Litz BT, Hofmann SG (2011) Gender differences in anxiety disorders. J Psychiatr Res 45(8):1027–1035

Modig K, Talbäck M, Torssander J, Ahlbom A (2017) Payback time? Influence of having children on mortality in old age. J Epidemiol Community Health 71(5):424–430

Nannini A, Lazar J, Berg C, Tomashek K, Cabral H, Barger M, Barfield W, Kotelchuck M (2008) Injury: a major cause of pregnancy-associated morbidity in Massachusetts. J Midwifery Womens Health 53(1):3–10

National Academies of Sciences, Engineering, and Medicine (NASEM) (2016) Parenting matters: supporting parents of children ages 0–8. The National Academies Press, Washington, DC

National Academies of Sciences, Engineering, and Medicine (NASEM) (2019) Vibrant and healthy kids: aligning science, practice, and policy to advance health equity. The National Academies Press, Washington, DC

Nepomnyaschy L, Waldfogel J (2007) Paternity leave and fathers' involvement with their young children: evidence from the American ECLS-B. Community Work Fam 10(4):427–453

Paulson JF, Bazemore SD (2010) Prenatal and postpartum depression in fathers and its association with maternal depression: a meta-analysis. JAMA 303(19):1961–1969

Persson P, Ross-Slater M (2019) When dad can stay home: fathers' workplace flexibility and maternal health. IZA Institute of Labor economics discussion paper no. 12386

Petts RJ, Carlson DL, Chris KC (2019) If I[take] leave, will you stay? Paternity leave and relationship stability. J Soc Policy 49(4):829–849. https://doi.org/10.1017/S0047279419000928

Philpott LF, Leahy-Warren P, FitzGerald S, Savage E (2017) Stress in fathers in the perinatal period: a systematic review. Midwifery 55:113–127

Philpott LF, Savage E, FitzGerald S, Leahy-Warren P (2019) Anxiety in fathers in the perinatal period: a systemic review. Midwifery 76:54–101

Pol HL, Koh SSL, He H (2014) An integrative review of fathers' experiences during pregnancy and childbirth. Int Nurs Rev 61(4):543–554

Ramchandani PG, Stein A, O'Connor TG, Heron J, Murray L, Evans J (2008) Depression in men in the postnatal period and later child psychopathology: a population cohort study. J Am Acad Child Adolesc Psychiatry 47(4):390–398

Richmond JB, Kotelchuck M (1983) Political influences: rethinking national health policy. In: McGuire CH, Foley RP, Gorr D, Richards RW (eds) Handbook of health professions education. Josey-Bass, San Francisco, pp 386–404

Rolling JK, Mascaro JS (2017) The neurobiology of fatherhood. Curr Opin Psychol 15:26–32

Roubinov DS, Luecken LJ, Gonzales NA, Crnic KA (2016) Father involvement in Mexico-origin families: preliminary development of a culturally informed measure. Cultur Divers Ethnic Minor Psychol 22(2):277–287

Saxbe DE, Edelstein RS, Lyden HM, Wardecker BM, Chopik WJ, Moors AC (2017) Fathers' decline in testosterone and synchrony with partner testosterone during pregnancy predicts greater post-partum relationship investment. Horm Behav 90:39–47

Saxbe D, Corner G, Khaled M, Horton K, Wu B, Khoddam H (2018) The weight of fatherhood: identifying mechanisms to explain paternal perinatal weight gain. Health Psychol Rev 12(3):1–38

Singley DB, Edwards LM (2015) Men's perinatal mental health in transition to fatherhood. Prof Psychol Res Pract 46(5):309–316

Smith JA, Braunack-Mayer A, Wittert G (2006) What do we know about men's help-seeking and health service use? Med J Aust 184(2):81–83

Steen M, Downe S, Bamford N, Edozien L (2012) Not-patient and not-visitor: a metasynthesis father's encounters with pregnancy, birth, and maternity care. Midwifery 28(4):362–371

Tollestrup J (2018) Fatherhood initiatives: connecting fathers to their children. Congressional Research Service. RL31025. www.crsreports.congress.gov.

Umberson D, Liu H, Mirowsky J, Reczek C (2011) Parenthood and trajectories of change in body weight over the life course. Soc Sci Med 73(9):1323–1331

United States Bureau of the Census (2018) Current population survey: annual social and economic supplement survey, United States, 2017 (ICPSR 37075). https://doi.org/10.3886/ICPSR37075.v1

Wise PH (2008) Transforming preconceptional, prenatal, and interconceptional care into a comprehensive commitment to women's health. Womens Health Issues 18(6 Suppl):S13–S18

Yogman MW, Eppel AM (2021) The role fathers in child and family health. In: Grau-Grau M, las Heras M, Bowles HR (eds) Engaged fatherhood for men, families and gender equality. Springer, Cham, pp 15–30

Yogman MW, Garfield CF, the Committee on Psychosocial Aspects of Child and Family Health (2016) Fathers' roles in the care and development of their children: the role of pediatricians. Pediatrics 138(1):e20161128

Open Access This chapter is licensed under the terms of the Creative Commons Attribution 4.0 International License (http://creativecommons.org/licenses/by/4.0/), which permits use, sharing, adaptation, distribution and reproduction in any medium or format, as long as you give appropriate credit to the original author(s) and the source, provide a link to the Creative Commons license and indicate if changes were made.

The images or other third party material in this chapter are included in the chapter's Creative Commons license, unless indicated otherwise in a credit line to the material. If material is not included in the chapter's Creative Commons license and your intended use is not permitted by statutory regulation or exceeds the permitted use, you will need to obtain permission directly from the copyright holder.

Steps in Developing a Public Health Surveillance System for Fathers

Clarissa D. Simon and Craig F. Garfield

In 2014, fatherhood experts from Northwestern University and reproductive health experts from the Centers for Disease Control and Prevention (CDC) Division of Reproductive Health (DRH) collaborated to conduct formative research to inform development of a public health surveillance system for fathers in the United States. This system would bridge from the Pregnancy Risk Assessment Monitoring System (PRAMS), which collects site-specific, population-based data on self-reported *maternal* attitudes and experiences before, during, and shortly after pregnancy. PRAMS was established in 1987 through a collaboration between CDC and 5 states and the District of Columbia (Colley et al. 1999). Over the past 30+ years, PRAMS has expanded to 47 states, the District of Columbia, New York City, and Puerto Rico, representing approximately 83% of all births in the United States (Shulman et al. 2018). PRAMS data have been used to measure progress towards achieving Healthy People 2020 objectives (Suellentrop et al. 2006) and Title V National Performance Measures (US Department of Health and Human Services 2019), such as pre-conception health care (Robbins et al. 2018) and infant sleep positioning (Hirai et al. 2019). Our goal was to develop a parallel system for new fathers to improve understanding of their health, experiences, and behaviors before, during, and after the birth of their child (Garfield et al. 2018).

C. D. Simon
Family and Child Health Innovations Program, Smith Child Health Outcomes, Research, and Evaluation Center, Ann & Robert H. Lurie Children's Hospital, Chicago, IL, USA
e-mail: csimon@luriechildrens.org

C. F. Garfield (✉)
Family and Child Health Innovations Program, Smith Child Health Outcomes, Research, and Evaluation Center, Ann & Robert H. Lurie Children's Hospital, Chicago, IL, USA

Department of Pediatrics, Northwestern University Feinberg School of Medicine, Chicago, IL, USA
e-mail: c-garfield@northwestern.edu

Three main issues for conducting public health surveillance with new fathers emerged: (1) how to reach the greatest number of fathers; (2) what questions and content areas are fathers willing to answer; and, (3) what methods of data collection are most effective at reaching fathers. To address these issues we utilized a multi-pronged approach to inform development of a public health surveillance system for fathers: (1) reviewed the literature to identify what is known about fatherhood, including gaps in knowledge on male and family health and current national-level fatherhood surveillance data; (2) assessed feasibility of identifying fathers to participate in a national-level public health surveillance system; (3) conducted formative research to develop methodology; and (4) piloted a public health surveillance system for fathers called the Pregnancy Risk Assessment Monitoring System for Dads or "PRAMS for Dads." Our approaches are described in detail in the following section.

1 Review of the Role of Fatherhood in Male and Family Health and Current National Surveillance Data on Young Men and Fathers

As men increasingly play integral family and parenting roles (Bianchi et al. 2006), research on fathers' roles and contributions to families has expanded. Father involvement with their children is linked to better maternal health during pregnancy and in the postpartum period, as well as to improved health for children (Teitler 2001; Yargawa and Leonardi-Bee 2015 see also, in this volume, chapters by Kotelchuck and Yogman & Eppel). Fathers' involvement has been associated with early prenatal care initiation and breastfeeding initiation and continuation (Teitler 2001; Hunter and Cattelona 2014), and also improved child developmental, psychological, and cognitive outcomes (Sarkadi et al. 2008; Cabrera et al. 2018).

Evidence suggests the quality of father involvement changes depending on how healthy men are; for example, depressed fathers are less likely to read to children and more likely to use corporeal punishment with their children (Ramchandani et al. 2005; Davis et al. 2011). Keeping men healthy during the preconception period (before their partner's pregnancy) and throughout their transition to fatherhood is important for improving reproductive health outcomes for fathers and their partners (Frey et al. 2008). Healthy fathers are more likely to have healthy offspring, support partners in parenting, and participate more fully in childrearing (Yogman et al. 2016). Becoming a father has been shown to influence men's health including effects on paternal mental health and physical health (Body Mass Index) (Garfield et al. 2016; see also chapter "The Impact of Father's Health on Reproductive and Infant Health and Development" by Kotelchuck in this volume). While men have become more involved with their children and within their families (Parker and Wang 2013), less is known about the transition to fatherhood as a distinct phenomenon, and how this might serve as a lever for improving men's health. An ongoing public health surveillance system at the state and national level could be used to address the gaps in knowledge around the transition to fatherhood and to inform efforts to improve the health and well-being of fathers, mothers, and their families.

A number of family-centered public health surveillance systems have led the way towards better understanding the health of men and fatherhood in the United States. The National Health Interview Survey (NHIS), which has monitored national trends in illness and disability since 1957 (Schiller et al. 2012), and the Behavioral Risk Factor Surveillance System (BRFSS), which has collected state-specific data on health-related risk behaviors since 1984 (Balluz et al. 2008), both provide information on health status and use of health services by women and men. Neither of these surveys, however, directly examine the transition to fatherhood or are specific to fathers. Since 1973, the National Survey of Family Growth (NSFG) has provided information on the health status and behaviors of reproductive-aged women through periodic surveys (Groves et al. 2009). Starting in 2002, a parallel survey for men (ages 15–44) was initiated to collect data on attitudes and experiences around marriage, childrearing, sexual behaviors, and contraceptive use (Marcell et al. 2016).

Currently, data on paternal involvement is mainly limited to the Fragile Families and Child Wellbeing Study (FFCWS)[1] and the Early Childhood Longitudinal Study of Birth (ECLS).[2] The FFCWS is a birth-cohort study of children living in major U.S cities, first interviewing fathers shortly after the birth of a child and an additional interview at the hospital or following baby's hospital discharge. The FFCWS collects important data on father involvement over time directly from both resident and non-resident fathers, including time with children, financial support for unmarried parents (Carlson and McLanahan 2010). The ECLS-B (Birth Cohort) is a nationally representative cohort study with fathers first interviewed when children were 9 months old, and also including measures of father involvement such as infant engagement and identification with the fathering role (Planalp and Braungart-Rieker 2016). Early Head Start, a program providing family-centered services for low-income families with children up to age 3,[3] developed fatherhood demonstration projects[4] evaluations that showed incredible success of father-centered programming to more fully involve fathers in the lives of their young children (Burwick et al. 2004). Aside from the aforementioned, there is currently no public health surveillance system collecting site-specific and population-based datafocused on the transition to fatherhood during the perinatal period.

---

[1] The FFCWS is a joint effort from Princeton University's Center for Research on Child Wellbeing and the Columbia Population Research Center.

[2] The ECLS is sponsored primarily by the U.S. Department of Education, National Center for Education Statistics.

[3] Early Head Start is funded by the Administration for Children and Families (ACF), a division of the Department of Health & Human Services.

[4] The 21 Early Head Start fatherhood demonstration projects were funded by the ACF and the Office of Child Support Enforcement.

2 Assessing the Feasibility of Sampling Fathers for a National-Level Public Health Surveillance System

The first step in developing a public health surveillance system for fathers was to determine the feasibility of sampling fathers to participate. Our aim was to determine whether it would be feasible to adapt the existing PRAMS sampling methodology for a public health surveillance system for fathers.

2.1 Use of Birth Records

PRAMS sites randomly selects new mothers using birth certificate data, to participate in the PRAMS survey. The standard certificate of live birth in the United States has 58 data fields, most of which relate to the mother (including her contact information) and infant. Only seven data points on the standard U.S. birth certificate relate to fathers, and these are all reported second hand by mothers, including the father's name and his date of birth (Centers for Disease Control and Prevention 2016). Data collected on births at the state level are entered into the Electronic Birth Registration System (EBRS). No separate contact information for the father, apart from what is reported by mothers, is included on a standard U.S. birth certificate, although the address listed will match the father if he lives with the mother. Married couples are assumed to live together, and non-married couples are encouraged to complete a separate Acknowledgment of Paternity (AOP, alternatively called the Voluntary Acknowledgement of Paternity) form in order for the father's information to be included on the birth certificate. More information on the AOP is provided below.

2.2 State input

State health department representatives from Connecticut, Florida, Illinois, Louisiana, Michigan, Minnesota, Oklahoma, Utah, and Washington provided information about birth certificate data collection and information available related to fathers. This information sharing process highlighted challenges in collecting new father information nationally. Table 1 displays the availability of this information from the following three sources: (1) typical, standard U.S. birth certificate, (2) paternity form information from Illinois and (3) paternity form information from Georgia, the first state to pilot PRAMS for Dads. Father data from these sources varies widely in completeness and quality, both between and within states, since each state has its own process and policies. Further, while the birth certificate lists the mother's address, an unmarried father who does not live with the mother has no separate address listing, unless the AOP form is completed.

Table 1 Availability of institutional parental data from birth certificates and acknowledgement of paternity forms from two sample states

	Standard U.S. Birth Certificate	Illinois Voluntary Acknowledgment of Paternity	Georgia Paternity Acknowledgment Form
Mother demographic information			
Name	Yes	Yes	Yes
Name prior to marriage	Yes	Yes	No
Address	Yes	Yes	Yes
DOB	Yes	Yes	Yes
Place of birth	Yes	Yes	Yes
Mailing address	Yes	No	No
Marital status	Yes	No	No
Married to person other than father listed	No	Yes	No
Social security number	Yes	Yes	Yes
Education	Yes	No	No
Race/ethnicity	Yes	No	No
Phone number	No	Yes	No
Employer	No	No	Yes
Employer address	No	No	Yes
Father demographic information			
Name	Yes	Yes	Yes
Address	No	Yes	Yes
DOB	Yes	Yes	Yes
Place of birth	Yes	Yes	Yes
Social security number	Yes	Yes	Yes
Education	Yes	No	No
Race/ethnicity	Yes	No	No
Phone number	No	Yes	No
Father acknowledges that he is the biological father	No	Yes	Yes
Employer	No	No	Yes
Employer address	No	No	Yes

Although this information is not required on the standard U.S. birth certificate, phone number availability for fathers is important for reaching fathers directly, rather than indirectly using mother demographic information. Furthermore, while Illinois refers to this form as a "Voluntary Acknowledgment of Paternity" form, Georgia has a "Paternity Acknowledgement Form." AOP form completeness varies due to factors such as father being absent at the hospital where most AOPs are signed since both the mother and father must sign the AOP form, either the mother or father not wanting the AOP signed, and uncertainty about biological parentage (Osborne and Dillon 2014).

Data collected on the AOP—if it is indeed of high quality—may allow fatherhood researchers to reach unmarried U.S. fathers who do not live with their infant's mother. Since 40% of births in the U.S. are to unmarried mothers, gathering data on this large group of fathers is important (Martin et al. 2019). Unmarried fathers may be different than married fathers, including in their fatherhood experiences and how they may impact mothers and babies (Carlson and McLanahan 2010).

In summary, it was determined that PRAMS methods for sampling participants could be adapted to identify fathers to participate in a public health surveillance system for fathers. The majority of fathers and at least partial contact information could be identified using the birth certificate for fathers who were either married or were unmarried and an AOP had been completed in the hospital.

3 Formative Research to Develop Methodology

To assess the willingness of men to participate in a PRAMS-like survey, Northwestern University conducted a short survey with two groups: (1) men who were expecting a baby in the next 6 months ("expectant fathers"), and (2) fathers whose babies were born in the last year ("new fathers"). Expectant fathers were recruited from a fatherhood course at a large, urban birthing hospital with over 13,000 deliveries per year. During a one-time evening course held bi-monthly over an 8 month period, men were invited to complete a short one-page survey about their willingness to answer questions on a variety of topics related to their experience as fathers including, physical health, access to health care, mental health, pregnancy intendedness, partner support, involvement in childrearing, breastfeeding, and vaccines.

New fathers were recruited through a large, urban, federally qualified health center (FQHC) organization serving communities with high rates of poverty and poor health outcomes on Chicago's south and west sides. The FQHC provides preventive and primary health care, with a goal to address significant health challenges, including lack of access and variable levels of health literacy. Ninety-six percent of the FQHC patients live below 200% of the Federal Poverty Level. FQHC staff invited clients who were fathers with babies less than a year old to complete the survey. The survey for new fathers was similar to the expectant father survey, with some modifications since these were current, not prospective parents. The survey addressed willingness to answer questions about new fatherhood, demographics, and contact preferences for a prospective survey.

Below are the survey results for both groups:

3.1 Expectant Father and FQHC New Father Demographics

Men in the expectant father classes (n = 57) were primarily in their 30s (74%), with equal amounts of fathers in their 20s and 40s. These fathers were mostly married (84%) or cohabiting (12%). The FQHC new fathers (n = 36) were younger, with 63% in their 20s and 16% between 32 and 37. These fathers were also much less likely to be married, with only 35% married and 27% cohabiting.

Mode of contact. To find out how best to reach fathers, men in both groups were asked "Which of the following methods of contact is acceptable to you?" Among expectant fathers, nearly half preferred contact within 3 months of their infant's birth via either email (34%), text messaging with a link (24%), phone/cell call (24%), or postal mail (15%). In contrast, FQHC new fathers selected phone (41%) over mail (31%), texting with a link (16%) or email (10%). Overall, men in both groups preferred either phone contact or email, with texting a close third preferred mode of contact. See Fig. 1.

Time of contact. Men were asked "What is the best time after the birth of your baby to contact you for a survey about becoming a father?" Most of the fathers in both groups chose the early prenatal period as the best time to be contacted for a study on fatherhood. Expectant fathers overwhelmingly chose either the 1–3 month (47%) or 3–6 month (29%) postnatal time period as the preferred time to be reached for a survey, while new fathers also chose the 1–3 month (35%) and 3–6 month (22%) postnatal time period. See Fig. 2.

Interest in answering questions. Men in both groups were largely willing to answer questions on a variety of topics (75–85% overall), although there was some variability in topics, particularly among the FQHC new fathers. One of the major differences was a high level of willingness to answer health access questions, but a lower willingness to answer questions about breastfeeding. Some variability was evident around the importance of these individual topics, as seen in Fig. 3.

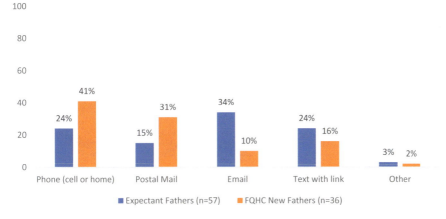

Fig. 1 Preferred mode of contact among expectant and new fathers

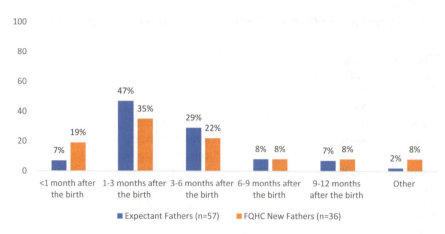

Fig. 2 Time of contact to complete a survey about becoming a father among expectant and new fathers

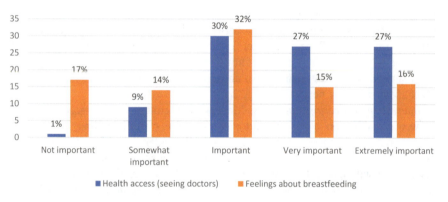

Fig. 3 Importance of health access and breastfeeding questions

Further, while all fathers answered questions about the importance of individual topics (N = 93), five fathers did not report whether they would be willing to answer questions on these topics.

In summary, survey data from this sample of expectant and new fathers revealed high levels of willingness to answer questions on new fatherhood, a preference for contact in the early post-natal period, with mixed preferences for mode of survey contact.

4 Focus Groups with New Parents

To explore in more depth and in their own voices, focus groups were conducted with current fathers and mothers at the FQHC to examine their experiences as men and women becoming parents. In particular, we asked how the logistics of a survey for fathers in the newborn period might be received by mothers as well as fathers. Two groups of mothers (total of eight mothers) and one group of fathers (five fathers) attended the focus groups with researchers to talk about parenting and father involvement. The parents described strong commitment to their families and children, with fatherhood reported as a joyful event by fathers.

Parents reported a number of barriers to completing a survey, and concerns about financial and employment responsibilities. Mothers with male partners who do not live with them (non-cohabiting) suggested that email is best for fathers due to frequent moves. As emails generally do not change, contacting men by email may be an effective way to reach men who move often. Mothers with residential partners supported the use of postal mail for the survey. While fathers report a willingness to be contacted via email or phone, they preferred phone to email or text for a survey.

Parents highlighted that the survey should promote the fathers' role in his child's life, an approach that focuses on health promotion, and the inclusion of incentives that were sports themed or baby-themed. Although such incentives were not included in the current pilot, to help streamline initial field efforts, we hope to tailor incentives for fathers in the future. They also suggested emphasizing the importance of fathers, including the rights of fathers and value of involvement with their children. Both mothers and fathers reported that fathers can be contacted indirectly through mothers using a "mothers-as-gatekeepers" approach. They reported that this would be an effective approach if parents have a good relationship, something both parents mention could be in flux. Nonetheless, overall, fathers and mothers both affirmed their willingness to complete surveys related to their child's wellbeing (fathers) or to make sure the survey was given to the fathers (in the case of mothers).

In summary, focus groups with new mothers and fathers provided data to inform best practices for survey completion, recruitment, and questionnaires, including surfacing some potential barriers for the PRAMS for DADS survey. Fathers reported willingness to answer a variety of questions and interest in providing their "father's voice" to a survey of new parents. Similar to the survey results, a flexible multi-method contact approach may be best for reaching new fathers. A number of barriers to reaching new fathers emerged including moving to a new home (transience), a poor co-parenting relationship, and intensive work responsibilities.

5 Collecting Father Data: Methodological Findings and Recommendations

Based on the above formative work, we present five key findings for reaching fathers in the perinatal period:

(a) **Pilot multiple approaches:** Fatherhood researchers may reach more fathers through a variety of approaches including mail, email, text and phone contact. Some of these approaches may have different responses rates depending on factors such as whether the father lives with his infant or the current quality of the relationship with the baby's mother. Fathers also have different preferences for completing a survey using mail or by entering information on-line. Fathers who move frequently may be easier to reach using email and texting, while others may prefer traditional paper surveys sent through snail mail.

(b) **Contact multiple times:** Fathers may be more difficult to contact than mothers, so the number of times expected to reach new fathers should be at minimum assumed the same as that required for new mothers. Contact may be especially challenging for unmarried fathers and those who do not live with their children, since the mailing address and phone number listed on the birth certificate may not work for these fathers or even be available at all. If mothers are asked for father's information, they may be less likely to provide or have father information if they don't live with the father. Focus groups with new mothers and fathers also suggested that some fathers may move frequently, so resources may be needed to not only contact fathers more often, but also to obtain more current addresses and phone numbers.

(c) **Provide adequate rewards and/or incentives:** Father participants should receive similar incentives to those that mother participants receive; however, given that men can be difficult to enroll in research studies, additional or different incentives may be needed (Patel et al. 2003). Some of these options include additional gift cards for completion by a certain date or using an approach that requires less staff time, such as completing the survey online. Other non-monetary incentives like celebrity or sports star endorsements may also help increase response rates for fathers.

(d) **Make special efforts to enroll hard-to-reach fathers:** Some groups of fathers will likely be difficult to reach, such as those who live apart from their children or those who move frequently. Additional efforts to reach these fathers, such as increasing the number of contacts or higher value incentives may needed to ensure representativeness of the data. Otherwise, research on fatherhood may be heavily biased toward fathers who are easy-to-reach. Certain groups of fathers, such as incarcerated, adoptive, surrogate, social, and uninvolved fathers will already be lost to studies that utilize birth certificates for enrollment, so it is necessary to focus efforts and provide additional resources to increase response rates for the most difficult to reach fathers.

(e) **Include a variety of survey topics, ideally in parallel to those asked of mothers.** To provide both mother and father perspectives on parenting within the same family, questions domains should be similar where relevant, in addition to fatherhood-centered domains to provide the unique father perspective. These topics could include: (1) demographic questions such as relationship status and employment; (2) health-related questions such as birth control use, safe sleep practices and health care access/usage; and (3) father-specific questions such as father involvement, feelings about breastfeeding, and family leave.

(f) **Carefully weigh whether to reach fathers directly or indirectly:** We identified two sampling approaches to reaching fathers, which are displayed in Fig. 4.

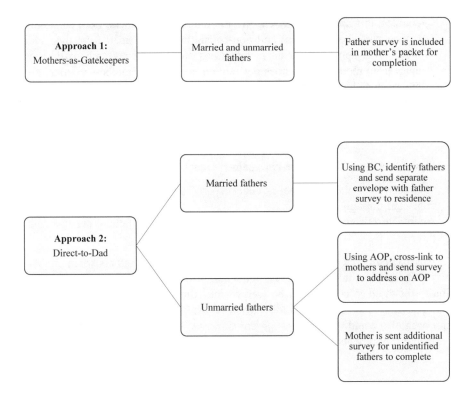

*BC = Birth Certificate; AOP = Acknowledgement of Paternity

Fig. 4 Two approaches to reach fathers after the birth of their child. *BC* birth certificate, *AOP* acknowledgement of paternity

- The first approach, "Mothers-as-Gatekeepers," requires including a separate survey for fathers in the mother's survey envelope. This approach is less time and cost intensive but reaches fathers indirectly. Two assumptions are implicit: (1) that the new mother will provide the survey to the father, and (2) that the father will elect to participate. This may introduce bias toward responses of those fathers actively involved with mother and infant, particularly for fathers who do not live with their children.
- The second approach, "Direct-to-Dads," requires contacting fathers directly without requiring involvement from the mother. This approach would require additional effort and resources to identify new fathers, as the address listed for mothers on the birth certificate may not necessarily be that of fathers. While married fathers can be reached directly through the address listed on the birth certificate, unmarried fathers would be reached through the information collected on the AOP form, if available, or by sending mothers an additional survey under separate cover. With 40% of births in the U.S. to unmarried

couples, this approach may capture more unmarried fathers, both cohabiting (living with their children) and non-cohabiting (living apart from their children). This approach considers fathers as parents and research participants apart from mothers, as it does not rely on the need for mothers to contact or approach fathers. In other words, the "Direct-to-Dads" approach allows for independent contact of fathers without using the mother as a gatekeeper of the survey.

Figure 4 below illustrates the two main approaches to reaching new fathers:

1. Approach 1 is the "Mothers-as-Gatekeepers" approach in which fathers are contacted through mothers.
2. Approach 2 is the "Direct-to-Dads" approach in which fathers are contacted directly.

Approach 1 and 2 will both reach married and unmarried fathers when an AOP was completed in the hospital. The advantages of these approaches include the ability for the data collected to be merged into already-existing vital records data and maternal contact information currently available in mother surveys. This approach also could yield interesting comparisons between mothers and fathers on particular topics, where both parents choose to participate.

6 Piloting a Public Health Surveillance System for Fathers: PRAMS for Dads

In October 2018 we put these findings into the field with a pilot study of PRAMS for Dads. Working with the Georgia Department of Public Health (GDPH), monthly samples of new mothers using recent birth certificates were drawn, from which fathers were identified and contacted. As with the maternal PRAMS protocol, fathers are contacted first by mail, initially with a pre-letter, then with three mailed surveys, and a "tickler" reminder mailer (Shulman et al. 2018). After this mail phase, participants move into phone phase and are contacted by phone to complete the survey. Unlike the maternal PRAMS protocol, the pre-letter includes a link to complete the survey electronically, and the three mailed surveys have the electronic link as well. A shortened URL link was created for inclusion in the letters to ease use of electronic completion. Figure 5 shows the monthly operations employed in the PRAMS for Dads pilot study.

In the pilot survey, fathers were asked a total of 71 questions, including domains such as health care access and usage, contraceptive use, cigarette and alcohol use, safe sleep practices, work leave, and father involvement. A specific section questions relevant for non-residential fathers included questions such as time spent with babies and material contributions. Questions were derived mainly from PRAMS, Fragile

Steps in Developing a Public Health Surveillance System for Fathers

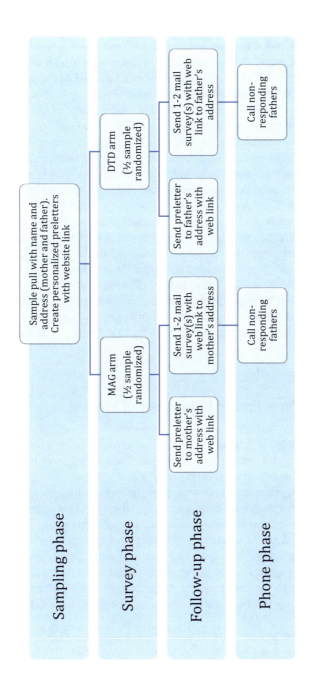

Fig. 5 PRAMS for dads pilot study multi-phase protocol

Families and Child Wellbeing Study, and the National Survey of Family Growth. Surveys were available in both English and Spanish.

Sampled fathers were randomized such that half of the fathers were contacted using Approach 1, the "Mothers-as-Gatekeepers" or MAG approach as shown above. For these fathers, surveys were sent to the mother's address listed on the birth certificate. The PRAMS for Dads survey was included in the packet mothers were asked to complete for the larger PRAMS study. Phone contacts were also made through the mother's contact information. The second half of the fathers were randomized and contacted using Approach 2, the "Direct-to-Dads" (DTD) approach. These fathers were sent their own blue envelope with a survey included, and attempts were made to find additional contact information specifically for fathers. Fathers are therefore considered independently of mothers as part of the study.

As of early 2020, we are currently in the field collecting data for the PRAMS for Dads pilot. Eventually, results from this pilot study will allow us to compare completion rates by the MAG and DTD approaches as well as the three survey completion options (e.g., mail, electronic, and phone). Best methods, as measured by highest response rates, may then be used to "scale up" the project, moving PRAMS for Dads into multiple states across the country and providing valuable data on the public health and behaviors of new fathers. Researchers and clinicians should continue to focus on the importance of hearing the voices of new fathers, both to better understand families and to promote men's health. Data devoted to the fatherhood experience is sorely needed, and PRAMS for Dads aims to help meet that need (Garfield et al. 2018).

7 Collecting New Father Data: Overall Findings

Based on our cumulative findings from our formative research, information gathered, and pilot study, we present five overall key findings and recommendations:

Fathers are involved and want their voices heard.

Our findings suggest that fathers want to participate in research aimed at better understanding the needs and experiences of new fathers and how to help their baby. Participation in survey research was considered by our focus group fathers a valid use of time, particularly as it relates to pathways towards helping children. With limited information on the transition to fatherhood from fathers themselves, our formative research supports that there interest in participation from fathers. We hope other researchers and clinicians pursue the challenging field of new fatherhood research, with an aim to better understand and support fathers, mothers, children, and families.

Make extra efforts to reach both fathers who live with their children (cohabiting) and fathers who live apart from their children (non-cohabiting)

In order to properly represent both sets of fathers, fatherhood research must be able to reach both groups effectively. Non-cohabiting fathers represent a large minority of fathers and less is known about how these fathers influence their children, in part because they are more difficult to contact. They are, however, an important group, underserved and disadvantaged, compared to fathers who live with their children and consequently their offspring may be at higher risk for poor outcomes. Since cohabiting fathers will likely be easier to reach, additional efforts must be made to reach non-cohabiting fathers.

Use acknowledgment of paternity (AOP) forms to reach more unmarried and non-cohabiting fathers, which are supplementary forms completed by unmarried fathers around the time of the birth of a child.

Utilizing address and phone information listed on paternity acknowledgement forms in order to contact non-cohabiting and unmarried fathers may be the most effective method of contact for these fathers. Although married fathers should be relatively easy to reach, given that they likely share the address listed on the birth certificate with mothers, many unmarried fathers and mothers sign an acknowledgement of paternity form, which contains contact information that may be utilized. Rates of completed acknowledgement forms do, however, vary by state and information may have to be separately requested through vital records or child support offices.

Reach fathers early, since the highest likelihood of success in reaching new fathers depends on having contact early in the postnatal period.

If reaching fathers in the hospital immediately following the birth of their child is not possible, aim to reach fathers early in the postnatal period, either between 1 and 3 months or 3–6 months after the birth of the infant, as fathers may be more receptive to answering questions at that time. Surveys of both expectant and new fathers suggest that these are the time periods when fathers prefer to be contacted for a study on fatherhood. In our PRAMS for Dads pilot survey, the main PRAMS study already reaches mothers during this time (2–4 months postpartum), so contact at this time promotes a cross-link between the new mother and new father surveys. We therefore recommend similar ability to cross-link by asking mothers and fathers at the same postnatal time.

Bring added value to existing surveillance systems.

PRAMS for Dads bridges directly from the ongoing PRAMS surveillance system for mothers. By integrating and adapting the PRAMS system for fathers, information can be collected on mother-father dyads, forming a family-centered, rather than individual-centered, new parenthood surveillance research project. Further, PRAMS for Dads benefits from a stream-lined approach to data collection, as no additional institutional data has to be collected beyond the birth certificate data already collected as part of PRAMS. Contacting fathers using the MAG approach also benefits from lowered staff requirements, since these mothers are already being contacted to complete the PRAMS survey; pilot data may confirm this. Researchers should evaluate whether complete development of a new system is necessary for fathers, or if they can similarly work in parallel to an already existing surveillance system.

This innovative line of research, while nascent, allows the voices of fathers to be heard in the public health arena. Through full integration of fathers in the formative research of this work, the data collected can inform programs and efforts to prepare men for the transition to fatherhood in such a way to optimize their health and that of their partners and children. Further, this approach can be used as a tool to monitor public health issues across the country and provide state, regional, and national level data on fathers and families before, during, and after the birth of a new baby. Ultimately, a more comprehensive understanding of perinatal public health within the context of contemporary families may lead to improved health and wellbeing of fathers, mothers, and infants.

References

Balluz L, Easton A, Garcia D, Garvin W, Kambon M, MacDonald G, Ramsey F, Ussery-Hall A, Vigeant J (2008) Prevalence of selected risk behaviors and chronic diseases—behavioral risk factor surveillance system (BRFSS), 39 steps communities, United States, 2005. MMWR Surveil Summ 57(11):1–20. https://www.cdc.gov/mmwr/preview/mmwrhtml/ss5711a1.htm

Bianchi SM, Robinson JP, Milke MA (2006) The changing rhythms of American family life. Russell Sage Foundation, New York

Burwick A, Bellotti J, Nagatoshi C (2004) Paths to father involvement: the early head start fatherhood demonstration in its third year. Final report. US Department of Health and Human Services, Head Start Bureau, Washington, DC

Cabrera NJ, Volling BL, Barr R (2018) Fathers are parents, too! Widening the lens on parenting for children's development. Child Dev Perspect 12(3):152–157

Carlson MJ, McLanahan SS (2010) Fathers in fragile families. In: Lamb ME (ed) The role of the father in child development, vol 5. Wiley, New York, pp 241–269

Centers for Disease Control and Prevention (2016) Mother's worksheet for child's birth certificate. https://www.cdc.gov/nchs/data/dvs/moms-worksheet-2016.pdf

Colley BJG, Johnson CH, Morrow B, Gaffield ME, Ahluwalia I (1999) Prevalence of selected maternal and infant characteristics, Pregnancy Risk Assessment Monitoring System (PRAMS). MMWR CDC Surveil Summ 48(5):1–37

Davis NR, Davis MM, Freed GL, Clark SJ (2011) Fathers' depression related to positive and negative parenting behaviors with 1-year-old children. Pediatrics 127(4):612–618

Frey KA, Navarro SM, Kotelchuck M, Michael CL (2008) The clinical content of preconception care: preconception care for men. Am J Obstet Gynecol 199(6):S389–S395

Garfield CF, Duncan G, Gutina A, Rutsohn J, McDade TW, Adam EK, Coley RL, Lindsay Chase-Lansdale P (2016) Longitudinal study of body mass index in young males and the transition to fatherhood. Am J Mens Health 10(6):NP158–NP167

Garfield CF, Simon CD, Harrison L, Besera G, Kapaya M, Pazol K, Boulet S, Grigorescu V, Barfield W, Lee W (2018) Pregnancy risk assessment monitoring system for dads: public health surveillance of new fathers in the perinatal period. Am J Public Health 108(10):1314–1315

Groves RM, Mosher WD, Lepkowski JM, Kirgis NG (2009) Planning and development of the continuous National Survey of Family Growth. Vital Health Stat 1 48:1–64

Hirai AH, Kortsmit K, Kaplan L, Reiney E, Lee W, Parks SE, Perkins M, Koso-Thomas M, D'Angelo DV, Shapiro-Mendoza CK (2019) Prevalence and factors associated with safe infant sleep practices. Pediatrics 144(5):e20191286. https://doi.org/10.1542/peds.2019-1286

Hunter T, Cattelona G (2014) Breastfeeding initiation and duration in first-time mothers: exploring the impact of father involvement in the early post-partum period. Health Promot Perspect 4(2):132–136. https://doi.org/10.5681/hpp.2014.017

Marcell AV, Gibbs SE, Choiriyyah I, Sonenstein FL, Astone NM, Pleck JH, Dariotis JK (2016) National needs of family planning among US men aged 15 to 44 years. Am J Public Health 106(4):733–739

Martin JA, Hamilton BE, Osterman MJK (2019) Births in the United States, 2018. NCHS Data Brief 346:1–8

Osborne C, Dillon D (2014) Dads on the dotted line: a look at the in-hospital paternity establishment process. J Appl Res Child 5(2):10

Parker K, Wang W (2013) Modern parenthood: roles of moms and dads converge as they balance work and family. Pew Research Center, Washington, DC

Patel MX, Doku V, Tennakoon L (2003) Challenges in recruitment of research participants. Adv Psychiatr Treat 9(3):229–238

Planalp EM, Braungart-Rieker JM (2016) Determinants of father involvement with young children: evidence from the early childhood longitudinal study–birth cohort. J Fam Psychol 30(1):135

Ramchandani P, Stein A, Evans J, O'Connor TG, ALSPAC Study Team (2005) Paternal depression in the postnatal period and child development: a prospective population study. Lancet 365 (9478):2201–2205

Robbins C, Boulet SL, Morgan I, D'Angelo DV, Zapata LB, Morrow B, Sharma A, Kroelinger CD (2018) Disparities in preconception health indicators—behavioral risk factor surveillance system, 2013–2015, and pregnancy risk assessment monitoring system, 2013–2014. MMWR CDC Surveill Summ 67(1):1–16

Sarkadi A, Kristiansson R, Oberklaid F, Bremberg S (2008) Fathers' involvement and children's developmental outcomes: a systematic review of longitudinal studies. Acta Paediatr 97 (2):153–158

Schiller JS, Lucas JW, Peregoy JA (2012) Summary health statistics for US adults: national health interview survey, 2011. Vital Health Stat Ser 10 (256) 1–218

Shulman HB, D'Angelo DV, Harrison L, Smith RA, Lee W (2018) The pregnancy risk assessment monitoring system (PRAMS): overview of design and methodology. Am J Public Health 108 (10):1305–1313

Suellentrop K, Morrow B, Williams L, D'Angelo D, Centers for Disease Control and Prevention (CDC) (2006) Monitoring progress toward achieving maternal and infant healthy people 2010 objectives—19 states, pregnancy risk assessment monitoring system (PRAMS), 2000-2003. MMWR CDC Surveill Summ 55(9):1–11

Teitler JO (2001) Father involvement, child health and maternal health behavior. Child Youth Serv Rev 23(4–5):403–425

US Department of Health and Human Services (2019) Health resources and services administration national performance measures. https://grants6.tvisdata.hrsa.gov/PrioritiesAndMeasures/NationalPerformanceMeasures. Accessed 14 Nov 2019

Yargawa J, Leonardi-Bee J (2015) Male involvement and maternal health outcomes: systematic review and meta-analysis. J Epidemiol Community Health 69:604–612

Yogman M, Garfield CF, Committee on Psychosocial Aspects of Child and Family Health (2016) Fathers' roles in the care and development of their children: the role of pediatricians. Pediatrics 138(1):e20161128

Open Access This chapter is licensed under the terms of the Creative Commons Attribution 4.0 International License (http://creativecommons.org/licenses/by/4.0/), which permits use, sharing, adaptation, distribution and reproduction in any medium or format, as long as you give appropriate credit to the original author(s) and the source, provide a link to the Creative Commons license and indicate if changes were made.

The images or other third party material in this chapter are included in the chapter's Creative Commons license, unless indicated otherwise in a credit line to the material. If material is not included in the chapter's Creative Commons license and your intended use is not permitted by statutory regulation or exceeds the permitted use, you will need to obtain permission directly from the copyright holder.

Fatherhood and Reproductive Health in the Antenatal Period: From Men's Voices to Clinical Practice

Raymond A. Levy and Milton Kotelchuck

1 Introduction

Fatherhood as a positive and critically important topic has not been taken seriously in academia, health communities, obstetrical clinical practice, social policy or business until recent decades, despite the publications of Kotelchuck et al. (1975), Kotelchuck (1976), Lamb (1975), Lamb and Lamb (1976) and others starting in the 1970s. President Barack Obama initiated a federal program, *My Brother's Keeper* (Obama 2014), which helped to generate credibility for the importance of fatherhood. Now, in the public-health, federal funding, and research worlds, more attention is being paid to fathers as a central component of family life, including their frontline parenting functions, in addition to their economic contribution to children and families. However, it still remains true that little attention has been paid to fathers in prenatal care, the emphasis of this chapter.

R. A. Levy (✉)
The Fatherhood Project, Department of Psychiatry, Massachusetts General Hospital, Harvard Medical School, Boston, MA, USA
e-mail: rlevy2@mgh.harvard.edu

M. Kotelchuck
The Fatherhood Project, Department of Psychiatry, Massachusetts General Hospital, Boston, MA, USA

General Academic Pediatrics Department, Center for Child and Adolescent Health Policy and Research, Department of Pediatrics, Massachusetts General Hospital for Children, Boston, MA, USA

Vincent Department of Obstetrics and Gynecology, Massachusetts General Hospital, Boston, MA, USA

Department of Pediatrics, Harvard Medical School, Boston, MA, USA
e-mail: mkotelchuck@mgh.harvard.edu

© The Author(s) 2022
M. Grau Grau et al. (eds.), *Engaged Fatherhood for Men, Families and Gender Equality*, Contributions to Management Science,
https://doi.org/10.1007/978-3-030-75645-1_6

This chapter presents and discusses the results of two combined waves of Father Surveys conducted by The Fatherhood Project (Kotelchuck et al. 2016, 2017) during prenatal care visits at the Vincent Obstetrics Department at the Massachusetts General Hospital, Boston, Massachusetts. This study's survey of 959 fathers accompanying their wives and partners for prenatal care at a large urban tertiary hospital system, we believe, is the largest sample to date of direct men's voices on their prenatal experiences, condition and preparedness. The results are followed by a targeted discussion of practice implications to increase men's involvement during prenatal care and to make pregnancy and birth a healthier, more family-oriented event.

We began by exploring men's voices and perspectives in prenatal care, as early in the family life course as practically possible, and we hoped that their voices might lead to enhanced clinical care. First, we present a more detailed history of the treatment of men in prenatal care within academic and service provision circles to further justify the importance of this study.

1.1 History of Men and Prenatal Care

There is a substantial and growing literature documenting that increased father involvement during the perinatal period is important for healthier births (Kotelchuck 2021a), healthier infants and children (Yogman et al. 2016), healthier families and partners, as well as healthier men themselves (Garfield 2015; Kotelchuck and Lu 2017). The broader Maternal and Child Health (MCH) life course and preconception health professional communities in the U.S. encourage early and continuous paternal involvement in the parenting process, (Kotelchuck and Lu 2017), as do national federal family and social policies and community-based fatherhood initiatives (Administration for Children and Families 2019).

The course of prenatal care services is an important time in the pregnancy and birthing period, and conceptually a possibly important period for paternal involvement and development (Kotelchuck 2021a, b). Yet pregnancy and birth are not usually conceptualized as a father-inclusive family event. Obstetric and prenatal care services are seen primarily as women's or mother's domains as reflected in the names of our fields of study and care (Maternal and Child Health, Maternal Fetal Medicine; Obstetrics as *women's* primary health care.)

Despite these negative factors, there is a changing reproductive health services reality on the ground; men are increasingly presenting for prenatal care and ultrasound visits, and now nearly 90% join their partners in the labor and delivery room (Redshaw and Heikkilä 2010; Redshaw and Henderson 2013) and are increasingly eligible for, and using, post-partum paternal leave (In the U.S., seven states and Washington DC now have paid family leave). Fathers are increasingly welcomed into pediatric practice as well (Yogman et al. 2016).

These may in part reflect the evolving transitions from men's and women's traditional prescribed gender-based parental roles to more shared and equitable parental roles, with men assuming more engagement with infant care responsibilities (Kotelchuck 2021a). Yet existing programmatic and policy promotion efforts to encourage this transformation in the U.S. seem weak and underdeveloped—and especially not focused on the pre-birth roots of fatherhood.

Moreover, there is very limited prenatal attention to men's own health or development as a father, his generativity (e.g., Kotelchuck and Lu 2017; Garfield 2015; Kotelchuck 2021b). Paternal engagement and commitment don't just begin at birth; fatherhood, like motherhood, may be a developmental stage of life and health (Kotelchuck 2021b). Yet current understanding of the impact of pregnancy experiences on men's health and family health as well as the impact of contemporary institutional practices on men's own health development are critical under-studied topics.

Men's voices and perspectives in the prenatal period are too rarely assessed and are generally missing from the Maternal and Child Health literature (Garfield et al. 2018; Simon and Garfield 2021), limiting knowledge about their potential needs, perceptions, contributions, and involvement. Fathers are often discouraged from involvement with MCH-related services and sometimes assumed to be uninterested (Steen et al. 2012; Davison et al. 2019). This data could provide an important basis for enhanced national and local father-friendly clinical practices. The earlier men are involved with their infants, the more likely they are to remain involved (Redshaw and Henderson 2013) and the more likely their involvement will yield improved family outcomes (Sarkadi et al. 2008; Lamb 2010).

1.2 Aims

This research study has six goals:

1. To learn about men's paternal involvement, needs, and concerns during the time of prenatal care appointments
2. To learn the status of men's health and mental health in the prenatal period
3. To assess how fathers were treated by the Massachusetts General Hospital Obstetrics staff during their partners' prenatal care visit for quality improvement purposes
4. To learn what additional fatherhood information and skills they might like to acquire and through what formats and modalities
5. To learn how men feel about the fatherhood study and potential fatherhood prenatal care initiative
6. And finally, to discuss the implications of the results and offer practical recommendations for improved prenatal care and obstetric practice, to ensure earlier and enhanced paternal involvement

2 Methodology

2.1 Sample

The target sample for each of the two 2-week, cross-sectional cohort study waves were all men attending prenatal services, including ultrasound, with their partners at the Obstetric Services of Massachusetts General Hospital (MGH), a large urban tertiary hospital system in Boston, Massachusetts with multiple community health centers (CHC) and offsite satellite clinics. The MGH Obstetric Services operates as a single hospital-wide practice, with centralized ultrasound, Maternal-Fetal Medicine specialty and delivery services, and approximately 3200+ births per year. Subjects were recruited at the central MGH prenatal clinic and at two of its major CHCs, in Chelsea and Revere, which serve communities with disproportionately large immigrant populations. The study took place during the first 2 weeks of August 2015 and the first 3 of September 2016. MGH Obstetrics sees approximately 100 prenatal care and ultrasound appointments daily.

2.2 Recruitment Methodology

When fathers arrived in the prenatal care waiting room accompanying their partners to prenatal medical visits, they were approached by one of the study's research assistants or primary investigators and told about the voluntary, anonymous fatherhood study. They were then asked if they were willing to participate, and if so, take the fatherhood survey immediately, with no rewards offered for participation. If they agreed, they were given a mini-iPad tablet computer on which to complete the survey. If they preferred not to participate or could not be engaged in the recruitment efforts, they were not asked a second time.

2.3 Survey Instrument and Survey Collection Methodology

The fatherhood survey was developed by the researchers associated with The Fatherhood Project at MGH (Levy et al. 2012) The survey instrument was a 15–20 min self-administered survey. It was composed of a series of closed-ended questions with an opportunity for open-ended comments at the end. It was available in multiple languages—English, Spanish, and Arabic in 2015; and also Portuguese and Serbian in 2016. The survey was formally reviewed and approved by the MGH Internal Review Board.

The survey, completed in the prenatal waiting room, was composed of two sections: prior to the prenatal clinical visit, the survey questions addressed broad fatherhood issues including paternal preparation and engagement, needs and concerns, and their physical and mental health status. After the prenatal visit, the survey questions assessed the men's immediate prenatal care treatment experiences, their needs and desires for additional fatherhood information, their preferences for how that information should be delivered, and their assessment of the MGH fatherhood study and potential initiative.

A paper copy of the survey was offered to those unable to complete it electronically in the waiting area, 14 in total. All iPad survey data was transferred electronically to an online data system for analysis at the time of completion.

The survey instruments and recruitment procedures were very similar across the two waves of data collection. There were however some minor differences from the first to the second wave: Subjects information was now also collected at two MGH-affiliated community health centers—Chelsea and Revere Health Centers—in addition to the main MGH Obstetrics hospital campus. There were some minor edits in the survey instrument to improve clarity and response options, and some additional questions added on father's roles, emotions, and attitudes. And the survey was also available in additional languages as described above.

2.4 Analysis

For this chapter, the results of the two waves of data collection are combined for analysis. Prior data analyses (not presented) had demonstrated a remarkable degree of similarity of responses across the two administrations of the survey, and we therefore combined them to obtain a larger single sample size. We further only examine those questions here that the two surveys had in common, the overwhelming majority of the survey items.

This study utilizes standard descriptive statistics to examine the overall findings. The results for each of the study aims will be presented in turn, immediately followed by a commentary on their meaning.

2.5 Methodologic Limitations

While we believe this study provides a successful methodologic framework for assessing father's voices and experiences during the prenatal care period, we also recognize that this study has some limitations, especially around its study sample, that may restrict its full generalizability.

Specifically, first, the study sample is not fully representative of all men during the prenatal period; it is a convenience sample from a single urban tertiary hospital in Boston, MA—a state and region with a slightly higher SES population, less racial diversity, and more immigrants than the U.S. as a whole. Second, and probably most significant, this survey represents only those fathers who chose to accompany their partners to MGH Obstetric prenatal services during the study periods. While we estimated that we had surveyed a broad and substantial proportion (43–46%) of all potential male partners (data not included), we obviously cannot ascertain the opinions of the non-attendees. Third, the prenatal policies and practices of the MGH Obstetric Services that the fathers experienced and assessed may not be representative of all prenatal practices in the U.S.

And finally, fathers are a very heterogeneous population; responses were explored across a wide variety of sub-populations, but given the complexity of the analyses and findings, this specialized line of research was not more actively pursued for this chapter.

In sum, despite the limitations noted above, this study succeeded in obtaining the perspectives and voices of a very large and broad cross-sectional sample of fathers during the prenatal period. The study provides for important initial baseline estimates of paternal topics heretofore under-studied.

3 Results and Results Discussion

Sample: The final sample of fathers who provided data during the two waves of data collection was $N = 959$. All men accompanying a woman into the prenatal care waiting room ($N = 1412$) were approached. One thousand one hundred seven fathers were eligible for the study; 959 provided data on the first part of the survey and 899 provided complete survey data, including 14 fathers who mailed in the second half of their survey. Overall, the study achieved a very high acceptance rate: 86.6% of eligible fathers (959/1107) participated in the survey, with only 148 fathers (13.4%) not providing answers to the survey, including 69 (6.2%) who formally declined.

Men who were not eligible included those whose partners were receiving non-prenatal care OB/GYN services, such as pre- or post-partum fertility or genetics counseling or post-partum follow-up care; those who had filled out the survey at a previous visit during the study period; and those who were not the father.

Given that this was an anonymous, voluntary survey, we were unable to systematically record the specific reasons for non-participation or the men's or their partner's demographic characteristics. Informally, we noted reasons varied from being too busy on a cell phone call, language issues, not wanting to be distracted from the primary maternal focus of the visit, late arrivals, child caretaking, or simply no explanation given.

Additionally, we have no knowledge about the fathers who did not come with their partners for prenatal care; nor were we able to ascertain the characteristics of women who came without a male partner or had no male partners.

3.1 Study Population Characteristics

3.1.1 Results

The majority of study fathers (76.3%) were over 30 years of age, with fathers 31–35 (39.7%) and 36–40 years old (24.5%) the larger age groups. Our cohort was slightly older than the overall Massachusetts fatherhood births population; with 68.3% above 30 years old, 34.4% 31–35 years old and 21.5% 36–40 years old. Relatively few fathers were either younger or older (calculated from Massachusetts Department of Public Health 2018).

The majority (61.9%) of the study participants were White, with 11.7% Asian fathers, 14.6% Hispanic fathers, and 6.6% Black fathers; relatively similar to the overall Massachusetts birth population (59.5%; 9.3% 18.4%; 9.9% respectively; calculated from Massachusetts Department of Public Health 2018).

The study fathers were well-educated: 41.3% had a post-BA degree and only 15.9% had high school or less education. The vast majority were married (84.5%), worked full-time (88.6%) and had private insurance (82.1%). Fewer MGH fathers (13.9%) utilized Medicaid than the overall state birth population (33.7%; calculated from Massachusetts Department of Public Health 2018) (Table 1).

The majority of study participants were disproportionately first-time fathers (61.2%), much higher than Massachusetts fathers in general (45.0%). While there was good representation across the trimesters of pregnancy when fathers were surveyed, the sample skewed slightly toward older gestational ages.

Overall, the surveyed fathers attending prenatal care visits at MGH Obstetrics are a diverse population that skewed towards older, higher socioeconomic status (SES) and first-time father populations, though racially and ethnically similar to all Massachusetts births.

3.2 Fatherhood Preparation and Engagement in Reproductive Health Services

3.2.1 Results

First, the survey reveals that the prenatal period is a time of active engagement and joy for men as they are becoming fathers and creating families, a potentially transformative period in men's development. Over 98% of fathers say they are excited about becoming a father, 93.2% very excited, and almost 92% have spent time thinking about their emerging fatherhood, 57.2% a lot. Over 92% of expectant fathers have spoken with their partner or wife about becoming a father (60.7% a lot, and only 8% little or no time). And over 90% of the fathers plan to be in the delivery room and take time off after the birth of their child. Second, the fathers express a balance of general confidence and a recognition of needing more knowledge and practical fatherhood caretaking skills. While 94% say they are confident in their

Table 1 Sample demographics

	Percent
Age	
18–25	5.9
26–30	17.8
31–35	39.7
36–40	24.5
41+	12.1
Race/ethnicity	
White	61.9
Hispanic or Latino	14.6
Black or African American	6.6
Asian/Pacific Islander	11.7
Other	5.2
Education	
Less than high school	7.3
High school diploma	8.6
Some college or vocational/tech program	13.2
Bachelors degree	29.6
Masters degree (MA/MS)	24.9
Doctorate or professional terminal degree	16.4
Relationship status	
Married	84.5
Not married but living together	12.4
Involved but not living together/other	1.4
Employment status	
Full time	88.6
Part time	6.1
Not working/student	5.3
Income	
Less than 20,000	6.7
20,000–40,000	12.9
40,001–75,000	12.2
75,001–100,000	8.5
More than 100,000	49.0
Prefer not to answer	9.6
Health insurance	
Private insurance	82.1
Public insurance	13.9
No health insurance	4.1
First time father?	
No	38.8
Yes	61.2
Timing of pregnancy at interview	

(continued)

Table 1 (continued)

	Percent
Less than 3 months	24.2
3–6 months	33.1
More than 6 months	42.8

N = 959

fathering abilities (37.6% agree and 39.7% somewhat agree), it is also true that the fathers are asking for either a lot or some help with practical parenting skills (77.3%). Third, fathers demonstrate high levels of involvement in their partner's prenatal care and future delivery health services. In our sample, fathers always or almost always (79.2%) accompany their partners or wives to prenatal visits and another 13% sometimes attend. And 19% of fathers took unpaid time off work to attend this study prenatal visit (Table 2).

3.2.2 Results Discussion

Our study findings on father's involvement in maternal reproductive health services—ultrasound visits, PNC, and delivery attendance expectations—is consistent to what others have also reported about fathers' increasing presence for ultrasound and delivery (Redshaw and Heikkilä 2010; Redshaw and Henderson 2013).

The strong and consistent involvement of fathers with their wives and partners in prenatal care reflects their interest in active fatherhood, from thinking about and discussing impending fatherhood with partners to attending prenatal visits, taking unpaid time off work and being in the delivery room. Fathers' interest establishes the foundation for an increase of paternal services and attention in prenatal care, which we elaborate on further in the Recommendations section.

3.3 Father's Health, Health Care and Mental Health

3.3.1 Health and Health Care

Results

The vast majority of fathers profess an awareness of the importance (81.4% feel it is very important) of their health for the health of the newborn infant (15.2% feel it is somewhat important). However, despite this awareness, only 65.2% of fathers had a routine physician exam in the past year. Second, fathers coming to prenatal care visits were substantially overweight (49%) or obese (23%). These figures appear to be consistent with men's elevated BMIs in the U.S. Third, excessive substance use was relatively uncommon in this sample of fathers, though possibly under-reported.

Table 2 Father preparation, engagement and participation in birth related services

	Strongly agree	Somewhat agree	Neutral	Somewhat disagree	Strongly disagree
Excited about becoming a father	93.2	5.4	1.2	–	0.1
Becoming a father is stressful	16.3	39.6	21.5	8.9	13.5
Confident in fathering abilities	67.7	26.5	4.6	1.0	0.3
How much...	**A lot**	**Some**	**Very little**	**Not at all/none**	
Time spent thinking about becoming a new father?	52.7	39.1	6.3	1.8	
Talked with the baby's mother about becoming a father?	60.7	31.5	6.6	1.3	
Do you feel you need help with practical parenting skills?	37.6	39.7	13.4	9.2	
How often do you go with the baby's mother to prenatal care visits?	Percent				
Always	42.1				
Almost always	37.1				
Sometimes	13.8				
Rarely	1.1				
This is my first prenatal visit	5.8				
Did you have to take UNPAID time off work to attend this appointment?	Percent				
Yes	19.0				
Unsure	5.3				
No	75.8				
Do you plan to be in the delivery room?	Percent				
Definitely	89.1				
Most likely	7.6				
Not sure	2.6				
Not likely/no	0.8				
Are you planning to take time off work once the baby is born?	Percent				
Yes	90.9				
Unsure	6.2				
No	2.9				

N = 959

Smoking was much less common (9.1%) than drinking (62.5%) with 16.8% of men reporting 4 or more alcohol drinks per week and 10.6% men reporting 7 or more drinks per week. Fourth, 65.4% of pregnancies in this sample occurred at "the right time," a potential indicator of good family planning. Still 14.0% of pregnancies occurred sooner than expected and 8.5% were not expected at all (Table 3).

Table 3 Men's prenatal health and health habits

How important do you think your health is to the health of the newborn infant?	Percent		
Very important	81.4		
Somewhat important	15.2		
A little important	3.0		
Not important	0.4		
Routine physical examination in the past year?	**Percent**		
Yes	65.2		
No	34.8		
Body mass index	**Percent**		
Underweight	0.3		
Healthy weight	27.1		
Overweight	49.2		
Obese	23.3		
Smoke cigarettes?	**Percent**		
Yes	9.1		
No	90.9		
Drinks in past week	**Percent**		
0	37.5		
1	11.4		
2–3	23.7		
4–6	16.8		
7+	10.6		
Pregnancy expectation	**Percent**		
Sooner than expected	14.0		
At the right time	65.4		
Later than expected	12.1		
Not expected at all	8.5		
PHQ-2 Depressive Symptoms	**Percent**		
Little interest or pleasure in doing things	20.9		
Down, sad or hopeless	15.3		
Any Depressive Symptom	26.0		
Any Severe Symptoms	8.0		
	Yes	Not Sure	No
Do you have any people or place(s) to go for fatherhood encouragement?	64.6	16.3	19.0

Results Discussion

Overall, the survey findings suggest that fathers have substantial health and health service utilization needs during the prenatal period, reinforcing sporadic similar reports of men's poor health and service needs pre-conceptually (Frey et al. 2012; Choiriyyah et al. 2015).

The study results should reinforce the emerging interest in encouraging men to attend to their own preconception and prenatal health care (Kotelchuck and Lu 2017; Garfield 2015; CDC 2019), in order to enhance his own life course health, as well as to his infant and partner's well-being (Kotelchuck 2021a). That almost 35% of men have not had a routine physical exam in the past year is a missed opportunity to have a pre-birth check-up and learn about and address any existing, significant health issues.

3.3.2 Mental Health

Results

Although virtually all fathers in our study experience joy in the pregnancy period (98.6%), our findings show a significant presence of depressive symptoms as well. The survey's PHQ-2 two question screener (Kroenke et al. 2003) yielded findings worthy of concern. Over 21% (21.4%) of fathers said they find little interest or pleasure in doing things while 15.5% described themselves as down, sad, or hopeless. In total, 26% of fathers endorsed one or more of these two symptoms, while 8% described themselves as having severe depressive symptoms as measured by at least one of the symptoms occurring more than half the time. At any given time in the US, 7.2% of adults are diagnosed with depression (SAMHSA 2019), which might suggest that our sample of fathers in the prenatal period have higher rates than average. The study also found that over 35% of men don't have, or are uncertain about having, people and places to go to for fatherhood encouragement, potentially suggesting a feeling of isolation at a critical period of emotional vulnerability.

In addition, 56% of fathers endorsed the statement that the pregnancy period was a source of stress. Analyses using only our 2016 study participants (Levy et al. 2017), where we had explored the sources of the paternal stress more deeply, showed the concerns were focused on financial pressure (44%), the ability to care for the baby (29%), decreased time for oneself (20%), and the changing relationship with the mother (15%) (Data not presented in the tables). Additionally, a group of men (15%) were worried that they would repeat the mistakes of their father, mistakes that they likely experienced in their own development, perhaps abuse, neglect or absence at their most extreme.

Results Discussion

Our data reveals that the prenatal period is marked by substantial mental health needs for the majority of fathers. Entering and negotiating the unknown world of pregnancy and prenatal services can contribute to men feeling insecure and uncertain about expectations.

Joy: The overwhelming majority of men are trying hard to meet the challenges and are experiencing the joys of fatherhood. We observe men embracing their newfound fatherhood role as an opportunity for growth, for the realization of long-held dreams and the healing of past disappointments and even traumas. Others see fatherhood as an opportunity for increased capacity to love and for the expansion of identity, a discovery of a previously unexpressed part of the self.

Stress: The current survey findings of elevated levels of prenatal paternal stress are consistent with other research, which similarly has noted greater stress among new fathers (Philpott et al. 2017; Gemayel et al. 2018). One's circle of concern needs to expand to include the welfare of the new baby; and one needs to derive gratification from the sacrifices for and pleasures of another. These psychological challenges are welcome for many, daunting for some, and insurmountable for others.

Additionally, the fathers are facing practical financial and childcare demands that can be challenging. There are financial pressures, changes in the demands of work-life balance, and less time availability to enjoy the marital or partner relationship (Kotelchuck 2021b).

Isolation: In this study sample, over 35% of men don't have or are uncertain about having people and places to go for fatherhood encouragement. Other paternal mental health researchers have also noted that fathers often feel isolated during the prenatal period, and that paternal isolation is a risk factor for pre- and postpartum depression and anxiety (Gameyal et al. 2018). With major changes to fathers' lives, additional social supports can be helpful.

Depression: This study's finding that 26% of fathers endorsed one of two depressive symptoms adds to the growing literature about men and depression during the perinatal period (Paulson and Bazemore 2010). Using our 2016 data (Levy et al. 2017), we found that elevated paternal stress, both overall and by specific source, was significantly associated with the father's depressive symptoms. This finding suggests that fathers can be overwhelmed by the stresses of impending fatherhood, and they often struggle to master the internal and practical demands. The finding that 26% of the fathers endorsed one or both of the depression items on the PHQ-2 in our study does not confirm a diagnosis of clinical depression, although it certainly does indicate that further evaluation is warranted.

Currently, there appears to be little professional awareness about this level of stress and depression in fathers during the prenatal period. Of critical importance, some men who won't allow themselves to ask for help externalize their problems and become angry, blaming friends, loved ones or society (Rowan 2016) and use substances to self-medicate, although curiously our sample seems relatively free of this phenomenon. Psychological evaluation of fathers in the prenatal period, when men clearly have mental health stresses while feeling vulnerable, could potentially prevent multiple problems in the family.

The voices of the fathers in this study, when asked, are expressing their mental health needs loudly. As we will describe in the Recommendations section, integrating mental health evaluation and referral for fathers into the Obstetric service may increase the likelihood that fathers will want to seek needed mental health services.

3.4 Perceptions of the Father-Friendliness of MGH Obstetric Services

3.4.1 Results

One of the goals of the Father Survey was to determine the current experience of fathers in the MGH Obstetric Services as they accompanied their partners and wives to prenatal visits, analogous to a continuous quality improvement effort, and one of the justifications for the department's support of this study. We were interested in learning directly from fathers about what areas of the service and the interpersonal experience needed to be addressed to help it become more father and family friendly. Our Father Survey is perhaps the first time men visiting prenatal care have been asked how they were treated (Table 4).

Overall, fathers perceived their welcome and inclusion at MGH Obstetrics prenatal care services very positively, though there were some notable indications suggesting needed improvements. While there was some slight variation across the various specific staff roles, between 57.1% and 61.3% of men reported being made to feel both very included and very important during the prenatal care visit, with an additional 18.6–27.9% somewhat included and important. Between 15 and 20% of men explicitly noted their neutrality or dissatisfaction with an individual obstetric provider or service.

Second, strikingly, large numbers of fathers were not asked (21.4%) or weren't sure (20.1%) they were directly asked, a single question by an MGH Obstetrics staff member during their partner's clinical encounter, representing clear missed opportunities for greater father engagement.

Table 4 Perception of father-friendliness of MGH prenatal/obstetric services

During your pre-natal visit, did the following people make you feel that you are included and are an important part of the visit and birth?	Very included	Somewhat included	Neutral	Somewhat unimportant	Very unimportant
Front desk staff	61.3	18.6	18.6	1.0	0.4
Doctor (ob/gyn) or midwife	57.1	27.9	11.7	3.1	0.2
Full MGH obstetrics staff	52.7	30.9	13.2	2.5	0.6
	Yes	No	Unsure		
Did the doctor (OB) or midwife ask you questions during the visit?	58.5	21.4	20.1		
Does the waiting area offer resources for fathers?	39.1	35.3	25.6		
[If yes or unsure], were the resources helpful	56.6	2.0	41.5		

N = 899

Third, at the time of our father survey, MGH Obstetrics Services did not offer any written or media resources specifically directed at fathers in the waiting area. Despite that fact, 39.1% of fathers incorrectly reported that they were offered such resources. Of those who said that MGH did offer resources, 56% felt that they were very helpful and 42% somewhat helpful. These findings perhaps reflect some positive patient satisfaction bias. Fathers also may have equated information for mothers with resources for themselves.

3.4.2 Results Discussion

The study results suggest that overall, fathers perceived that they were very well treated at MGH Obstetric prenatal services; they felt included and an important part of their partner's prenatal care visit—despite the widely remarked on observation in the literature that men often feel excluded from reproductive health services (Steen et al. 2012). No single staff role stood out for engaging men.

There are several reasons, however, to be cautious in over-interpreting the very positive overall paternal responses. First, the MGH Obstetrical Services may already be especially father-friendly, and its providers may be at their father-friendliest when we are conducting our fatherhood survey. Second, most surveys of clinical care provider satisfaction generally reveal very positive responses. Third, maybe the fathers had very low expectations of involvement in their partners' prenatal care services, which historically are not usually directed at them, beyond being welcomed and treated courteously. And fourth, men may be very reluctant to say anything too critical that might reflect negatively on their partner's important upcoming delivery care.

Yet, there were also clearly some indications of missed opportunities for service improvement and greater paternal and family engagement. First, despite the fathers professed satisfaction with the prenatal care visit, when asked objectively about their own informational and skill development needs, substantial numbers indicated a desire to receive information about a wide range of fatherhood and reproductive pregnancy topics not currently being provided them at these visits. (See next section, 3.5.) Secondly, at MGH, when the study began, fathers were not represented and mirrored in the waiting area. There were no pictures of men as fathers on the waiting room walls, nor targeted brochures for them, nor any special explicit fatherhood-focused prenatal care activities or programs. Third, a small but sizable number of the fathers explicitly noted their neutrality or dissatisfaction with individual obstetric providers or services. And finally, some of the fathers added written survey comments indicating that they wanted more involvement and were aware of not being included. Others were simply pleased to be recognized and treated as though they mattered through the attention of the Father Survey. (See Sect. 3.6.)

These perceptions of the Obstetric Services friendliness and opportunities for practice improvements are potentially readily remediable. In the subsequent Recommendations section, we propose several ways that an Obstetric Service can potentially provide father-specific resources during their partner's prenatal care visit.

3.5 Paternal Information Needs and Potential Formats for Delivery

3.5.1 Results

The fathers report a balance of confidence and of recognition of needing more skills. Although only 35.5% of fathers initially said they wanted more information about being a father, (25.4% unsure, 39% no), it is clear that as more specific content areas were presented in the Father Survey, more fathers (33.2–59.7%) acknowledged the need for information topics and skills that they could potentially learn (Table 5).

Specifically, fathers were most interested in how to support their wives and partners prenatally (59.7%), and in learning about the stages of pregnancy (54.6%). They expressed strong interest in learning about their role in infancy (54.3%) and about their baby's emotions and needs (52.5%), both suggesting that fathers plan to be on the frontline of caretaking. Fathers also wanted to know more about their contribution to healthy pregnancy and childbirth (53.2%). Plus, 46.5% stated they wanted to learn more about practical parenting skills. Fathers were relatively less interested in specialized father topics of finances and paternal health impacts. There was a relatively similar distribution of responses between first-time and experienced fathers (data not included).

Table 5 Paternal information needs and potential methods of delivery

Want more information about being a father?	Percent
Yes	35.5
Unsure	25.4
No	39.1
What fatherhood information would you like?	**Percent**
How to support my partner during pregnancy and early parenthood	59.7
My own contribution to a healthy pregnancy and childbirth	53.2
Fathering and fathers' role in early infancy	54.3
What to expect at each stage of pregnancy	54.6
How to better understand my baby's emotions and needs	52.5
Practical parenting skills (diapers, feeding, bathing)	46.5
The financial costs of parenting	33.2
The impact of pregnancy and parenting on my own health	35.2
Which of the following would you find helpful?	**Percent**
Information for fathers at prenatal visits	41.4
More time and attention to fathers in childbirth classes	19.2
Learning from other expectant or recent fathers	27.7
A prenatal visit specifically for expectant fathers	22.9
Reading printed materials on fatherhood	46.6
Viewing fatherhood materials on the web	43.3
Emails or text messages with fatherhood information	30.7

N = 899

The fathers most preferred methods for receiving desired paternal information is through written materials: publications (46.6%) or social media (43.3% on the web; 30.7% via texts), though similar numbers (41.4%) also desired this information from health professionals at the prenatal care visit. Fathers desire more reproductive health and fatherhood information and skills at prenatal visits (41.4%) from across a wide range of fatherhood-related topics. Study participants were currently much less interested in direct experiential sharing modalities. These results are similar to other studies of father's information method preferences (DeCosta et al. 2017).

3.5.2 Results Discussion

Fathers' voices clearly inform us that they desire more parenting skills and knowledge, suggesting that they want to participate more actively and knowledgably in the pregnancy and beyond. We believe that most fathers are unaware of the multiple areas of potential and complex learning needed to effectively interact with and care for their infants, as they have not been historically socialized to care for infants and children. Seeing the list of possibilities mentioned in the Father Survey excited fathers' interest for specific topics.

We believe that the fathers' requests for more specific fatherhood information and skills prenatally is a further indication that their attitudes toward reproductive health, their parental roles and responsibilities, and child development are in the process of significant cultural transformation; i.e., that we are witnessing a new era of increased paternal commitment to caretaking roles and potentially a stronger emotional engagement with their families and infants.

Currently, there is very limited information directed at fathers here at MGH Obstetric Services, nor likely elsewhere at other Obstetric Services. Like mothers, fathers are clearly desirous of similar prenatal information, and usually are less familiar with it. That 35% of fathers had no known person or places to go to for fatherhood motivational encouragement and information further emphasizes the potential importance of prenatal care visits as a realistic site to learn more about fatherhood.

3.6 Father's Assessment of the MGH Fatherhood Prenatal Care Initiative

3.6.1 Results

Free Form Father Quotes from the Father Survey

- "I strongly think that obstetrics should increase fathers' involvement during pregnancy. Thank you for doing this. It's about time obstetrics involve fathers. Thank you again."

Table 6 Men's judgment of the importance of the prenatal fatherhood initiative

Do you think father involvement in prenatal and obstetric care is important?	Percent
Very important	79.5
Somewhat important	15.4
Neutral or less	5.1

N = 899

- "Love the way you guys are thinking. Incredibly impressed with MGH and proactive initiatives like this."
- "I'm excited you are even asking these questions!"
- "It's a wonderful experience."
- "Very good initiative. I'm proud to be a father."
- "Would be nice to see if system also considers and recognizes fatherhood equally important!"
- "Try to include them (fathers) as much as possible and explain how important they can be to both the mother and baby throughout the pregnancy and childbirth.

In addition to these comments, one father said proudly to his wife that his conversation with one of the study's primary investigators was "just for daddies." And another returned with twins, one on each arm, 4 days after their birth, asking if he could finish the second half of the Father Survey.

Fathers overall were very supportive of this initial MGH fatherhood prenatal care study, with over 86% agreeing to participate in this baseline fatherhood survey. The fathers who responded to our survey were very enthusiastic about the involvement of men in prenatal and obstetric care: 79.5% thought the initiative was very important, 15.4% somewhat important (combined 94.9%), while only 5.1% thought it was of neutral or lower importance (Table 6).

3.6.2 Results Discussion

The very high rate of survey completion and the general positive and cooperative affective tenor of the fathers both indicate that the fathers were pleased to have interest and attention during their prenatal visits. Indeed, just hearing fathers' voices and perspectives in prenatal care is already an initial form of positive inclusion.

Overall, these findings suggest that fathers no longer think of themselves as merely chauffeurs to their partner's prenatal visits, but as active participants in the support to their wives and partners during the birth process and childcare. Their voices are actively requesting support toward these goals. This evolution of men's paternal interests far surpasses what Obstetric Services currently are aware of and have planned for. Programmatic changes in Obstetric Services to enhance father inclusion could help improve reproductive outcomes and men's own health and early family involvement.

4 Discussion

The fathers' very positive response to this study's survey should help further refute any notions that fathers are relatively unaffected or disengaged by the pregnancy; that pregnancy is not a family event; that they are not present at reproductive health services; that they have limited interest in prenatal care services; or that they will not participate in reproductive health services research. The men in our study were highly engaged, curious, and eager for prenatal involvement and information and skill acquisition.

Specifically, this study documents:

1. that men have come of age as frontline, engaged fathers who expect themselves to be actively involved with their partners during the prenatal and birth process. Engaged fathering is the new norm and reflects an expansion of men's identity.
2. that the prenatal period is also marked by substantial paternal physical and mental health needs. This period reveals elevated paternal obesity, insufficient family planning, and lack of primary care health services. Fathers are also burdened with substantial paternal stress, elevated depressive symptoms, and personal isolation.
3. that fathers perceive they were made welcome and included by professional staff during their partners prenatal care visits, though many men (~40%) were not asked a single question at the prenatal care visit and no targeted fatherhood resources, information, or services were offered them.
4. that fathers desire more fatherhood information and skills training at the prenatal care visit—across a wide range of fatherhood-related topics—which they would prefer to receive from publications, social media, online education or health professional counseling rather than through experiential fatherhood sharing modalities.
5. that fathers demonstrate an active and engaged "voice" during prenatal care, and are strongly supportive of initiatives, like at MGH, to enhance their involvement in reproductive health services.
6. and finally, that men are willing to participate directly in research and surveys about fatherhood, and that the important and unique information they provide (fathers' voices) can serve to help develop interventions that foster earlier and more enhanced paternal involvement and engagement in reproductive and child health care, family-centric pregnancy and childbirth, and men's own health and health care.

The Father Survey findings detailed above potentially reflect major changes in male identity in which fatherhood responsibilities are becoming more important and have expanded to become a broader and deeper part of fathers' psychological life. Fathers now more often include their nurturing capacity and the development of a bond and emotionally engaged relationship with their children as part of their parenting role. Fathers' self-esteem, anxiety, pleasure, and sense of responsibility are extended to various fatherhood pursuits. Perhaps this is to be expected as families often have two adults working and sharing parenting duties, placing fathers in frontline caretaking roles.

5 Father-Friendly Obstetric Prenatal Care Practice Recommendations

From its conception, The Fatherhood Project sought to build a collaboration with staff at MGH Obstetrics, to address men's involvement with fatherhood in the prenatal period and to assess the widely held view that Obstetric Services were not father and family friendly. The Fatherhood Surveys were intended to collect data to provide father-specific guidance to these efforts. As this chapter shows, we believe that we have successfully researched and heard father's voices at MGH about a set of themes that might lead to enhanced reproductive health services, improved fathers' health, and increased father involvement with their partners, and ultimately their infants, during prenatal and delivery care.

Based on the fatherhood survey results, an MGH Obstetric Practice Task Force on Fatherhood was created that meets monthly to discuss the implementation of the lessons learned and put them into practice. Based on the joint discussions between The Fatherhood Project and the Task Force, we developed a set of potential practice interventions to enhance obstetric prenatal care and make it more father-friendly and more family-centric, without diminishing the traditional maternal and infant focus of obstetrics. None of the proposed interventions replaces or interferes with existing care or emphasis.

These proposed interventions fall into five broad practice categories that can be conceptualized as sequential steps of increasingly greater father involvement:

1. Staff Training about Father Inclusion
2. Father-Friendly Clinic Environment
3. Explicit Affirmation of Father Inclusion
4. Development of Educational Materials for Fathers
5. Specialized Father-focused Reproductive Health Care Initiatives

5.1 Staff Training About Father Inclusion

5.1.1 Rationale

Currently, many obstetric staff may not think of father inclusion as a practice goal and may not be comfortable interacting with men (Davison et al. 2017). Over 40% of fathers in our study said no questions were directed at them during their partner's prenatal visit. Staff training can offer new approaches to including men in the obstetric practice.

5.1.2 Recommendations

1. At the practice level, we believe that consistent nursing and clinical staff training that emphasizes the importance of relating to fathers is important for enhanced fatherhood involvement. Training of Obstetric staff by fatherhood experts has the potential to influence providers to talk with fathers regularly and directly during visits and to overcome implicit and explicit biases about fathers as fully competent caretakers.
2. Formal presentations and father engagement trainings need to emphasize the research-based, improved emotional, social, behavioral, and academic outcomes for children with greater father engagement.
3. Training on relating to fathers can help some female staff feel less anxious and more competent when addressing fathers. Since the Father Survey was implemented, The Fatherhood Project conducts an annual fatherhood staff training for all nursing and nursing-associated staff in the Obstetrics Department.
4. Reaching beyond the practice site is recommended as well. Critical staff training can start earlier at provider educational institutions. Obstetrics can be taught with an inclusive attitude toward fathers in medical, nursing, and midwife programs. Knowledge about the improvement in reproductive health when fathers are engaged in the prenatal period should be emphasized.

5.2 Father Friendly Office Environment

5.2.1 Rationale

Many men don't feel comfortable in clinical settings for women's reproductive health services or prenatal care (Steen et al. 2012).

5.2.2 Recommendations

1. The waiting area can display photographs on the wall that reflect all configurations within families, including fathers with babies, which will communicate inclusion and importance.
2. An educational video that includes fathers and discusses the critical areas of prenatal and infant care can be running in the waiting room.
3. There can be educational materials specifically directed at fathers—pamphlets and magazines—that focus on topics related to fathers' role in the prenatal and early postnatal period.
4. A chair for a second adult or father can be routinely provided in all exam rooms.

5.3 Explicit Affirmation of Father Inclusion

Rationale: Men are hesitant to enter into what is widely perceived as a woman's traditional world (Johansson et al. 2015; Jomeen 2017).

5.3.1 Recommendations

1. To make the concept of family-centric obstetric care real, obstetric practices must make it explicitly clear to both the mothers and fathers (or other partners) that they are both *wanted* and *expected* to participate in all prenatal services. Inclusion of fathers needs to begin with the first contact with the obstetric clinical service, the welcoming script that nurses use in their initial phone medical evaluation of new pregnant mothers. At the MGH Obstetric Service, fathers or partners are now actively welcomed and expected to attend services, especially the first visit, thereby establishing the norm for his inclusion throughout the pregnancy. Explicitly saying "you and your husband or partner" rather than solely "you" signals to the mother that the orientation of the service is inclusive of the father, partner, and family, contributing to more positive reproductive outcomes. We recognize that this may seem problematic for evaluation of domestic abuse, but this critical information can be ascertained in many ways without excluding fathers from routine prenatal visits.
2. Fathers' information is not generally collected in the obstetric records, except perhaps for his name and insurance status. We propose recording fathers' information on all enrollment forms and especially in the EPIC-based Electronic Medical Record. This modification would help define the family as a unit of interest and enable providers to cross reference fathers when they are recording information about mothers.
3. It would be helpful to document fathers' and others' attendance at prenatal visits. Family-centric pregnancy care necessarily would require family-centric medical records, which currently don't exist—and father's health records are not ever linked to their child's records. Frequently, knowing about the father can be helpful to a provider's service to the mother. We recognize, of course, that waivers of confidentiality would need to be obtained to share this information.
4. Prenatal care clinics could conduct annual anonymous (Continuous Quality Improvement) cross-sectional surveys of the father's perceptions of their experiences at OB prenatal care services—similar to the second half of the current MGH Fatherhood Surveys—and publicize the results. This would help demonstrate to fathers that the prenatal care practice valued fathers and their opinions.
5. To enhance father involvement, when fathers are present in the exam room, nurses, midwives, and doctors should talk directly to them, in addition to the usual conversation between mothers and providers. As we have noted, nearly 40% of fathers didn't recall being asked any questions during their MGH prenatal accompanying visit.

6. Providers can include father-directed information during appointments, i.e., how to support their partners in the prenatal period (highly desired by the men in our study). If fathers are not present at a visit, mothers can be encouraged to have the father come to the next appointment.
7. The importance of co-parenting can be highlighted when both parents are present.

5.4 Development of Educational Materials for Fathers

5.4.1 Rationale

There is very limited educational material directed at fathers, in the obstetric office and online (Albuja et al. 2019).

5.4.2 Recommendations

1. The fathers' voices in this study documented the extensive desire for more paternally oriented pregnancy, childbirth, parenting, and partnering information and skills. The MGH Obstetric Nursing Practice Task Force on Fatherhood has encouraged The Fatherhood Project to create brochures for their practice relating to fathers' interest in their partner's pregnancy and delivery as well as infant caretaking and development. Over 50% of men in this survey desired more information and skills.
2. We recommend that practices also develop father-specific electronic educational materials. For example, practices may want to offer expectant fathers weekly text messages that they can choose to receive. These text messages can contain the kinds of information fathers requested in our study.
3. Additionally, obstetric practices that currently have a dedicated webpage for mothers can develop a similar webpage for fathers. The webpage can allow for interactive question and answer responses and address the fathers' areas of interest. Referrals for coaching, psychotherapy, and medical evaluation can be available through the website. Most fathers indicated on our survey that they prefer to receive information through electronic means. We recognize that a website and text messages can also serve the fathers who are unable to attend prenatal care visits or whose interest would increase with viewing educational materials they are unaware of.
4. Experienced expectant fathers or men who recently became fathers could also be engaged in being peer mentors, working individually, or as a leader of a class or support groups. Announcements of these possibilities can be made available to fathers at the time of visits, or by text and webpage.

5.5 *Special Father Reproductive Health Care Initiatives*

5.5.1 Rationale

Our current survey documented substantial health and mental health needs among fathers in the prenatal period.

5.5.2 Recommendations

1. One idea that we strongly encourage and have proposed is the creation of a specific prenatal visit, perhaps named "The Family Visit," during which the father (or other partner) will be offered an opportunity to speak confidentially with a dedicated professional about his prenatal fatherhood concerns, hopes, and related health and social issues. We conceptualize this meeting possibly in conjunction with the fourth maternal prenatal visit, the lengthy Glucose Tolerance Test (GTT) visit. Fathers would be invited and informed in advance. During this appointment, fathers would have the opportunity to be evaluated for health and mental health related concerns. This can include drug and alcohol use, obesity, financial concerns, anxiety, depression, anger dysregulation, and other, perhaps more severe, mental health issues. Referrals can be made following evaluation.
2. Alternatively, some of these father-targeted health concerns could be addressed with an enhanced primary care visit scheduled during the early pregnancy period. However, most primary care visits do not inquire about potential paternity concerns, plus a man-only visit, however good, is less likely to foster a sense of family-oriented pregnancy. A father visit held through the Obstetric Service as described above during the prenatal period that is about the pregnancy and his needs would be more ideal.

In this section, we presented a sequence of five practical and limited cost interventions to make obstetric prenatal services more father-friendly and more family-centric in order to ensure earlier and enhanced fatherhood engagement and experiences. These suggestions are all responsive to the fathers' voices that emerged from our Father Survey.

6 Concluding Comments

From the beginning, our Fatherhood Survey was intended as a public health initiative aimed at gathering fathers' voices to guide us in the important work of suggesting interventions and alterations in health service delivery at obstetric practices.

This study attempted to hear the direct perspectives and voices of fathers about their experiences and needs during the prenatal period. The results, we believe, have proven to be very informative—for improving fatherhood experiences, men's health, and the creation of more father-friendly health services. Fathers' direct voices are critical—for creating new scientific knowledge about their perinatal conditions, for shaping the new emerging more family-friendly clinical programs (such as the prior obstetric practices recommendations), and for developing the political will to help transform current Maternal and Child Health (MCH) services (Richmond and Kotelchuck 1983). We hope it will be one of many such systematic paternal listening efforts across a wide range of MCH programs and policies.

This study further documents the health, and especially the added mental health, needs of men during the prenatal reproductive period. The isolation, stress, anger dysregulation, and depression expressed by the men can be addressed through father-friendly prenatal initiatives for the improvement of reproductive health outcomes. As we have suggested, fathers' voices inspired practice interventions designed to respond to fathers' needs in the obstetric service without interference with pre-existing care for pregnant women.

We believe that our study results can lead to a recognition that there is a fatherhood revolution hiding in plain sight that needs to be welcomed and supported in obstetric practices around the country. Fathers and fathers' health are important to their families' lives and, in this historical moment, fathers have become eager to engage in the reproductive prenatal care period, presumably leading to their greater engagement with their children and families as frontline caretakers and breadwinners.

Hopefully, Obstetric Services beyond MGH will find the study's new data on men's reproductive health needs valuable and will implement some of the proposed paternal health service changes, perhaps altered to fit the particular needs of individual practices.

We hope that this descriptive study of fathers' prenatal "voices" inspires many more similar perinatal research studies to explore men's impact on infants', mothers', families', and men's own health. We hope that others will be motivated to develop and create more father-friendly MCH health services. Ultimately, the critical issue is to hear fathers' voices—and to engage and uplift the millions of interested fathers while improving reproductive health.

Acknowledgements The authors thank the members of the larger research and nursing practice teams at MGH Obstetric Services and The Fatherhood Project: Hiyam Nadel, John Badalament, Erika Cheng, Jennifer Doherty, Susan Gamble, Chandra Khalifian, Michelle Lee, Janika Gates, John Knutsen, Anne Maguire, Lisa Masciulli, Karen Paul, Alison Rosen.

References

Administration for Children and Families (2019) Healthy marriage and responsible fatherhood. https://www.acf.hhs.gov/ofa/programs/healthy-marriage

Albuja AF, Sanchez DT, Lee SJ, Lee JY, Yadava S (2019) The effect of paternal cues in prenatal care settings on men's involvement intentions. PLoS One 14(5):e0216454. https://doi.org/10.1371/journal.pone.0216454

Centers for Disease Control and Prevention (CDC) (2019) Preconception health and health care. https://www.cdc.gov/preconception/index. Accessed 15 Jan 2019

Choiriyyah I, Sonenstein FL, Astone NM, Pleck JH, Dariotis JK, Marcell AV (2015) Men aged 15–44 in need of preconception care. Matern Child Health J 19(11):2358–2365

Davison KK, Charles JN, Khandpur N, Nelson TJ (2017) Fathers' perceived reasons for their underrepresentation in child health research and strategies to increase their involvement. Matern Child Health J 21(2):267–274

Davison KK, Gavarkovs A, McBride B, Kotelchuck M, Levy R, Taveras EM (2019) Engaging fathers in early obesity prevention during the first thousand days: policy, systems and environmental change strategies. Obesity 27(4):523–533

DeCosta P, Møller P, Frøst MB, Olsen A (2017) Changing children's eating behaviour—a review of experimental research. Appetite 113(1):327–357

Frey KA, Engle R, Noble B (2012) Preconception healthcare: what do men know and believe? J Men's Health 9(1):25–35

Garfield CF (2015) Supporting fatherhood before and after it happens. Pediatrics 135(2):e528–e530

Garfield CF, Simon CD, Harrison L, Besera G, Kapaya M, Pazol K, Boulet S, Grigorescu V, Barfield W, Lee W (2018) Pregnancy risk assessment monitoring system for dads: public health surveillance of new fathers in the perinatal period. Am J Public Health 108(10):1314–1315

Gemayel DJ, Wiener KKK, Saliba AJ (2018) Development of a conception framework that identifies factors and challenges impacting perinatal fathers. Heliyon 4(7):e00694

Johansson M, Fenwick J, Premberg A (2015) A meta-synthesis of the father's experiences of their partner's labour and birth. Midwifery 31(1):9–18

Jomeen J (2017) Fathers in the birth room: choice or coercion? Help or hinderance? J Reprod Infant Psychol 35(4):321–323

Kotelchuck M (1976) The infant's relationship to the father: experimental evidence. In: Lamb ME (ed) The role of the father in child development. Wiley, New York, pp 161–192

Kotelchuck M (2021a) The impact of father's health on reproductive and infant health and development. In: Grau-Grau M, las Heras M, Bowles HR (eds) Engaged fatherhood for men, families and gender equality. Springer, Cham, pp 31–61

Kotelchuck M (2021b) The impact of fatherhood on men's health and development. In: Grau-Grau M, las Heras M, Bowles HR (eds) Engaged fatherhood for men, families and gender equality. Springer, Cham, pp 63–91

Kotelchuck M, Lu M (2017) Father's role in preconception health. Matern Child Health J 21(11):2025–2039

Kotelchuck M, Zelazo PR, Kagan J, Spelke E (1975) Infant reaction to parental separations when left with familiar and unfamiliar adults. J Genet Psychol 126(2):255–262

Kotelchuck M, Levy RA, Nadel H (2016) Fatherhood prenatal care obstetrics survey, Massachusetts General Hospital 2015: what men say, what we learned. In: Oral presentation at the annual meetings of the APHA, Denver CO, November 2016. www.thefatherhoodproject.org/research

Kotelchuck M, Khalifian CE, Levy RA, Nadel H (2017) Men's perceptions during prenatal care: the 2016 MGH fatherhood obstetrics survey. In: Oral presentation at the annual meetings of the APHA, Atlanta GA, November, 2017. www.thefatherhoodproject.org/research

Kroenke K, Spitzer RL, Williams JBW (2003) The patient health questionnaire-2: validity of a two-item depression screener. Med Care 41(1):1284–1292

Lamb ME (1975) Fathers: forgotten contributors to child development. Hum Dev 18(4):245–266

Lamb ME (ed) (2010) The role of the father in child development, 5th edn. Wiley, New York

Lamb ME, Lamb JE (1976) The nature and importance of the father-infant relationship. Fam Coord 25(4):379–385

Levy RA, Badalament J, Kotelchuck M (2012) The Fatherhood Project. Massachusetts General Hospital, Boston. www.thefatherhoodproject.org

Levy RA, Khalifian CE, Nadel H, Kotelchuck M (2017) The impact of fatherhood stress on depression during the prenatal period at the intersection of race and SES. Poster presentation at the annual meetings of the APHA, Atlanta GA, November, 2017. www.thefatherhoodproject.org/research

Massachusetts Department of Public Health (2018) Massachusetts births 2016. https://www.mass.gov/doc/2016-birth-report/download

Obama B (2014) My brother's keeper. https://obamawhitehouse.archives.gov/my-brothers-keeper

Paulson JF, Bazemore SD (2010) Prenatal and postpartum depression in fathers and its association with maternal depression: a meta-analysis. JAMA 303(19):1961–1969

Philpott LF, Leahy-Warren P, FitzGerald S, Savage E (2017) Stress in fathers in the perinatal period: a systematic review. Midwifery 55:113–127

Redshaw M, Heikkilä K (2010) Delivered with care. A national survey of women's experience of maternity care 2010. Technical report. National Perinatal Epidemiology Unit, University of Oxford, United Kingdom. https://researchonline.lshtm.ac.uk/id/eprint/2548656

Redshaw M, Henderson J (2013) Father engagement in pregnancy and child health: evidence from a national survey. BMC Pregnancy Childbirth 13:70

Richmond JB, Kotelchuck M (1983) Political influences: rethinking national health policy. In: McGuire CH, Foley RP, Gorr D, Richards RW (eds) Handbook of health professions education. Josey-Bass, San Francisco, pp 386–404

Rowan ZR (2016) Social risk factors of black and white adolescents' substance use: the differential role of siblings and best friends. J Youth Adolesc 45:1482–1496. https://doi.org/10.1007/s10964-016-0473-7

Sarkadi A, Kristiansson R, Oberklaid F, Bremberg S (2008) Fathers' involvement and children's developmental outcomes: a systematic review of longitudinal studies. Acta Paediatrica 97(2):153–158. https://doi.org/10.1111/j.1651-227.2007.00572.x

Simon CD, Garfield CF (2021) Developing a public health surveillance system for fathers. In: Grau-Grau M, las Heras M, Bowles HR (eds) Engaged fatherhood for men, families and gender equality. Springer, Cham, pp 93–109

Steen M, Downe S, Bamford N, Edozien L (2012) Not-patient and not-visitor: a metasynthesis father's encounters with pregnancy, birth, and maternity care. Midwifery 28(4):362–371

Substance Abuse and Mental Health Services Administration (SAMHSA) (2019) Results from the 2018 national survey on drug use and health: detailed tables. Center for Behavioral Health Statistics and Quality, Rockville. https://www.samhsa.gov/data/sites/default/files/cbhsq-reports/NSDUHDetailedTabs2017/NSDUHDetailedTabs2017.htm

Yogman MW, Garfield CF, the Committee on Psychosocial Aspects of Child and Family Health (2016) Fathers' roles in the care and development of their children: the role of pediatricians. Pediatrics 138(1):e20161128

Open Access This chapter is licensed under the terms of the Creative Commons Attribution 4.0 International License (http://creativecommons.org/licenses/by/4.0/), which permits use, sharing, adaptation, distribution and reproduction in any medium or format, as long as you give appropriate credit to the original author(s) and the source, provide a link to the Creative Commons license and indicate if changes were made.

The images or other third party material in this chapter are included in the chapter's Creative Commons license, unless indicated otherwise in a credit line to the material. If material is not included in the chapter's Creative Commons license and your intended use is not permitted by statutory regulation or exceeds the permitted use, you will need to obtain permission directly from the copyright holder.

Part II
Social Policy

Fathers and Family Leave Policies: What Public Policy Can Do to Support Families

Alison Koslowski and Margaret O'Brien

> *"In a rapidly changing world, we will continue witnessing the growing momentum and recognition of the importance of men for gender equality, reconciling work-family life and impacting the future of their children"* United Nations (2011)

1 Types of Family Leave Available to Fathers

The first global form of paid leave from employment was introduced in 1919 under the auspices of the International Labour Organization's Maternity Protection Convention (ILO 2014). Female focused, this measure was concerned with the health and safety of employed women just before and after childbirth. Subsequently, the late twentieth and early twenty-first centuries have witnessed an expansion of various forms of leave for men and women as managing work-life balance has become more difficult especially as more mothers return to paid employment in their child's first year (Moss and Deven 2015; World Bank 2018). Across the world, many countries have witnessed a deepened role for governments and employers in developing parental leave and other family leave policies, extending their duration and increasing the payment level, for fathers as well as mothers.

In this context, infant care is no longer purely a private family matter as employed parents attempt to accommodate 24/7 infant care within a 24/7 globalised working

---

A. Koslowski (✉)
School of Social and Political Science, University of Edinburgh, Edinburgh, UK
e-mail: alison.koslowski@ed.ac.uk

M. O'Brien
Thomas Coram Research Unit, UCL Institute of Education, University College London, London, UK
e-mail: m.obrien@ucl.ac.uk

© The Author(s) 2022
M. Grau Grau et al. (eds.), *Engaged Fatherhood for Men, Families and Gender Equality*, Contributions to Management Science,
https://doi.org/10.1007/978-3-030-75645-1_7

environment, involving a trade-off between the time spent on infant care and the time spent in the labour market, in the context of maintaining household financial security. At a macro level, a country's family leave regime is an important facilitating setting for achieving a sustainable work-life arrangement for financial wellbeing and family care.

Working parents across countries are entitled to a range of family leave types, the most common being maternity leave, paternity leave, parental leave, and leave to care for children who are ill. Maternity leave is leave generally available to birth mothers only, with other provision available to adoptive parents. Paternity leave is generally available to fathers only (or in some cases a same sex co-parent), usually to be taken soon after the birth of a child, and intended to enable the father to spend time with his partner, new child, and older children. In some countries, parental leave and paternity leave are synonymous. Parental leave is generally intended to give both parents an equal opportunity to spend time caring for a young child. Where available, leave to care for children who are ill would typically be available to both mothers and fathers (Bartel et al. 2018; Blum et al. 2018). Some countries aim for an almost gender-neutral leave policy overall (e.g., Sweden), with most of the leave available designated as parental leave. Other countries have a family leave system that clearly presumes the mother as a primary carer (e.g., Ireland).

Paternity leave and father-targeted parental leave schemes are expanding rapidly, across the world. Parental leave is a period of longer leave available to either parent, usually after maternity or paternity leave finishes, ranging from months to 3 years, and often, but not always, unpaid. Its provision has been found in 66 countries surveyed by ILO, mostly in developed economies, Eastern Europe, and Asia but only paid in 36, most generously in the Nordic countries. Although Sweden was the first country (in 1974) to introduce parental leave open to fathers as well as mothers, Norway was the first country (in 1993) to reserve 4 weeks of well-paid parental leave exclusively for fathers -- the non-transferable "daddy month" (Eydal et al. 2015; see also Kvande's chapter in this volume).

By 2014, the International Labour Organisation (ILO) found a statutory right to paternity leave in 79 of 167 countries, paid in 71 of the cases (ILO 2014). While a global minimum ILO standard on duration of maternity leave exists—14 weeks, met by 53% of countries—no such standard exists for paternity leave, which globally ranges from 1 day to periods over 2 weeks. Company or government payment ranges from strong compensation, as found in Finland with 9 days at 70% of earnings to a minimal flat rate coverage as in the UK (Koslowski et al. 2016).

Leave policies provide job protection for a period of time so that a worker can be available to care for a dependent, and after this period of time, return to employment with the same employer. They can also include an element of wage replacement during this period (Ray et al. 2010). Seen as a key instrument for maintaining the presence of mothers in the labour market (Pronzato 2009; Ciccia and Verloo 2012; Dearing 2016), they are increasingly also seen as a key instrument for increasing the opportunities for fathers to spend more time caring for their young children (O'Brien 2009; Caracciolo di Torella 2014). In addition to supporting gender equality, leave policies can be seen as important policy instruments for supporting child health and well-being, maternal and paternal health and well-being, fertility rates, and various labour market outcomes such as reduced gender pay gaps (Kamerman and Moss 2009; Andersen 2018; Moss et al. 2019).

Leave can be unpaid, paid at a low flat rate similar to social assistance, or paid as a form of (usually approximate) wage replacement. Leave paid at a level that approximates wage replacement, is associated with increased uptake by all parents, but in particular by fathers (Pull and Vogt 2010; Ray et al. 2010; Lapuerta et al. 2011). Sometimes a nominal wage replacement system becomes similar to a low flat rate if ceilings are set too low or are not uprated over time.

Family leave policies can be categorised as either "equality-impeding," "equality-enabling," or as actively "equality-promoting" policies (Brighouse and Wright 2008). As discussed in the following chapter by Kvande, an individual entitlement is equality-promoting, whereas an individual entitlement with a transferable or family entitlement is equality-enabling, and a mother-only leave is equality-impeding. Leave can be available for both parents at the same time, or require them to be the primary carer for this period of leave. Evidence suggests that such immediate and simultaneous father involvement such as that facilitated by paternity leave is relevant to later gender equality outcomes such as female labour market participation (Farré and Gonzalez 2017). However, evidence also suggests that fathers taking leave alone on parental leave is correlated with more gender equal sharing of childcare throughout the life course (O'Brien and Wall 2017).

Across the world paid leave from employment policies continue to evolve. Their design is responsive to new cultural, economic, and political issues as well as early influences from health and social insurance and post-war, welfare regime path dependencies.

2 Policy Design and Leave Use by Fathers

In some countries, men's behaviour has been receptive to public policies developed to extend their engagement with infants. Key ingredients which enhance utilization appear to be high-income replacement combined with designated father-targeted or reserved schemes rates. Evidence shows that blocks of time which are labelled "daddy days" or "father's quota" are attractive to men and their partners (Eydal et al. 2015). Designs with low-income replacement or based on maternal transfer, both features of the UK's additional paternity leave and its successor, *Shared Parental Leave*, are known not to encourage paternal uptake.

Since the late 1990s, strategies to enhance the visibility of fathers' entitlements to parental leave have accelerated, particularly in Europe. There has been experimentation with a range of policy instruments, based on incentive, penalty, and even compulsion. Part of the policy innovation has involved a form of re-branding where periods of leave time within individual or family entitlements have become reserved for fathers or father-targeted (sometimes referred to as a "father's quota"). Through the reconfiguration, fathers' access to a period of parental leave, previously implicit, within an individual gender neutral entitlement, becomes explicit. The group includes the well-established father-sensitive regimes embedded in the majority, but not all, of the Nordic countries, and the enhanced schemes come from countries as diverse as Germany, Portugal, Spain, and Slovenia.

Within Nordic countries, one of the most innovative father-targeted leave entitlements so far developed, in terms of combined time (3 months) and economic compensation (80% of prior salary) is to be found in Iceland (Einarsdóttir and Pétursdóttir 2007). In 2000, the Icelandic government introduced a total of 9 months paid post-birth leave (to be taken in the first 18 months) organized into three parts: 3 months for mothers (non-transferable), 3 months for fathers (non-transferable) and 3 months which could be transferred between parents as they choose. In addition there is 13 weeks unpaid parental leave available each year for each parent. The Bill *Maternity, Paternity and Parental Leave* was passed by the Icelandic government in 2000, following several years' deliberation about men's societal role and gender equality, including a government committee on the "Gender Role of Men" (Eydal and Gíslason 2008).

The Iceland 3 + 3 + 3 month model has significantly shifted male behaviour in a relatively short period of time. By 2006, over 90% of Icelandic fathers took parental leave. Gíslason (2007: 15) notes: "Probably, there have never been more Icelandic fathers active in caring for their children than there are today." Kolbeinn et al. (2008: 153) describe how the normative pattern is for Icelandic men to take most of their dedicated days but typically not to utilise the shared component: "You may well be regarded as weird if you don't use the paternity leave, but the same does not hold for using the shared entitlement." However, leave taking by fathers declined following the 2009 economic crisis, in particular those (higher earners) most hit by the implementation of a ceiling on the flat rate payment (Júlíusdóttir et al. 2018).

In the same decade, a radical break in family policy to create an incentive for fathers to take leave was introduced in Germany against a leave policy background which supported mothers to stay out of the labour market for 3 years after the birth of a child (Erler 2009). A new highly paid 2 months, "Elterngeld," was added to a shorter 12-month parental leave period. The reform concentrated high payment onto a shorter 12-month parental leave period, with an extra 2 months of high payment if fathers take 2 months of leave. The proportion of fathers taking leave more than tripled from 3.5% in the last quarter of 2006 to 13.7% in the second quarter of 2008 and has risen incrementally since (Blum et al. 2016).

In general, take up of leave increases as household income increases. This is in part linked to eligibility to leave being higher for those on steady (non-precarious) incomes, as picked up by Ratele in this volume. In the UK, for example, not all workers qualify for leave entitlements, due to being self-employed or not having a certain kind of employment contract. In addition, some fathers may be entitled to enhanced leave entitlements as a result of their employer offering extra-statutory occupational benefits, or linked to collective agreements. In such cases, leave uptake maybe facilitated by this top-up in provision.

In summary, fathers' access to individual and paid entitlement is strongly associated with increased take up of the leave (e.g., Haas and Rostgaard 2011; Duvander and Johansson 2012), though this design needs to be complemented by sustained political work and cultural change. Other incentives include the couple being eligible for an extended duration of leave if fathers take a certain amount of leave (e.g., as is the case in Austria, Croatia, France, Germany, Italy, and Portugal). It is also worth mentioning that successful leave systems are integrated with public childcare systems. For example, in Denmark, Finland, Germany, Slovenia and Sweden, the maximum duration of leave available to parents dovetails with the provision of publically subsidised childcare, so that there is no childcare gap for parents to have to fill.

3 Impact of Fathers on Leave

Whilst the study of fathers on leave has been of interest to researchers now for some decades (e.g., Haas 1992), empirical enquiry into the specific personal and family experiences and impact of maternal, paternal, and paternity leave is still relatively undeveloped. Macht explores in her chapter in this volume the dynamics of father-child emotional wellbeing. There is still surprisingly little empirical research on what parents "do" during parental leave, and even less specifically on what fathers "do"' (Seward et al. 2006; Haas and Hwang 2008). As such, understanding the processes by which parental leave may operate to promote or hinder gender equity or child and family well-being are still unclear. In part, this is linked to a lack of data on parental leave use.

In addition, in attempting to understand the impact of parental leave policies there are important macro- and micro-level methodological considerations. At a macro level, parental leave is a black box of diverse arrangements, which vary both within and between countries despite common nomenclatures. As mentioned above, eligibility criteria also vary; although, in general, they tend to exclude insecure and informal workers. Also, in attempting to understand the specific impact of parental leave it is important to contextualize parental leave as part of societal level public investment.

In most countries, public investment in paid leave policies is often highly associated with more general public spending on family benefits as a proportion of GDP (Adema and Ali 2015). As such, claims from macro-level studies of impact have been academically controversial, with pathways of influence difficult to disentangle, particularly as any gains can be linked to prior characteristics of fathers (gender egalitarian and child-oriented) rather than the policy itself. Methodological issues, for example about sample selectivity, are also relevant for micro-level analyses, although qualitative research has the advantage of fine-tuned dimensional sampling not always available for large-scale administrative or survey data sets.

Where impact research does exist the focus has been mainly on the effects of maternity leave provision with several studies showing child health benefits in, for instance, immunization uptake and employment retention (Tanaka 2005; Han et al.

2009). Positive health gains for children are maximized when the maternity leave is paid, provided in a job-secure context, and with a duration of at least 10 weeks.

In terms of fathers and leave, the logic has been that giving fathers the opportunity to spend more time at home through leave after childbirth should result in greater involvement in domestic life and childcare. More studies on fathers taking leave have been published over last decade spanning both comparative and within country policy analysis, particularly concerning implementation and impact at a macro-level (e.g., Nepomnyaschy and Waldfogel 2007; Huerta et al. 2013; Kotsadam and Finseraas 2011; Rege and Solli 2010; Bünning 2015).

The Nordic countries and Germany have provided fertile ground for "before and after" studies of impact at a country level (Ekberg et al. 2005; Duvander and Johansson 2012; Schober 2014; Bünning 2015). The natural experiment paradigm, which has framed many of these studies, has produced evidence of greater engagement of fathers in the care of children after policy reforms, in comparison with fathers who do not take leave. For instance, Kotsadam and Finseraas (2011) found that men whose last child was born in the year after Norway's father quota introduction in 1993 reported 11% lower levels of conflict over household division of labour and were 50% more likely to share in clothes washing than men whose last child was born just before the reform. However, there has been some concern that greater engagement by fathers who have taken leave may be short-lived rather than long-term and so have a weak impact on the gendering of care. Indeed, German longitudinal analysis by Schober (2014) suggested that fathers increased their participation in childcare only temporarily during the first year after taking parental leave, but subsequent research has suggested sustained longer term effects up until the third year of the child's life (Bünning 2015; Reimer et al. 2015).

Notably, Reimer et al.'s (2015) study also found a large effect of paid parental leave taken alone by the father. In particular, an observed relationship between fathers' use of leave and their time for childcare only persisted when at least one leave month was taken alone by the fathers: an important selection criterion for this book's qualitative sample. Both Bünning (2015)and Reimer et al.'s (2015) studies were able to use nationally representative German panel data sets (*German Socio-Economic Panel* and *Families in Germany*) which include items on duration and whether leave is taken alone or with a partner. Also, the data sets allow the same fathers to be tracked before and after they take parental leave which enables exploration of selection effects.

Other country level natural experiments have assessed "duration" effects of fathers' leave on a wide range of outcomes. In a further Norwegian case, it has been found that 4 weeks' exposure to the leave quota during a child's first year was associated with a 1–3% drop in fathers' earnings over the next 5 years (Rege and Solli 2010). In an another study of duration and fathers' engagement in childcare, research in Australia has found that taking some leave (2 or 4 weeks) increased the likelihood of fathers engaging in sole care at week-ends when the child was older (4–9 months) (Hosking et al. 2010). Notably, studies are emerging on child outcomes in families where fathers do not take leave in countries where it is expected that they do; for instance, Flacking et al. (2010) found that Swedish infants whose fathers *did not* take family leave in the first year were significantly less likely to be breast fed at 2- and 6-months.

Although the body of macro-level research is still emergent, it does suggest that fathers' as well as mothers' leave taking has direct as well as indirect influences on infants, family, and work life. Moreover, there are indications that leave taking alone by fathers may be especially salient in priming subsequent greater engagement in the care of infants. Earlier qualitative studies, primarily in Nordic countries, have suggested that being home alone sensitizes or enhances fathers' awareness of infant life "slow time" (Brandth and Kvande 2002). A recent set of cross-national case studies of fathers taking leave alone (O'Brien and Wall 2017) has extended these observations into a wider set of country contexts.

4 A Good Quality of Infant Life

Leave policies are instruments for realising children's rights to both their parents' time and care (Haas and Hwang 1999). Infant life has not traditionally been considered the province of social policy, possibly because of an historic gendered assumption (but an enduring one—see chapter by Borgkvist) that only mothers can provide the permitting circumstances. In the field of parental leave policies, the focus has not so much been on the state of infancy per se but on the parenting or care processes perceived as necessary for infant life.

In terms of classic father involvement constructs in the developmental psychology literature, leave available for fathers can be conceptualised as a way to enhancing attachment by potentiating paternal availability and interaction with infants and young children (Lamb et al. 1987). But specification of the dimensions of a good quality of life for an infant is fraught with political dilemmas, economic considerations, and, of course, relates to the models of optimal infant development dominant in any one culture at a particular historical juncture. As Waldfogel (2006: 180) states: "The tensions between respecting choice, promoting quality, and supporting employment are higher in the first few years of life than at any other period."

Contemporary hallmarks of "a good enough" infancy depend to some extent on cultural factors and the theoretical models of psychologists or sociologists. Psychologists tend to research the personal characteristics of the parents in providing the care environment, such as their parenting style, whereas sociologists pay more attention to resource and community influences on child development. An ecological-parental capital approach (Pleck 2007) requires a multi-layered and multi-dimensional framework, attempting to incorporate governmental, community, family, and individual levels for understanding infancy.

In the ecological context of early childhood and parental employment, the quality of life which infants experience, is made up of a complex set of processes and resources (some of which are explored by Macht in this volume). The daily life of the infant is organized around regular feeding on 6–8 (or more) occasions in a 24 h cycle, holding, soothing, diaper changing, bathing, dressing as well as sociable interaction, in between regular phases of infant sleeping. In this highly dependent phase of childhood the infant needs at least one carer (not necessarily the same person, although cultural norms vary) to be in close physical proximity. A century of psychological research evidence shows that the nature of adult care (in particular its sensitivity, stability, and attentiveness) fosters infant sociability although there is not a linear association between parental time availability and the quality of emergent human relationships (Cabrera and Tamis-LeMonda 2013). At a more distal level, the infant needs economic care for material resources. In essence an adequate quality of infant life, as discussed in Yogman's chapter in this volume, requires both economic and emotional investment.

5 Supporting Fathers in the Workplace to Take Leave

Far fewer eligible fathers take leave, in contrast to eligible mothers (Blum et al. 2018). Clearly then, new mothers and fathers have a very different experience in how they harmonise their work and their family responsibilities. Consider your own workplace, it is likely that you can quickly identify the leave-taking norms and that they will be different for mothers and fathers. This is discussed further in the following chapters by Bueno and Oh and by Borgkvist. While many organisations have programmes to support new mothers—offering them mentoring, back-to-work schemes and maternity replacement cover—this support intent is typically not available to new fathers.

Fathers often report feeling worried and even embarrassed to use offered leave entitlements (Koslowski and Kadar-Satat 2019; Moran and Koslowski 2019). Fathers are worried about what it might mean for their career prospects if they go against what is normal in their workplace (Rudman and Mescher 2013; Tanquerel and Grau-Grau 2020). A number of policies can help with this, including making sure fathers have adequate cover for their job responsibilities whilst on leave, and insuring that individual line managers support a father's efforts to combine work and family life (including being aware of who is a father of an infant). Fathers also need time from work to attend antenatal appointments.

Employers who are not offering paid family leave may be choosing not to do so because they worry that it could be too expensive. Research suggests that costs may balance out because of the boost in staff engagement and retention (see also chapter by Macht). Increasingly, companies with higher participation in programmes designed to support working fathers have higher employee retention and job satisfaction (Appelbaum and Milkman 2011). The good news is that employers should experience a double benefit from supporting fathers in the workplace. In addition to attracting and retaining talented fathers, they also create opportunities for mothers. As working fatherhood becomes normalised, women are less often penalised for the ways they seek to combine work and family. Because of this, firms with strong policies and cultures supporting working parents should see their gender pay gaps lessen.

Low-income fathers are even less likely to take meaningful time off, feeling unpaid or reduced-pay time off might adversely impact their family's finances. In the absence of well-paid family leave, fathers are likely instead to take paid vacation time, therefore taking less leave to spend time with their children than they would be legally entitled to.

6 Practical Recommendations

The world of work and family life has transformed since the ILO's Maternity Protection Convention in 1919. As well as support for employed mothers, paid paternity leave and father targeted parental leave schemes are now important measures for parents of very young children in their daily negotiation of care, time, and money. While governments, organisations, and civil societal actors are indeed attempting to fit fathers into work-family polices the "cost" of male care can hinder innovation especially in uncertain economic times.

Unchallenged maternalism is commonplace, and so this gender gap in leave provision and take up is more socially acceptable than in many other parts of social life (such as education or the gender pay gap). Despite this, "Fathers undertaking a more active role in caregiving is likely to be one of the most significant social developments of the twenty-first century" (International Labour Organization 2014: 1).

More research is needed to understand maternal and paternal policies in unison, as what is available to mothers and fathers affects how caring is shared by parents. In particular, the interaction of maternity and paternity leave arrangements and experiences requires further scrutiny. We know that dual-earner couples negotiate parental leave use in part depending on both partners' job characteristics. Similarly, more mixed methods research programmes, combining qualitative and quantitative designs, are required in order to explore underlying familial and work-place cultural processes. Bueno and Oh consider this couple dimension across different country contexts in their chapter in this volume.

Key Recommendations for:

– **Policy makers** wishing to increase the proportion of fathers taking leave would be to consider the success of reforms in Germany and Iceland, as presented earlier, and ensure that there are clear incentives to families for fathers to take leave. Key ingredients which enhance leave utilisation are high-income replacement and the presence of an individual entitlement and a non-transferable component. Branding matters: Father-targeted reserved schemes such as "daddy days" are effective.
– **Organizations** should examine and challenge their gendered cultural practices around take up by fathers at all levels: CEO, supervisors, and peers. Fathers are parents as well as employees. Men's behaviour is very receptive to workplace culture and norms about what makes a good worker and a good father.

- **Fathers** themselves: Given the growing evidence base that early father involvement matters for child development and couple wellbeing, be bold, be pioneers, take the leave you are entitled to!

References

Adema W, Ali N (2015) Recent changes in family outcomes and policies in OECD countries: the impact of the economic crisis. Community Work Fam 18(2):145–166

Andersen SH (2018) Paternity leave and the motherhood penalty: new causal evidence. J Marriage Fam 80:1125–1143

Appelbaum E, Milkman R (2011) Paid family leave pays off in California. Harv Bus Rev. https://hbr.org/2011/01/paid-family-leave-pays-off-in

Bartel AP, Rossin-Slater M, Ruhm CJ, Stearns J, Waldfogel J (2018) Paid family leave, fathers' leave-taking, and leave-sharing in dual-earner households. J Policy Anal Manage 37(1):10–37

Blum S, Erler D, Reimer T (2016) Germany country note. In: Koslowski A, Blum S, Moss P (eds) International review of leave policies and research 2016. http://www.leavenetwork.org/lp_and_r_reports/

Blum S, Koslowski A, Macht A, Moss P (2018) International review of leave policies and research 2018. https://www.leavenetwork.org/fileadmin/user_upload/k_leavenetwork/annual_reviews/Leave_Review_2018.pdf

Brandth B, Kvande E (2002) Reflexive fathers: negotiating parental leave and working life. Gend Work Organ 9(2):186–203

Brighouse H, Wright EO (2008) Strong gender egalitarianism. Polit Soc 36(3):360–372

Bünning M (2015) What happens after the 'daddy months'? Fathers' involvement in paid work, childcare, and housework after taking parental leave in Germany. Eur Sociol Rev 31(6):738–748. https://doi.org/10.1093/esr/jcv072

Cabrera NJ, Tamis-LeMonda CS (2013) Handbook of father involvement: multidisciplinary perspectives. Routledge, New York

Caracciolo di Torella E (2014) Brave new fathers for a brave new world? Fathers as caregivers in an evolving European Union. Eur Law J 20(1):88–106

Ciccia R, Verloo M (2012) Parental leave regulations and the persistence of the male breadwinner model: using fuzzy-set ideal type analysis to assess gender equality in an enlarged Europe. J Eur Soc Policy 22(5):507–528

Dearing H (2016) Gender equality in the division of work: how to assess European leave policies regarding their compliance with an ideal leave model. J Eur Soc Policy 26(3):234–247

Duvander A-Z, Johansson M (2012) What are the effects of reforms promoting fathers' parental leave use? J Eur Soc Policy 22(3):319–330

Einarsdóttir T, Pétursdóttir GM (2007) The Iceland report. In: Moss P, Wall K (eds) International review of leave policies and related research 2007 employment relations research series no. 80. Department for Business Enterprise and Regulatory Reform (BERR), London, pp 179–186. https://www.leavenetwork.org/fileadmin/user_upload/k_leavenetwork/annual_reviews/2007_annual_report.pdf

Ekberg J, Eriksson R, Friebel G (2005) Parental leave: a policy evaluation of the Swedish "Daddy-Month" reform. IZA, Bonn. http://ftp.iza.org/dp1617.pdf

Erler (2009) Germany: taking a nordic turn? In: Kamerman SB, Moss P (eds) The politics of parental leave policies: children, gender, parenting and the labour market. Policy Press, Bristol, pp 119–130

Eydal GB, Gíslason IV (2008) Paid parental leave in Iceland—history and context. In: Eydal GB, Gíslason IV (eds) Equal rights to earn and care—parental leave in Iceland. Félagsvísindastofnun Háskóla Íslands, Reykjavík

Eydal GB, Gíslason IV, Rostgaard T, Brandth B, Duvander A-Z, Lammi-Taskula J (2015) Trends in parental leave in the nordic countries: has the forward march of gender equality halted? Community Work Fam 18(2):167–181

Farré L, Gonzalez L (2017) The effects of paternity leave on fertility and labor market outcomes. Institute of Labor Economics (IZA) discussion paper no. 10865. https://www.iza.org/publications/dp/10865/the-effects-of-paternity-leave-on-fertility-and-labor-market-outcomes

Flacking R, Dykes F, Ewald U (2010) The influence of fathers' socioeconomic status and paternity leave on breastfeeding duration: a population-based cohort study. Scandinavian J Public Health 38(4):337–343

Gíslason IV (2007) Parental leave in iceland bringing the fathers in. Developments in the wake of new legislation in 2000. Centre for gender equality, ministry of social affairs

Haas L (1992) Equal parenthood and social policy: a study of parental leave in Sweden. State University of New York Press, Albany

Haas L, Hwang P (1999) Parental leave in Sweden. In: Moss P, Deven F (eds) Parental leave: progress or pitfall? Research and policy issues in Europe, vol 35. NIDI/CGBS Publications, The Hague, pp 45–68

Haas L, Hwang P (2008) The impact of taking parental leave on fathers' participation in childcare and relationships with children: lessons from Sweden. Community Work Fam 11(1):85–104

Haas L, Rostgaard T (2011) Fathers' rights to paid parental leave in the Nordic countries: consequences for the gendered division of leave. Community Work Fam 14(2):177–195

Han W-J, Ruhm C, Waldfogel J (2009) Parental leave policies and parents' employment and leave-taking. J Policy Anal Manage 23(1):29–54

Hosking A, Whitehouse G, Baxter J (2010) Duration of leave and resident fathers' involvement in infant care in Australia. J Marriage Fam 72(5):1301–1316

Huerta MdC, Adema W, Baxter J, Han W-J, Lausten M, Lee RH, Waldfogel J (2013) Fathers' leave, fathers' involvement and child development: are they related? Evidence from four OECD countries. OECD social, employment and migration working papers, no 140. https://doi.org/10.1787/5k4dlw9w6czq-en

ILO (International Labour Organization) (2014) Maternity and paternity at work: law and practice across the world. ILO, Geneva

Júlíusdóttir Ó, Rafnsdóttir GL, Einarsdóttir Þ (2018) Top managers and the gendered interplay of organizations and family life: the case of Iceland. Gend Manage 33(8):602–622

Kamerman SB, Moss P (eds) (2009) The politics of parental leave policies: children, gender, parenting and the labour market. Policy Press, Bristol

Kolbeinn S, Eydal GB, Gíslason IV (2008) Summary and conclusions. In: Eydal GB, Gíslason IV (eds) Equal rights to earn and care—parental leave in Iceland. Félagsvísindastofnun Háskóla Íslands, Reykjavík, pp 97–121

Koslowski A, Kadar-Satat G (2019) Fathers at work: explaining the gaps between entitlement to leave and uptake. Community Work Fam 22(2):129–145

Koslowski A, Blum S, Moss P (2016) International review of leave policies and research 2016. https://www.leavenetwork.org/fileadmin/user_upload/k_leavenetwork/annual_reviews/2016_Full_draft_20_July.pdf

Kotsadam A, Finseraas H (2011) The state intervenes in the battle of the sexes: causal effects of paternity leave. Soc Sci Res 40(4):1611–1622

Lamb ME, Pleck J, Charnov EL, Levine J (1987) A biosocial perspective on paternal behavior and involvement. In: Lancaster JB, Altmann J, Rossi AS, Sherrod LR (eds) Parenting across the lifespan: biosocial dimensions. Aldine de Gruyter, Hawthorne, pp 111–142

Lapuerta I, Baizán P, González M (2011) Individual and institutional constraints: an analysis of parental leave use and duration in Spain. Popul Res Policy Rev 30(2):185–210. https://doi.org/10.1007/s11113-010-9185-y

Moran J, Koslowski A (2019) Making use of work-family balance entitlements: how to support fathers with combining employment and caregiving. Community Work Fam 22(1):111–128

Moss P, Deven F (2015) Leave policies in challenging times: reviewing the decade 2004–2014. Community Work Fam 18(2):137–144. https://doi.org/10.1080/13668803.2015.1021094

Moss P, Duvander A-Z, Koslowski A (2019) Parental leave and beyond. Policy Press, Bristol
Nepomnyaschy L, Waldfogel J (2007) Paternity leave and fathers' involvement with their young children. Community Work Fam 10(4):427–453
O'Brien M (2009) Fathers, parental leave policies and infant quality of life: international perspectives and policy impact. Ann Am Acad Pol Soc Sci 624(1):190–213
O'Brien M, Wall K (eds) (2017) Comparative perspectives on work-life balance and gender equality: fathers on leave alone. Springer International Publishing, Cham
Pleck JH (2007) Why could father involvement benefit children? Theoretical perspectives. Appl Dev Sci 11(4):196–203
Pronzato C (2009) Return to work after childbirth: does parental leave matter in Europe? Rev Econ Househ 7(4):341–360
Pull K, Vogt A-C (2010) Much ado about nothing? The effects of the German parental leave reform. Soziale Welt-Zeitschrift Fur Sozialwissenschaftliche Forschung Und Praxis 61(2):121–137
Ray RR, Gornick JC, Schmitt J (2010) Who cares? Assessing generosity and gender equality in parental leave policy designs in 21 countries. J Eur Soc Policy 20(3):196–216
Rege M, Solli I (2010) The impact of paternity leave on long-term father involvement. University of Stavanger, Stavanger
Reimer T, Warnholtz L, Pfau-Effinger B (2015) Daddy months' as a sustainable policy? Discerning the long-term influence of a new parental leave legislation in Germany on fathers' engagement in childcare. Paper presented at workshop "fathers' involvement in the life course" Berlin, September 3 and 4, 2015
Rudman LA, Mescher K (2013) Penalizing men who request a family leave: is flexibility stigma a femininity stigma? J Soc Issues 69(2):322–340
Schober PS (2014) Parental leave and domestic work of mothers and fathers. A longitudinal study of two reforms in west Germany. J Soc Policy 43(2):351–372
Seward RR, Yeatts DE, Zottarelli LK, Fletcher RG (2006) Fathers taking parental leave and their involvement with children. Community Work Fam 9(1):1–9
Tanaka S (2005) Parental Leaves and child health across OECD countries. Econ J 115(501):F7–F28
Tanquerel S, Grau-Grau M (2020) Unmasking work-family balance barriers and strategies among working fathers in the workplace. Organization 27(5):680–700. https://doi.org/10.1177/1350508419838692
United Nations (2011) Men in families and family policy in a changing world. UN, New York. http://social.un.org/index/Family/Publications.aspx
Waldfogel J (2006) What children need? Harvard University Press, Cambridge
World Bank (2018) Women, business and the law report. International Bank for Reconstruction and Development—The World Bank, Washington, DC. http://wbl.worldbank.org/

Open Access This chapter is licensed under the terms of the Creative Commons Attribution 4.0 International License (http://creativecommons.org/licenses/by/4.0/), which permits use, sharing, adaptation, distribution and reproduction in any medium or format, as long as you give appropriate credit to the original author(s) and the source, provide a link to the Creative Commons license and indicate if changes were made.

The images or other third party material in this chapter are included in the chapter's Creative Commons license, unless indicated otherwise in a credit line to the material. If material is not included in the chapter's Creative Commons license and your intended use is not permitted by statutory regulation or exceeds the permitted use, you will need to obtain permission directly from the copyright holder.

Individual Parental Leave for Fathers: Promoting Gender Equality in Norway

Elin Kvande

1 Introduction

How to increase fathers' use of parental leave is a relevant question for countries that want to promote men's involvement in childrearing and gender equality more broadly. As countries are searching for instruments that can effectively promote a greater involvement of fathers in care work, the Nordic parental leave experiences may be useful. The Nordic countries, Denmark, Finland, Iceland, Norway and Sweden, have followed similar trajectories of development, not exactly following the same timeline, but clearly inspired by each other. All of them have introduced special incentives for fathers to use leave after having experienced that simply offering shared parental leave was not enough to get fathers to use it. Norway was the first country to introduce a fathers' quota in 1993, followed by Sweden 2 years later, Denmark in 1998 (until 2002 when it was discontinued) and Iceland in 2000. Finland had a bonus system providing fathers with 12 extra days if they used 12 days of the shared parental leave. This was changed to an individual, non-transferable right, a father's quota in 2013.

In comparative research on gender equality, the Nordic welfare states are analysed as including regulations that support both working mothers and fathers (Pascall 2012). Equality between men and women is encouraged through an individual earner-carer regime (Sainsbury 1999). Important policy measures in this regime include publicly funded parental leave schemes, universal, high quality daycare, and access to reduced work hours. These are the same social arrangements

---

E. Kvande (✉)
Department of Sociology and Political Science, Norwegian University of Science and Technology, Trondheim, Norway
e-mail: elin.kvande@ntnu.no

© The Author(s) 2022
M. Grau Grau et al. (eds.), *Engaged Fatherhood for Men, Families and Gender Equality*, Contributions to Management Science,
https://doi.org/10.1007/978-3-030-75645-1_8

as Gornick and Meyers (2009) pinpoint as important in order to create a dual-earner/dual-caregiver society.

A comprehensive research literature on parental leave has evolved during the last 20 years. In fact, the study of parental leave is in the forefront of comparative social policy research focusing on gender equality (Ray et al. 2010). This strong interest in parental leave policies must be understood on the basis of these policies having the potential to change women's position in employment and engaging men in caregiving. Parental leave policy rights and designs vary substantially across countries (Blum et al. 2018) and the effect of the different leave systems on gender equality is also debated (Morgan 2008; Moss and Deven 1999; Moss et al. 2019).

In their analysis of what is needed to achieve "strong gender equality" in family and working life, Brighouse and Wright (2008) distinguish between three types of policies: (1) equality-impeding policies (e.g., unpaid caregiving leaves), (2) equality-enabling policies (e.g., paid caregiving leaves given to families), and (3) equality-promoting policies (e.g., paid caregiving leaves given to individuals rather than families). According to them, shared parental leave granted to the family enables parents to adopt egalitarian strategies, but do not represent strong incentives for fathers to use the leave rights. Leave policies that promote equality are exemplified by paid leave granted to individual parents, which lapses if it is not used. Brighouse and Wright find that this type of leave is necessary for breaking down the cultural barriers to gender equality in family and working life.

Using this as a point of departure, this paper will describe the design elements of the Norwegian parental leave system for fathers and examine how it works as a regulatory measure to promote equality in care work. The paper will thus address the request put forward by Ray et al. (2010), in which they point out that surprisingly little research has been carried out that links the design of leave policies to their outcomes. There are especially few empirical studies assessing which parental leave schemes are gender egalitarian by design (Bartel et al. 2018; Dearing 2016), and this has left a gap in cross-national literature on leave policies.

2 Designing Individualized Parental Leave for Fathers

Research on social policy in European welfare states has increasingly focused on the norm of individualization, thus indicating a social policy that treats women and men as individual workers (Lewis 2015). Similarly Daly (2011) suggests applying the concept of "individualization processes" in order to capture change in family policies which implies a shift away from policy assumptions based on the male breadwinner/female carer model and, instead, expecting all adults to be both breadwinners and carers. Individualistic policy designs, however, do not necessarily include gender equality (Ray et al. 2010). Therefore, how social policies relate to this parameter dictates whether they are classified as supporting an individualistic or familistic model according to Daly (2011).

Research has documented that to give parental leave rights to individuals, rather than to families, is more effective when it comes to getting fathers to take leave (Duvander and Lammi-Taskula 2012; Haas and Rostgaard 2011; Eydal and Gíslason 2013). In their analyses of institutions that support gender equality in parenthood and employment, Gornick and Meyers (2009) point to the importance of individualized parental leave, as well as the principle of non-transferability, as in the fathers' quota. They suggest a period of 6 months leave to each parent, which cannot be transferred to the other parent. This is also what was suggested in a white paper produced by an expert committee for the Norwegian government in 2017 (NOU 2017).

The international literature on specific policy provisions for parental leave is expanding (McKay and Doucet 2010), particularly concerning fathers. Within research based on Nordic experiences, there is a consensus that parental leave rights given to individuals, rather than to families, are most likely to get fathers to take leave (Rostgaard 2002; Duvander and Lammi-Taskula 2012; Haas and Rostgaard 2011; Eydal et al. 2015). The father's quota in Nordic countries has been successful in involving fathers in taking care of their young babies (Haas and Rostgaard 2011; Brandth and Kvande 1998, 2018). These results are also found internationally (Moss and Kamerman 2009; Gornick and Meyers 2009; Miller 2013; Harvey and Tremblay 2019). Documented findings from a number of countries have shown that the shared parental leave (and thus optional for fathers) is mostly used by mothers (O'Brien and Wall 2017; Ray et al. 2010; Fougner 2012; Gíslason and Eydal 2013). Fathers taking leave challenge the traditional gender norm that mothers are the primary caregivers of small children.

This chapter explores fathers' understandings and experiences with the father's quota (i.e., the leave programs), which, according to Brighouse and Wright (2008), may promote equality. Studies of the Norwegian leave programme comparing the father's quota to the more optional schemes of shared parental leave and cash allowances were conducted some years after the introduction of the father's quota (Brandth and Kvande 2009) This research documented that mandatory leave for fathers made it easier for them to use the father's quota to set boundaries against the demands of work, thus reserving uninterrupted father-child time. It was also pointed out that a statutory earmarking of the father's quota lifts the decision of who should take leave from the family up to the institutional level, where it would apply to "all" fathers. The father's quota became a pre-negotiated right for men also in terms of the workplace, and it was supposed to eliminate the need to negotiate individually with the employer over the use of the father's quota.

This chapter examines the impact of the expansion and maturation of the father's quota. Using Brighouse and Wright's conceptual framework the chapter explores how the Norwegian leave policies which are an individual right are experienced by the fathers in our latest study.

3 The Norwegian Parental Leave System for Fathers

In 1978 the leave rights in Norway were changed so that most of the leave could be shared between the parents, moving away from the idea of maternity leave as a special right only for women. By granting fathers the right to shared leave, legislation signaled a new view of men's responsibilities and participation in caregiving. In the years to come, fathers, however, rarely used shared parental leave so the policy did not promote more equal parenting. To advance that goal, an earmarked, non-transferable leave of 4 weeks for fathers was introduced in 1993. At the same time the total leave period was extended from 35 to 42 weeks with 100% wage compensation. Proponents argued that a quota would give a strong signal to parents as well as to employers that men as well as women are parents with obligations and rights as caregivers. Children's need for their fathers was also emphasized in the debate. Since then the father's quota has developed gradually, extended to 14 weeks and then reduced to 10 weeks in 2014 following the politics of the parties in power.

Both mothers and fathers have individual, non-transferable leave rights in addition to shared leave rights. Currently, mothers have an earmarked period of 13 weeks, of which 3 must be taken before the child's birth. Beginning in 2014, 26 weeks are sharable between mothers and fathers. If the parents choose lower pay (80% of wages), the leave is extended by 10 weeks. The fathers' quota is now 10 weeks. In addition to parental leave, fathers have 2 weeks of paternity leave to be taken after the birth of the child to assist the mother. There are no public records of the usage of paternity leave, as wage compensation is based on collective agreements and paid by employers.

The fathers' quota gives male employees the right and obligation to provide care during the child's early years of life. The principal aim of this leave is to break away from the norm that men serve as breadwinners and women as caregivers even if they, too, are employed outside the home. The system is based on the principle that parents "earn" the right through participation in working life. To qualify for parental leave, both mothers and fathers have to be in the workforce for 6 of the last 10 months prior to the birth. If the mother is not eligible, the father loses his right to the fathers' quota but not to the shared leave if the mother returns to studies or takes on employment. This type of eligibility encourages both parents to combine work and family obligations as it is built on a model in which both mothers and fathers are employed. Since its introduction, the fathers' quota has been widely used, and more than 90% of eligible fathers use all or part of this leave (Kitterød et al. 2017). Mothers take most of the shared leave days, and, for most couples, mothers' leave is considerably longer than fathers'.

4 Data and Method

The analysis is based on a qualitative study in which 22 fathers who had taken parental leave were interviewed in 2012 and 2013. The interviews were carried out during the second year after the child's birth. Thus, the fathers in the sample had rights to 10 or 12 weeks of individual leave and 27 or 26 weeks of shared leave if they chose 100% compensation. If they chose the 80% compensation option, the leave would have been prolonged accordingly. The fathers were recruited by contact with various workplaces and then snowballing. The interviewees had to have become fathers after the fathers' quota was expanded to 10 weeks in 2009, as we were interested in their experiences of relatively long leaves. The length of the leave taken by the sample varied; most fathers had taken the father's quota of 10 or 12 weeks, but 8 had also taken all or part of the shared parental leave.

The research team endeavoured to find interviewees with varied social backgrounds. Half had higher education (masters level), while the other half either had a medium level education at the bachelor level (6) or no education beyond high school (5). The fathers had a wide range of occupations, including engineers, artisans, teachers, office workers, consultants, and administrative, healthcare, and technical staff. They worked in organizations of various sizes and composition.

As Norwegian leave rights are employment based (i.e., accrued by the participation of both parents in working life), all the fathers and most of their children's mothers (except for three) were in paid employment prior to the birth of their child and had a right to parental leave. Half of the fathers were employed by private companies, but only one was self-employed, and one, a student, was temporarily employed. Except for this father, all worked full time. All the fathers lived together with the mother and their child, and the child who triggered the interview could be the father's first, second, or third child. Most fathers were in their 30s, though they ranged between 27 and 43. Eight of the fathers (36%) had taken shared parental leave. Two of them had taken all the shared parental leave available, as the mothers were not eligible due either to having returned to work or school.

The interviews were semi-structured and lasted between 1 and 2 h. The data was collected by a research team, in which the author participated. To preserve anonymity, the full name and contact details of the interviewees were not recorded, and fictitious names have been used. The fathers were mostly interviewed in their homes. The fathers' understandings were based on their own experiences and what they observed with colleagues and friends. The recorded transcripts were examined to identify each father's stories about their experiences at their respective workplaces. We also asked hypothetical questions about what would have happened if there were no father's quota. The next stage was interpreting these themes in a dialogue with the literature. The findings are illustrated by quotations.

5 Experiencing the Fathers' Quota Design

5.1 The Fathers' Quota as a Norm

The fathers' quota enjoys a high degree of support among fathers in Norway (Hamre 2017), and studies on fathers' quota usage have pointed out that it has become a norm among men in Norway to take leave when they have become fathers (Halrynjo and Kitterød 2016; Naz 2010). Our findings also support this claim.

"There was no doubt that I should take the fathers' quota," said Steinar, an engineer with two daughters. According to Ivar, "For fathers to have 12 weeks is quite natural in a way.... It has become incorporated." Their viewpoints illustrate that the fathers' quota is a matter of fact. Twenty-five years after it was introduced, taking leave seems to be taken for granted among fathers in Norway. That it is based in law, earmarked, and non-transferable identifies this leave with fathers and defines it as their right and 'property.'

It is also interpreted as an obligation and seen as a signal from the welfare state that fathers are expected to engage in taking care of small children. "Society reacts if you don't take it, right," Harold said. Lars, an engineer, claimed that the quota "feels like something you ought to ... that it's something you should take, really.... It feels like there's pressure on you to take it. That ... if you want to be a good parent, or a good father, then you have to take the daddy leave." Several fathers indicated that if they had not taken the fathers' quota, they would have to explain themselves to others.

Fathers' leave-taking is supported by social norms of good fatherhood that these fathers seem to have incorporated into their identities. As the next section shows, fatherhood has also been incorporated into their practices as employees.

5.2 Employers' Support of Fathers' Caregiving Responsibilities

Many of the fathers in the sample strongly felt that having a quota given to them as employees was an unconditional strength in relation to work, and that it would have been much more difficult to gain support from employers if it were not for their legal right to the fathers' leave. "It makes your position stronger when the quota is based in law," said Geir. Kristoffer and many others believed that if the father's quota was not retained as a father-specific right, they would fail in their negotiations over leave with their employer. Since the fathers' quota is statutory, employers have little leeway to adopt discriminatory practices.

The fathers' sense of entitlement becomes explicit when Steinar reflects on how he would have had to argue in his previous job as a consulting engineer with a small company. "It was very intense with a call on us to work 80 h a week and perform all we could with lots of pressure and bonuses. In this place, taking leave would have been frowned upon. But still, should you have to fight for your rights?" Moreover, the fathers' leave is paid by the state rather than the employer. Comparing his right to the fathers' quota with his right to paid holidays, Steiner said that if he did not take his "3 months 'holiday' with pay," he would lose it. Entitlements to paid time off are acceptable in working life. To have to argue with his employer about his childcare responsibilities would not work as well, Steinar claimed.

None of the fathers in the study reported that they had experienced any serious problems with their current employers when planning to use their entitlement (Brandth and Kvande 2019a, b). Indeed, men seem to be expected to take the fathers' leave by their employers and colleagues. Harold, a schoolteacher, said: "It was all right, and it was expected! It would have been more of an issue if I hadn't taken it. Public workplaces have to play by the rules." For fathers, it seems inevitable that working life must adapt to the regulations of the welfare state. Christian, a senior advisor in the municipal administration, pointed out that even though the fathers' quota might sometimes represent challenges for workplaces, organizations do adapt to this legislation.

The fathers' quota has existed for a quarter century, which means that men who have advanced to management positions in some organizations have taken fathers' leave themselves. That experience influences what is considered fair and feasible. Tore, a doctor in a large hospital, described how his leave-taking was received by his director, a 60-year-old chief physician: "He is up to date on the father's quota.... He has had young children himself.... And I am not the first father to be in this situation." Steinar, too, explained that his bosses are fathers: "They are 54 and 62, and both were home with their children at a time when it was much less common than now. So, they pushed me, saying 'Steinar, it is clear that you must stay home,' and 'Are you sure you won't take a bit longer leave?' They said so even if it was bad for the job." Likewise, Sivert described his boss as very positive: "He understood me very well. I suppose he is 50 years, so he is very up to date." His boss was eager to help him find out about the regulations concerning the father's quota and the rest of the parental leave system. Sivert considered him a "modern" man who regarded fathers' involvement with children as important. Another father interviewed, Hans, said:

> I think most employers today live in the modern world and understand that they must live up to that. This is how it is. They need employees who are happy with their job and have a good family life. Now, we see that both managers and middle managers in companies, 35 to 40 years old, experience the same tensions concerning career, childcare, parental leaves and work hours. I have a mate who is manager of marketing, only a few years older than me in a top job; he had four months daddy leave, so that says a lot.

Fathers are more likely to take up family friendly working practices if they can "compare themselves with other fathers and realize that it is feasible to do so" (Lewis and Stumbitz 2017: 230). The fathers we interviewed reported that as leave takers they did not stand out in any way. Hans, a communications advisor in a transport company, told us that at his workplace "many of my male colleagues had a child at about the same time as me, which was great! We were about three or four who had kids within a 2- or 3-month span. In addition, many employees here have small children." The norms that are produced by these practices make it easy for fathers to take leave and for organizations to plan for it. Dahl et al. (2014), who studied the peer effect of father quota usage, found that fathers are even more likely to take the quota if their colleagues did. The effect was greatest if a manager at a higher level in the organization had taken the fathers' leave.

Many of the fathers confidently portrayed the quota as *their* leave. In so doing, they conveyed a sense of entitlement and beliefs about what is right and fair. Hobson and Morgan (2002: 14) hold that family friendly policies provide men with discursive resources with which they can make claims upon their employers. For instance, Ivar communicated that it was he who controlled how much and when he would work, and he was not afraid to insist on his priorities.

5.3 Empowered as Caregivers

The fathers communicated an identity as competent caregivers and attributed this to their time on leave when they had gotten to know the child well. They thought that children benefit from close contact with fathers, and that fathers are significant caregivers for children. Erlend said:

> "It is quite unfair that only mothers are regarded as important for the children. Speaking as a man I think this is a new situation for gender equality.... I have been able to prove that I can be just as good a carer as the mother. I think it is super important! It increases men's self-confidence and society's confidence in men as caregivers."

Regarding it as unfair that only mothers are given support as caregivers, these men see the fathers' quota as remedying this injustice. They justify their entitlement to leave as based on their ability to care for their small children and think the fathers' quota contributes to their being seen as needed and important caregiving parents. They feel entitled to both the joys and burdens of childcare, and they stress that the fathers' quota represents an opportunity to develop an autonomous relationship with their children. "Being home on leave has in a way laid the foundation for the contact we [father and child] have today. A lot will happen later in life, but this is the basis," Didrik said.

The quota as a father-specific right simplifies negotiations with the mother. Sivert realized that this was the point of earmarking it: "This is why they designed it like that. If not, nothing would have come of it. Then the mother would have taken the whole leave." He thought that to many people it is still not obvious that the father will choose to stay home with the child. To avoid making parental leave only mothers' leave, he said, it was important that things were not "made completely flexible."

Employed fathers view the fathers' quota as an entitlement, a support from the welfare state for them to be active caregivers. There are strong moral obligations for fathers to take the father's quota and for employers to accept it. This finding seems important in understanding the high use of the quota among fathers in Norway.

6 Practical Recommendations

These findings illustrate that the design of the father's quota as a statutory, earmarked, and non-transferrable right for fathers *promotes* the fathers' use of leave and hence equality. The earmarking, and the fact that it cannot be transferred to the mother, renders it unnecessary for fathers to negotiate with the mother about this leave. The father's quota is also an important bargaining chip in relation to the job. Even if fathers have stories about situations where the employers do not want the father to take leave, employers are most often described as positive towards the father's leave, and the interviews include few personally experienced stories about employers impeding the fathers from taking leave. We interpret this as a sign that the father's quota as a legal earmarked right may have contributed to making visible and promoting the fact that employed men are also fathers and "encumbered" with caregiving responsibilities as much as employed mothers. Thus, in order to promote gender equality, policy makers should choose paid parental leave given to individuals rather than to families. These policies help the equality processes in work organizations through normalizing that both female and male employees are parents.

Much of the evidence indicates that if there were no earmarked and non-transferrable leave for the father that was based in law, reluctant fathers would not have taken any leave and mothers may have been unwilling to give up leave to share with them. There are ambivalent and hesitant fathers who would then choose differently. This also shows that leave for many fathers is not something that is fully in place as an accepted and taken-for-granted practice. These findings thus support other research on fathers' use of leave which have shown that the design characteristics of father's quota represents a strong incentive for greater involvement on the part of fathers.

Considering these findings, it is interesting that the EU Commission in 2019 introduced a new package on work-life balance to ensure better leave provisions and care facilities for working parents in all EU member states. The existing EU Directives on maternity and parental leave are regarded as outdated as they have largely failed to improve gender equality, neither expanding women's participation in the labour market, nor encouraging men to use leave provisions and take a greater share of caring responsibilities.

References

Bartel AP, Rossin-Slater M, Ruhm CJ, Stearns J, Waldfogel J (2018) Paid family leave, fathers' leave-taking, and leave-sharing in dual-earner households. J Policy Anal Manage 37(1):10–37

Blum S, Koslowski A, Macht A, Moss P (2018) 14th annual international review of leave policies and research 2018. International network on leave policies & research. https://www.leavenetwork.org/annual-review-reports/archive-reviews/

Brandth B, Kvande E (1998) Masculinity and child care: the reconstruction of fathering. Sociol Rev 46(2):293–313

Brandth B, Kvande E (2009) Gendered or gender neutral care policies for fathers? Ann Am Acad Polit Social Sci 624(1):177–189

Brandth B, Kvande E (2018) Masculinity and fathering alone. Men Masculinities 21(1):72–90

Brandth B, Kvande E (2019a) Fathers' sense of entitlement to ear-marked and shared parental leave. Sociol Rev 67(5):1154–1169

Brandth B, Kvande E (2019b) Workplace support of fathers' parental leave use in Norway. Community Work Fam 22:43–57

Brighouse H, Wright EO (2008) Strong gender egalitarianism. Polit Soc 36(3):360–372

Dahl GB, Løken KV, Mogstad M (2014) Peer effects in program participation. Am Econ Rev 104 (7):2049–2074

Daly M (2011) What adult worker model? A critical look at recent social policy reform in Europe from a gender and family perspective. Soc Polit 18(19):1–24

Dearing H (2016) Gender equality in the division of work: how to assess European leave policies regarding their compliance with an ideal leave model. J Eur Soc Policy 26(3):234–247

Duvander A-Z, Lammi-Taskula J (2012) Parental leave. In: Gíslason IV, Eydal GB (eds) Parental leave, childcare and gender equality in the Nordic countries. Nordic Council of Ministers, Copenhagen, pp 31–64

Eydal GB, Gíslason IV (2013) Tredelt permisjon og lang fedrekvote: Erfaringer fra Island. In: Brandth B, Kvande E (eds) Fedrekvoten og den farsvennlige velferdsstaten. Universitetsforlaget, Oslo, pp 222–237

Eydal GB, Gíslason IV, Rostgaard T, Brandth B, Duvander A-Z, Lammi-Taskula J (2015) Trends in parental leave: has the forward march of gender equality halted? Community Work Fam 18 (2):161–181

Fougner E (2012) Fedre tar ut hele fedrekvoten - også etter at den ble utvidet til ti uker. [Fathers use the whole father's quota – also after extension]. Arbeid og velferd 2:71–77

Gíslason IV, Eydal GB (2013) Parental leave, childcare and gender equality in the Nordic countries. Nordic Council of Ministers, Copenhagen

Gornick JC, Meyers MK (eds) (2009) Gender equality. Transforming family divisions of labor. Verso, London

Haas L, Rostgaard T (2011) Fathers' right to paid parental leave in the Nordic countries: consequences for the gendered division of care. Community Work Fam 14(2):177–195

Halrynjo S, Kitterød RH (2016) Fedrekvoten – norm for fedres permisjonsbruk i Norge og Norden: En litteraturstudie. Report 2016:06. ISF, Oslo. https://samfunnsforskning.brage.unit.no/samfunnsforskning-xmlui/handle/11250/2442339

Hamre K (2017) Fedrekvoten – mer populær enn noen gang. *Samfunnsspeilet*, 1. Statistics Norway. https://www.ssb.no/befolkning/artikler-og-publikasjoner/fedrekvoten-mer-populaer-enn-noen-gang

Harvey V, Tremblay D-G (2019) The workplace: challenges for fathers and their use of leave. In: Moss P, Duvander A-Z, Koslowski A (eds) Parental leave and beyond. Recent international developments, current issues, future directions. Policy Press, Bristol, pp 223–240

Hobson B, Morgan DHJ (2002) Introduction. In: Hobson B (ed) Making men into fathers. Cambridge University Press, Cambridge, pp 1–23

Kitterød RH, Halrynjo S, Østbakken KM (2017) Pappaperm? Fedre som ikke tar fedrekvote – hvor mange, hvem og hvorfor? Report 2017: 2. ISF, Oslo

Lewis J (2015) The decline of the male breadwinner model. Soc Polit 8(2):152–169

Lewis S, Stumbitz B (2017) Research on work and family: some issues and challenges. In: Liebig B, Oechsle M (eds) Fathers in work organizations. Barbara Budrich, Berlin, pp 227–244

McKay L, Doucet A (2010) "Without taking her leave": a Canadian case study of couples' decisions on fathers' use of paid parental leave. Fathering 8(3):300–320

Miller T (2013) Shifting out of neutral on parental leave. Making fathers' involvement explicit. Public Policy Res 19(4):258–262

Morgan KJ (2008) The political path to a dual earner/dual carer society: pitfalls and possibilities. Polit Soc 36(3):403–420

Moss P, Deven F (1999) Parental leave: progress or pitfall? Research and policy issues in Europe. Vlaamse Gemeenschap, Brussels

Moss P, Kamerman SB (2009) Introduction. In: Kamerman S, Moss P (eds) The politics of parental leave policies. Policy Press, Bristol, pp 1–13

Moss P, Duvander A-Z, Koslowski A (eds) (2019) Parental leave and beyond: recent developments, current issues, future directions. Policy Press, Bristol

Naz G (2010) Usage of parental leave by fathers in Norway. Int J Sociol Soc Policy 30(5/6):313–325

NOU (2017) NOU 2017:6 Offentlig støtte til barnefamiliene [Public support for families with children]. Government of Norway. Ministry of Children and Equality, Oslo. https://www.regjeringen.no/no/dokumenter/nou-2017-6/id2540981/

O'Brien M, Wall K (eds) (2017) Comparative perspectives on work-life balance and gender equality: fathers on leave alone. Springer, London

Pascall G (2012) Gender equality in the welfare state? The Policy Press, Bristol

Ray R, Gornick JC, Schmitt J (2010) Who cares? Assessing generosity and gender equality in parental leave policy designs in 21 countries. J Eur Soc Policy 20(3):196–216

Rostgaard T (2002) Setting time aside for the father: father's leave in Scandinavia. Community Work Fam 5(3):343–370

Sainsbury D (1999) Gender, policy regimes and politics. Chapter 8. In: Sainsbury D (ed) Gender and welfare state regimes. Oxford University Press, New York

Open Access This chapter is licensed under the terms of the Creative Commons Attribution 4.0 International License (http://creativecommons.org/licenses/by/4.0/), which permits use, sharing, adaptation, distribution and reproduction in any medium or format, as long as you give appropriate credit to the original author(s) and the source, provide a link to the Creative Commons license and indicate if changes were made.

The images or other third party material in this chapter are included in the chapter's Creative Commons license, unless indicated otherwise in a credit line to the material. If material is not included in the chapter's Creative Commons license and your intended use is not permitted by statutory regulation or exceeds the permitted use, you will need to obtain permission directly from the copyright holder.

How Do Men Talk about Taking Parental Leave? Evidence from South Korea, Spain, and the U.S.

Xiana Bueno and Eunsil Oh

1 Introduction

Allowing working fathers, as well as mothers, to combine family and work responsibilities has contributed to a closing of the gender gap at home and in the labor market (Bünning 2015) and improves the bond between parents and their children (O'Brien 2009). However, the use of parental leave by men is still far from a common practice in many societies. The persistence of traditional gender-role ideology and its social norms, the rigidity of labor markets and organizational culture, and existing gender inequality in public institutions, such as in family policies, are part of the explanation. The gender dimension at the individual and institutional levels is highly interconnected.

In recent decades, some countries have made an effort to provide parental leave benefits to employed men. We know little, however, about how men talk about the leave system and use parental leave. In this chapter, we aim to extend our understanding of men's views on parental leave use by putting their individual narratives in the macro-level context where they live in order to better understand how institutions and individuals are connected. To do this, we analyze how childless men and fathers of one child talk about taking leave and use leave policies. Using 80 personal in-depth interviews, we compare men's narratives and reasoning in South Korea, Spain, and the United States. These three countries represent distinctive macro-institutional contexts, labor market structures and cultures, and

X. Bueno (✉)
Centre d'Estudis Demogràfics, Carrer de Ca n'Altayó, Edifici E2, Universitat Autònoma de Barcelona, Barcelona, Spain
e-mail: xbueno@ced.uab.es

E. Oh
University of Wisconsin-Madison, Madison, WI, USA

© The Author(s) 2022
M. Grau Grau et al. (eds.), *Engaged Fatherhood for Men, Families and Gender Equality*, Contributions to Management Science, https://doi.org/10.1007/978-3-030-75645-1_9

gender-role models, and the findings suggest how these three features are linked to interviewees' narratives in different ways.

Although this paper focuses on men, we acknowledge that men's decision making regarding parental leave cannot be understood outside the couple dimension. Both partners' ideologies and employment characteristics are crucial for fertility decisions and childcare arrangements (Bueno and Grau-Grau 2021; Singley and Hynes 2005; Bygren and Ann-Zofie 2006; Kaufman and Almqvist 2017). In this chapter, we examine the couple dimension based on what our male interviewees reflect about their partners. This work contributes to a better understanding of the reasoning behind couples' use of parental leave from men's perspectives and will offer insight for the design of future policies and strategies to reduce gender inequality.

2 Theoretical Approaches and Literature Review

To understand men's intentions and use of parental leave under their macro-level context, we draw on the main theoretical approaches that past literature has highlighted as influencing the use of parental leave. We agree that gender is at the center of understanding how individuals use parental leave (Singley and Hynes 2005; Valarino et al. 2018). However, we need to understand other dimensions – labor market and financial conditions, cultural aspects, and institutional factors – to fully understand the role gender plays in how people understand parental leave and use it.

2.1 Workplace Environment

Numerous studies have shown how labor market structure and workplace environment shape the use of parental leave by men. For example, working in the private sector implies additional constraints not present in the public sector (Beglaubter 2017). Additionally, studies emphasize the role of organizational culture and employers in explaining how men use parental leave (Haas et al. 2002; Bygren and Ann-Zofie 2006). The use of leave by other coworkers (Lapuerta et al. 2011), an employer's willingness to facilitate work-life balance (Crompton 2006), or working in a family-friendly environment (Escot et al. 2012) have positive effects on men's parental leave use. A recent study comparing intentions with parental leave use showed that men who received organizational support from their companies to plan parental leave ended up realizing their parental leave plans (Horvath et al. 2017). Although higher income positively relates to leave-taking behavior (Lapuerta et al. 2011), the higher the job status (i.e., managerial positions) the less likely leave-taking becomes, mainly because the opportunity costs for a career increase (Escot et al. 2012). For this analysis, we expect that in settings with rigid work norms such as Korea and, to a lesser extent, the U.S., respondents would be more reticent to use family policies regardless of job status, than in Spain.

2.2 Individual- and Couple-level Dynamics

Beyond individual characteristics, couple or household characteristics are crucial to obtain a full understanding of men's parental leave use. Based on household income, couples evaluate the affordability of taking childcare leave (Reich 2010; Meil et al. 2017). Additionally, men and women evaluate their educational and occupational status to determine the comparative advantages of the partners and their opportunity costs (Becker 1981). Similarly, fathers with partners who have a stronger position in the labor market are more likely to take parental leave than other fathers are (Reich 2010). The bargaining model predicts that each partner has *power* to trade with the other resulting from their relative earnings and time availability (Lundberg and Pollak 1996). According to this model, we expect that in countries where the dual-earner model persists as the most common couples' economic arrangement even after parenthood, as in Spain and the U.S., men would be more prone to take parental leave than in Korea.

2.3 Cultural Explanations

There is wide agreement among scholars on how individuals' subjective characteristics, such as identity, individual norms, or ideology, influence parental leave behaviors (Doucet 2009). In particular, what has been traditionally considered "good" mothering (caregiving) and fathering (breadwinning) relates to cultural norms (Craig and Mullan 2010; Kühhirt 2012). Conversely, some studies observing emerging unconventional patterns in parents' childcare arrangements have claimed that structural factors, such as an economic crisis, might force a gender-role change at the societal or institutional level (Chesley 2011; Dominguez-Folgueras et al. 2018). The emerging pattern of gender-egalitarian fathers that adopt an active role in childcare and subscribe to the "new fatherhood ideal" (Petts et al. 2017) is associated with higher educational levels and younger ages (Escot et al. 2014). At the interactional level, men and women match their behaviors according to what they expect from each other and socially with respect to parental responsibilities (Singley and Hynes 2005). In this sense, we expect higher involvement of men in taking parental leave in countries where gender-role attitudes have evolved toward greater egalitarianism, such as Spain or the U.S., compared to more traditional gender-role settings like Korea.

2.4 Welfare System and Policies

The institutional context - characteristics of leave, length, wage replacement rate, and requirements to qualify - shapes individuals' attitudes toward welfare programs (Valarino et al. 2018). A gendered paid parental leave system, by which mothers get longer leaves than fathers, reinforces traditional gender roles (Lapuerta et al. 2011). In the U.S. context, the fact that paid childcare leave is often offered only to mothers leads women to take further responsibilities in childcare after the end of the leave (Fox 2009). Beyond the parental leave system, the provision of public childcare supply or tax benefits after parenthood are important factors to be considered (Baizán 2009). In countries in which the welfare state does not promote gender equality, more traditionalism in gender roles occurs after parenthood (Neilson and Stanfors 2014). Therefore, we expect to observe a significant divergence between the Spanish respondents, whose parental leave system is expanding in favor of men's rights, and the Korean and American respondents, whose available options are limited in this regard.

3 Three Macro-Institutional Contexts: Korea, Spain, and the U.S.

3.1 Labor Force Participation and Gender Equality

Among the three countries, and despite having a population with highest proportion of highly educated women in the world, Korea also has the lowest female participation rate: 63.4% of females between 25 and 34 years old were in the labor force in 2012 (the reference year of our sample) (OECD 2018a). A high gender wage gap—men earn 36.3% more than women, compared to 19.1% and 8.6% in the U.S. and Spain, respectively—is also a distinguishing pattern for Korea. The high level of unemployment in Spain during the peak of the 2008 global recession is noteworthy, at 28.7% in 2012 for men (slightly lower for women), compared with 5.3% and 8.2% for Korean and American males, respectively. The instability of the Spanish labor market and the economy cannot be neglected as a key factor driving women to be economically active regardless of their gender-role attitudes. The lower gender wage gap in Spain should cause this factor to interfere less in Spanish parents' parental leave use negotiation than in that of parents in the other two countries. Spain has the highest female participation rate of the three countries (85.3%). The U.S. falls between Korea and Spain, with 74.1% female labor force participation.

The Gender Gap Index (GGI) from the World Economic Forum (WEF) measures countries' gender inequality based on economic participation, educational attainment, health and survival, and political empowerment. According to the GGI (Hausmann et al. 2012), Spain and the U.S. hold similar rankings, 26 and 22 (out of 135), respectively. Korea, however, reflects a context in which gender inequality is high, ranking 108. Additionally, gender-role attitudes reflect that Spain is the most gender egalitarian, followed by the U.S. and Korea (World Values Survey 2010-2014). Lastly, the division of household labor shows that Korean men spend only 45 min per day in unpaid work, while their American and Spanish counterparts spend 150 min and 146 min, respectively. In terms of paid work, Korean men spend 422 min in paid work per day on average, American men spend 335 min, and Spanish men spend 236 min (OECD 2018b).

3.2 Family Policies

Fully paid statutory allowances for mothers and fathers exist only in Korea and in Spain. In 2012, in both countries, policies provided mothers with a longer period of paid leave than fathers. Maternity leave lasts almost 13 weeks (90 days) for Korean mothers and 16 weeks for Spanish mothers. In the Spanish case, 10 out of the 16 weeks were able to be transferred to the father in 2012 (year of the interviews). However, between 2008 and 2011, less than 2% of fathers used transferable weeks from maternity leave (Flaquer and Escobedo 2014).

Regarding parental leave, it is important to distinguish between paid and unpaid leave. Paid paternity leave is substantially shorter. Korean fathers as of 2021 can take 10 days of paid paternity leave. Conversely, although Spain has offered two paid days to new fathers since the 1930s, in recent times, a progressive effort has been made to improve fathers' leave length. In 2007, two-week paternity leave was implemented; in 2017, the government approved four-week leave for fathers, which became 5 weeks in July 2018, 8 weeks in April 2019, 12 weeks in January 2020 and 16 weeks in January 2021, achieving parity with maternity leave. In the U.S., there is no national legislation in this regard, although some states and municipalities offer paid leave policies at the local level. Paid leave, if any, is generally provided at employers' discretion and is often intended exclusively for mothers and not fathers. Nevertheless, according to a Department of Labor Survey from 2000, only 24% of private U.S. employers offered some kind of paid maternity-related leave, and only 12% offered "leave for parents to care for a newborn" (Ray et al. 2008) (Table 1).

The characteristics of parental leave differ substantially across countries. Childcare leave in Korea and Spain can be taken full-time or part-time. For the latter, there is a salary reduction proportional to the reduction in working hours. However, while Korea offers wage replacement in the full-time version, in Spain and the U.S., full-time leave is unpaid. Additionally, leave length differs substantially. Korea offers up to 52 paid weeks (1 year). The first 13 weeks are paid at 80% and from the 14th to 52nd week at 40%. In contrast, Spain is one of the most generous countries offering unpaid leave. Regarding full-time leave, Spanish parents can take

Table 1 Country context indicators: Korea, Spain and the U.S.

	Korea	Spain	U.S.
Labor market and time use			
• Female labor force participation rate, 25–34 years old [1]	63.4	85.3	74.1
• Male unemployment rate, 25–34 years old [1]	5.3	28.7	8.2
• Gender wage gap [1,2]	36.3	8.6	19.1
• Men's time spent in unpaid work (minutes per day) [3]	45	145.9	150.2
• Men's time spent in paid work (minutes per day) [3]	421.9	236.2	334.8
Gender inequality and attitudes			
• Country ranking (1–135) on the gender gap index (GGI) [4]	108	26	22
• Percent of males considering that the best childcare option for children under school age is "Both mother and father part-time" [5]	5	16	4
• Disagreement with the statement *"When jobs are scarce, men should have more right to a job than women"* (%) [6]	22.7	82.1	69.9
Family policies			
• Paid maternity leave (in weeks, in 2012)	12.9	16	0
• Paid paternity leave (in weeks, in 2012)	0.4	2.1	0
• Paid parental leave (in weeks, in 2012)	52	0	0
• Unpaid parental leave (in weeks, in 2012)	0	156	12

Source: [1] OECD Stats 2012; [2] The gender wage gap is defined as the difference between male and female median wages divided by the male median wage; [3] OECD Stats (Korea 2009; Spain 2009–10; U.S. 2014); [4] World Economic Forum 2012; [5] International Social Survey Programme (ISSP) 2012 - Family and Changing Gender Roles IV [6] World Values Survey 2010-2014

52 weeks with protection of their former job position and up to 156 weeks (3 years) with job protection, though they are not guaranteed the same position. For part-time leave, Spanish parents could reduce their working hours between 1/8 and 1/2 until the child is 8 years old (in 2012).[1] Despite these policies, for the period 2005–2009, fathers in Spain started unpaid parental leave for 0.3% of yearly births compared with 5–6% for mothers (Escot et al. 2014). American parents face much less beneficial conditions. The federal Family Medical Leave Act (FMLA) has provided 12 full-time continuous weeks of unpaid leave to new parents since 1993. Employees only qualify for FMLA leave if they have been working for at least 1 year at the company and the company has more than 50 employees. Such restrictions imply that approximately 40% of U.S. workers in 2012 were not covered by the FMLA (Klerman et al. 2014), and those workers largely belong to low-income families (Ray et al. 2008). Some states complement the FMLA by offering partial-payment or more flexible conditions.

---

[1]Unpaid part-time leave can be taken until 12 years old as of 2020.

4 Data and Methods

Our data were drawn from 80 in-depth interviews conducted in three countries in 2012. The interviewees were recruited through snowball sampling. Interviews were conducted face-to-face and typically lasted between 60 and 120 min. All interviews were voice-recorded and transcribed in full by a native speaker from each country. Sampling and interviewing in Korea and Spain were carried out by the authors, who are both sociologists. Fieldwork in the U.S. was performed by sociology graduate students. The sample includes 43 childless males and 37 fathers with one child. Given the small sample size, we sought to avoid having too much heterogeneity within our sample. All the respondents are highly educated, heterosexual, native-born, urban men aged 24–35 in stable unions.[2] Higher education is defined as the completion of tertiary education (a university degree or post-secondary vocational program). The selected ages—24-35 years old—capture the life-stage period in which family formation is highly prominent. In addition, we restricted the sample to individuals who are not full-time students, who are not expecting a child, do not have children from a previous relationship, and who are not separated, divorced, or widowed. Equal numbers of interviews were conducted in large urban areas in each country: Seoul and Busan in Korea, Madrid and Barcelona in Spain, and Boston and New York City in the U.S. The interview questions touched on various topics: current or most recent employment of the interviewee and his/her partner; union formation, fertility ideals, intentions, and reasoning; household and childcare division of labor; gender-role attitudes; and views on family policies.

In the first stage, thematic coding was performed using qualitative software (*Dedoose*). In the second stage, we inductively coded and wrote extensive detailed memos about the narratives offered by participants. In the third stage, the authors shared their analyses and had an in-depth discussion. The data were rigorously revisited as many times as necessary to ensure the correct interpretation of each interview.

5 Results

5.1 Spain and the U.S.: The Salience of Leave Availability

As Table 2 summarizes, our analysis reveals three important findings. First, for both Spanish and American interviewees who use and plan to use parental leave, the rationale behind their intentions is often the partner's relative resources on the labor market and whether leave is paid or unpaid. In Spain, none of the males (and very

---

[2]While all respondents in the Korean and American samples are married, the Spanish sample includes both married and stable cohabiting couples to reflect the diverse union formation patterns of the European context.

Table 2 Results

	Korea	Spain	U.S.
Usage and intention	**Paid paternity leave (5 days):** Taken or plan to take it **Partially paid parental leave (1 year):** No intention of using leave by childless and none of the fathers (except one) used it	**Paid paternity leave (2 weeks):** Taken (plan to take it) almost by all **Full-time unpaid parental leave (up to 3 years old):** Not an option (economic uncertainty) **Part-time unpaid parental leave (up to 8 years old):** Childless more flexible than fathers (none used it)	**Paid paternity leave:** Taken when available **Childcare arrangements after paid leave:** Childless more rigid than fathers (many made job adjustments)
Narratives	Policies are good, but workplace norms (rigidity and long-working hours) do not legitimate use of parental leave for men There are strong gender-essentialist norms	High unemployment and economic uncertainty lead men to talk about the cost and benefit of using leave Gender egalitarian norms are prevalent	There are strong gender-essentialist norms regarding motherhood for young children Individuals' responsibility is highlighted due to the lack of policies

Source: Project interviews

few of their partners, according to interviewees) considered taking (or took) full-time parental leave. Regardless of couples' gender ideology, the economic uncertainty that has arisen in the Spanish context due to the economic crisis and the lack of wage replacement during childcare leave explain the very low usage of this policy option. Childless respondents show more flexible opinions regarding part-time unpaid parental leave or reduction of working hours. Nevertheless, those who expressed positive intentions to take part-time leave—as well as their partners—seem to be aware that their ultimate decision will be subject to two conditions: his and his partner's job situation and employers' willingness at the time of making the decision and their economic circumstances at that time. Bruno is an example. He is 27, childless, and works as a primary school teacher.

> [Would you take part-time unpaid parental leave?] If I could afford it, I would not mind at all. Of course! But, as I've said before, the school administration is not very flexible in these cases, not even with women. I can't even imagine how they would be with men.

Among Spanish fathers, those who actively engage in childcare express that this is mainly due to their partners' employment circumstances rather than to their ideological commitment to gender egalitarianism. Interestingly, a majority of Spanish fathers who adjust their working conditions instead of using parental leave are self-employed. Likewise, those fathers who report an arrangement in which he did not take unpaid leave and she did do not necessarily hold traditional gender-role attitudes.

Compared with more traditional narratives among American childless men, many fathers from the U.S. sample made some labor-market adjustments when they had their first child. The actual childcare arrangements employed by the American fathers in the sample indicate three different strategies. The first strategy is that of dual-earner couples in which both partners hold occupations with a relatively similar status and male respondents report having a gender-egalitarian distribution of tasks at home. Both partners return to work after their paid leave allowance. A second common strategy is that of couples in which the female partners take a much longer parental leave than their husbands. Some of these women have unpaid parental leave available in their work place, while others take a deliberately extended period of unemployment or stop working for an open-ended period of time. These women act as primary caregivers for periods that range between 6 and 15 months or until their child(ren) goes to school. Some fathers expressed a hope that their partners would return to the labor market in the near future to continue their career development. There is also a small group of involved fathers. Fathers who are more involved in their child's care and who make adjustments to their labor force participation—taking FMLA leave and switching to a part-time job—have partners who hold a more stable and better paid position in the labor market than them. Often after considering the cost of daycare or nannies, these couples decide that it will be the man that will make the adjustment.

In the American sample, a clear majority of childless respondents expressed that they had no intention of stopping full-time work. In general, respondents intend to change their work hours, but these changes often consist in cutting back overtime rather than reducing work hours. For example, childless American respondents plan to respect their 40-h work week but said that they might adjust their schedules by travelling less for work, arriving home earlier, eliminating weekend or after-hours work, or trying to work remotely from home. There is an assumption of intensive mothership during early childhood that leads childless men to not even envision themselves as parental leave-takers. Edward put it this way: *"I'm really looking forward to having little kids, but I'm not looking forward to having a baby."* Nevertheless, a small group held more gender-egalitarian attitudes, such as Jeffrey, a 30-year-old childless actor and acting teacher.

> I don't have any kind of preconceptions about which parent should be taking care of the kids. I really don't think that matters … I would say if you can arrange it so either you're both working part-time and with complimentary schedules so that you can spend a lot of time with the child, then that would be great, or if one parent is working and the other's not—although I guess that would be less ideal because I certainly wouldn't want to get into an arrangement where I was working 80 hours a week, and Laura wasn't working at all, and I never saw my child. I wouldn't find that acceptable.

Nevertheless, rational choice based on partners' relative resources was often present among American respondents with a more egalitarian ideology. Some of them stated that the partner who would make job adaptations would be the one whose adjustment would make more sense economically for the finances of the family.

With few exceptions, the majority of our interviewees in the three countries took or plan to take the paid paternity allowance after the birth of their child. Money is an important driving motivation to fully utilize the available leave system. However, despite having a paid leave system, not taking days off after a child's birth is a practice more common in Korea than in Spain or the U.S. This is related to workplace-influenced attitudes and assumptions surrounding the legitimacy of using leave, such as feeling unable to stop working (often among the self-employed or those in higher status positions) or being afraid of penalties for taking leave (i.e., weak relationship with employer). As Kitae, a 33-year-old journalist and father of one child, argues, *"When no one uses leave and it is kind of awkward to use leave, it is obviously hard to utilize a long leave."* Even though Korea has one of the most generous childcare leave policies in the world, the rigidity of its labor market norms and long working hours position men's intentions and actions far from considering taking childcare leave. Paradoxically, in the U.S., with no statutory policies, fathers in our American sample took longer paternity leaves than fathers in Korea. Regardless of recent changes in the family policy system, the comparison shows that workplace culture as well as attitudes toward who should use leave strongly shape the ways in which men use and imagine using leave.

5.2 Korea and the U.S.: The Salience of Gender-Role Attitudes

The belief in gender-essentialist norms—the male breadwinner, female caregiver model—emerged in most of the interviews with the Korean men. Ascribing to relatively more gender-essentialist attitudes, Korean men see the gendered pattern of using parental leave as natural and believe that leave should be used only by mothers because they are more fit for child rearing. There are strong and internalized social and cultural expectations that being a good father means sustaining a stable income. For Minho, a 31-year-old childless architect, this is clear: *"It is natural to focus on working when you become a father. I will be working harder for my family, for my child, as a head of the family."*

In contrast to the Korean males, none of the males in the Spanish sample are in a partnership that reflects traditional gender-roles. Highly educated men do not expect to have a stay-at-home partner, mostly because of their relatively egalitarian gender-role attitudes but also because of the convenience of having both partners economically support the household. As noted before, some childless Spanish men have positive intentions of taking leave, as do their partners (according to them). It is notable that all those who reported negative intentions – except two – also expressed their belief that their female partners would be willing to take part-time leave (or sometimes full-time). While some of these males and their partners hold gender-traditional values, others show more gender-egalitarian conceptions. For the latter, it is the weaker position of their female partners in the labor market (i.e., unemployed, working part-time or precariously) that explains their negative intention to take leave rather than preconceived ideas about their gender roles within the family. Interestingly, men who reported that they and their partners would not take leave were highly educated and career-oriented, and their partners had similar trajectories.

Conversely, many of the childless American respondents emphasize the ideal arrangement as one in which they "can afford that she can stay at home." Gender-essentialist beliefs about the ideal childcare arrangement are taken for granted, leading many American males to see intensive mothership during very early childhood as *normal* and, as a result, that they have no responsibility to take parental leave. Indeed, several childless respondents in their narratives imply that their active involvement as fathers will be more needed when their children are toddlers or older. Relying on a "biological discourse" based on the breastfeeding argument and a "strong bond between the mother and the child'" these males consider themselves less useful for childcare during the early childhood period. Thomas, a 33-year-old substitute teacher, represents an extreme case of this idea.

> I think that I would not want to change diapers. [Laughter] I think that would be her job. When it comes to like guy stuff like teaching him to play sports and how to ride a bike, I said earlier, you know that, I would definitely be happy to take responsibility when it comes to that.
>
> [Can you imagine what proportion of the child rearing she might do versus you?]
>
> I think it would be 50/50. She'll do the female stuff, I'll do the male stuff. [Chuckles] I think it would be half and half.

Among childless American respondents, it is easy to identify the "flexible egalitarian" attitude in which couples emphasize individual freedom as their rationale. Taylor, among others, clearly reflects this stance: *"It's really a choice, so if she wants to pursue being a full-time mother, that's fine. If she wants to pursue having a career, that's fine as well."* Male ambivalence about the female's role—as long as it makes financial sense—reinforces the assumption that the role of main caregiver continues to be a woman's. However, while some of our interviewees affirmed that their partners have always desired to become full-time mothers, others emphasized that their partners were conflicted about whether to continue their careers or become stay-at-home mothers. Some males expressed their feeling of needing to know that they could be the sole provider for their family if necessary, while others with a flexible egalitarian attitude expressed a feeling of regret at the idea that their female partners might abandon their careers and education efforts to become full-time mothers.

5.3 Institutional Context and Individual Narratives

The macro-institutional contexts interfere substantially with parental leave use and intentions in Spain and the U.S. There is a distinct difference between childless men and fathers in Spain: Respondents in both groups mentioned a desire for equal and longer maternity and paternity leaves, but only fathers desired longer leaves for mothers. American respondents have a much more limited vision of ideal family policies. For American interviewees, ideal policies often involved paid maternity leave, and it was rare to insist on longer available leave for fathers.

Both Spanish and American respondents emphasize the need for workplaces to offer more time flexibility in allowing employees to manage their own schedule, work remotely, or work compressed schedules. Spanish respondents in particular complained about the inequality between the public and private sector regarding the application of statutory policies. It is known that many employees in the private sector, mainly men but also women, experience penalties when taking parental leave (Lapuerta et al. 2011).

The scenario is quite different for the American context, since the U.S. does not provide statutory paid parental leave (except for some states and municipalities), and benefits generally depend on employers. Many of the childless American interviewees are not aware of the family policies that their companies offer, and such policies did not play any particular role in their decision to join their companies. When asked about how family-friendly their workplaces are, parental leave is not the first thing they mention; rather, they discuss flexible working hours or the ability to leave work when an emergency occurs. These men do not think about childcare on a daily basis. They know about their companies' parental leave policies only from workmates that have transitioned to parenthood recently. Most of the time, they refer exclusively to maternity leave. Indeed, the idea is so uncommon that some males use the term "male maternity leave" to refer to paternity leave. David, for example, who is an accountant, never heard about a man taking time off in his company: *"I've never come across anybody taking off, a man taking off. I don't know. I've never brought it up to anybody, but I've never known anybody that has."* Many of these men reported that they would feel uncomfortable asking for time off. David adds later, *"I might feel a little uncomfortable actually going to them saying, 'Hey can I take a few months off cuz I've got kids.' [Why?] Again I feel that's just more of a, I don't know. Sometimes I feel they might look at me the wrong way. 'You're not the woman, so why are you taking time off?'."* For many interviewees, the reason that stops them from using the policies is their anticipation that this will hurt their careers or limit promotion possibilities. Most of them declare that they would feel comfortable using time off if they saw other male employees using it. Some of the fathers found out after becoming fathers the work-life reconciliation measures that their company provides. Flexible time, on-site daycare, or financial assistance to pay for childcare were some of the measures available to fathers working in more family-friendly companies.

6 Implications

This study finds three important narratives about the intended use and use of parental leave among childless men and fathers from three different countries – Korea, Spain and the U.S. First, in the Korean context, strong masculinity norms and workplace norms make Korean men unwilling to take parental leave. They work (or plan to work) even harder after parenthood as a result of their more traditional gender-role values, which makes the gender approach prevalent in this context. This creates a mismatch between labor-market institutions and family policies because implementing paid parental leave has not resulted in more frequent leave-taking by men. Second, in the Spanish context, the lack of wage replacement in a scenario of economic uncertainty makes the relative resources perspective prevalent regardless of respondents' gender-role ideology and gender dynamics at home. Spanish policies fall short in supporting dual-earner couples in resolving work-life conflict. Nevertheless, some involved fathers made unofficial adjustments to their careers, most of them working in self-employment. Third, in the U.S., the lack of statutory policies and the prevalence of a gendered culture in companies, combined with a strong liberalized and individualistic labor market, reinforce gender essentialist norms towards family. This work culture in a context of more gender egalitarian attitudes gives place to flexible egalitarian attitudes toward women among male respondents. While most American respondents do not envision a change in their full-time work schedules, they show a preference for, or at least an ambivalence about, their female partners working part-time or leaving the workforce after childbirth.

Our findings point to both scholarly and practical recommendations. Future study should investigate how "good" fatherhood is shaped by and, in turn, shapes the available parental leave for men. In relation to this, our results indicate the power of institutions and policies. Gender-equal statutory policies shape how workers think about being treated equally at the workplace. When the usage of leave is legitimized for both men and women, we expect to see a merging of ideals about a good worker and a good parent.

References

Baizán P (2009) Regional child care availability and fertility decisions in Spain. Demogr Res 21(27):803–842

Becker GS (1981) A treatise on the family. Harvard University Press, Cambridge

Beglaubter J (2017) Balancing the scales: negotiating Father's parental leave use. Can Rev Sociol 54(4):476–496

Bueno X, Grau-Grau M (2021) Why is part-time unpaid parental leave (still) gendered? narratives and strategies of couples in Spain. J Fam Issues 42(3):503–526. https://doi.org/10.1177/0192513X20918286

Bünning M (2015) What happens after the 'daddy months'? Fathers' involvement in paid work, childcare, and housework after taking parental leave in Germany. Eur Sociol Rev 31(6):738–748

Bygren M, Ann-Zofie D (2006) Parents' workplace situation and fathers' parental leave use. J Marriage Fam 68(2):363–372

Chesley N (2011) Stay-at-home fathers and breadwinning mothers: gender, couple dynamics, and social change. Gend Soc 25(5):642–664

Craig L, Mullan K (2010) Parenthood, gender and work-family time in the United States, Australia, Italy, France, and Denmark. J Marriage Fam 72(5):1344–1361

Crompton R (2006) Employment and the family. The reconfiguration of work and family life in contemporary societies. Cambridge University Press, Cambridge

Dominguez-Folgueras M, Jurado-Guerrero T, Botía-Morillas C (2018) Against the odds? Keeping a nontraditional division of domestic work after first parenthood in Spain. J Fam Issues 39(7):1855–1879

Doucet A (2009) Dad and baby in the first year: gendered responsibilities and embodiment. Ann Am Acad Pol Soc Sci 624(1):78–98

Escot L, Fernández-Cornejo JA, Lafuente C, Poza C, Jurado-Guerrero T, Botía-Morillas C (2012) Willingness of Spanish men to take maternity leave. Do firms' strategies for reconciliation impinge on this? Sex Roles 67(1–2):29–42

Escot L, Fernández-Cornejo JA, Poza C (2014) Fathers' use of childbirth leave in Spain. The effects of the 13-day paternity leave. Popul Res Policy Rev 33(3):419–453

Flaquer L, Escobedo A (2014) Licencias parentales y política social de la paternidad en España. Cuadernos de Relaciones Laborales 32(1):69–99

Fox B (2009) When couples become parents: the creation of gender in the transition to parenthood. University of Toronto Press, Toronto

Haas L, Allard K, Hwang P (2002) The impact of organizational culture on men's use of parental leave in Sweden. Community Work Fam 5(3):319–342

Hausmann R, Tyson LD, Zahidi S (2012) The global gender gap report 2012. World Economic Forum, Geneva

Horvath LK, Grether T, Wiese BS (2017) Fathers' realizations of parental leave plans: leadership responsibility as help or hindrance? Sex Roles 79(3–4):163–175

Kaufman G, Almqvist A-L (2017) The role of partners and workplaces in British and Swedish Men's parental leave decisions. Men Masculinities 20(5):533–551

Klerman JA, Daley K, Pozniak A (2014) Family and medical leave in 2012: technical report. Abt Associates, Washington, DC. https://www.dol.gov/sites/dolgov/files/OASP/legacy/files/FMLA-2012-Technical-Report.pdf

Kühhirt M (2012) Childbirth and the long-term division of labour within couples: how do substitution, bargaining power, and norms affect parents' time allocation in West Germany? Eur Sociol Rev 28(5):565–582

Lapuerta I, Baizán P, González MJ (2011) Individual and institutional constraints: an analysis of parental leave use and duration in Spain. Popul Res Policy Rev 30(2):185–210

Lundberg S, Pollak RA (1996) Bargaining and distribution in marriage. J Econ Perspect 10(4):139–158

Meil G, Romero-Balsas P, Rogero-García J (2017) Why parents take unpaid parental leave: evidence from Spain. In: Česnuitytė V, Lück D, Widmer ED (eds) Family continuity and change: contemporary European perspectives. Palgrave Macmillan, London, pp 245–267

Neilson J, Stanfors M (2014) It's about time! Gender, parenthood, and household divisions of labor under different welfare regimes. J Fam Issues 35(8):1066–1088

O'Brien M (2009) Fathers, parental leave policies, and infant quality of life: international perspectives and policy impact. Ann Am Acad Pol Soc Sci 624(1):190–213

OECD (2018a) Population with tertiary education (indicator). https://doi.org/10.1787/0b8f90e9-en. Accessed 22 May 2018

OECD (2018b) Time spend in paid and unpaid work, by sex (indicator). https://stats.oecd.org/. Accessed 22 May 2018

Petts RJ, Shafer KM, Lee E (2017) Does adherence to masculine norms shape fathering behavior? J Marriage Fam 80(3):704–720

Ray R, Janet C. Gornick, John Schmitt (2008) Parental leave policies in 21 countries. Assessing generosity and gender equality. Report. Center for Economic and Policy Research. http://cepr.net/publications/reports/plp

Reich N (2010) Who cares? Determinants of the fathers' use of parental leave in Germany, HWWI research paper 1–31, Hamburg

Singley SG, Hynes K (2005) Transitions to parenthood: work-family policies, gender, and the couple context. Gend Soc 19(3):376–397

Valarino I, Duvander A-Z, Haas L, Neyer G (2018) Exploring leave policy preferences: a comparison of Austria, Sweden, Switzerland, and the United States. Social Politics: International Studies in Gender, State & Society 25(1):118–147

World Values Survey (2010-2014) World Values Survey Wave 6: 2010–2014. http://www.worldvaluessurvey.org/wvs.jsp

Open Access This chapter is licensed under the terms of the Creative Commons Attribution 4.0 International License (http://creativecommons.org/licenses/by/4.0/), which permits use, sharing, adaptation, distribution and reproduction in any medium or format, as long as you give appropriate credit to the original author(s) and the source, provide a link to the Creative Commons license and indicate if changes were made.

The images or other third party material in this chapter are included in the chapter's Creative Commons license, unless indicated otherwise in a credit line to the material. If material is not included in the chapter's Creative Commons license and your intended use is not permitted by statutory regulation or exceeds the permitted use, you will need to obtain permission directly from the copyright holder.

Part III
Work & Organizations

Impossible Standards and Unlikely Trade-Offs: Can Fathers be Competent Parents and Professionals?

Jamie J. Ladge and Beth K. Humberd

> *This is the worst period in history to be a dad.*
> *– Adam Carolla, in his book* Daddy Stop Talking *(2016).*

The topic of fatherhood has garnered increased scholarly attention over the past several decades. Initially limited primarily to sociology, developmental psychology, and the humanities (Lamb 2004), management scholars are now focused on understanding fatherhood given the rise in dual career couples (e.g., Masterson and Hoobler 2015; Shockley and Allen 2018), and the availability of family friendly organizational policies (Allen 2001; Kossek and Lautsch 2018). Where prior literature recognized the important role that fathers play in the psychological wellbeing of their children (Yeung et al. 2001), the family unit (Lamb 2004; Yeung et al. 2001), and society as a whole (Dowd 2003), management literature considers the impact of fatherhood, and in particular, "involved fathers" – those who are more engaged, accessible and nurturing in their children's lives – in the workplace. Research finds that when fathers are more involved with their children, they may experience increased job satisfaction, greater work-family enrichment and lower work-family conflict (Ladge et al. 2015). However, they may also face a backlash if involved fathering detracts from perceptions that they are ideal workers that can be fully present and devoted to work above all else (Coltrane et al. 2013; Williams et al. 2013; Rudman and Mescher 2013).

While fathers today are becoming more involved at home than in prior generations, scholars question just how "involved" involved fathering truly is (Wall and Arnold 2007), and the extent to which workplace and societal norms may limit a

J. J. Ladge (✉)
D'Amore-McKim School of Business, Northeastern University, Boston, MA, USA

University of Exeter Business School, Exeter, UK
e-mail: j.ladge@northeastern.edu

B. K. Humberd
Manning School of Business, University of Massachusetts Lowell, Lowell, MA, USA
e-mail: beth_humberd@uml.edu

father's ability to actually enact such involvement (Williams et al. 2016). When men take their involvement in their child(ren)'s lives "too far," they may personally feel they are out of their comfort zone or may put others out of their comfort zone, particularly in contexts where traditional views of fatherhood (e.g., as household provider) persist. As the opening quote suggests, this could be considered "the worst" time to be a dad because now there is an expectation that fathers will not only be competent and committed professionals, but also competent and committed parents.

Comedian and author of *Daddy, Stop Talking*, Adam Carolla further lamented in an interview with *Men's Health* Magazine, *"A certain amount of interaction between a father and his kids is necessary...but...it's not about logging the minutes you're spending with your kids...My kids, here's what they need. They need a lot of interaction with their mommy. And they need some interaction with their daddy. But mainly, they need to respect their dad. They need to say, 'I don't see my dad as much as I see my mom, but that's okay because my dad busts his tail for this family.'"* While Carolla's sentiments are certainly not reflective of all dads' perspectives, in our own research of working fathers, we noted some implicit protests around the expectations facing dads today (Humberd et al. 2015; Ladge et al. 2015). One research participant, who was a relatively new father, admitted that he was surprised and even annoyed by his high level of involvement with his child relative to his spouse. Such views may be a reflection of outdated gender norms, or they could suggest that we are creating impossible standards for fathers, similar to those that have long plagued working mothers.

Many questions remain with respect to what it actually means to be an involved father today and the ways in which organizations can encourage a more holistic view of men as ideal parents *and* professionals. In this chapter, we reflect on these considerations by drawing from prior research and set an agenda for further examining fatherhood in an organizational context.

1 Traditional Notions of the Ideal Father in Work and Family Contexts

Idealized views of fatherhood have been characterized by a "deep-seated ambivalence" since the early 1800s (Pleck 1997:351, as cited in Burnett et al. 2011). Traditionally, an ideal father was a man viewed as the primary breadwinner (O'Brien and Shemilt 2003). While mothers were expected to intensely focus on children, fathers were expected to focus solely on work. In this traditional sense, the notion of an ideal father coincides with the notion of an ideal worker – someone who is fully devoted to one's organization taking little time for himself or family (Reid 2015; Williams 2001). To be an ideal worker, a father's primary responsibility to the family can only be to provide financial support with minimal caregiving expectations. Fathers who did engage in more childcare responsibilities than expected or take time off for paternity leave might be seen as weak or "liberal sissy men" because "a real man works" (Weber 2013). While these views are largely seen as outdated, they continue to persist in depictions of fathers on television, in movies, and in the popular press, which emphasize the father as the sole provider of the family, who is often portrayed as a lazy, irresponsible, incompetent "part-time" parent (Nathanson and Young 2006; Wall and Arnold 2007).

Traditional expectations of fatherhood exist in response to masculine cultural norms tied to workplace norms that stipulate less involvement with family and more time in the office for men in particular (Cooper 2000; Coltrane 1997). A good dad, in the traditional sense, was someone who simply showed up to school events and engaged in few other childcare activities (Hochschild 1989), given his primary site of engagement was the workplace. Research finds that fathers receive a "fatherhood premium" at work, garnering higher earnings than childless men, because having children signals they have a family to support (e.g., Hodges and Budig 2010; Killewald 2013). Due to traditional beliefs that a father's central role is to provide for his growing family, Dahl and colleagues suggest that male executives may "have an impulse to husband his firm's resources for himself and his growing family, potentially at the expense of his employees by reducing their wages or increasing them less than he otherwise would have done" (Dahl et al. 2012:672). This research found that when male CEOs have children of their own, they pay themselves more, particularly when fathering a son; they also pay their employees "less generously" even more so when they have a daughter first rather than a son (Dahl et al. 2012). Thus, the transition to fatherhood influences men's own values in ways that may reinforce traditional notions of fatherhood, and these reinforced views can have unintended organizational impacts.

On the home front, traditional notions of fatherhood are also reinforced by feminine norms and gender ideologies, which often determine paternal involvement (Bulanda 2004). In the United States, individuals are socialized to believe that men and women are associated with particular roles in the household, with women engaging in more of the housework and childcare activities than men (Coltrane and Ishii-Kuntz 1992). Even in couples with more egalitarian views, research suggests that after the birth of their first child, many couples tend to fall back on traditional gender roles (Coontz 1997). Similarly, in the most egalitarian societies where paternity leave is widely available and encouraged (e.g., Nordic countries), women still take substantially more time off after childbirth (OECD 2017). Research suggests that when men do engage in a high degree of parental involvement, it can lead some women to prevent their husband's involvement because it violates the perception that a woman's primary domain is in the home (e.g., Allen and Hawkins 1999). As Bulanda (2004:40) notes, "it may be that the gender ideology of a traditional wife leads to a lack of reinforcing behavior for a less traditional husband who attempts to become more involved with his children. Her belief that a man is not capable of nurturing or caring for children may lead her to limit the amount of her husband's involvement." Even when mothers welcome their spouses's involvement, they may still believe that it infringes on their primary role or they may think that fathers do not have the skillset or ability to nurture their chidren (Allen and Hawkins

1999). Additionally, mothers are often shamed when they do not provide the primary care for their children (Cain Miller 2018). Together, these reinforcing dynamics make traditional notions of fathering – tied to work and masculinity – difficult to change.

2 Contemporary Fathers in Work and Family Contexts

"I'm a dad, not a hero. I'm also not babysitting them. I'm their dad." – Peter Mountford.

Despite the cementing of traditional notions of fathering in societal and organizational contexts, recent scholarship explores the changing role of the father. Some suggest as a result of the Great Depression, men may have begun to be seen as poor, ill-fated providers (Lamb 2004), encouraging them to become more active, involved and nurturing parents (Griswold 1993; Pleck 2004). Further, the changing nature of family structures and increases in the number of dual career couples necessitated a multidimensional view of a father's role, beyond simply a provider but also that of caregiver, role model/teacher, and protector (Lamb 2004). Researchers have documented the "modern" father from Western conceptualizations, where views have shifted from the father as the sole breadwinner and provider towards an idealized view of fathers as more involved in caregiving and emotionally present for their children (Burnett et al. 2011; Cabrera et al. 2000). The "involved father" is one who "should be flexible enough to both earn a wage and be able to help fix dinner and read a bedside story" (Burnett et al. 2011:164). In many ways, this new dad is beholden to similar expectations facing working mothers.

2.1 *The Upside of Involved Fathering*

Ensuing narratives suggest that the "involved father" benefits not only their children, but also their spouse and themselves. Greater paternal involvement may be a positive contributing factor to children's educational attainment, adolescent behavior, and overall psychological well-being (Furstenberg Jr. and Harris 1993; Marsiglio et al. 2000). More involvement can also have positive impacts on the family's overall well-being (Glass 1998), particularly when shared caregiving alleviates the burden experienced by many working mothers (Hochschild 1989). When fathers are active caregivers, they create a more equitable household (Coontz 2009, 2016) where children benefit from having two parents they can equally connect with (Deutsch 1999) and each partner feels less stressed, less guilty, and less career impact from family strains (Holcomb 2000). There are also intrinsic benefits for fathers when they are directly involved with their own children (Deutsch et al. 1993). Anecdotal experiences of fathers reflect such benefits: On a fathers blog, James Norton notes, "Speaking personally, I like changing diapers. Let me restate that: I take satisfaction in changing diapers. Since breastfeeding isn't an option, it's an aspect of childcare where my own limited talents can contribute, if not actually shine. I like the post-diaper smiles. And I like taking my son on walks, and being around to catch all those silly-but-significant little developmental milestones. But most of all, I like knowing that I'm participating actively in raising him – we've been having dude time together since he was born, something that I hope continues for the rest of my life" (Norton 2013).

Involved fathering may also have positive impacts to organizations. In our own research, we found that the more time fathers spent with their children on a typical day, the more satisfied they were with their jobs and the less likely they were to want to leave their organizations (Ladge et al. 2015). Greater involvement was also associated with less work-family conflict and greater work-family enrichment for these fathers. In another study, we found that new fathers can benefit interpersonally at work with colleagues viewing them as more mature and serious, but with a softer side, once they become parents (Humberd et al. 2015). Recognizing fathers as involved parents can build camaraderie and support amongst working parents in organizations more broadly.

Given these positive outcomes, work-family support in organizations has become less about organizations solely supporting mothers, and more about considering how to help all workers in organizations thrive in their work and family lives through both policy reform and informal support (Harrington and Ladge 2009); Kelly et al. 2008). When fathers have access to and feel they can utilize workplace flexibility policies, they report increased job satisfaction, productivity and organizational commitment, and report having better relationships with their co-workers (Bowers 2014). These shifts may be attributed in particular to Millennial generation fathers in the workplace, who report a stronger desire than any other generation to be more involved with their children, viewing their fathering role as a combination of both breadwinner and caregiver (Harrington and Fraone 2016).

Even with these promising shifts, there are open questions as to what constitutes involvement. Many studies that track the household division of labor in families combine all aspects of childcare and housework, making it difficult to assess which aspects of fatherhood men spend the most time engaging in (Bulanda 2004). Further, there may be gender differences in terms of the type of involvement men have with their children, as compared to women, with fathers engaging in "play" with their children, while mothers are often focused on the caretaking and nurturing aspects of parenting (Lamb 2004). Some research finds that when fathers have less traditional attitudes about gender roles, they are more involved in a wide breadth of interactions with their children including leisure activities away from the home, working on projects, helping with homework or playing, having one-on-one conversations and watching television (Bulanda 2004). These complexities lend to questions about the boundaries of fathers' involvement, and potential downsides that can arise from expectations of involvement.

2.2 The Downside of Involved Fathering

While the above discussion certainly recognizes the positive aspects of involved fathering, fathers in dual career couples still face similar work-family balance challenges that mothers face, such as "always feeling rushed" (Livingston and Parker 2019) and never feeling fully engaged in either domain (Humberd et al. 2015). Unlike mothers however, men have fewer role models to look to for support and guidance on balancing work and family (Ladge and Greenberg 2019), and fathers may be less likely to express their desires for involvement fear of being seen as less of an ideal worker or less of a man (Behson 2013). Even though workplace flexibility are purported to be available for all employees, most managers and employees still associate these benefits with women more so than with men, contributing to beliefs that men will not need to adapt their careers to manage family as much as women (Burnett et al. 2011).

When fathers do make use of flexible work arrangements, they face a greater "flexibility stigma" – an informal penalty resulting from perceptions that one is uncommitted to their work if they make use of such arrangements – than women (Williams et al. 2016). Working fathers may even "fake" their hours to manage their needed flexibility while still appearing as a committed worker (Reid 2015); yet in doing so, these men may feel less authentic, and subsequently less engaged in their work. In some ways, it's a difficult dilemma for working dads in organizations: if they make use of the work-family benefits available to them, they are seen as uncommitted, yet if they manage their flexibility in stealth ways, they feel less engaged and perhaps are less productive with their work. Some men have fought against these biases by protesting unequal treatment and taking legal action against their employers (Levs 2015; Johnston 2018), with over a quarter of child-care related discrimination cases filed by men in the past decade (Calvert 2016).

While workplaces may espouse to be receptive to men's role as fathers, many organizations do not actually support these men in being active and involved caregivers, particularly as it relates to paternity leave. In the United States, only 12% of private sector employees have access to paid parental leave (U.S. Department of Labor 2015) and when it is offered, it is typically short, unpaid, or requires the use of vacation and sick time. Although the number of companies offering paternity leave has increased in the past decade (Harrington et al. 2014; Livingston 2014b), most American fathers still return to work within 2 weeks of their child's birth (Harrington et al. 2014) and many choose to not even use any paternity leave at all, even when they have access to it (Williams 2013). Some research suggests that men may experience biases that can lead to decreased earnings when they do take paternity leave (Rege and Solli 2013), so it is not surprising that many fathers who do have access to leave say that they do not make use of such policies due to informal norms and workplace pressures in their organizations (Harrington et al. 2014). While maternity leave has become a generally accepted option for women, many organizations (including managers, and colleagues of the employees) still do not expect fathers to take leave; doing so, violates implicit norms of masculinity, leaving men unable to benefit from any policies that may actually be offered to them.

Together, these norms and social pressures can result in longer-term career consequences for men who want to be involved dads, such as being passed up for promotions and depressed earnings (Coltrane et al. 2013), more harassment and general mistreatment (Berdahl and Moon 2013), and overall perceptions that they are uncommitted to their work (Behson 2013).

3 Reconciling the Old and New: Redefining Fatherhood

The picture for working fathers today is complex. Involved fathering is perhaps more accepted and encouraged today than ever before, yet the fatherhood role is still associated with the work domain more so than the family domain. Men face such high expectations of the type of fathers they should be, that it is hard to tell if it is even possible to reconcile these complexities in practice. Likewise, some argue that the father's role in a family has in fact not changed much at all (Wall and Arnold 2007), while other work suggests that fathers are taking on more family and childcare responsibilities in dual-income households (Parker et al. 2017). Further, fathers may perform specific tasks (e.g., watching children at a sporting event or assisting them with technologies) that are a unique form of involvement than is typically assessed or captured (Parker et al. 2017).

Given these variations in how involved fathering is understood and assessed, men themselves may be confused as to how best to reconcile these old and new fathering expectations. Fathers may receive more praise than women for completing ordinary parenting tasks, but face biases at work when adjusting their work to accommodate their family life (Coltrane et al. 2013; Rudman and Mescher 2013). Our own research findings about the positive workplace outcomes associated with involved fathering suggest that there may be an "optimal" amount of time that allows for such benefits to arise: In our study, fathers spent an average of only 2.5 h with their children during a typical work day (Ladge et al. 2015). A New York Times article aptly stated: "the power of expectations sheds light on why employers reward fatherhood—but only if they don't think men are spending too much time on it" (Cain Miller 2014). Further, even if men espouse a more involved fatherhood, their actual practices often diverge from such notions (Hochschild 1989). A key finding of study we collaborated on found that "while fathers believe that caregiving should be divided equally, they acknowledge that this is not the current reality in their families" (Harrington et al. 2011; Ladge et al. 2015).

There is no question that competing views of fathering exist, and men in professional careers in particular are likely to experience tension around these conflicting expectations. Although fathers may be expected to be more involved in caregiving in the home, images of the ideal, devoted worker are still entrenched in our broader societal expectations and institutional arrangements (Gerson 2009), creating multiple, and seemingly conflicting, expectations of what it means to be a father (Humberd et al. 2015). Our research has found that men don't necessarily hold one image of themselves as fathers but instead hold multiple images of themselves as fathers that are sustained through norms and expectations in their day-to-day work and personal contexts. In a qualitative study of 31 first time fathers, our analysis revealed that participants express several different images of themselves as fathers, which represent the various internalized meanings and expectations they hold of how they view themselves and hope to be viewed by others as fathers. The meanings coalesced around four common fathering images – provider, role model, partner, and nurturer – that comprise the content of their fathering identities (Humberd et al. 2015). As these images span from more traditional to more involved notions of fathering, men in our study seemed to maintain the multiplicity of meanings.

Not surprisingly, men express confusion and ambivalence around how to enact their fathering role while trying to preserve an appropriate work image (Reid 2015). For example, outside of work, fathers may emphasize their involvement to increase other's perceptions of kindness and compassion for working dads (Richards 2014), while downplaying their caregiving role at work in order to seem committed to their careers. This confusion and ambivalence has cross-domain effects such that men may adopt a work-family image that may or may not align with their actual identity (Ladge and Little 2019). Thus, even if more involved fathering may be the expected standard today (Ladge et al. 2016), there is little empirical evidence that men are able to truly enact these new expectations in their day to day lives across work and home domains (Coltrane 1997; Gregory and Milner 2011; LaRossa 1988).

4 Where Can We Go from Here? Bolstering Paternal Competence at Work and at Home

When referring to mothers, we don't add the term "involved" as we do with fathers – for mothers, involvement is implied, yet for fathers, it has to be assessed. In applying that term, it assumes that there is variation in the extent to which fathers should focus on their child(ren). The question then becomes, how do we get to the point where involvement is implied for fathers and not something that needs to be evaluated or speculated? Can expectations of fathers change so that we always assume they are competent, dedicated parents, just in the same way we see them as competent and dedicated professionals? Much research and practical advice considers how women should deal with the guilt that may be associated with being a working mother and build confidence in their abilities to have both a successful career and family life (e.g., Holcomb 2000; Sandberg 2013; Ladge and Greenberg 2019). Similar conversations to guide working fathers toward building a sense of confidence across both domains is necessary; yet this research needs to take into account multiple areas that we consider below.

First, while research is beginning to explore what men can do to manage work and family effectively, there is a need to also examine what women, and couples together, can do to support involved fathering in their everyday lives. Recent research has considered the negotiations that spousal couples engage in to decide whose career takes priority (Livingston 2014a) as well as how partners in dual-career couples shape each other's professional identities (Petriglieri and Obodaru 2018). How can we build on these lines of work to truly consider the couple as a unit engaging in the work and home domains? There is much room truly understand the intersections between each partners' sense of confidence and competence in work and home domains. In our own research, we find that fostering new mothers' maternal confidence is important to their experiences of work-family conflict, and ultimately their ability to stay in the workforce (Ladge et al. 2018); but, what does this say about fostering men's paternal confidence? Perhaps part of mothers' ability to build their own sense of confidence in managing work and family could be supported by also recognizing that men need to build similar sense of confidence. It may also be useful to consider the confidence and competence of the parental unit together. Focusing on the parental unit more broadly could also help to move away from dividing gender and further reinforcing traditional norms.

Secondly, future research must also focus on the complexity of family structures that exist today, because understanding what constitutes involvement will differ greatly for different types of families. Indeed, much of the existing literature draws from samples of upper middle class, white fathers in traditional family structures. Some work has begun to acknowledge the different challenges facing fathers in dual-career couples compared to couples with stay-at-home spouses (e.g., Hammer et al. 1997), or men in heterosexual marriages compared men in gay marriages (e.g., Richardson et al. 2012). There are even more complexities to understand with respect to involvement for fathers with one child, fathers with multiple children, single fathers, widowed fathers, and other increasingly complex and diverse family structures. Similarly, more research can focus on the challenges of involvement across the life cycle of parenting; while current conversations focused on paternity leave are important, we must also extend our research to understand what involved fathering means at middle and later stages of parenting.

Lastly, beyond a focus on the men themselves, more research should consider specifically what can be done within work domains to shift the narrative on what fathering means today. While organizations are seemingly more friendly to working parents today, perhaps the biggest impediment for working fathers is the informal culture in many organizations. Indeed, much research discusses the difficulty in "dislodging the norm of the ideal worker who receives backstage support of a stay-at-home wife" (Williams et al. 2013:210). One way to shift the informal culture is having managers and leaders that are "vocal, consistent, and transparent about support for men's caregiving responsibilities" (Humberd et al. 2015:264). Beyond simply support, though, research suggests that leaders need to model behavior (e.g., a CEO that enacts "involved fathering" freely and openly) that opens up the space for all employees to engage in their work and home lives (e.g., Burke and Major 2014; Litano et al. 2014). Thus, leaders who are working parents can play an important role in changing the culture by demonstrating support *and* acting as role models by utilizing family-friendly practices, talking openly about their own experiences managing work and family demands, and encouraging others to do the same. Further, organizations that offer various levels of support for working mothers such as affinity groups and individualized coaching, should offer and encourage the same so that fathers also have the space to participate in discussions about work-family needs. Additionally, organizations may need to take further steps to enforce policies in order to shift the cultural norms: A recent Wall Street Journal article highlighted some organizations that have begun enforcing a mandatory paternity leave for fathers in their organizations (Lipman 2018). Multiple approaches will be necessary to change taken-for-granted performance expectations and cultural norms that support the view of ideal workers as those that are always present and available.

5 Concluding Thoughts

Changes in families have been precipitating changes in the workplace for decades now. While we have paid important attention to the shifts necessary to support working mothers, we owe similar focus to the shifts necessary to support working fathers. Fathers today face similar challenges in managing work and family, albeit often in unexpected or alternative ways from mothers. Without attention to the pressures on both men and women, as well as on the parental unit as a whole – in whatever complex and unique form it comes – we run the risk of reinforcing the long-standing gendered expectations that underpin both work and home domains.

References

Allen TD (2001) Family-supportive work environments: the role of organizational perceptions. J Vocat Behav 58(3):414–435
Allen SM, Hawkins AJ (1999) Maternal gatekeeping: Mothers' beliefs and behaviors that inhibit greater father involvement in family work. J Marriage Fam 61(1):199–212
Behson S (2013) What's a working dad to do? Harvard Business Review. https://hbr.org/2013/08/whats-a-working-dad-to-do. Accessed Aug 2021
Berdahl JL, Moon SH (2013) Workplace mistreatment of middle class workers based on sex, parenthood, and caregiving. J Soc Issues 69(2):341–366
Bowers K (2014) A mother's work: special report. Working Mother. April–May 2014 Z(Issue 32) https://www.workingmother.com/special-report/mothers-work-special-report
Bulanda RE (2004) Paternal involvement with children: the influence of gender ideologies. J Marriage Fam 66(1):40–45
Burke RJ, Major DA (eds) (2014) Gender in organizations: are men allies or adversaries to women s career advancement? Edward Elgar Publishing, Cheltenham
Burnett S, Gatrell C, Cooper C, Sparrow P (2011) Fatherhood and flexible working: a contradiction in terms? In: Kaiser S, Ringlstetter MJ, Eikhof DR, Cunha MPE (eds) Creating balance? International perspectives on the work-life integration of professionals. Springer, Berlin, pp 157–172
Cabrera N, Tamis-LeMonda CS, Bradley RH, Hofferth S, Lamb ME (2000) Fatherhood in the twenty-first century. Child Dev 71(1):127–136

Cain Miller C (2014) Being a father is good for your career, but don't get carried away. In: The Upshot, New York Times. https://www.nytimes.com/2014/11/14/upshot/being-a-father-is-good-for-your-career-but-dont-get-carried-away.html. Accessed Nov 13

Cain Miller C (2018) The relentlessness of modern parenting. The Upshot, New York Times. https://www.nytimes.com/2018/12/25/upshot/the-relentlessness-of-modern-parenting.html. Accessed Dec 25

Calvert CT (2016) Caregivers in the workplace: family responsibilities discrimination litigation update. Center for Work Life law, University of California – Hastings

Carolla A (2016) Daddy Stop Talking. Dey Street Books, New York

Coltrane S (1997) Family man: fatherhood, housework, and gender equity. Oxford University Press, New York

Coltrane S, Ishii-Kuntz M (1992) Men's housework: a life course perspective. J Marriage Fam 54 (1):43–57

Coltrane S, Miller EC, DeHaan T, Stewart L (2013) Fathers and the flexibility stigma. J Soc Issues 69(2):279–302

Coontz S (1997) The way we really are: coming to terms with America's changing families. Basic Books, New York

Coontz S (2009) Sharing the load. In The Shriver report: a woman's nation changes everything. New York: Free Press. http://shriverreport.org/sharing-the-load/

Coontz S (2016) Gender equality and economic inequality: impact on marriage. In: McHale SM, King V, Van Hook J, Booth A (eds) Gender and couple relationships. Springer, New York, pp 29–90

Cooper M (2000) Being the 'go-to guy': fatherhood, masculinity, and the Organization of Work in Silicon Valley. Qual Sociol 23(4):379–405

Dahl MS, Dezső CL, Ross DG (2012) Fatherhood and managerial style: how a male CEO's children affect the wages of his employees. Adm Sci Q 57(4):669–693

Deutsch FM (1999) Halving it all: how equally shared parenting works. Harvard University Press, Cambridge

Deutsch FM, Lussier JB, Servis LJ (1993) Husbands at home: predictors of paternal participation in childcare and housework. J Pers Soc Psychol 65(6):1154–1166

Dowd NE (2003) Redefining fatherhood. New York University Press, New York

Furstenberg FF Jr, Harris KM (1993) When fathers matter/why fathers matter: the impact of paternal involvement on the offspring of adolescent mothers. In: Lawson A, Rhode DL (eds) The politics of pregnancy: adolescent sexuality and public policy. Yale University Press, New Haven, pp 189–215. https://repository.upenn.edu/cgi/viewcontent.cgi?article=1042&context=sociology_papers

Gerson K (2009) Changing lives, resistant institutions: a new generation negotiates gender, work, and family change. Sociol Forum 24(4):735–753

Glass J (1998) Gender liberation, economic squeeze, or fear of strangers: why fathers provide infant Care in Dual-Earner Families. J Marriage Fam 60:821–834

Gregory A, Milner S (2011) What is 'new' about fatherhood? The social construction of fatherhood in France and the UK. Men Masculinities 14(5):588–606

Griswold RL (1993) Fatherhood in America: a history. Basic Books, New York

Hammer LB, Allen E, Grigsby TD (1997) Work–family conflict in dual-earner couples: within-individual and crossover effects of work and family. J Vocat Behav 50(2):185–203

Harrington B, Fraone JS (2016) The new Millenial dad: understanding the paradox of Today's fathers. Boston College Center for Work and Family, Chestnut Hill

Harrington B, Ladge JJ (2009) Work-life integration: present dynamics and future directions for organizations. Organ Dyn 38(2):148–157

Harrington B, Van Deusen F, Fraone JS, Eddy S, Hass L (2014) The new dad: take your leave. Boston College Center for Work and Family, Chestnut Hill

Harrington B, Van Deusen F, Humberd B (2011) The new dad: caring, committed and conflicted. Boston College Center for Work and Family, Chestnut Hill

Hochschild AR (1989) The second shift: working parents and the revolution at home. Penguin, New York

Hodges MJ, Budig MJ (2010) Who gets the daddy Bonus? Organizational hegemonic masculinity and the impact of fatherhood on earnings. Gend Soc 24(6):717–745

Holcomb B (2000) Not guilty!: the good news for working mothers. Simon and Schuster, New York

Humberd BK, Ladge JJ, Harrington B (2015) The 'new' dad: navigating fathering identity within organizational contexts. J Bus Psychol 30(2):249–266

Johnston K (2018) More fathers are protesting unequal treatment at work. Boston Globe. https://www.bostonglobe.com/business/2018/01/02/more-fathers-are-protesting-unequal-treatment-work/TwmdCd60XyvETvwIX7jDUN/story.html. Accessed Jan 2017

Kelly EL, Kossek EE, Hammer LB, Durham M, Bray J, Chermack K, Murphy LA, Daskubar D (2008) Getting there from here: research on the effects of work-family initiatives on work-family conflict and business outcomes. Acad Manag Ann 2:305–349

Killewald A (2013) A reconsideration of the fatherhood premium: marriage, Coresidence, biology, and fathers' wages. Am Sociol Rev 78(1):96–116

Kossek EE, Lautsch BA (2018) Work-life flexibility for whom? Occupational status and work-life inequality in upper middle, and lower level jobs. Acad Manag Ann 12(1):5–36

Ladge J, Greenberg D (2019) Maternal optimism: forging a positive path through work and motherhood. Oxford University Press, New York

Ladge JJ, Humberd BK, Eddleston KA (2018) Retaining professionally employed new mothers: the importance of maternal confidence and workplace support to their intent to stay. Hum Resour Manag 57(4):883–900

Ladge JJ, Humberd BK, McNett J (2016) The other half: views of fatherhood in organizations. In: Matthews R, Spitzmueller C (eds) Perspectives on work and the transition to motherhood. Springer Books, Berlin, pp 267–285

Ladge JJ, Humberd BK, Watkins MB, Harrington B (2015) Updating the organization MAN: an examination of involved fathering in the workplace. Acad Manag Perspect 29(1):152–171

Ladge J, Little LM (2019) When expectations become reality: work-family image management and identity adaptation. Acad Manag Rev 44(1):17–40

Lamb ME (2004) The role of the father in child development. Wiley, New York

LaRossa R (1988) Fatherhood and social change. Fam Relat 37(4):451–458

Levs J (2015) All in: how our work-first culture fails dads, families, and businesses--and how we can fix it together. HarperCollins, New York

Lipman J (2018) Want equality? Make new dads stay home: mandatory paternity leave would help close the wage gap and strengthen family bonds. Wall Street J. https://www.wsj.com/articles/want-equality-make-new-dads-stay-home-1538151219

Litano ML, Myers DP, Major DA (2014) How can men and women be allies in achieving work-family balance? The role of coping in facilitating positive crossover. In: Burke RJ, Major DA (eds) Gender in organizations: are men allies or adversaries to women's career advancement. Edward Elgar, Cheltenham, pp 365–384

Livingston BA (2014a) Bargaining behind the scenes: spousal negotiation, labor, and work–family burnout. J Manag 40(4):949–977

Livingston G (2014b) Growing number of dads home with the kids: biggest increase among those caring for family. Pew Social and Demographic Trends. Pew Research Center. http://www.pewsocialtrends.org/2014/06/05/growing-number-of-dads-home-with-the-kids/

Livingston G, Parker K (2019) 8 facts about American dads. Pew Research Center, Fact Tank: News in the Numbers. https://www.pewresearch.org/fact-tank/2019/06/12/fathers-day-facts/

Marsiglio W, Amato P, Day RD, Lamb ME (2000) Scholarship on fatherhood in the 1990s and beyond. J Marriage Fam 62:1173–1191

Masterson CR, Hoobler JM (2015) Care and career: a family identity-based typology of dual-earner couples. J Organ Behav 36(1):75–93

Nathanson P, Young KK (2006) Legalizing misandry: from public shame to systemic discrimination against men. McGill-Queen's Press, Montreal

Norton J (2013) I'm a dad, not a hero: Thoughts on tom Stocky's Facebook post. Family: modern parenthood, blog, Christian Science Monitor. July 12. https://www.csmonitor.com/The-Culture/Family/Modern-Parenthood/2013/0712/I-m-a-dad-not-a-hero-Thoughts-on-Tom-Stocky-s-Facebook-post

O'Brien M, Shemilt I (2003) Working fathers: earning and caring. Equal Opportunities Commission, London. http://www.fatherhoodinstitute.org/uploads/publications/280.pdf

OECD (2017) How's life? 2017: measuring Well-being. OECD Publishing, Paris. https://doi.org/10.1787/how_life-2017-en

Parker K, Horowitz JM, Stepler R (2017) On gender differences, no consensus on nature vs. Nurture: Americans say society places a higher premium on masculinity than on femininity. Pew Social Trends. Pew Research Center. http://www.pewsocialtrends.org/2017/12/05/on-gender-differences-no-consensus-on-nature-vs-nurture/

Petriglieri J, Obodaru O (2018) Secure-base relationships as drivers of professional identity development in dual-career couples. Adm Sci Q 27:1–43

Pleck JH (1997) Paternal involvement: levels, sources, and consequences. In: Lamb ME (ed) The role of the father in child development. Wiley, New York, pp 66–103

Pleck EH (2004) Two dimensions of fatherhood: a history of the good dad–bad dad complex. In: Lamb ME (ed) The role of the father in child development, 4th edn. Wiley, New York, pp 32–57

Rege M, Solli IF (2013) The impact of paternity leave on fathers future earnings. Demography 50(6):2255–2277

Reid E (2015) Embracing, passing, revealing, and the ideal worker image: how people navigate expected and experienced professional identities. Organ Sci 26(4):997–1017

Richards D (2014) Daddy Doin' work: empowering mothers to evolve fatherhood. Jollyfish Press, Provo

Richardson HB, Moyer AM, Goldberg AE (2012) 'You try to be superman and you don't have to be': gay adoptive Fathers' challenges and tensions in balancing work and family. Fathering 10(3):314–337

Rudman LA, Mescher K (2013) Penalizing men who request a family leave: is flexibility stigma a femininity stigma? J Soc Issues 69(2):322–340

Sandberg S (2013) Lean in: women, work, and the will to Lead. Alfred A. Knopf, New York

Shockley KM, Allen TD (2018) It's not what I expected: the association between dual-earner Couples' met expectations for the division of paid and family labor and Well-being. J Vocat Behav 104:240–260

U.S. Department of Labor (2015) DOL factsheet: paid family and medical leave. https://www.dol.gov/wb/resources/paid_leave_fact_sheet.pdf

Wall G, Arnold S (2007) How involved is involved fathering? An exploration of the Contemporary culture of fatherhood. Gend Soc 21(4):508–527

Weber L (2013) Why dads don't take paternity leave: more companies offer new fathers paid time off, but many fear losing face back at the office. Wall Street J. https://www.wsj.com/articles/SB10001424127887324049504578541633708283670

Williams JC (2001) Unbending gender: why work and family conflict and what to do about it. Oxford University Press, New York

Williams M (2013) 40% of fathers do not to take paternity leave. The Guardian News and Media January 06. https://www.theguardian.com/careers/fathers-choose-not-to-take-paternity-leave

Williams JC, Berdahl JL, Vandello JA (2016) Beyond work-life 'integration'. Annu Rev Psychol 67:515–539

Williams JC, Blair-Loy M, Berdahl JL (2013) Cultural schemas, social class, and the flexibility stigma. J Soc Issues 69(2):209–234

Yeung WJ, Sandberg JF, Davis-Kean PE, Hofferth SL (2001) Children's time with fathers in intact families. J Marriage Fam 63(1):136–154

Open Access This chapter is licensed under the terms of the Creative Commons Attribution 4.0 International License (http://creativecommons.org/licenses/by/4.0/), which permits use, sharing, adaptation, distribution and reproduction in any medium or format, as long as you give appropriate credit to the original author(s) and the source, provide a link to the Creative Commons license and indicate if changes were made.

The images or other third party material in this chapter are included in the chapter's Creative Commons license, unless indicated otherwise in a credit line to the material. If material is not included in the chapter's Creative Commons license and your intended use is not permitted by statutory regulation or exceeds the permitted use, you will need to obtain permission directly from the copyright holder.

The New Dad: The Career-Caregiving Conundrum

Brad Harrington

1   Introduction and Research Overview

Over the last decade, the Boston College Center for Work & Family has completed a series of research studies on the changing face of fatherhood in the United States of America. We began our series in 2009 to fill the gap we observed in high quality, in-depth research that existed on American fathers. We saw that this dearth of research had led to many unfortunate misconceptions, including:

- Outdated workplace assumptions about the caregiving roles that fathers play
- Employer work-family programs targeted, explicitly or implicitly, at women, making men reluctant to take advantage of these offerings
- Increased work-family conflict for fathers that is not widely recognized or understood
- Inaccurate portrayals of fathers in the media

Perhaps the most troubling problem was that fathers' voices were often absent from, or even seen as irrelevant to, work-family conversations. In an effort to address this, we began our journey with a relatively small sample, a qualitative study of fathers of very young children to better understand their experiences transitioning to fatherhood. We titled our first report *The New Dad* for the obvious reason that the men in the sample were all new dads. But we did this also because we were trying to explore whether the role of fathers was, in fact, changing and a new model was emerging. This report became the first step in a 10-year journey, with a new

B. Harrington (✉)
Boston College Center for Work and Family (CWF), Carroll School of Management, Boston College, Chestnut Hill, MA, USA
e-mail: harrinb@bc.edu

© The Author(s) 2022
M. Grau Grau et al. (eds.), *Engaged Fatherhood for Men, Families and Gender Equality*, Contributions to Management Science,
https://doi.org/10.1007/978-3-030-75645-1_11

publication each year, exploring different perspectives of the role today's father play at work and in the home.

Not surprisingly, we have observed that fathers' roles are indeed in a state of transition in the U.S. Also, not surprisingly, this period of change brings with it accompanying dilemmas. The most fundamental dilemma the dads we have studied face is finding the sweet spot between a focus on their careers vs. their caregiving responsibilities. The results of all our studies show that a very significant percent of today's fathers struggle with this conundrum and knowing where they should be on the career vs caregiver spectrum in order to do the right thing for their partners and themselves. This chapter will highlight results from our studies, and some other noted scholars, that bring to light fathers' caregiving dilemma.

Our research samples over this time have focused almost exclusively on U.S., college educated, white-collar fathers who work in large corporations. As such, we do not assert that the results are generalizable to all fathers.

We have been gratified that *The New Dad* series has contributed to a growing body of knowledge about the experiences and expectations of today's fathers. We feel that it has also catalyzed a significant increase in our national dialogue on this important subject.

2 Comparing Dads' and Moms' Caregiving Responsibilities

The historic, often stereotypical, division of labor in which men go off to work and women take care of children and the home is no longer the common model of today's American family. Significantly, more families are dual-career, with both mothers and fathers working. There are even more single-parent headed households in the U.S. than the historical model of the "traditional American family." As a result, there is increasing pressure on men to do a greater share of childcare and housework than was the case in previous generations. Mothers' increased labor force participation demands this. According to a 2015 EY global workforce study, Millennials are almost twice as likely to have a spouse/partner working full-time than Baby Boomers were (78% for Millennials vs. 47% of Baby Boomers). The Bureau of Labor Statistics (2014) reports that in 2013 both parents were employed in 59.1% of all married couples with a child under 18 years old.

Time use data indicate that men have nearly tripled their time spent providing primary childcare, (i.e., the amount of time when childcare is their primary activity) over the last few decades (Wang and Bianchi 2009). Although women continue to spend more hours providing childcare than men do, fathers spent about 2.5 h in primary childcare activities per week from 1965 to 1985, and that number had grown to nearly 7 h per week by 2000 and to 7.5 h by 2015. In 2013, the Pew Research Center identified a similar increase in fathers' involvement in the home (Pew 2013a). Pew reported that when one combines child care, housework, and paid work time, fathers dedicate approximately the same number of total hours to the family as mothers do, but mothers still spend approximately two times as many hours on childcare and housework as their male partners (in heterosexual couples).

It is also interesting to examine whether men's participation in caregiving is different for men whose wives are in the paid labor force versus those whose wives are not. Wang and Bianchi (2009) found that:

- Fathers whose spouses worked for pay spent significantly more time in <u>solo care activities</u> (i.e., without their spouse present) than men whose wives were at-home full time.
- Fathers with spouses in the paid workforce were more involved in childcare, particularly when their children were infants and toddlers, than fathers whose wives did not work.

A 2015 study by Ohio State University researchers using time diary data from 182 couples who participated in the *New Parents Project* found that 95% of both men and women who were about to have their first child agreed that mothers and fathers should equally share the childcare responsibilities (Yavorsky et al. 2015). In the same vein, Knight and Brinton (2017) found that 93% of Europeans agree that "men should take as much responsibility as women for home and children" and 78% agree, "fathers are as well-suited to look after their children as mothers." According to the Ohio State study however, after the arrival of their child, men did about 10 h a week of physical childcare – the "less fun work" such as changing diapers and bathing the baby – while women spent 15 h per week engaged in those activities. Men spent about 4 h and women about 6 h per week in the more "fun" part of parenting, which included activities such as reading to the baby and playing. (Yavorsky et al. 2015).

Is the division of labor also problematic for same-sex couples? A Families and Work Institute study of both same-sex and different-sex couples indicated that men in same-sex couples have significantly higher satisfaction with the division of household and childcare responsibilities. As these tasks cannot be divided solely based on traditional gender roles, more conversations occur about how the responsibilities are fulfilled. In both same-sex and different-sex couples, those who have conversations about the divisions of household responsibilities have a higher satisfaction with the division of labor than those who do not explicitly address such concerns (Matos 2015).

3 How Do Fathers See their Roles?

Historically, most people assumed that a father's role was clear – he was the breadwinner, providing his family with the much-needed economic means to make other family objectives possible – from the basic necessities of food and shelter, to the longer term, more strategic investments in funding children's college educations and mom and dad's retirement. But times have changed.

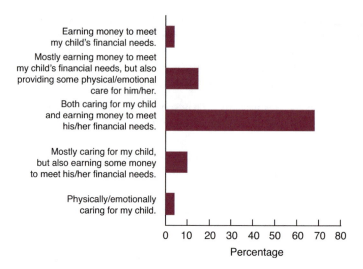

Fig. 1 How fathers see their role: Caregiving vs. breadwinning. Source: Boston College Center for Work & Family. *The New Dad: Caring, Conflicted and Committed.* 2011

In 2013, the Pew Research Center released a report (2013b) stating that in the U.S., women now made up 40% of primary household earners. In response to this, in June of the same year, the *New York Times* published a "Room for Debate" editorial titled *"What are Fathers For?"* The title suggested that as men's role as the family breadwinner was diminishing, it raised a question of how much and in what ways do fathers contribute to contemporary families (New York Times 2013). On closer examination, the most important detail from the Pew study behind the headline was glossed over – that in 5 out of 8 of the households where the mother was the primary breadwinner, she was also the only adult present (i.e., it was a single mother-led household). In homes where an unmarried woman was the sole breadwinner, the family's average income was only $23,000 a year. More than half of the children in such homes live in poverty. By contrast, female breadwinners who were living with and earning more than their husbands were in an entirely different income bracket; their median salary was $80,000. And for the remaining 60% of U.S. families where the woman is not the primary breadwinner, fathers are still the main financial provider.

So how do fathers today see their role as breadwinners vs. caregivers? In our 2011 study *The New Dad: Caring, Committed and Conflicted* (Harrington et al. 2011), which surveyed 963 fathers employed in one of four Fortune 100 organizations, fathers were asked to identify where they fell on the continuum between providing for their families' financial needs (the breadwinning role) and caring for their families' emotional and physical needs (the caregiving role). The result was surprising. More than 2/3 of the fathers believed the two were equally weighted – they did not see themselves solely or even primarily as financial providers as one might

Perceptions of Work Culture

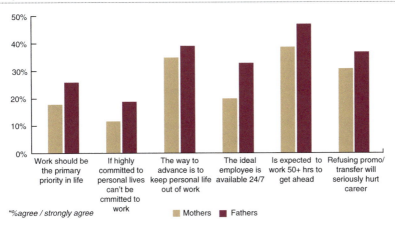

Fig. 2 How Millennial mothers and fathers respond to cues from their corporate culture. Source: Boston College Center for Work & Family. *The New Millennial Dad: Understanding the Paradox of Today's Fathers*. 2016

expect. In fact, as can be seen in Fig. 1 below, less than 5% of the fathers reported that they saw their role as being a financial provider alone.

How does this more balanced view manifest itself in action? Do organizations and society as a whole support fathers as caregivers? Are fathers more sensitive to organizational culture norms that their female counterparts? Are fathers still more ambitious and career focused than mothers? Are fathers likely to be, or even consider being, stay at home fathers than was the case in the past? How do men's actions align with their expressed desire to be more fully engaged caregivers? These are the topics that much of our research set out to explore.

In our 2016 study on Millennial fathers (Harrington et al. 2016), we explored the issue of how sensitive Millennial dads were to cues transmitted by their corporate culture regarding the so-called "ideal worker." This model would suggest that the ideal worker is one who goes to any length to be sure work is completed, is available beyond standard hours to focus on work projects, and will compromise time with one's family and personal life to meet their employer's expectations (Williams 2001). We compared their feelings with those of Millennials mothers.

As the Millennial dads strive to reach their professional goals, they seem to be keenly aware of and influenced by their workplace culture. In our study, the young fathers indicated greater awareness and sensitivity to the demands of their employers and to the vision of the ideal worker than their female counterparts. Men were more likely to characterize their work environments as requiring a great deal in terms of time, energy, and focus.

As can be seen in Fig. 2, the fathers were more likely than mothers to characterize their work environments as requiring work to be primary. Constant availability was seen as the expectation for one-third of fathers (vs. 20% of mothers), and nearly half of fathers saw 50 h as the baseline commitment expected in order to "get ahead."

Slightly more Millennial dads than moms believed keeping their personal life out of the workplace was important for advancement. Relative to their female peers, Millennial fathers were more likely to believe that turning down a promotion or transfer would seriously hurt their careers, and they were more inclined to believe that their employer felt work should be primary in one's life.

Despite the high hurdles for career success, fathers indicated a greater willingness to do what was necessary to succeed professionally and to make tradeoffs affecting their personal and family lives. Nearly 87% of men with children were willing to put in a great deal of effort at work beyond what was normally required (compared to 77% of mothers). Fathers characterized themselves as highly engaged with their work and expressed a deep sense of professional responsibility. Four-out-of-five described themselves as being very involved personally with their jobs and over half experienced their organization's problems as their own. Importantly, dads were twice as likely as mothers to want to advance even if it meant less time with their children (although that number was still quite small at 16%) and nearly twice as likely to be willing to relocate for career advancement.

The heightened sensitivity of fathers to organizational norms might be explained by the reality that men reap greater professional rewards – with regards to opportunities and compensation – than mothers. Research has shown, for example, that while women experience a "motherhood penalty" in terms of diminished earning after becoming a parent, men receive a "fatherhood bonus" (Hodges and Budig 2010; Budig 2014). This sensitivity may also come from understanding the costs that can be associated with more conspicuous family focus as we explain in the next section. While fathers portrayed the terms of engagement for professional growth as very demanding, and with attendant costs, they were more willing to meet those terms in their pursuit of career success. This can leave fathers with less time and energy for active involvement as caregivers and equal partners at home, thwarting their efforts to get closer to the egalitarian ideal of truly shared caregiving.

4 Is there a Career Penalty for Being a Committed Dad?

As we will explore later in this chapter, most fathers who participated in our research seek to be equal caregivers with their spouse. But does such caregiving inevitably mean career penalties for dads? Women have faced negative career consequences for many years as the result of their caregiving responsibilities. When women become parents, there is often an assumption that they will make compromises at work due to their family responsibilities, whether or not that is in fact the case. It is well documented that women pay a price for becoming mothers from pay losses (Budig and England 2001) to being viewed as less committed, less promotable, and even less competent in the workplace (Correll et al. 2007).

While research indicates the motherhood penalty is steep, the penalty for highly involved fathers may be even steeper. (Williams 2010; Berdahl and Moon 2013). For fathers who are the sole or primary breadwinners, the risks of prioritizing family at the cost of their focus on work, may simply seem too high. As women have historically struggled with these unfair suppositions, there has, at least, been an expectation that mothers are faced with difficult trade-offs due to the dual demands of work and family. There is little such expectation when it comes to men.

This could be due to gender stereotypes and the very short duration of men's parental leave patterns. For example, 16% of fathers in our 2011 study (Harrington et al. 2011) took no time off following the birth of their most recent child and 96% took 2 weeks or less. 96% of fathers reported that their supervisor expects no change to occur to their working patterns as the result of their becoming parents. While as mentioned, many fathers may experience a fatherhood bonus in terms of compensation, by contrast, those who take time off to be active caregivers often suffer lower long-term earnings.

In a 2013 study, Berdahl and Moon researched how workers of both genders were treated as the result of being "conspicuous caregivers." They found that while both women and men both faced stigma, men who were too conspicuous in their involvement in family were seen not just as lesser workers, but also "lesser men" (by contrast, women who did so were viewed as lesser workers but "better women"). This is because these men did not adhere to the breadwinning model of fatherhood, one where men are regarded as employees first who have little to no responsibilities outside of work. In spite of increased societal expectations around paternal involvement and the desire of many men to participate more fully in family life, Berdahl and Moon's research suggests that fathers who are heavily involved in caregiving, or take time off for to care for their families, can be subject to informal and formal professional sanctions.

The authors also found that fathers who were highly involved in childcare reported the greatest levels of harassment compared to other men in the sample, in particular fathers who provided minimal childcare. In a second study in the same article, fathers who were responsible for more domestic work at home experienced greater workplace mistreatment than non-fathers and fathers who participated less in housework (Berdahl and Moon 2013).

Similarly, Coltrane et al. (2013) found that men who took time off to care for family members had significantly lower long-term earnings than men who had not done so. The authors found that regardless of gender, leaving work for family reasons was associated with lower long-term earnings, indicating that both men and women who take time off to care for family members suffer financial consequences as a result.

5 Are Fathers Interested in Taking Paternity Leave?

Perhaps no work-life topic has garnered more attention in the U.S. recently than paternity leave. As some major employers began to offer paid paternity leave, a debate ensued about the validity of giving fathers time to provide caregiving to their new children. But as time has progressed it has become increasingly clear that more and more fathers want and need paid time off following the birth or adoption of a new child, and the issue of paternity leave has gained public support.

Research we conducted in 2014 (Harrington et al. 2014) looked at a sample of more than 1000 fathers from 286 different organizations in the U.S. and found that paternity leave is important to them: a full 89% of dads surveyed believed it is important that an employer provide paid paternity leave. Our research found that virtually all of the men who participated in the study felt employers should offer paid paternity leave. It also revealed that the vast majority of fathers, 86% of respondents, would not make use of paid paternity leave unless it covered at least 70% of their salaries, and most fathers were looking for 100% pay during this leave period.

A recent study of U.S. fathers (Petts et al. 2019) found that as little as 2 weeks or more of paternal leave-taking is positively associated with children's perception of fathers' involvement, father child closeness, and father-child communication. The results suggest that increased attention to improving opportunities for parental leave in the U.S. may help strengthen families by nurturing higher quality father-child relationships.

Unfortunately, in the U.S. only about 13% of private-sector workers are covered by formal paid leave policies (U.S. Bureau of Labor Statistics 2017). Most fathers would need to combine vacation time, holiday time, and personal days to take any time off following the birth of their children. There has, however, been a flurry of progress regarding paid paternity leave at many major U.S. corporations. Employers such as American Express, EY, Intel, IBM, KPMG, and Johnson & Johnson have increased their fully paid, gender-neutral parental leave policies to allow for bonding time for both mothers and fathers with durations ranging from 8 to 20 weeks.

In order for parents to truly be equal partners in caregiving, we believe it is essential that fathers be actively involved in hands-on care from the time their child arrives. Research in countries where paid parental leave is readily available for fathers have found that men who take more time off with their new children develop better parenting skills and are better prepared to accept the responsibilities that facilitate shared-parenting. When a pattern of "dad at work" and "mom at home" is set in place following the birth of a child, it is difficult to reverse this pattern, so it is important for dads to establish themselves as involved caregivers from the very beginning.

6 Are More Fathers Today Considering Being an at-Home Dad?

According to the U.S. Census Bureau, the percentage of at-home dads has risen from 1.6% of families with an at-home parent in 2001 to 3.8% in 2018 (U.S. Census Bureau 2019), a substantial increase albeit from a very small base. So while at-home dads continue to be more the exception than the rule, it is clear from our research that fathers' attitudes about caregiving, including full-time caregiving, are changing. In our 2011 study of working fathers, a surprisingly high percentage of fathers (53%) "agreed" or "strongly agreed" when asked, "If your spouse earned enough money to support your family's needs, would you consider being a stay-at-home dad?" (Harrington et al. 2011.) In our 2016 study of Millennial parents, 51% of Millennial fathers agreed with the same statement vs. 44% of Millennial moms (Harrington et al. 2017).

Through our study of at-home dads (Harrington et al. 2012) we learned that these fathers were comfortable in their role and generally assessed themselves as doing a good or very good job at caregiving and domestic tasks. The fathers reported that being an at-home parent initially took adjustment, and they stated they were faced with a number of challenges including:

- The loss of a social network. This is loss is felt most acutely by at-home fathers since their numbers continue to be low.
- Feelings of being stigmatized due to the continuing sense that the at-home parent role is still not appropriate for a man.
- The fear that their future employment opportunities would be jeopardized by the fact that they had taken on this nontraditional role.

In spite of these obstacles, we found evidence that the at-home dads we studied were very good parents and this assessment was strongly confirmed by their spouses' survey responses. They reported that the at-home fathers were devoted to their children and were highly active, involved parents. Much like our image of the competent and caring at-home mom, these fathers were committed to their children, supportive of their spouses and their careers, and doing the myriad of daily tasks needed to maintain their households, even if in some cases their assessment of a clean house fell slightly short of their wives' standards.

7 Are Fathers Living up to their Own Caregiving Expectations?

Over the course of our fatherhood studies, we have asked fathers about how their expectations of caregiving compare to their reality. We have done this by asking two questions:

- How do you believe caregiving *should be* divided between you and your spouse/partner?
- How *is* caregiving divided between you are your spouse/partner?

In our studies, we have seen a consistent pattern in the answer to these two questions. While more than two-thirds of men respond that caregiving should be divided 50–50, less than one-third of men say this is, in fact, the case. In all of those cases where there was a shortfall in shared caregiving, it was the fathers themselves who admitted they were coming up short and the wives/partners who were fulfilling

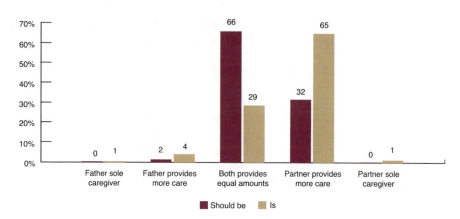

Fig. 3 How Fathers believe caregiving "should be" divided compared to their current division. Source: Boston College Center for Work & Family. *The New Dad: Career vs. Caregiving Conflict.* 2017

the majority of caregiving responsibilities. Therefore, it would be fair to suggest that for more than one-third of fathers in our sample, there is a very significant gap between their espoused caregiving goals and their current reality.

In order to better understand the impact this caregiving gap has on the father's career and life satisfaction, we broke fathers into three groups (Harrington et al. 2017). The first group of fathers responded that caregiving at home should be divided equally and that indeed it was. We labeled this group the ***egalitarian*** fathers and they comprised 30% of the study participants. A second group of fathers responded that their "spouse should provide more caregiving at home" and they were doing so. We labeled this group ***traditional*** fathers to reflect their more traditionally gendered views on parental roles and caregiving. They comprised approximately 32% of the sample. The third group responded that caregiving should be divided 50/50 but admitted that their spouse provided more care than they did. This group was labeled as ***conflicted*** fathers due to the dissonance between their caregiving aspirations (SHOULD be) and their reality (IS). Conflicted fathers comprised 38% of the sample (Fig. 3).

As researchers, we discovered that these categories presented a highly useful way to conceptualize the work-life experiences of today's fathers. When we broke our sample into the three fatherhood types, some interesting similarities and differences were evident.

- **Income levels of the three fatherhood types**: The traditional fathers' income was the highest and *Egalitarians'* income is the lowest. More than one-third (34.4%) of the *Egalitarians* earned less than $75,000 as compared to only 12% of the *Traditionals* and 22% of the *Conflicteds*. On the upper end of the earnings scale, nearly 3 out of 5 traditional fathers earned more than 100 K compared to 44% of conflicted fathers and 32% of egalitarian fathers.

- **Education levels of three father types:** Since our research was conducted with mainly "white-collar" professionals, the vast majority of the fathers in the sample attended college with most holding at least a bachelor's degree and/or a graduate degree (90% of the *Traditionals*, 77% of *Egalitarians* and 80% of the *Conflicteds*). Less than 1% possessed only a high school diploma. In general, the more educated a father is, the more likely he belongs to the Traditional fatherhood group.
- **Partners' work patterns of three father types:** Not surprisingly, there is a marked difference in the employment status of the partners of the three of fatherhood types. Slightly more than 90% of the *Egalitarians'* partners were employed, compared to 73% of *Conflicteds* and only 44% of *Traditionals'* partners. When we review partners' work hours (including those who did not work outside the home), the differences between spouses working hours by fatherhood type are significant. *Egalitarians'* spouses worked an average of 28 h per week, *Conflicteds'* spouses worked 20 h per week, and *Traditionals'* spouses worked just 9.

When we compared the responses to subsequent questions indicating, for example, the fathers' overall satisfaction on a number of work and life indicators, a clear pattern emerged. We discovered that overall, *Egalitarian* and *Traditional* fathers expressed higher levels of satisfaction in their jobs and their careers. For example:

Job Satisfaction & Commitment: On job satisfaction, a clear pattern that emerges. *Traditionals* and *Egalitarians* are consistently more satisfied than *Conflicted* fathers are. While all three fatherhood types showed high levels of satisfaction with their jobs (positive responses are consistently between 70–90%, which speaks highly of the employers whose organizations participated in the study), overall *Conflicted* fathers are the least satisfied in their jobs.

The Feeling of Belonging to a Group: When asked if they really felt a part of their workgroup, once again the *Conflicted* group reported the lowest levels of satisfaction. *Egalitarians* showed the highest levels of satisfaction.

Job Withdrawal Intentions: On items that explored discontent, *Conflicted* fathers showed the highest level of job withdrawal intentions. This included their intention to look for other jobs as well as their thoughts about quitting their present jobs outright. In general, *Conflicted* fathers were about 10% more likely than the other two fatherhood types to think about quitting their jobs and are 7–9% more likely to report looking for another job.

Career Satisfaction: Career satisfaction measures we used looked less at the fathers' satisfaction in their present role and more at their satisfaction with their career progression over time (e.g., satisfied with advancement, satisfied with their earnings growth, etc.). *Conflicted* fathers once again had the lowest levels of satisfaction on these career satisfaction items. In the area of career satisfaction, the *Traditionals* reported the highest levels of satisfaction on three items: progress toward career goals, income, and advancement.

8 What Impact Does Generational Cohort Play in Fatherhood Types?

In our years of researching the changing role of fathers from a work and family perspective, perhaps no question has emerged more frequently from the media and corporate groups than, "Isn't this all a generational thing?" The implication is that Millennials have grown up in a time of greater gender equality and that this had led younger fathers to seek these greater levels of engagement and parity with their spouses in caregiving.

While there is some evidence to support a generational shift, our research does not demonstrate dramatic differences between the fatherhood cohorts by generation. While there are a higher percentage of *Egalitarian* fathers in the Millennial generation than in the Baby Boomer generation (31% vs. 27%), there were slightly fewer *Egalitarians* in the Millennial sample vs. Generation X (31% vs. 32%). The number of *Conflicted* fathers in our samples was also 4% higher among Baby Boomers when compared to Generation X and Millennials (i.e., 40% of Baby Boomer fathers vs. 36% of Generation X and Millennials (Fig. 4).

When we analyze the career satisfaction of fathers, another interesting pattern emerges for *Egalitarian* fathers. When one reviews the scores by generations, there is a trend toward higher satisfaction for the younger *Egalitarian* fathers versus older ones, (i.e., Millennials are the most satisfied, followed by Generation X, followed by Baby Boomers).

For questions regarding involvement in caregiving, the three fatherhood types showed significant differences in their responses. When asked to choose one of the following statements "I would like to spend more time with my children," "I am satisfied with the amount of time I currently spend with my children," or "I would like to spend less time with my children," a clear pattern emerged that was consistent across all three generations. *Conflicted* fathers were the most likely to agree with the

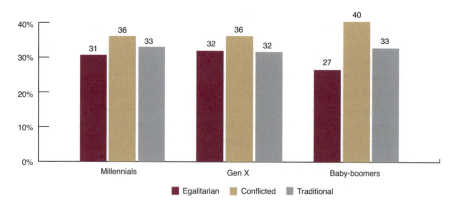

Fig. 4 "Fatherhood types" By generation. Source: Boston College Center for Work & Family. *The New Dad: Career vs. Caregiving Conflict.* 2017

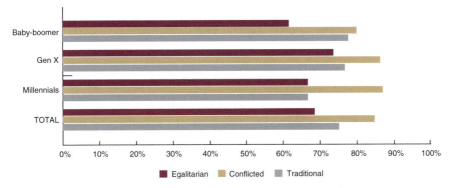

Fig. 5 Preference for more time with children by fatherhood type and generation. Source: Boston College Center for Work & Family. *The New Dad: Career vs. Caregiving Conflict.* 2017

statement that they would like to spend more time with their children. Overall, nearly 85% of *Conflicteds* responded they wanted more time, compared with 75% of *Traditionals* and 69% of *Egalitarians*. This suggests the relatively lower level of comfort *Conflicted* fathers feel towards the current state of their work-family balance when compared with the other two fatherhood types (Fig. 5).

9 Summary and Recommendations

As was stated in the introduction, the lack of focus on the experiences of fathers over the years has often led to a misunderstanding of the important role they play in American family life. From the absence of attention in research, to inaccurate portrayals in the media, to the outdated workplace assumptions about the caregiving roles that fathers play, men have continued to be seen as minor players in the family. While some progress is being made to better understand the roles fathers play today, much more research and greater insight is needed.

How can employers help fathers be more engaged caregivers? Here are a few thoughts:

- Consider having a fathers' employee network that provides dads the opportunity to discuss their concerns and needs regarding caregiving and balancing their work-family demands.
- Make parental leave policies gender neutral and offer the same amounts of paid leave for fathers that mothers currently receive (beyond the time birth mothers are given for delivery and recovery). This will demonstrate that the fathers' role in parenting is given the same weight as the mothers' role.

- Cultivate a flexible work environment at your organization. Offering flexible work options can support dads as they strive to meet both their professional and personal responsibilities.
- Consider establishing a voluntary mentoring program for fathers interested in not just career-related dialogue, but which also includes conversations regarding the work-family dilemmas and challenges men face.
- Conduct a survey with fathers in your organization to assess whether they feel the climate is as accepting of fathers' engagement in caregiving as it is for mothers.

There are also things that fathers themselves can do to enhance their caregiving role:

- Talk to other fathers formally or informally to share common struggles and brainstorm potential solutions. If a father's employee resource group does not exist in your organization, explore the possibility of establishing one. Dads groups are also growing in many local communities (see, e.g., City Dads Group: https://citydadsgroup.com/) for social connections and support.
- If your organization offers paternity leave, strongly consider taking this time off to bond with your child and to gain experience in "hands-on parenting." This will increase your confidence and competence in your parenting skills. It will also help you establish very early on your role as a co-caregiver with your partner.
- Have frequent conversations with your partner about your roles at home and at work and your goals for your family. Our research has demonstrated that couples who hold these discussions more frequently have higher life satisfaction (Harrington et al. 2015).
- Support other fathers at your workplace who are caregivers. Changing organizational culture requires more than changes in policies or even statements of support from senior leaders. Men who support colleagues in their effort to be engaged parents will help to shift the organizational culture to one that is more equitable and encouraging of men as caregivers. This will in turn, also promote the advancement of women in the organization.

We believe that it is time to do a "hard reset" – at home, in the workplace, and in society. It's time to ask ourselves why, as we've redefined the role of women in the workplace over the past 25 years, we have been much less able to do the same for men on the home front. No doubt, a major contributor to this situation is men themselves. For far too long, fathers' voices have been silent and nearly absent from work-family conversations. This has had a detrimental effect on fathers' ability to redefine their role in contemporary families. It's time to see more clearly what dads are doing in the family and ask how we can help them do it better. We have begun to see positive early results of men speaking out, particularly by men in at-home dads' networks. The change in how dads are being portrayed in the media is a good example of how change can come from research, media attention, and the voices of dads themselves. We are convinced that gender equity will never be attained until workplaces and society see men and fathers from a "whole person" perspective. When we achieve that aim, we will have enhanced workplaces, created a more equitable society, and strengthened the most important building block to ensure our country's prosperity – the American family.

Acknowledgments The author would like to acknowledge Jennifer Sabatini Fraone, Professor Jegoo Lee, Fred Van Deusen and the staff at the Boston College Center for Work & Family for their many contributions over the last decade to "The New Dad" research series.

References

Berdahl J, Moon S (2013) Workplace mistreatment of middle class workers based on sex, parenthood, and caregiving. J Soc Issues 69(2):341–366
Budig M, England P (2001) The wage penalty for motherhood. Am Sociol Rev 66(2):204–225
Budig MJ (2014) The fatherhood bonus and the motherhood penalty: parenthood and the gendergap in pay. Third Way
Bureau of Labor Statistics (2014) Economic News Release: Table 4. Families with own children: Employment status of parents by age of youngest child and family type, 2012–2013 annual averages. https://www.bls.gov/news.release/famee.t04.htm
Bureau of Labor Statistics (2017) 13 percent of private industry workers had access to paid family leave in March 2016. The Economics Daily. https://www.bls.gov/opub/ted/2016/13-percent-of-private-industry-workers-had-access-to-paid-family-leave-in-march-2016.htm
Coltrane S, Miller E, DeHaan T, Stewart L (2013) Fathers and the flexibility stigma. J Soc Issues 69 (2):279–302
Correll S, Bernard S, Paik I (2007) Getting a job: is there a motherhood penalty? Am J Sociol 112 (5):1297–1338
EY (2015) Global generations: a global study on work-life challenges across generations. EYGM Limited. https://www.ey.com/Publication/vwLUAssets/Global_generations_study/$FILE/EY-global-generations-a-global-study-on-work-life-challenges-across-generations.pdf
Harrington B, Fraone J, Lee J (2017) The new dad: the career caregiving conflict. Boston College Center for Work & Family, Chestnut Hill
Harrington B, Fraone J, Lee J, Levey L (2016) The new Millennial dad: understanding the paradox for today's fathers. Boston College Center for Work & Family, Chestnut Hill
Harrington B, Van Deusen F, Fraone J, Eddy S, Haas L (2014) The new dad: take your leave. Boston College Center for Work & Family, Chestnut Hill
Harrington B, Van Deusen F, Fraone JS, Morelock J (2015) How Millennials navigate their careers: young adult views on work, life and success. Boston College Center for Work & Family, Chestnut Hill
Harrington B, Van Deusen F, Humberd B (2011) The new dad: caring, committed and conflicted. Boston College Center for Work and Family, Chestnut Hill
Harrington B, Van Deusen F, Mazar I (2012) The new dad: right at home. Boston College Center for Work & Family, Chestnut Hill
Hodges M, Budig M (2010) Who gets the daddy Bonus?: organizational hegemonic masculinity and the impact of fatherhood on earnings. Gend Soc 24(6):717–745
Knight CR, Brinton MC (2017) One egalitarianism or several? Two decades of gender-role attitude change in Europe. Am J Sociol 122(5):1485–1532
Matos K (2015) Modern families: same- and different-sex couples negotiating at home. Families and Work Institute. http://www.familiesandwork.org/downloads/modern-families.pdf
New York Times (2013) Room for debate: what are father's for? New York Times. https://www.nytimes.com/roomfordebate/2013/06/03/what-are-fathers-for. Accessed 3 June 2013

Petts R, Knoester C, Waldfogel J (2019) Fathers' paternity leave-taking and children's perceptions of father-child relationships in the United States. Sex Roles 82:1–16. https://doi.org/10.1007/s11199-019-01050-y

Pew Research Center (2013a) Modern parenthood: roles of moms and dads converge as they balance work and family. https://www.pewsocialtrends.org/2013/03/14/modern-parenthood-roles-of-moms-and-dads-converge-as-they-balance-work-and-family/

Pew Research Center (2013b) Breadwinner moms: mothers are the sole or primary provider in four-in-ten households with children; public conflicted about the growing trend. https://www.pewsocialtrends.org/2013/05/29/breadwinner-moms/

US Census Bureau (2019) Historical families tables. https://www.census.gov/data/tables/time-series/demo/families/families.html. Accessed 8 Oct 2019

Wang R, Bianchi S (2009) ATUS fathers' involvement in childcare. Soc Indic Res 93(1):141–145

Williams JC (2001) Unbending gender: why work and family conflict and what to do about it. Oxford University Press, New York

Williams JC (2010) Reshaping the work-family debate: why men and class matter. Harvard University Press, Cambridge

Yavorsky J, Dush C, Schoppe-Sullivan S (2015) The gender division of labor across the transition to parenthood. J Marriage Fam 77(3):662–679

Open Access This chapter is licensed under the terms of the Creative Commons Attribution 4.0 International License (http://creativecommons.org/licenses/by/4.0/), which permits use, sharing, adaptation, distribution and reproduction in any medium or format, as long as you give appropriate credit to the original author(s) and the source, provide a link to the Creative Commons license and indicate if changes were made.

The images or other third party material in this chapter are included in the chapter's Creative Commons license, unless indicated otherwise in a credit line to the material. If material is not included in the chapter's Creative Commons license and your intended use is not permitted by statutory regulation or exceeds the permitted use, you will need to obtain permission directly from the copyright holder.

French Fathers in Work Organizations: Navigating Work-Life Balance Challenges

Sabrina Tanquerel

1 Introduction

In France, like many other developed countries, men increasingly seek a better work-life balance in order to spend more time at home, especially when fathers of young children (ORSE 2010, 2014; Gregory and Milner 2012; UNAF 2016). Studies about "new fathers" and "l'homme nouveau" ["*the new man*"] (Castelain-Meunier 2013) question whether France is heading to changing norms of masculinity. According to a national survey (OPE 2017), 64% of French fathers declare they do not have enough time to do what they wish with their children. Fathers also report that their employers do not help them combine their work and family life (69%). Fathers would like them to train supervisors to make them more aware of their teams' personal life, and more generally take into account their role as fathers. These new expectations are also visible in the increased paternal leave usage in France (14 days): 70% of French fathers benefit from it, an increase of 20% since its creation in 2002 (DREES 2016).

Nevertheless, fathers struggle between the desire to be involved fathers (spending time and engaging with their children during the working week) and their role as the main breadwinner in the family (facing and managing the demands of "greedy" organizational cultures [Kvande 2012]). Time use surveys show that men still spend more time at work and less time in childcare than women (Insee 2010), which suggests that the discourses of fathers on fatherhood may differ from their practices (LaRossa 1988; Dermott 2008; Hunter et al. 2017). Caught between traditional and modernized conceptions of fatherhood, they cope with ambivalence, tensions, and asynchronicities in the workplace (Liebig and Oechsle 2017).

S. Tanquerel (✉)
Ecole de Management de Normandie, Campus de Caen, France
e-mail: stanquerel@em-normandie.fr

France provides a particularly relevant and rich context for the analysis of fatherhood in organizations. Indeed, though France has a specific family policy based on natalism with a generous childcare system, it also has a 'hyper-maternalised' policy tradition, historically oriented towards mothers. The country maintains a strong male breadwinner culture, which may explain the underdevelopment of its fatherhood regime. However, as is happening in many developed countries, there is evidence of attitudinal change by fathers and organizations. The tensions triggered by this change are part of a long-term process of "lagged adaptation," a state of transition worthy of interest for many states and organizations.

Yet, little research is focused on fatherhood in work organizations in France. This chapter addresses this issue by focusing on deeply embedded and change-resistant gendered workplace practices and cultures that can undermine active fatherhood. More specifically, this chapter answers the questions: (1) What are the challenges/tensions between the simultaneous pressure of having a successful career and of embodying an involved fatherhood that French working fathers experience? (2) What practices and strategies do fathers leverage to face these challenges in the organizational context? The aim is to stimulate reflection regarding how to create and contribute to systemic change in workplaces (Lewis and Stumbitz 2017).

Based on 20 interviews conducted in France with fathers from heterogeneous backgrounds working in family-friendly companies, I present findings regarding their "talk" on work-life balance (WLB). I will first outline my theoretical approach and the state of current research, as well as the methods and data. I will then present empirical insights about their individual experiences of WLB. In the last section, based on the results, I will discuss the different ways fathers decide to combine work, non-work, fathering, and how different factors such as their professional ideals and self-concepts of fatherhood influence their degree of involvement. Finally, I will end with some further recommendations regarding how organizations can foster a truly father-friendly environment.

2 Men's New Aspirations: Juggling Traditional Male Identity and Organizational Constraints

Unlike women, men's difficulties managing work-life tensions have been understudied. Women's adaptations to work have been thoroughly examined and explained in light of their relation to work-family reconciliation and the difficulties they experience when challenging professional expectations (e.g., Blair-Loy 2003; Budig and England 2001; Hochschild and Machung 1989; Pocock 2005; Wood and Newton 2006). But men's uninterrupted full-time work model, exclusive of other life domains, has long been taken for granted. Although a plurality of masculinity models and practices are operating in the workplace (Carrigan et al. 1985; Collinson and Hearn 1994; Connell and Messerschmidt 2005), numerous studies reveal that men and masculinity still correlate strongly to gainful employment and occupational career. Men have few other ways to define their identity than by the (paid) work they do (Yancey Martin 2001). Yet, researchers have questioned the notion of working life as the main arena for constructing male identity and mastery — and particularly the aspiration for career success (Connell 1995; Collinson and Hearn 2005). In Europe, the traditional patterns of the workplace, being the primary requirement that structures men's time, persist (e.g., Blossfeld et al. 2006). As men often hold the most powerful positions, the pressure to work long hours (Kvande 2009) still exist, and workplaces are still 'greedy' (Coser 1974; Kvande 2012) for time use.

Recent research has problematized men's role as fathers with the request for a new father's role (Brandth and Kvande 2002; Kimmel 2004; Kugelberg 2006; Marsh and Musson 2008). Men have new aspirations, yearning to become more involved at home (Dermott 2008; Kaufman 2013), and the demands of work organizations sharply contrast with fathers' intentions of making working life adapt to family life (Brandth and Kvande 2002). Work organizations are rarely gender neutral and have a rather 'traditional' gender perspective of the couple, with women as primary caregivers, men as work-primary and breadwinners (Ladge and Greenberg 2019). Companies handle and interpret fathers' and mothers' parental claims differently. Research suggests that men experience a greater degree of bias compared to women when they take advantage of family friendly policies at work (Cain Miller 2014; see also Ladge and Humberd and Harrington in this volume). Companies frame fathers' parental leave as a luxurious addition to support mothers (Haas and Hwang 2019), who remain in the gender-specific position of the primary parent responsible for childcare (Neumann and Meuser 2017).

In addition, research indicates the existence of strong barriers to men taking up WLB measures (Tanquerel and Grau-Grau 2020). Due to strong dominant norms of masculinity constructed as breadwinner not as carer, men who take parental leave may suffer from stigmas ('poor worker' and 'femininity' stigmas; see Coltrane et al. 2013). As research increasingly reports the difficulties men experience when facing highly challenging employer expectations (Galinsky et al. 2009; Harrington et al. 2011), aspirations toward involved fatherhood (Harrington et al. 2011; Kaufman 2013) seem to be incompatible with the pattern of hegemonic masculinity (Murgia and Poggio 2013). When men dissociate themselves from the traditional masculine norm of being devoted to and continuing full-time work, they digress from the dominant gender order and challenge the norms of the work sphere. They question the prevalent expectation that men do not have any duties besides gainful employment. Even when fathers are granted rights, they still can encounter resistance to taking advantage of these rights within their company (Brandth and Kvande 2002; Liebig and Oechsle 2017). Reductions in working hours are still often interpreted as a lack of professional commitment. Fathers who request or take parental leave may still be considered by their employers to be less ideal workers than other men. Taking family leave can also be seen as an infringement of man's masculinity (Doucet and Merla 2007). The lack of alternative models to these traditional norms of masculinity and fatherhood, even if they are eroding, remains also a strong barrier to men's taking up of WLB initiatives.

In this ambivalent context of imposed masculinities and men's new aspirations, little research in France has considered fathers individual experiences and interpretations of work-life balance in the workplace and how they deal with these tensions. Research is abundant in demography (Brugeilles and Sebille 2009a, b, 2011, 2013) and sociology (Castelain-Meunier 2005, 2013; Le Talec 2016; Martial 2016) but are limited to describing sociological behaviors. However, little research in organization studies has considered how those tensions impact male employees in the workplace and which strategies fathers use to face those challenges. The goal of this study is therefore to understand how French men navigate their needs for flexibility to better balance their work and non-work responsibilities, within the normative (and hidden) rules that the organization implicitly imposes. It aims at highlighting men's subjective experiences, visions, practices of flexibility in challenging organizations.

3 Fatherhood in the French Social Context

France provides a particularly interesting case for the analysis of fatherhood in organizations because of its national family policy based on natalism with a generous childcare system, but an underdeveloped fatherhood regime (Gregory and Milner 2008).

3.1 A Natalism-Based and Mother-Centered Family Policy

France has a distinct family policy, based on significant support for childbirth or natalism, with generous family benefits for households with children and explicit support for larger families (Levy 2005; see also Fig. 1 below).

⇨ **Highly developed childcare system funded on average 80% by the State:**
- Daycare centers (*"crèches"*): where a child can be placed from the age of 2½ months to 3 years).
- Registered childminders (*"assistante maternelle"*): regulated and certified by the State, regularly inspected and trained, they are the main type of out-of-home childcare in France representing 69% of the total available places for children under 3 (DREES 2018).
- Public preschool: though the official age for school entry in France is 6 years, 97% of children aged 3 and 99% aged 4 attend preschool (*"école maternelle"*) which is free of charge (Gomajee et al. 2017).

⇨ **Family benefits for households with children and large families**.

⇨ This external support can explain in part the country's relatively **high fertility rate**: at 2.01 child per family, France had the second-highest fertility rate in the EU, behind Ireland (Moss 2013; SPSS 2013).

Fig. 1 France: a pro-natalism country

Nonetheless, France has had a mother-centered family policy, historically aimed at supporting working mothers with childcare provision, and which is widely held to entrench traditional gender roles. This context of a traditional 'hyper-maternalisation' of family policy (for 'hyper-maternalisation': see Castelain-Meunier 2005) has constituted a powerful constraint on the development of 'fatherhood policies' and the emergence of a strong fatherhood regime.

3.2 The Fatherhood Regime in France

Today, paternity leave in France consists of three "birth" days (available to all fathers on the birth of a child) added to eleven days' leave, none compulsory. 70% of French fathers benefit from it. In order to access the leave, fathers must notify their employer a month in advance, and they are entitled to a wage-related benefit funded by the health insurance scheme and administered by the family benefits agency. In addition to this advantage, fathers have also the possibility to take a long parental leave, conditions of access to which have been evolving in the last decades as detailed in Table 1.

The 2014 law aims to increase men's take-up of post-childbirth parental leave to 25% of eligible fathers from the take-up rate of 5% today. The main obstacle for men's usage of parental leave remains a low compensation payment, which makes the benefit only minimally incentivizing for them.

Table 1 Parental Leave in France

Family benefits	Introduction	Beneficiaries	Duration of the benefit
APE *Allocation Parentale d'Éducation* (parental education benefit)	1986	– Parents of children under 3 – Initially available from the third child only	– **1 year**, renewable twice
APE	1994	– Parents of two children	– **1 year**, renewable twice
APE	2004	– Parents from the first child	– **6 months**, renewable once
PreParE *Prestation Partagée d'Education de l'Enfant* (shared benefit for child's education)	2014	– Parents from the first child	– Extended to **1 year** if half of the existing parental leave is reserved for the **second parent**, on a 'use it or lose it basis' – Longer leave entitlement of two and a half years still applies to mothers expecting a second or third child, whilst fathers are entitled to 6 months

3.3 Difficult Articulation Between Fatherhood and Work

In the French case, even if the paternity leave of around 2 weeks has now become an accepted norm for male employees, particularly those working in larger firms (Gregory and Milner 2011; Milner and Gregory 2015), fathers still report difficulties in their articulation between fatherhood and work. The constant rate of take-up also indicates some difficulties for around a third of employees. Whilst paternity leave has become the norm for lower-paid employees, it is less widely used by higher-grade employees. This may be because these higher-paid employees are able to access flexible working without having to face the income ceiling of statutory paternity pay. It is also thought to reflect the culture of "presenteeism" (on which, see Gatrell 2011) which is thought to be affecting increasing numbers of managerial employees, of whom approximately 60% are men (Pak and Zilberman 2013; SPSS 2013), although reliable data are scarce precisely because it is a 'hidden phenomenon' which does not appear in working time statistics. This explains in part the low rate of usage of work-family policies among men and that no change occurs to fathers' working patterns as the result of their becoming parents. Unlike mothers, fathers rarely change their working schedule after child's birth and continue to work full-time (Pailhe and Solaz 2009).

The usage of WLB policies by men comes from a complex dynamic between national fatherhood regimes, organizational and sector characteristics, and the individual employee (Gregory and Milner 2011). That is why this paper aims to analyze how working fathers navigate the main challenges and tensions in trying to achieve WLB and which practices and strategies they leverage in the organizational context.

4 Methods and Data

This exploratory study is based on 20 semi-structured interviews of French working fathers from heterogeneous backgrounds selected in order to grasp a wide range of fathers' experiences: blue-collar (operators, technicians) and white-collar fathers (engineers, directors). The 11 companies where they work are certified as family-friendly employers. They are both public and private, of different sizes and sectors (delivery service sector, microelectronics, automotive, IT ...) and located in Normandy (France). All interviews were conducted face-to-face from 2014 to 2017. Each interview took about 1 h and was conducted in French. Each interview was based on a talk about WLB and fatherhood, perceptions of WLB initiatives, reasons for use, obstacles and facilitators, and strategies. Interviews were audio-recorded and transcribed.

The interview analysis consisted of an axial coding and a thematic analysis, both horizontal and vertical. The aim was to understand and to compare fathers' representations, experiences, and behaviors regarding WLB. The data analysis consisted of two steps: firstly, examining the individual unit of production of each interview, in

Table 2 Interviewees' characteristics

	Name	Age	Occupation	Marital Status	Working time
1.	Matthias	28	Operator	Perm. Relationship, 1 child	Full-time - staggered working hours 4 days a week
2.	Noël	35	Expert operator	Perm. Relationship, 2 children	Full-time 4 days a week
3.	Pierre	48	Operator	Married, 2 children	Full-time
4.	Simon	22	Operator	Single, 1 child	Full-time 4 days a week
5.	Stéphane	44	Operator	Married, 3 children	Full-time (has been on part-time)
6.	Tony	40	Expert operator	Blended family, 6 children	Full-time 4 days a week
7.	Bertrand	51	Sales assistant	Married, 2 children	Full-time
8.	Yvan	27	Operator	Perm. Relationship, 2 children	Full-time
9.	Francis	47	Team leader	Divorced, 2 children	Full-time
10.	Louis	37	Team leader	Married, 1 child	Full-time
11.	Olivier	47	IT technician	Married, 2 children	Part-time 80%
12.	Jean-Baptiste	43	Librarian	Married, 2 children	Part-time 80%
13.	David	41	Engineer	Perm. Relationship, 1 child	Full-time
14.	Frédéric	42	Engineer	Married, 2 children	Full-time (1 day teleworking)
15.	Yoann	30	Marketing analyst	Married, 1 child	Full-time
16.	Romuald	51	Director	Married, 2 children	Full-time
17.	Xavier	46	Engineer	Married, 2 children	Full-time (1 day teleworking)
18.	Sébastien	38	Sales representative	Married, 2 children	Full-time
19.	Jacques	53	Project leader	Married, 3 children	Full-time
20.	Jérémy	32	Electrician	Married, 2 children	Full-time

order to create categories and analyze themes, and secondly, extracting meaning from the data to understand the contents. We did an iterative coding of recurring first-order categories ("informant's voice") and identified both emerging second-order categories and aggregate dimensions (Gioia et al. 2013) that brought to light the main dimensions of fathers' beliefs, experiences, and strategies regarding WLB policies. All names are pseudonyms. See Table 2 for details.

5 Empirical Findings

5.1 Fathers' Talk on WLB: Combining Needs, Professional Challenges and Changing Social Expectations

5.1.1 Masculine Meanings of WLB for Differentiated Needs

Our research brings into focus the masculine meanings of WLB policies. Most of the men associate WLB with occasional and informal arrangements. In our interviews, men do not really ask their supervisor for time flexibility or long-term changes to their working schedules to adapt their children' needs. They rather reported occasional requests (WLB as an 'emergency').

> *"If one day, someone has a problem and tells us that he/she has to change his/her working schedule and/or leave earlier, we will say OK and be ready to help, insofar as possible, we will try. As an example, we now have an employee whose wife is training in Paris for two days. He usually starts work at 6:00 but he asked us to start later on these days to look after his three children. We cannot allow ourselves to refuse something like this..."* [Louis, 37, team leader; married, father of 1].

When referring to WLB, they often mention the social benefits (financial, material, banking facilities) provided by the company. They evaluate WLB initiatives in quantitative terms since social benefits contribute to family well-being.

> *"From a financial perspective, these initiatives are interesting for everybody. All these initiatives and help provide well-being for everybody, for the person who is working of course but also for his/her family, because the whole family can take advantage of all the benefits that we have for sport. It is the same for bonuses, the whole family will enjoy them"* [Pierre, 48, operator; married, father of 2].

5.1.2 Professional Ideals and the Role the Organization Should Play in WLB

The fathers interviewed generally see fatherhood as a "private matter" in the workplace. Some fathers do not necessarily view the organization as a source of solutions for a better WLB, as illustrated by Francis's discourse:

> *"Before working with this new director that we have now, it was 'you have to sort it out by yourself!' In the past, whether you started at 5:30 or 6:00 am, nobody cared, nobody wanted to hear about it. You have children, it is your choice, and you have to manage it. The company is not responsible for your personal choice."* [Francis, 47, team leader; divorced, father of 2].

For many of them, especially those in higher positions, work continues to determine primarily time use, highlighting a powerful work-devotion schema. Fathers added that they believe they have flexibility in their time schedule since they are managers, but they also recognize that this flexibility is a double-edged facility since it is difficult to put limits.

French Fathers in Work Organizations: Navigating Work-Life Balance Challenges   221

> *"When you are a manager, you have to adapt your life to your work... you have to adapt to the employees and the company, not the opposite! Managing people takes time and sometimes it is difficult to put limits."* [Louis, 37, team leader; married, father of 1].

Not everyone agrees with the role the organization has to play in WLB facilitation. Some reject the intrusion of the employer in their personal life. Others consider that communication and dialogue with supervisors is a mainstay for harmonizing both spheres. The fathers in lower professional positions seem to make their needs more visible than the fathers in higher status who do not express visible expectations.

> *"The lack of dialogue might be an obstacle for WLB. I think that here we have a lot of dialogue, which entails that for example, our director relatively knows about our personal lives, not everything of course, but she knows what happens. Therefore, yes, because of that, she always has an adapted response to our problems and difficulties. Compared to 4 or 5 years ago, we all had taken different ways, and she has always known how to respond to our problems, and this has improved considerably our quality of work, and by the way, our lives..."* [Matthias, 28, operator; permanent relationship, father of 1].

5.1.3 Self-Concepts of Fatherhood

The way men conceive fatherhood determines the degree of the father's involvement and influence the needs for WLB. In some cases, fathers decide to make their needs visible to the company and to ask for part-time adjustments.

> *"I have already worked part-time to take care of my three daughters. I could pick up my little daughter in the afternoon, she is 10 months and I looked after her and afterwards, I took care of my other 2 daughters, they are older, when they came back from school, I prepared the snack and then did some house chores..."* [Stéphane, 44, operator; married, father of 3].

We also observe that fathers negotiate their domestic role with partners, in particular when their partner works. Men's breadwinner role is shaped by their own gender role attitudes and aspirations as well as by their partners' expectations and constraints.

> *"Anyway, today, mothers and fathers have to work, if there are not two salaries, life is very complicated. Therefore, I think that men have to participate more in family and domestic life. My wife is passionate about her work and does not have as much as flexibility as me, that's why I adjust my schedule to hers and take advantage of the work-family initiatives that are available in my company."* [Tony, 40, expert operator; blended family, father of 6].

5.2 *Fathers' 'walk' on WLB: Three Ways of Combining WLB and Fatherhood*

One of the research questions of this chapter was to explore the strategies French fathers leverage in the workplace to manage their work and family interface. The results of this study highlight three main categories of fathers using diverse strategies to navigate WLB challenges, echoing research of typologies that categorize fathers in their attitudes and behaviors (old dads, new dads, and superdads (Kaufman 2013); traditional, transitionals, and superdads (Cooper 2000)).

5.2.1 The Breadwinner Father

The underlying cultural ideal in this first category is the traditional breadwinner model, the classic ideal of fatherhood. A father should be first a "good worker." Professional identity/role is salient to the other life roles. Even if the organizational environment is family-friendly and working-time regime favorable, the work-devotion schema is dominant. These fathers do not use formal family-friendly programs. Family and fatherhood are considered a "private matter." This model reproduces the gender order and reinforces hegemonic masculinity.

> "Asking for flexibility arrangements is not really compatible with a career, and by principle, I consider that we do not have children to take advantage of it..." [Romuald, 51, Director; married, father of 2].

5.2.2 The Caring Father

The underlying cultural model is the involved father. A "good father" is the one who wants to be involved at home. The desire to spend time and engage with children during the working week is important and prevails on career and professional priorities. These fathers use formal family-friendly programs, thinking that responsibility for achieving WLB is not assigned to women. Flexibility is visible because they desire it or because they have no choice (partner's position). They "challenge" the gender order and resist hegemonic masculinity, building caring masculinities (Elliott 2016). They are egalitarian in their opinions, attitudes and acts.

> "Today, I work at 80%... (When we had our second child), I really felt like spending time with my children and the idea of a day off a week to take care of them tempted me. It was really me who was calling for more qualitative time with my kids and it was naturally that I took this decision." [Jean-Baptiste, 43, librarian; married, father of 2].

5.2.3 The 'want to have it all' Father

The cultural model is hybrid: 'career oriented' and 'caring father'. He wants to be both: a good worker and a good father. He is aware of the "hidden rules" in organizations. The desire to balance different life areas is dependent on career. The ideal worker norm is accepted and internalized. They are egalitarian in their discourse but not necessarily in their acts. The will to emancipate from the gender order is present. They may use family-friendly policies but prefer informal arrangements since flexibility is seen as a risk to career. They "conform" to the gender order and maintain a type of complicit masculinity (Fig. 2).

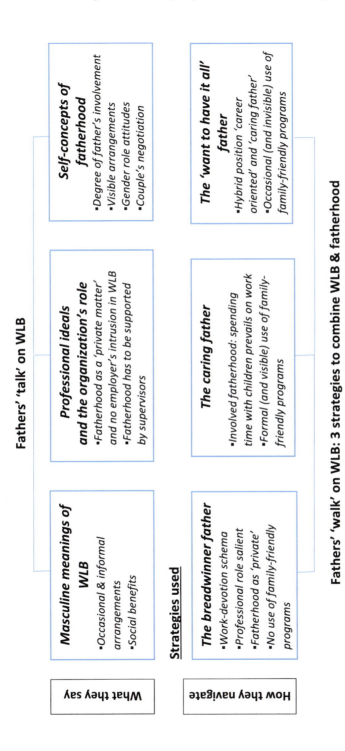

Fig. 2 French fathers facing work-life balance challenges

> "*I see that we might change more or less schedules when needed or take a day off [...] if I needed more flexibility than I have now, I would probably ask for it or maybe, before asking, I would look for a way... though I work as an analyst, I can do it here or at home. Therefore, before asking, I would probably think about a new work organization*" [Yoann, 30, marketing analyst; married, 1 child].

6 Discussion and Practical Recommendations

The results highlight a masculine construction of what means WLB and provide evidence that men increasingly seek a better balance between their professional and family lives, but have their own representations of what WLB covers for them. Fathers in our study have specific conceptions of what WLB means because their needs are specific, and they generally do not feel identified with the current WLB initiatives, viewed as basically geared towards women (Lewis and Stumbitz 2017).

The findings show that while fathers expect an increasing adaptability, support, and flexibility from their organizations, they also have to deal with challenging tensions related to their professional aspirations and the visibility of their fatherhood practice. Research indicates the existence of barriers (Coltrane et al. 2013; Possinger 2017; Tanquerel and Grau-Grau 2020) to men taking up WLB measures due to strong dominant norms of masculinity constructed as breadwinner not as caregiver. Organizational expectations on working time interact with gendered norms about the ideal worker and the ideal caregiver (Gregory and Milner 2011). Our findings support this view showing that fathers' cultural patterns of masculinity and fatherhood remain strongly linked to work. Working and leading a successful career are still part of contemporaneous masculine identity (Neumann and Meuser 2017).

Our results also show that fathers' expectations regarding the role the organization has to play in WLB facilitation are not homogeneous, some of them claiming an active organizational support and others rejecting the employer's interference. In that sense, class may be an important element in determining men's strategies to balance work and non-work spheres, as professional men are better able to take advantage of flexible work arrangements and organize their working schedules, passing as 'ideal workers' (Reid 2015), while working-class men more often use shift work to balance work and family demands (Kaufman 2013). As some studies argued (Williams 2010), as men occupy higher job positions, they also have more autonomy and ask for less formal flexibility. This research tends to show that the fathers in lower positions need more help and support from the organization and supervisor while fathers in managerial positions do not express this need. Men continue to negotiate and position themselves in relation to hegemonic masculinity as a taken for granted set of norms (Hunter et al. 2017). The degree of compliance with this set of norms determine which visible or invisible strategies fathers decide to leverage.

6.1 Practical Recommendations

Organizational policies must take account of men's positioning regarding traditional versus non-traditional masculinity and their heightened sensitivity to organizational norms (Harrington et al. 2015). Most men are so organization-centric that the organization has to provide them with more legitimacy (Kaplan et al. 2017). To do so, policies must tackle both societal expectations of men's roles (McDonald and Jeanes 2012) as well as implicit gender-coding of norms and policies to increase the feeling that men have the possibility to supportive measures (Hobson 2014).

A free choice approach would agree that if more men desire more time and if policies, which support mothers at work, are in place, men would access them. Yet, organizations tend to construct such policies in gender-neutral terms, which do not necessarily recognize structural or cultural barriers for their usage, and which tend to reinforce existing socio-economic inequalities (Williams 2010). Many fathers are somehow not fully enabled by their organizations to use policies (Moran and Koslowski 2019). Including men in the 'work-life' debate cannot simply be a matter of applying the same policies as those designed to help women to negotiate paid employment and motherhood. It is not enough. There is a need to challenge gendered ideal worker assumptions and traditional views of masculinity and fatherhood. As Harrington suggests in his chapter of this volume, employers should go further to help fathers be more engaged caregivers: *"having a father's employee network that provides dads the opportunity to discuss their concerns and needs regarding caregiving and balancing their work-family demands; offering flexible work options that support dads as they strive to meet both their professional and personal responsibilities; establishing a voluntary mentoring program for fathers interested in not just career-related dialogue but which also includes conversations regarding the work-family dilemmas and challenges men face...."*

In a general way, challenging deeply held convictions about women and men and their reproductive and economic roles in wider society would potentially involve support from a range of key stakeholders, including government, employers, and educational organizations. Research shows several measures to counter such barriers and to focus on targeted measures for men, which increase their visibility in the workplace (Burnett et al. 2013) and therefore create a sense of entitlement. Changes can also come from championing by male role models. Redefining fathers' roles – from a societal (national fatherhood regimes), organizational (supportive work environment), and individual perspective (new masculinity) – is necessary to change the hegemonic gender order. Future research could focus on whether or not changes in masculinity are merely cosmetic or whether they actually contribute to shifting gender norms' (Hunter et al. 2017).

The empirical work presented in this chapter, although exploratory, makes a significant contribution to our understanding of WLB policy and practice, particularly as it relates to French fathers. This research demonstrates that a shift in employer approaches to support fathers who seek access to family-friendly policies is necessary (Stovell et al. 2017). Organizations should accompany men in their changing roles and consider their WLB requests as legitimate as for women.

Acknowledgements The author thanks Harvard Kennedy School's Women and Public Policy Program (WAPPP), the Social Trends Institute (STI) and the International Center for Work and Family for initiating, funding and supporting the conference '*Elevating Fatherhood: Policies, Organizations and Health & Wellbeing*'. She also thanks all the participants of the conference for their enlightened suggestions and helpful comments to improve this chapter. She finally thanks all the fathers who kindly accepted to share their experience in this research.

References

Blair-Loy M (2003) Competing devotions: career and family among women executives. Harvard University Press, Cambridge
Blossfeld H-P, Mills M, Bernardi F (2006) Globalization, uncertainty and Men's careers: an international comparison. Edward Elgar, London
Brandth B, Kvande E (2002) Reflexive fathers: negotiating parental leave and working life. Gender, Work & Organization 9(2):186–203
Brugeilles C, Sebille P (2009a) La Participation des Pères Aux Soins et à L'éducation des Enfants. L'influence des Rapports Sociaux de Sexe Entre les Parents et Entre les Générations. Politiques Sociales et Familiales 95:19–32
Brugeilles C, Sebille P (2009b) Pères et Mères Face aux Activités Parentales: Un Partage Inégalitaire. in Régnier-Loilier A. (dir.), Portraits de Familles. L'enquête Étude des Relations Familiales et Intergénérationnelles, Ined, coll. « Grandes enquêtes », : 241-264
Brugeilles C, Sebille P (2011) Partage des Activités Parentales: Les Inégalités Perdurent. Revue des Poliques Socialesti et Familiales 103:17–32
Brugeilles C, Sebille P (2013) Le Partage des Tâches Parentales: Les Pères, Acteurs Secondaires. Informations Sociales 2(176):24–30
Budig MJ, England P (2001) The wage penalty for motherhood. Am Sociol Rev 66(2):204–225
Burnett SB, Gatrell CJ, Cooper CL, Sparrow P (2013) Fathers at work: a ghost in the organizational machine. Gender, Work & Organization 20(6):632–646
Cain Miller C (2014) Being a father is good for your career, but don't get carried away. The Upshot, New York Times. https://www.nytimes.com/2014/11/14/upshot/being-a-father-is-good-for-your-career-but-dont-get-carried-away.html
Carrigan T, Connell B, Lee J (1985) Toward a new sociology of masculinity. Theory Soc 14(5):551–604
Castelain-Meunier C (2005) Les Métamorphoses du Masculin. Presses Universitaires de France, Paris
Castelain-Meunier C (2013) Le Ménage: La Fée, la Sorcière et L'homme Nouveau. Stock, Paris
Collinson D, Hearn J (1994) Naming men as men: implications for work, organization and management. Gend Work Organ 1(1):2–22
Collinson D, Hearn J (2005) Men and masculinities in work, organizations, and management. In: Kimmel M, Hearn J, Connell RW (eds) Handbook of studies on men and masculinities. Sage, Thousand Oaks, pp 289–310
Coltrane S, Miller EC, Dehaan T, Stewart L (2013) Fathers and the flexibility stigma. J Soc Issues 69(2):279–302
Connell RW (1995) Masculinities. Polity Press, Cambridge
Connell RW, Messerschmidt JW (2005) Hegemonic masculinity: rethinking the concept. Gend Soc 19(6):829–859

Cooper M (2000) Being the 'go-to guy': fatherhood; masculinity; and the organization of work in Silicon Valley. Qual Sociol 23(4):379–405
Coser LA (1974) Greedy institutions: patterns of undivided commitment. Free Press, New York
Dermott E (2008) Intimate fatherhood: a sociological analysis. Routledge, London
Doucet A, Merla L (2007) Stay-at-home fathering: a strategy for balancing work and home in Canadian and Belgian families. Community Work Fam 10(4):455–473
DREES (2016) Le Congé de Paternité: Un Droit Exercé par Sept Pères sur Dix. Études et Résultats, n°957, Drees, Mars
DREES (2018) L'offre D'accueil Collectif des Enfants de Moins de Trois ans en 2015. Nadia Amrous et Françoise Borderies, Série « statistiques », n° 203, janvier 2018
Elliott K (2016) Caring masculinities: theorizing an emerging concept. Men Masculinities 19(3):240–259
Galinsky E, Aumann K, Bond JT (2009) Times are changing: gender and generation at work and at home. Families and Work Institute, New York
Gatrell CJ (2011) 'I'm a bad mum': pregnant Presenteeism and poor health at work. Soc Sci Med 72(4):478–485
Gioia DA, Corley KG, Hamilton AL (2013) Seeking qualitative rigor in inductive research notes on the Gioia methodology. Organ Res Methods 16(1):15–31
Gomajee R, El-Khoury F, Van Der Waerden J, Pryor L, Melchiorthe M (2017) Early life childcare and later behavioral difficulties: a causal relationship? Data from the French EDEN study. J Econ Behav Organ 181:344–359
Gregory A, Milner S (2008) Fatherhood regimes and father involvement in France and the UK. Commun Work Family 11(1):61–84
Gregory A, Milner S (2011) Fathers and work-life balance in France and the UK: policy and practice. Int J Soc Policy 31(1–2):34–52
Gregory A, Milner S (2012) Men's work life choices: supporting fathers at work in France and Britain. In: McDonald P, Jeanes E (eds) Men, wage work and family. Routledge, London
Haas L, Hwang CP (2019) Policy is not enough – the influence of the gendered workplace on fathers' use of parental leave in Sweden. Community Work Fam 22(1):58–76
Harrington B, Van Deusen F, Fraone JS, Morelock J (2015) How millennials navigate their careers: young adult views on work, life and success. Boston College Center for Work & Family, Chestnut Hill
Harrington B, Van Deusen F, Humberd B (2011) The new dad: caring, committed and conflicted. Boston College Center for Work and Family, Chestnut Hill
Hobson B (2014) Conclusion. In: Hobson B (ed) Worklife balance: the agency and capabilities gap. Oxford University Press, Oxford, pp 266–287
Hochschild A, Machung A (1989) The second shift: working parents and the revolution at home. Viking, New York
Hunter SC, Riggs DW, Augoustinos M (2017) Hegemonic masculinity vs. a caring masculinity: implications for understanding primary caregiving fathers. Soc Personality Psychol Compass 11(3):e12307
INSEE (2010) Enquête Emploi du temps en 2010. https://www.insee.fr/fr/statistiques/2118074
Kaplan D, Rosenmann A, Shuhendler S (2017) What about nontraditional masculinities? Toward a quantitative model of therapeutic new masculinity ideology. Men Masculinities 20(4):393–426
Kaufman G (2013) Superdads: how fathers balance work and family in the 21st century. NYU Press, New York
Kimmel MS (2004) Masculinity as homophobia: fear, shame, and silence in the construction of gender identity. In: Rothenberg PD, Mayhew KS (eds) Race, class, and gender in the United States: an integrated study. Worth, New York, pp 81–93
Kugelberg C (2006) Constructing the deviant other: mothering and fathering at the workplace. Gender, Work & Organization 13(2):152–173
Kvande E (2009) Work – life balance for fathers in globalized knowledge work. Some insights from the Norwegian context. Gender, Work & Organization 16(1):58–72

Kvande E (2012) Control in post-bureaucratic organizations-consequences for fathering practices. In: Oechsle M, Muller U, Hess S (eds) Fatherhood in late modernity: cultural images, social practices, structural frames. Verlag Barbara Budrich, Opladen, pp 233–248

Ladge J, Greenberg D (2019) Maternal optimism: forging a positive path through work and motherhood. Oxford University Press, New York

LaRossa R (1988) Fatherhood and social change. Fam Relat 37(4):451–457

Le Talec JY (2016) Des *Men's Studies* aux *Masculinity Studies*: Du Patriarcat à la Pluralité des Masculinités. *SociologieS* [En ligne], Dossiers, Sociétés en Mouvement, Sociologie en Changement, mis en ligne le 07 mars 2016, consulté le 10 avril 2018

Levy JD (2005) Redeploying the state: liberalization and social policy in France. In: Streeck W, Thelen K (eds) Beyond continuity. Institutional Change in Advanced Political Economies. Oxford University Press, Oxford

Lewis S, Stumbitz B (2017) Research on work and family: some issues and challenges. In: Liebig B, Oechsle M (eds) Fathers in work organizations, inequalities and capabilities, rationalities and politics. Verlag Barbara Budrich Publishers, Opladen, pp 227–244

Liebig B, Oechsle M (eds) (2017) Fathers in work organizations, inequalities and capabilities, rationalities and politics. Verlag Barbara Budrich Publishers, Opladen

Marsh K, Musson G (2008) Men at work and at home: managing emotion in telework. Gender, Work & Organization 15(1):31–48

Martial A (2016) Des Pères «En Solitaire »? Ruptures Conjugales et Paternité Contemporaine Aix-en-Provence: Presses universitaires de Provence

McDonald P, Jeanes E (eds) (2012) Men, wage and family. Routledge, New York

Milner S, Gregory A (2015) Fathers, care and family policy in France: an unfinished revolution? Families, Relationships and Societies 4(2):197–208

Moran J, Koslowski A (2019) Making use of work–family balance entitlements: how to support fathers with combining employment and caregiving. Community Work Fam 22(1):111–128

Moss P (ed) (2013) International review of leave policies and research 2013. International Network on Leave Policies and Research, London

Murgia A, Poggio B (2013) Fathers' stories of resistance and hegemony in organizational cultures. Gender, Work & Organization 20(4):413–424

Neumann B, Meuser M (2017) Changing fatherhood? The significance of parental leave for work organizations and couples. In: Liebig B, Oechsle M (eds) Fathers in work organizations, inequalities and capabilities: rationalities and politics. Verlag Barbara Budrich publishers, Opladen, pp 83–102

OPE (2017) Baromètre 2017 de la Conciliation entre Vie pro et Vie perso (volet « Salariés »)

ORSE (2010) Livre 'Patrons papas, paroles de 10 dirigeants sur l'équilibre travail et vie privée'

ORSE (2014) Rapport 'Les hommes, sujets et acteurs de l'Egalité professionnelle'

Pailhe A, Solaz A (2009) Entre Famille et Travail. Des Arrangements de Couples aux Pratiques des Employeurs. La Découverte, Paris

Pak M, Zilberman S (2013) La Durée du Travail des Salariés à Temps Complet. DARES Analyses, no.047. https://dares.travail-emploi.gouv.fr/IMG/pdf/2013-047.pdf

Pocock B (2005) Work/care regimes: institutions, culture and behaviour and the Australian case. Gender, Work & Organization 12(1):32–49

Possinger J (2017) The 'Daddy Months' in the German fatherhood regime: a step towards an equal share of work and care? In: Liebig B, Oechsle M (eds) Fathers in work organizations, inequalities and capabilities, rationalities and politics. Verlag Barbara Budrich publishers, Opladen, pp 185–204

Reid E (2015) Embracing, passing, revealing, and the ideal worker image: how people navigate expected and experienced professional identities. Organ Sci 26(4):997–1017

SPSS (2013) Projet de Loi des Finances de la Sécurité Sociale. Partie I: Données de cadrage, Paris: SPSS. http://www.assemblee-nationale.fr/14/projets/pl0235.asp

Stovell C, Collinson D, Gatrell C, Radcliffe L (2017) Rethinking work-life balance and wellbeing. The perspectives of fathers. In: Cooper CL, Leiter MP (eds) The Routledge companion to wellbeing at work. Routledge, London

Tanquerel S, Grau-Grau GM (2020) Unmasking work-family balance barriers and strategies among working fathers in the workplace. Organization 27(5):668–700

UNAF (2016) Réseau national des Observatoires des Familles, 2016. Note de synthèse n°8 « *Etre père aujourd'hui !* » 16/06/2016 https://www.unaf.fr/IMG/pdf/bro_20p_obsv_familles_8-finale_2_.pdf. Etude n°8 de l'Observatoire des familles menée par 42 UDAF et 2 URAF en 2015 dans 48 départements auprès d'une sélection de 3000 ménages allocataires de CAF ayant au moins un enfant à charge âgé de 4 à 20 ans

Williams JC (2010) Reshaping the work-family debate: why men and class matter. Harvard University Press, Cambridge

Wood G, Newton J (2006) Childlessness and women managers: 'choice', context and discourses. Gender, Work & Organization 13(4):338–358

Yancey Martin P (2001) 'Mobilizing masculinities': Women's experiences of men at work. Organization 8(4):587–618

Open Access This chapter is licensed under the terms of the Creative Commons Attribution 4.0 International License (http://creativecommons.org/licenses/by/4.0/), which permits use, sharing, adaptation, distribution and reproduction in any medium or format, as long as you give appropriate credit to the original author(s) and the source, provide a link to the Creative Commons license and indicate if changes were made.

The images or other third party material in this chapter are included in the chapter's Creative Commons license, unless indicated otherwise in a credit line to the material. If material is not included in the chapter's Creative Commons license and your intended use is not permitted by statutory regulation or exceeds the permitted use, you will need to obtain permission directly from the copyright holder.

'It Would Be Silly to Stop Now and Go Part-Time': Fathers and Flexible Working Arrangements in Australia

Ashlee Borgkvist

1 Introduction

The rates of men taking up formal flexible working arrangements in Australia, including parental leave, are relatively low when compared to women in Australia and when compared with men in other countries (Baxter 2013; Craig and Mullan 2010; Huerta et al. 2013). Flexible working arrangements, sometimes referred to as flexibility, are generally understood to be any working arrangements where the employee has some influence over where, when, how much, and how work is conducted (Williams 2010). Some barriers that impact men's use of flexible working arrangements include: a lack of support from managers and co-workers; career consequences such as missing out on promotions and pay raises; organizations' expectations in relation to men's use of flexibility; and the ideal worker norm (Acker 1990; Kelly et al. 2010). Investigating men's use of flexible working arrangements in Australia revealed a strong link between masculine identity and paid work. The importance of masculine identity among Australian men impacted decisions regarding work, family, and the uptake of flexible working arrangements (see Borgkvist et al. 2018).

In this chapter I present findings from semi-structured interviews with 15 working fathers in South Australia (see Table 1 for descriptive statistics). I discuss the link between masculinity, fathering, paid work, and men's uptake of flexibility. I further discuss the reciprocal influence of these factors on the development of Australian family policy, and some of the broader implications for policy and practice.

A. Borgkvist (✉)
Safe Relationships and Communities Research Group, The University of South Australia, Adelaide, SA, Australia
e-mail: ashlee.borgkvist@unisa.edu.au

Table 1 Participant information

Participant #/ Pseudonym	Age	Occupation	Relationship Status	Number/Age of children	Flexible Working Arrangement
1. Mike	40	Program officer	Married	2/6, 4	No
2. Mark	38	Call Centre	Married	3/5, 3, 0.5	Informal
3. Carl	33	Administration officer	Married	1/3, 1 on way	No
4. David	45	Community planner	Married	3/10, 8, 3	Informal
5. Ernie	52	Community planner	Married	2/16, 12	Informal
6. Frank	43	Journalist	Married	2/9, 6	No
7. Gary	33	Financial manager	Married	2/8, 6	No
8. Harry	39	Senior lecturer	Married	3/10,8,3	No
9. Jerry	46	IT consultant	Married	3/21,19,7	No
10. Kieran	39	Communications	Married	2/2, 4, 1 on way	Part time – 4 days per week
11. Larry	36	Researcher	Married	2/5, 3	Part time – 4 days per week
12. Nick	42	Team leader	Married	2/8, 6	No
13. Oscar	41	Administration officer	Married	1/ 2	Part time – 4 days per week
14. Phil	51	Social worker	Married	3/17, 14, 17 m	No
15. Ross	46	Scientist/ manager	De facto	4/15, 13, 4, 3	No

2 The Link Between Masculinity, Fathering, and Paid Work

Expectations of fathers and some fathering practices have changed over time (Miller 2017). The past few decades have seen changes in father's expressed desires to be involved, and expectations that fathers will be more involved in all aspects of child rearing (Dolan and Coe 2011; Miller 2017; O'Brien et al. 2007; Suwada 2017). These changing expectations likely reflect the complex and evolving nature of society and of what is considered good or normative fathering at different times.

The concept of hegemonic masculinity (Connell 2005b) suggests that within societies and cultures there is a dominant idea of what it is to be masculine, and the achievement of this kind of masculinity impacts the way fathering is performed (Coltrane et al. 2013; Shirani et al. 2012; Suwada 2017). In other words, to legitimise their status as both fathers and men, men are influenced to perform fathering in certain ways. These performances have traditionally included financial provision and engagement with paid work – almost to the exclusion of engagement with activities within the home, which has been considered more suitable for women (Connell 2005a; Pedulla and Thébaud 2015). Some research has found that men still associate manhood with having a job (Edley and Wetherell 1999; Shirani et al. 2012), and being a father with being able to financially provide for their family and children (Brandth and Kvande 2002; Harrington et al. 2010).

Further, the link between masculinity, fathering, and paid work influences what actions men feel are acceptable in the workplace – including taking periods of leave and using flexibility for family reasons (Brandth and Kvande 1998; Coltrane et al. 2013; Kelly et al. 2010). Men perceiving a need to work in a way which shows their dedication to paid work can be explained by a concept called the ideal worker norm, which was first proposed by Joan Acker (1990). The concept refers to the idea that the ideal worker is someone who is dedicated to work with no outside distractions, including family. This has historically been the male worker because their female partners have been held responsible for the private sphere of the home and for children. The concept of the ideal worker norm continues to have a large influence on the ways in which men perform work, because 'living up to the ideal worker norm is an important way to enact masculinity – and protect a privileged position' (Kelly et al. 2010:283; see also Cooper 2000) both in the workplace and at home. Organizational cultures are affected by what occurs outside of them in society and wider culture (Acker 1990). The association between paid work, masculine identity, and fathering which exists culturally also exists within organizations, and men are encouraged to behave in ways consistent with the provider role – within as well as outside of organizations.

The fathering role has historically been associated with different things than the mothering role – authoritarianism and breadwinning rather than emotion and caring (Halford 2006). These cultural divisions have different practical consequences. Research in the United States, for example, found that some fathers have 'difficulty seeing themselves in the role of stay-at-home spouse and primary caregiver. Part of this derived from their own sense of career identity' (Harrington et al. 2010:20; see also his chapter this volume for further discussion). In this research, fathers reported a strong connection between their careers and their identities. Many stated that:

> 'being a stay at home spouse did not fit with their views of themselves as a primary breadwinner. Equally important was the feeling that for a man to choose this option might be seen as not living up to his financial provider role in the eyes of others.' (p. 20).

A historical reliance on, and expectation of, women to conduct care work and on men to perform the role of the ideal worker and financially provide, can therefore be seen not only to be prescriptive for women but to restrict men's abilities to deviate from gendered expectations as well (see Correll et al. 2014). Men's use of flexible working arrangements for family reasons can be seen as transgressing the normal role they are expected to inhabit in an organization and within families.

3 Fathering and Paid Work in Australia

The association between paid work and fathering identity is important in the Australian context because of the special expression of masculinity in Australia. The historical influences on the formation and performance of masculinity in Australia will be explored briefly here to contextualise the findings presented later in this chapter.

Australian researcher and academic Raewyn Connell noted that masculinity expectations in Australia encourage men to behave in certain socially and culturally specific ways (Connell 2005a, b, 2014). Mateship—a kind of social contract in which men are expected to support other men who display appropriate and accepted masculinity—is something perceived as a core aspect of Australian masculinity. Connell has argued that mateship specifically has had a large influence on how Australian men interact with one another, and the social and cultural expectations of Australian men (see also Murrie 1998).

Masculine identity in Australia and mateship stems from historical legends that came to represent archetypal masculinity. Australia is a colonial society with a convict history. Manual labour, physical strength, stoicism, and endurance came to be culturally valued and revered (Dyrenfurth 2015; Summers 1975). Mateship grew out of these conditions, and can be seen to rest on the same kind of tenants as Connell's (2005a) conception of a dominant or hegemonic form of masculinity. This dominant form of masculinity involves the inclusion of accepted and revered masculine behaviours and the exclusion of what is considered feminine behaviour, in order to uphold a gender structure which privileges the masculine. This means a focus on what Australian men do rather than what they might feel (Connell 2014).

Thus, the performance of Australian masculinity has come to be heavily reliant on what men are able to achieve in the public sphere – that is, through engagement with and in paid work. Australian masculinity, then, is in part maintained by the dedication of Australian men to financial provision within families. Stepping away from full-time paid work in order to engage more fully in caregiving could therefore be viewed in opposition to what it means to be masculine in Australia.

4 The Development of Policy in Australia

The development and progression of Australian legislation in relation to family life and parenting has had a large impact on Australian masculinity, in part by making explicit the roles that Australian men and women should play within the family unit (Brennan 2011). Parenting roles in Australia have arguably been 'configured in relation to pro-natalist discourses and policies which shape maternal and paternal domains'. Historically, these have '... [had] a central focus on women as mother, reinforcing binary dimensions' (Miller and Nash 2016:2). The masculinist history surrounding Australian families and the development of family policies such as the

Family Tax Benefit and Paid Parental Leave within this culture, reinforced the breadwinner/caregiver dichotomy. Subsequently, the development of a particular kind of masculine and fathering identity in the Australian culture was encouraged and reinforced.

Australia lacked a national system of Paid Parental Leave (PPL) until 2011, despite previous efforts to create one (Pocock et al. 2013). The delay has been argued to have 'largely reflected three things: a strongly masculinist general culture; the dominance of a "male breadwinner" model of the worker; and the absence of a contributory insurance-based system of workplace benefits' (Pocock et al. 2013:599). The historically difficult nature of employees' access to paid leave and access to flexibility (Charlesworth and Heron 2012; Pocock et al. 2013), and the patriarchal social climate of Australia (Connell 2014; Miller and Nash 2016; Summers 1975) has meant that a reliance on gendered patterns, particularly the male breadwinner model, has been etched into Australian families' work and care arrangements.

The male breadwinner model, and the focus on altering women's ways of working but not men's, is reflected in the government-funded parental leave policies currently available to mothers and fathers in Australia. The Australian Government-funded PPL scheme offers 18 weeks leave to the primary carer, paid at minimum wage. In 2013, Dad and Partner Pay (DPP) was introduced for secondary carers, to be taken at the same time as the primary carer, and again paid at the minimum wage. Employers can also offer their own paid parental leave should they choose, although not all do.

While the PPL scheme for primary carers is gender neutral, these parental leave policies facilitate women taking time off from work to care while not providing adequate support for fathers to do the same (see, for example, Brandth and Kvande 2018). The primary carer for the first 18 weeks of a child's life is much more likely to be a woman, in part because women need to physically recover after giving birth and also may choose to breastfeed, and in part because women are likely to earn less than their male partners. Women are consequently much more likely to take the whole 18 weeks of paid leave, and this is reflected in the very low numbers of Australian men who utilise any PPL – approximately 2–3% (OECD 2016). Further, if a father's employer does not offer paid secondary carer's leave, they are put in the position of taking unpaid leave or using annual or personal leave if they want to take more than 2 weeks off from work when their child is born.

With a focus on increasing father's use of parental leave for the past 40 years, Sweden in particular has seen a large increase in fathers using parental leave and flexible working arrangements after the birth of children as a result of policy change. This has come to be an accepted and expected norm (see Suwada 2017). Due to the way it is set up, Australia's current PPL and DPP scheme essentially encourages one carer to be at home providing care – and this is usually the mother. Further, taking unpaid leave, or even leave paid at minimum wage, is often not enough to support families financially. Compared with most Scandinavian countries where men receive numerous months of paid parental leave under a 'use it or lose it' policy (OECD 2016), Australia's family policies seem conservative.

5 Men's Uptake of Flexible Working Arrangements in Australia

In Australia, evolving fathering expectations, and the seeming recognition of these expectations by Australian fathers, has seen them reporting an increase in care activities (see Baxter 2013; Baxter and Smart 2011). This increase in performing caregiving tasks points to a possible renegotiation and expansion of Australian masculinity. However, despite this increase in involvement, research has found that mothers are still primarily held responsible for care and for the emotional and mental work associated with this care, such as co-ordinating when and how fathers engage in caregiving and other unpaid labour (Singleton and Maher 2004; Riggs and Bartholomaeus 2018). Recent research also found that fathers thought they were not helpful to infants and would not be helpful at home after the birth of their children (Rose et al. 2015; Borgkvist et al. 2018).

Australian men have been found to express a need to increase their work hours when their children are born, which can be seen as an enactment of fathering identity linked to breadwinning (Gray 2013). On the other hand, Australian women decrease their involvement with paid work after children are born (Baxter and Hewitt 2013). A multitude of research shows that after the birth of a child, traditional gender roles become more delineated in relationships, and specifically 'in the Australian context fathers widen the gender gap by extending their paid work time upon becoming a father' (Gray 2013:172).

Though it appears that Australian men are engaging in relatively more caregiving behaviours than in the past, women are still held responsible for the majority of caregiving. This gendered dynamic is not specific to Australia (Miller 2011; Suwada 2017), however the distinct nature of Australian masculinities helps us to understand the association between fathering and paid work, and the barriers in utilising flexible working arrangements. Our research (Borgkvist et al. 2018), upon which this chapter is based, indicates that fathers do recognise changes in parenting expectations and express a desire to be more involved fathers. It is important, therefore, to examine how Australian men (and men in general) are negotiating these expectations and the support available to them. Furthermore, we need to determine how men who are using flexibility to engage in involved fathering are able to do so.

My research focused specifically on gender (masculinity) and how this might relate to the decisions that fathers make about using flexible working arrangements. Fifteen interviews were carried out with working fathers in which they were asked about how they managed their work and home lives, looking at what barriers and facilitators these fathers identified to flexibility use and how they talked about their decisions to use or not use flexibility. Their responses were then analysed with a gender lens.

A main finding from this research is that the ideal worker norm remains a significant barrier to fathers utilising flexible working arrangements. The construction of the ideal worker as dedicated to their jobs with no outside distractions and as able to work long hours was reinforced by organizational culture and was internalised by employees. While some fathers were using flexibility, such as coming in later after dropping kids off at school and a few who were working part-time, they were aware of a need to visibly minimise their time away from paid work. One father, for example, was doing school visits with his wife and child, but for the last visit had 'decided just to let them go to it' because he had taken too much time off. Another stated he did not 'want to be seen as someone who tries to get out of doing work,' and so he had decided not to approach his manager about using flexibility. Other participants of the research noted that within the organizational environment it was not considered unusual for women to use flexibility, though it was considered unusual for men. It seemed that the internalisation of these organizational expectations was an important aspect of men's decisions around flexibility; their value as organizational citizens is linked to productivity, and their identities being derived from this encouraged them to meet organizational expectations that they would be ideal workers (see also Tanquerel and Grau-Grau 2020).

Another factor identified as continuing to have an influence over men's decisions around the use of flexibility is the pervasive influence of masculinity. The interviewed fathers were more involved in care work than traditional masculinity would prescribe (Connell 2005b) and stated that they wanted to be involved in feeding, bathing, changing nappies, and other care-related activities. However, they positioned work as a more important aspect of their fathering identities. Fathers emphasised the importance and seniority of their positions at work and the resolve they had in overcoming difficulties in the workplace, firmly grounding their identities in paid work. One participant stated that if he worked part-time and his wife worked full-time, they would be better off financially, but he had worked hard to get to where he was 'so it would be absolutely silly to stop now and go part-time.' Participants also emphasised their roles as breadwinners and their female partners' roles as carers, with one participant stating that 'I can't imagine her going back to work and letting me look after the children when they were very young.' These kinds of statements were common, with participants tending to reinforce the gendered division of work and care in their interviews.

Though there were participants who were working part-time or using a formal form of flexibility so that they could be more involved in caregiving, they were not the majority. However, these men are of particular interest because they are stepping away from full-time paid work and creating a need to negotiate both their fathering identities and masculine identities. In this research, these men presented the most distinct attempt at a negotiation of an alternative masculine identity, one which more fully incorporated involved fathering. I termed these men 'ground-breakers.'

Of note, the 'ground-breaker' fathers were currently, or had previously been, working part-time, and they noted the difficulties they had faced in the workplace. One participant told of the assumption by his co-workers that he was still a full-time worker after he had been working part-time for over a year. He stated that he 'maybe was a little bit judged by some who had different attitudes towards men taking time off to do that' and that these 'were primarily people who had fairly strong ideas about what a male in a relationship or a father did, as opposed to what a mother did.'

These 'ground-breaker' participants, though, inverted these difficulties. For example, they emphasised their psychological strength, spoke of themselves as having power and control over their behaviour, and of not caring what others thought of their choices. Another participant, Kieran, stated:

> 'For the most part it didn't bother me that much because I just thought, well, you know, maybe in some respects I might be a bit of a front runner in, you know, men being able to do this a bit more .... I wanted to do it. I wanted to spend time with my kids, and if other people thought badly of it or didn't do it themselves, ... it didn't bother me'.

Talking about being a 'front runner' and making things easier for other men, can be understood to reproduce traditional notions of masculinity. These participants described themselves as having strength, perseverance, and a sense of power in not caring what others thought of them and exercising agency. However, talking about their behaviour in relation to caretaking and part-time work which is usually associated with femininity provides an example of an alternative masculine identity. That is, fathers are stepping outside of the norm which presents the need for them to negotiate an identity which deviates from this norm. What a reliance on these traditional notions of masculinity also accomplishes, though, is similar to what has been found in research into how men who work in 'feminized' occupations negotiate masculine identity. Their emphasis on attributes which reaffirm masculinity allows them to distance themselves from femininity (Hrženjak 2013; Pullen and Simpson 2009).

Finally, fathers primarily talked about the use of flexibility, and particularly parental leave, as a privilege and a choice as opposed to a right. Taking time off for the birth of their children and using flexibility later on to assist in managing work-life conflict (Pocock 2005) was discussed as an individual choice and therefore their own responsibility to manage, rather than as something that should be supported by organizations and government policy. Fathers' accounts of leave-taking around the time of their children's birth was framed as a privilege, with one participant stating, 'I was very fortunate, probably 99 percent of the population don't get that opportunity.' Among these participants it seemed there was a distinct lack of 'sense of entitlement' (Lewis 1997) to time off and use of flexibility for family reasons. Fathers' lack of 'sense of entitlement' was further evidenced by their discussions of the normality of women using flexibility, and women's use of flexibility being framed as a right. However, as Lewis and Smithson (2001) noted, the type of welfare state that individuals experience has an influence on their expectations regarding support from both employer and state. As Australia is highly patriarchal and support for the breadwinner/carer dichotomy is apparent in both culture and social policy (Connell 2014), these participants' responses and general lack of 'sense of entitlement' to organizational support is in keeping with expected gender roles within the Australian social climate.

6 Implications and Recommendations

What these results point to is that fathering expectations are changing in Australia and abroad, but there remains a strong connection between fathering identity and paid work which contributes to father's resistance to utilise flexibility for family reasons. Previous policy has also contributed to a gendered division of labour, and there is little policy support for men wanting to engage in shared or primary caring (Brennan 2011; Pocock et al. 2013). However, increasing men's use of flexibility will not come simply from policy change, particularly in the Australian climate. Other factors will be of relevance in encouraging a change in the way men work – namely a cultural shift is required to motivate men, and fathers specifically, to challenge and reject traditional gender roles and attitudes. To work towards this, the barriers to men's ability to work in (what are currently considered) non-normative ways need to be tackled. Without adequate financial and cultural support for fathers to take periods of leave throughout children's lives, Australian families will continue to fall back on traditionally gendered patterns of work and care (Baxter 2013; Miller 2011).

Tackling cultural issues outside of workplaces will provide more insight in to how to break the link between masculinity and paid work that operates within them. Fathers may be encouraged to become aware of and challenge workplace structures which maintain gendered practices. Naming and challenging gendered stereotypes and processes, for example, has been found to have an impact on the ways in which male employees relate to male peers as well as to their families (Ely and Meyerson 2010). In particular, if it is considered that the men in my research did not appear to have a sense of entitlement to use flexibility, and that flexibility, like child-care, is still considered to be 'for women,' it makes sense that we see this reflected in lower numbers of Australian men using a formal form of flexible working arrangement. Changing broad Australian policy and encouraging organizations to change their own policies to provide more support, sends a message to men that their participation in child rearing and care taking activities is valued and valuable. Other countries have also found that the introduction of parental leave policy targeted at fathers has encouraged challenge and re-definition of ideas about what father's roles are, as well as underscoring the importance of father's involvement in the first year of the child's life. These policies have been successful in increasing men's short and longer term use of flexibility for family reasons (Brandth and Kvande 2009; Suwada 2017), and O'Brien (2013) suggested that a targeted policy initiative can be successful even in countries with a strong breadwinner ideology.

Brandth and Kvande (2009) also discuss the need to filter out policies which are presented as gender neutral. They showed that these policies do not challenge gender inequality because it is usually the mother who ends up utilising them. This is true of the current PPL scheme in Australia and of many flexibility policies within organizations (Ahmed 2007). The effect of this is that flexibility is still implicitly considered to be 'for women' within organizations (see also Borgkvist et al. 2021). Making this visible is something which needs to occur to allow fathers to feel an entitlement to use flexible working arrangements.

Our research, like other research from around the world, has identified that many fathers remain reluctant to use flexibility, with numerous barriers to this use being cultural and gendered in nature. Scandinavian countries have demonstrated that culture change is vital, and changes in social norms and expectations can be facilitated by government policy. Therefore, I suggest that tangible and practical policy change in Australia will play a key role in encouraging more fathers to use flexible working arrangements and parental leave. Evidence-based research tells us that when fathers are provided with well-compensated, targeted, and extended parental leave, they are very likely to take it (Brandth and Kvande 2009; O'Brien 2013; Wall 2014). This is an important consideration given that when fathers are involved early on in an infant's life, they are more likely to maintain that involvement as the child grows and throughout the child's life (Huerta et al. 2013; Miller 2017).

As a country, there is a need to show fathers that their involvement is valuable and that time off from paid work for family reasons is a workplace benefit that should be used by all. This needs to start with more inclusive and supportive policy. I conclude with some suggestions for policy makers, organizations, and fathers in Australia:

- Policy makers should implement a specified period of paid parental leave for fathers
- Policy makers should consider quotas for the use of flexible working arrangements by male employees within mid-large size organizations
- Organizations should maintain transparency with all employees regarding flexible and paid parental leave policies
- Organizations should consider a top down approach to culture change, such that senior managers model and support flexible working arrangements
- Fathers should be willing to challenge organizational and cultural norms, and request support from their managers to balance work and family responsibilities

Acknowledgements This research was conducted as part of my PhD program at the University of Adelaide, South Australia. I would like to extend my gratitude to my PhD supervisors, to Dr. Elizabeth Hoon who read and provided feedback on an earlier version of this chapter, and to the editors and reviewers for their supportive feedback.

References

Acker J (1990) Hierarchies, jobs, bodies: a theory of gendered organizations. Gend Soc 4(2):139–158
Ahmed S (2007) The language of diversity. Ethn Racial Stud 30(2):235–256
Baxter J (2013) Parents working out work. In: Australian Family Trends. No. 1. Australian Institute of Family Studies, Melbourne. https://aifs.gov.au/publications/archived/864
Baxter J, Hewitt B (2013) Negotiating domestic labor: Women's earnings and housework time in Australia. Fem Econ 19(1):29–53

Baxter JA, Smart D (2011) Fathering in Australia among couple families with young children. In: Family Matters No. 88. Australian Department of Families, Housing, Community Services and Indigenous Affairs, Melbourne. https://aifs.gov.au/sites/default/files/fm88b.pdf

Borgkvist A, Eliott J, Crabb S, Moore V (2018) 'Unfortunately I'm a massively heavy Sleeper': an analysis of fathers' constructions of parenting. Men and Masculinities. https://doi.org/10.1177/1097184x18809206

Borgkvist A, Moore V, Eliott J, Crabb S (2018) 'I might be a bit of a front runner': an analysis of Men's uptake of flexible work arrangements and masculine identity. Gend Work Organ 25(6):703–717

Borgkvist A, Moore V, Crabb S, Eliott J (2021) Critical considerations of workplace flexibility "for all" and gendered outcomes: men being flexible about their flexibility. Gend Work Organ. https://doi.org/10.1111/gwao.12680

Brandth B, Kvande E (1998) Masculinity and child care: the reconstruction of fathering. Sociol Rev 46(2):293–313

Brandth B, Kvande E (2002) Reflexive fathers: negotiating parental leave and working life. Gend Work Organ 9(2):186–203

Brandth B, Kvande E (2009) Gendered or gender-neutral care politics for fathers? Annals of the American Academy of Political and Social Science 624(1):177–189

Brandth B, Kvande E (2018) Masculinity and fathering alone during parental leave. Men Masculinities 21(1):72–90. https://doi.org/10.1177/1097184x16652659

Brennan D (2011) Australia: the difficult birth of paid maternity leave. In: Kamerman SB, Moss P (eds) The politics of parental leave policies: children, parenting, gender and the labour market. The Policy Press, Bristol, pp 15–32

Charlesworth S, Heron A (2012) New Australian working time minimum standards: reproducing the same old gendered architecture? J Ind Relat 54(2):164–181. https://doi.org/10.1177/0022185612437840

Coltrane S, Miller EC, DeHaan T, Stewart L (2013) Fathers and the flexibility stigma. J Soc Issues 69(2):279–302. https://doi.org/10.1111/josi.12015

Connell RW (2005a) A really good husband: work/life balance, gender equity and social change. Aust J Soc Issues 40(3):369–383

Connell RW (2005b) Masculinities. Allen & Unwin, Crows Nest

Connell RW (2014) Feminist scholarship and the public realm in postcolonial Australia. Aust Fem Stud 29(80):215–230

Cooper M (2000) Being the "go-to guy": fatherhood, masculinity, and the Organization of Work in Silicon Valley. Qual Sociol 23(4):379–405

Correll S, Kelly E, O'Connor LT, Williams J (2014) Redesigning, redefining work. Work Occup 41(1):3–17

Craig L, Mullan K (2010) Parenthood, gender and work-family time in the United States, Australia, Italy, France, and Denmark. J Marriage Fam 72(5):1344–1361

Dolan A, Coe C (2011) Men, masculine identities and childbirth. Sociol Health Illn 33(7):1019–1034. https://doi.org/10.1111/j.1467-9566.2011.01349.x

Dyrenfurth N (2015) Mateship: a very Australian history. Scribe Publications, Australia

Edley N, Wetherell M (1999) Imagined futures: young Men's talk about fatherhood and domestic life. Br J Soc Psychol 38(2):181–194. https://doi.org/10.1348/014466699164112

Ely R, Meyerson D (2010) An organizational approach to undoing gender: the unlikely case of offshore oil platforms. Res Organ Behav 30(C):3–34. https://doi.org/10.1016/j.riob.2010.09.002

Gray E (2013) Fatherhood and Men's involvement in paid work in Australia. In: Baxter AEAJ (ed) Negotiating the life course: stability and change in life pathways. Springer Science and Business Media, Dordrecht, pp 161–174

Halford S (2006) Collapsing the boundaries? Fatherhood, organization and home-working. Gend Work Organ 13(4): 383-402. doi:10.1111j.1468-0432.2006.00313.X

Harrington B, Van Deusen F, Ladge J (2010) The new dad: exploring fatherhood within a career context. Boston College Center for Work & Family, Boston

Hrženjak M (2013) Negotiating masculinity in informal paid care work. Int Rev Sociol 23(2):346–362. https://doi.org/10.1080/03906701.2013.804296

Huerta M d C, Adema W, Baxter J, Han W-J, Lausten M, Lee RH, Waldfogel J (2013) Fathers' leave, Fathers' involvement and child development: are they related? Evidence from four OECD countries. In: OECD Social, Employment and Migration Working Papers, No. 140. OECD Publishing, New York. https://doi.org/10.1787/5k4dlw9w6czq-en

Kelly EL, Ammons SK, Chermack K, Moen P (2010) Gendered challenge, gendered response. Gend Soc 24(3):281–303. https://doi.org/10.1177/0891243210372073

Lewis S (1997) 'Family Friendly' employment policies: a route to changing organizational culture or playing about the margins? Gend Work Organ 4(1):13–23

Lewis S, Smithson J (2001) Sense of entitlement to support for the reconciliation of employment and family life. Hum Relat 54(11):1455–1481. https://doi.org/10.1177/00187267015411003

Miller T (2011) Falling Back into gender? Men's narratives and practices around first-time fatherhood. Sociology 45(6):1094–1109. https://doi.org/10.1177/0038038511419180

Miller T (2017) Making sense of parenthood: caring, gender and family lives. Cambridge University Press, Cambridge

Miller T, Nash M (2016) 'I just think something like the "bubs and pubs" class is what men should be having': paternal subjectivities and preparing for first-time fatherhood in Australia and the United Kingdom. J Sociol 53(3):541–556. https://doi.org/10.1177/1440783316667638

Murrie L (1998) The Australian legend: writing Australian masculinity/writing 'Australian' masculine. Journal of Australian Studies 22(56):68–77

O'Brien M (2013) Fitting fathers into work-family policies: international challenges in turbulent times. Int J Sociol Soc Policy 33(9/10):542–564

O'Brien M, Brandth B, Kvande E (2007) Fathers, work and family life. Community, Work and Family 10(4):375–386

OECD (2016) Parental leave: where are the fathers? Men's uptake of parental leave is rising but still low. https://www.oecd.org/policy-briefs/parental-leave-where-are-the-fathers.pdf

Pedulla D, Thébaud S (2015) Can we finish the revolution? Gender, work-family ideals, and institutional constraint. Am Sociol Rev 80(1):116–139. https://doi.org/10.1177/0003122414564008

Pocock B (2005) Work-life 'Balance' in Australia: limited Progress, dim prospects. Asia Pac J Hum Resour 43(2):198–209. https://doi.org/10.1177/1038411105055058

Pocock B, Charlesworth S, Chapman J (2013) Work-family and work-life pressures in Australia: advancing gender equality in "good times"? Int J Sociol Soc Policy 33(9/10):594–612

Pullen A, Simpson R (2009) 'Managing difference in feminized Work': men, otherness, and social practice. Hum Relat 62(4):561–587

Riggs D, Bartholomaeus C (2018) 'That's my job': accounting for division of labour amongst heterosexual first time parents. Community Work Fam 23(1):107–122. https://doi.org/10.1080/13668803.2018.1462763

Rose J, Brady M, Yerkes MA, Coles L (2015) 'Sometimes they just want to cry for their mum': Couples' negotiations and Rationalisations of gendered divisions in infant care. J Fam Stud 21(1):38–56. https://doi.org/10.1080/13229400.2015.1010264

Shirani F, Henwood K, Coltart C (2012) Why Aren't you at work?: Negotiating economic models of fathering identity. Fathering 10(3):274–290

Singleton A, Maher J (2004) The "new man" is in the house: young men, social change, and housework. J Men Stud 12(3):227–240. https://doi.org/10.3149/jms.1203.227

Summers A (1975) Damned whores and God's police: the colonization of women in Australia. Penguin Books, Ringwood

Suwada K (2017) Men, fathering and the gender trap: Sweden and Poland compared. Palgrave Macmillan, Cham

Tanquerel S, Grau-Grau M (2020) Unmasking work-family balance barriers and strategies among working fathers in the workplace. Organization 27(5), 680–700. https://doi.org/10.1177/1350508419838692

Wall K (2014) Fathers on leave alone: does it make a difference to their lives? Fathering 12 (2):196–210. https://doi.org/10.3149/fth.1202.196

Williams JC (2010) Reshaping the work-family debate: why men and class matter. Harvard University Press, Cambridge

Open Access This chapter is licensed under the terms of the Creative Commons Attribution 4.0 International License (http://creativecommons.org/licenses/by/4.0/), which permits use, sharing, adaptation, distribution and reproduction in any medium or format, as long as you give appropriate credit to the original author(s) and the source, provide a link to the Creative Commons license and indicate if changes were made.

The images or other third party material in this chapter are included in the chapter's Creative Commons license, unless indicated otherwise in a credit line to the material. If material is not included in the chapter's Creative Commons license and your intended use is not permitted by statutory regulation or exceeds the permitted use, you will need to obtain permission directly from the copyright holder.

Small Changes that Make a Great Difference: Reading, Playing and Eating with your Children and the Facilitating Role of Managers in Latin America

María José Bosch and Mireia Las Heras

1 Introduction

Time is a scarce resource. We get it at the rate of 24 h per day. How we allocate it affects our satisfaction and the relationships we build with the people we care about. The use of time becomes most relevant when we talk about parenting. Technology has facilitated that boundaries between work and non-work hours almost disappear. Globalization has led to 24/7 demands on many employees. More women in the workforce and more single-parent families mean no backup for child and elder care at home. Rapid changes in competition, unrest in social and legal structures, and volatility in market valuation means that companies and individuals need to be agile and adaptable. For all these reasons, how we distribute time between work and family has become increasingly challenging. Also, time allocation impacts not only family life but also work life, health, satisfaction, and social behaviors.

Researchers have long studied how to facilitate both, that women enter in the work force and balance their professional career and home life. However, they have not put the same effort into studying how to foster that men enter the home sphere and balance it with their professional work. This has created an imbalance. More and more women are getting into the workplace, yet men are not entering the home sphere at the same pace. This is an unsolved issue, as men continue to feel some social pressure to be breadwinners, and since workplaces still often see balance as a women's issue (Ladge et al. 2015) and much legislation presumes that women

M. J. Bosch (✉)
ESE Business School, Universidad de los Andes, Las Condes, Chile
e-mail: mjbosch.ese@uandes.cl

M. Las Heras
International Center for Work and Family, University of Navarra, Barcelona, Spain
e-mail: mlasheras@iese.edu

© The Author(s) 2022
M. Grau Grau et al. (eds.), *Engaged Fatherhood for Men, Families and Gender Equality*, Contributions to Management Science, https://doi.org/10.1007/978-3-030-75645-1_14

primarily take care of children instead of men. The study of fatherhood is likely to have a positive influence on gender equality in the workplace, and the amount of time that both parents spend with their children.

Parenting provides unique rewards, and it serves as a buffer against work problems (Kirchmeyer 1992). Family involvement helps in developing skills that are transferrable to the workplace, such as time management and patience. According to Greenhaus and Powell (2006), work-family enrichment improves life quality both in the family and work.

Fathers' involvement at home has a positive impact on the developmental outcomes of their children (Sarkadi et al. 2007; see also earlier chapters in this volume). Lamb (2010) shows that there is not only a positive effect of fathers' involvement, resulting in higher cognitive competencies, more empathy and more internal locus of control of their children, they also shows that the absence of the fathers results in negative outcomes, such as having lower school performance. Pleck's research (2010) shows that interactive activities (e.g., playing and reading) between the father and his children results in children with fewer behavioral problems and better cognitive development.

In this chapter, we intend to contribute to our collective knowledge about the impact of managers on the time fathers (collaborators of those managers) spend with their children. We will focus on three significant positive engagement activities: family dinners, playing, and reading. We use data from seven Latin American countries that reveals differences between countries.

2 The Role of Fathers in Family Life

The father figure has changed through time, and it still differs across cultures. (Sarkadi et al. 2007). From an Occidental perspective, beginning in ancient Greece and Rome, the father symbolizes authority and exteriority of the family core. In ancient Greece, the *polis*, the public space, the politics, and war were the places where men could perform and transcend, while the home (*Oikos*) was the feminine place (Roy 1999). Similarly, in ancient Rome, the father (*pater familias*), was a symbol of power and authority over his wife and children (Amunategui 2006).

The social and economic changes in the following centuries derive from an important rural economy, where family became a productive community. Although there was a division of labor by gender, and the father was the breadwinner, his presence was constant. It was in the industrial society that the presence of the father decreased. As men started to fulfill their labor role outside the home, Lamb and Tamis-LeMonda (2004) suggest that in that change, the nature of fatherhood evolved from being the moral teacher to becoming a distant breadwinner.

The study of child and adult development has mainly focused on the impact of the mother on his or her development and socialization. The research on the father's role started in the mid-twentieth century, mostly studying the outcomes of his presence vs. absence, as well as the impact of him co-residing with the child and the mother at home, as well as that of his economic support toward the mother (Pleck 2010).

Within the last two decades, with the increase of women in the labor force and the increase of dual-earner households, we have witnessed the rise of new expectations on the father figure. These expectations relate to his co-responsibility, his parenting impact (Pleck and Pleck 1997) and his involvement in his children's development (McGill 2014). Yet, while the expectations on the father have grown, fathers' role performance has changed only slowly and in low proportions (Lamb and Tamis-Lemonda 2004). In parallel, long working hours, the increase of divorces and the increase of single parent families, have all raised the concern of the absent-parent effect that may explain some contemporary social problems (Yeung et al. 2001).

Research related to the relevance of fathers in the human and social development of their children has become more critical. Research should not only focus on the outcomes of the co-residence of the father with his children, or on the effects of material support he gives to them, but research should focus on relevant issues such as the quantity and the quality of time he spends with them. To do so, researchers can use theories of parental involvement, which study a series of positive engagement activities that fathers can participate in with their children, such as spending time in family dinners, playing, and reading with them (Pleck 2007; Pleck 2010).

In the next section, we will present how the involvement of the father, in addition of that of the mother, represents an essential benefit for the child and, as a result, also to society at large. Later, we will show how positive engagement activities influence the child and adult development, and how managers can shape the time male employees who are fathers spend with their children.

3 The Importance of Fathers

Psychology literature defines family dinners, playing, and reading as positive engagement activities that the parents, and consequently the father, can have with his children. In this chapter we'll focus on these activities, as they are relevant to understand the role of the father in human development.

The father's involvement activities promote a secure attachment between the father and the child, which leads to positive outcomes at early ages, like self-control, and personal assurance (Cassidy and Shaver 1999; Pleck 2010). Moreover, when we consider the family social capital (Coleman 1988), parenting styles (Maccoby and Martin 1983), and proximal processes (Bronfenbrenner 1994), the father's involvement also influences the child's academic performance, relationships with his/her peers, and interaction with the environment.

Playing and reading provide a context where the father develops an authoritative parental style, and in turn allows the child to explore and make decisions based on his/her own reasoning. Playing and reading allow the development of proximal processes, which favor fundamental social interactions with other people and the environment. This is very relevant as interactions with other people and society help in developing the child self-confidence, conduct, and sociability. Engagement activities, such as family dinners, playing, and reading with the children, are the ideal scenarios to promote proximal processes (Bronfenbrenner 1994; Pleck 2010).

Fathers' involvement in playing, reading, and having dinner with their children allows them to transfer family social capital, which in turn promotes cognitive development, academic achievement, and educational aspirations (Coleman 1988; Pleck 2010).

We have justified the importance of parents spending time with their children. Next, we will move to study the importance of each of the proposed activities, having family dinners, playing, and reading on the children's development and the quality of life in adulthood. We will then move to study what influences the amount of time they spend playing with their children, and frequency they have dinner with them.

4 Positive Engagement Activities Between Fathers and Children

4.1 Family Dinners

Eating is an essential key biological function that any living being must perform. Yet, there is a key element that differentiates humans as we fulfill this activity: we are the only ones who do it as a social activity. All animals eat, but humans are the only ones that cook. So, eating together, and eating cooked food, becomes more than a necessity; it is the symbol of our humanity, what marks us off from the rest of nature. Our eating together is known as commensality. Commensality has different social functions: it strengthens the bonding of kinship; it revitalizes kinship; and it even develops significant relationships between people outside the family circle. Additionally, eating puts order to one's social life and individual behavior at the biological level and the social level. This order does not have a universal look but happens all over the world.

Not every culture has the same rules for eating, but each culture has its own guidelines of accepted behaviors; these are known as manners. Manners are one of the first exposures of culture transference, social skills, ethics, and resource access. Lastly, one of the main functions of commensality is the socialization of individuals to follow specific rules associated with cooperation and coexistence (Fischler 2011).

Therefore, several studies catalog family dinners as one of the critical components in the development of healthy children, adolescents, and adults. This practice offers a routine that has a positive impact on the person's quality of life and the relationship with one's father (Buswell et al. 2012; Kalil and Rege 2015). It also allows a setting in which fathers to transfer resources to children and adolescents, such socializing them in communicative skills, manners, nutrition, and good alimentary habits,

Family dinners, in which the father is present, show to be protecting children from risky behaviors, depression symptoms, and stress (Eisenberg et al. 2004). Family dinners (or any family meal in general) are one of the primary contexts in which fathers can get involved with their children. Family meals allow the development of authoritative parental styles, proximal processes, and transference of family social capital to children (Pleck 2010). However, family dinners is a practice that is in regression in more individualistic societies (Fischler 2011) because of several demographic and organizational factors, like longer times in transportation and commuting and the increase of dual career families (Anderson and Spruill 1993).

Spending time with children during dinner increases family unity and the adaptability that families have towards changes or problems. Family dinners reduce the problems related to work-family balance because family dinners increase the probability of the father perceiving a successful personal life, despite long working hours.

There is a broad range of literature that explains the importance of family dinners with the presence of both parents for the health of children and adolescence. Evidence shows that it reduces the risk of obesity (Taveras et al. 2005) and eating disorders (Eisenberg et al. 2004). The quality of the diet increases, and healthy habits are formed (Gillman et al. 2000; Taveras et al. 2005; Videon and Manning 2003): increasing the intake of fruits, vegetables, dairy products, and reducing the probability of skipping meals such as breakfast. Besides, these effects persist to adulthood (Larson et al. 2007).

Children who eat with their fathers tend to have a considerably better relationship with them than children who do not have a father figure frequently at family dinners. This activity works as a protecting factor to drugs, alcohol and tobacco consumption, and to depressive episodes and suicidal behaviors (Eisenberg et al. 2004). An adolescent who has a bad relationship with his father is four times more likely to abuse marijuana. Adolescents that do not share dinner with their fathers have higher probabilities of abusing tobacco and alcohol than the ones who have family dinners with both parents (The National Center on Addiction and Substance Abuse at Columbia University 2012; Eisenberg et al. 2004).

Long working hours (Neumark-Sztainer et al. 2003; Mallan et al. 2014) negatively relate to the frequency of family dinners. Managers also play a crucial role in facilitating (vs. hindering) support to employees, as they are the gatekeepers of access to flexible conditions. Supervisor can display family-friendly supervisor behaviors. Supervisor family friendliness may consist of emotional support; being a role-model for effective balancing; and coming up with creative solutions to work-family challenges (Hammer et al. 2009). These types of supervisory behaviors result in higher frequency of employees' family dinners, and lower frequency of fast food consumption (Allen et al. 2008).

4.2 Playing

Children's development requires acquiring the conscience of oneself. Playing is one of the main social activities that allow the development of one's own consciousness (self) and a social consciousness (me). Games provide role-playing contexts (i.e., embodying a police officer and/or a thief, playing mothers and fathers, etc.) and require understanding the rules of specific games. Playing helps to shape an identity, to understand the different roles that can be associated with being a human being, and how social expectations influence us (Mead 1934).

Psychology has linked playing more to fathers than to mothers. Even though fathers spend less time with their children than mothers do, on average they spend more time playing than mothers (Lamb and Tamis-Lemonda 2004).

Research shows that playing has an effect at an individual level for the child or adolescent, but it also has an effect at the family level. At the individual level, the frequency and quality of the game explains a higher development of cognitive and academic skills (MacWayne et al. 2013). The co-residency of the father and his child is very relevant in the case of the game because the fathers that live with their children tend to spend more time playing with them (Tamis-Lemonda et al. 2004).

Playing is also very important for a child's conduct and relationship with his/her peers. Similar to reading, fathers who play with their children positively influence their development of self-control and reduce behavioral problems (MacWayne et al. 2013), while also improving the relationship with their peers (Kennedy et al. 2015).

Families in which fathers play with their children have better-quality life indicators and show more cohesion and family adaptability under challenging situations. Games help children to be flexible, as they are not only moments of recreation but also instances for the development of adaptability skills (Buswell et al. 2012).

Work Interfering with Family (WIF) negatively relates to the time children spend playing with their fathers (Cho and Allen 2012). Colleagues' support is critical for parents with long working hours in allowing them to spend more time with their children (Roeters et al. 2012). However, other organizational support, like access to flexible policies, does not ensure an increase in the hours that fathers spend with their children (Kim 2018).

4.3 Reading

Shared book reading allows the child to develop his/her vocabulary since the words used in the written language are generally more complex than the oral language used by adults. Also, this activity allows the use of decontextualized language which is the language that it is used to communicate information to a person with little experience on the topic of discussion (Duursma 2014).

The quantity and the quality of the hours that a father spends reading to his children positively relates to his children's levels of language learning (Duursma

2014). A father reading to his children shows a positive correlation to the child's cognitive and academic skills in general. It is essential to recognize that the socio-economic level of the father acts as a moderator on this relationship (MacWayne et al. 2013)

The greater the frequency of father-child reading, the lower the child's behavioral problems (MacWayne et al. 2013), independently of socio-economic level and maternal attachment. For this reason, behavioral parent training in vulnerable populations in the U.S. uses father-child reading in its programs (Chacko et al. 2018). Fathers who participate in these studies improved their self-reported level of discipline and their positive parenting over time. Children in this study showed higher levels of listening comprehension skills and better expressive communication (Chacko et al. 2018).

Organizations also play a role in the amount of time fathers spend with their children. Working hours are negatively related to the time fathers spend with their children. However, to the best of our knowledge, studies show that as fathers' work hours increase, there is no change in the time they spend reading to their children (Hofferth and Goldscheider 2010).

5 The Importance of the Organizational Life on Father's Involvement with their Children

Work and family are interconnected. The experiences in one domain (e.g., family) impact the other domain (e.g., work) (Barnett and Rivers 1996). Organizations play an essential role in promoting a positive interface between work and family and reducing the conflict between these two domains (Kossek et al. 2011).

Role accumulation theory shows that holding multiple roles (e.g., being a father and an employee) produces positive qualities for both the organization and employee, such as family commitment, strong leadership skills, and stronger welfare of employees (Ruderman et al. 2002). Holding several roles also increases productivity and satisfaction with the father's professional career (Graves et al. 2007; Wallace and Young 2008). Researchers attribute these outcomes to work-family enrichment, or "the extent to which experiences in one role improve the quality of life in another role" (Greenhaus and Powell 2006:73). Enrichment mediates the relationship between being an involved father, and job performance (Graves et al. 2007) and the family context positively relates with work environment (Duxbury and Higgins 1991) and the benefits are bi-directional (Lapierre et al. 2018).

Organizational life affects employees work-life balance through three main dimensions: organizational policies; managerial behaviors; and values and culture. Organizational policies can promote flexibility in working hours, facilitate working from alternative places, support family care, and support personal and specific situations for sick relatives or emergencies. The implementation of policies is important in reducing the conflict between work and family.

Managerial behaviors can foster, vs. hinder, work-life balance and integration. The higher Family Supportive Supervisor Behaviors (FSSB), the lower the Work-to-Family Conflict (WFC), turnover intentions, and burnout. FSSB positively impacts job satisfaction and satisfaction with work-family balance among other positive employee outcomes.

The organizational culture expresses the way supervisors and peers treat people who work in the organizations, and the expectations of what the employees should be doing. Thompson et al. (1999) identified three dimensions of such culture: 'managerial support for work-family balance, career consequences associated with utilizing work-family benefits, and organizational time expectations that may interfere with family responsibilities.' They found that the higher the support level of work-family culture, the lower the family-to-work and work-to-family conflict.

6 The Impact of Managers on Father's Involvement with their Children

Family Supportive Supervisor Behaviors (FSSB) are those behaviors the supervisor displays to support the family life of their employees (Hammer et al. 2009). These behaviors include emotional and instrumental support as well as role-modeling behaviors, and instrumental support. The higher the FSSB, the lower work-family conflict and turnover intentions, and the higher work-family positive spillover, job satisfaction, and sleep quality. FSSB offers employee resources and flexibility (Rofcanin et al. 2018).

Managers' work and home engagement influence subordinates physical and attitudinal well-being at work (Rofcanin et al. 2018). Muse and Pichler's (2011) study of low-skilled workers finds that FSSB is negatively related to work-family conflict and positively related with job performance.

6.1 Managers and the Time Fathers Spend with their Children

There are two crucial dimensions we would like to highlight where managers affect organizational dynamics: First is time demands, and second is the impact on employees' career.

First, organizations tend to be demanding. For such reason, how we allocate our time and resources is crucial. Supervisors set expectations in terms of whether employees should put work before family responsibilities; and how much time they should work. Second, supervisors set expectations about what is considered as good work, and who can in turn, be promotable. Thus, the supervisors set

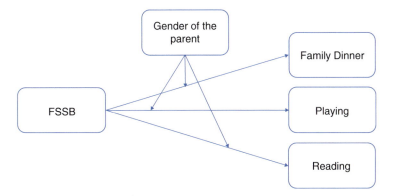

Fig. 1 Relationship between FSSB, gender of the parent and family dinner, playing and reading

expectations about whether or not displaying commitment to family can harm one's career.

We pose that FSSB is likely to promote the integration of work and family roles, thus leading to father's higher frequency of family meals, playing, and reading. We measure if this impact is the same for fathers and mothers. Therefore, we use the gender of the parent as a moderator in this relationship.

In Fig. 1 we present the relationships we will test.

6.2 The Importance of the Context: The Female Percentage of the Labor Force of a Country

Although globalization impacts how we work, employee motivation, organizational work-family policies, national regulation, and social norms are still different from one country to another (Bosch et al. 2018). Thus, it is relevant that context features in the analysis of these differences (e.g., Matthews et al. 2014; Shor et al. 2013). We know form research that the context in which work-family support occurs influences its effect on individual outcomes (Las Heras et al. 2015).

We test the influence of FSSB displayed by the manager on the time fathers spend in positive engagement activities with his children, and we controlled for the context, measured by the female labor force participation of the country. We do so because culture and gender affect how men and women distribute their time. Therefore, a variable that can reflect how men and women distribute their roles is the female labour force participation. To our knowledge, it is unclear how this variable will influence the amount of time fathers spend with their children. It is an indicator of the social development of the country; therefore, we expect a positive result on the hours that both men and women spend with their children.

7 The Case of Latin America

Culture influences how people perform roles in any society. The father figure has changed over time differently in each culture. Most studies on the role of the father focus on Anglo-Saxon cultures. These countries tend to be economically developed; fathers tend to live exclusively with their nuclear family; and often times they tend to display individualistic behaviors and tendencies (Spector et al. 2004). This is rather different from the context in which most people live in Latin America. Latin American countries tend to be collectivistic (Hofstede insights 2019). In these societies family groups and ties are very strong. People expect that those of their kin will offer care, protection, and loyalty (Hofstede and Hofstede 2005). Parents usually raise their children together with the grandparents, uncles, and extended family (Hofstede and Hofstede 2005). This increases the pressure on the father figure. According to Spector et al. (2004), in these societies, family welfare is very important. Work is not and individual activity, but rather an obligation to provide for family. This might often result in fathers feeling pressure to work long hours, in which case, not seeing their children is a minor externality suffered for a greater good. In these contexts, fatherhood is recognized as one important sign of responsibility (Vigoya 2001). Latin American countries have social norms that explicitly divide the roles of men and women, with the direct consequence of fewer women in the workforce (Unterhofer and Wrohlich 2017).

Considering the specific context of Latin American culture, we want to test the relationship between FSSB and the positive engagement activities of fathers: family dinner, playing, and reading. Thus, we took data from 22,070 individuals from 55 companies based in Latin America who participated in the IFREI 1.5 study from 2011 to 2015. This study is part of a larger research project managed by a leading European business school, whose is focused in measuring different variables of work life balance, and how this impacts individuals, families, organizations and the society. These companies operate in Argentina, Chile, Colombia, El Salvador, Guatemala, Mexico, and the Dominican Republic. Participants in the survey represent a wide range of Latin American countries that have different female labor force, and various levels of welfare. Participation was voluntary and anonymous. Our sample includes employees working in different industries, diverse hierarchical levels and in the public as well as in the private sector. Our sample is a convenience sample using electronic and physical surveys sent out to different databases in each country and posted in the social media networks: LinkedIn, Facebook and Twitter.

7.1 Measures

FSSB (Family Supportive Supervisor Behaviors): We used seven items from the Hammer et al. (2009) scale to measure the subordinates' perception of the family supportive supervisor behaviors. Items included, for example: "My supervisor is willing to listen to my problems in juggling work, and non-work life" and "My supervisor thinks about how the work in my department can be organized to benefit employees and the company jointly." Responses were measured on a seven-point scale (1 = strongly disagree; 7 = strongly agree).

Family Dinners, Playing and Reading: The outcome variables "Reading" and "Playing" were expressed in the number of hours, and the outcome variable "Dining" was expressed in number of days a week.

Female Labor Force Participation (FLFP): We used the percentage of labor force participation for female from the ILO.

Controls: We also control for other variables like gender, gender of the supervisor, if the couple works, age, tenure, responsibility, number of kids, and country.

7.2 Descriptive Statistics

Our final sample includes parents from the seven Latin American countries discussed. Table 1 provides details of the sample broken down by country.

Our group of interest is parents, specifically fathers, but for the first analysis, we included fathers and mothers to test if there is a difference between men and women and our variables of interest. Therefore, our sample was reduced to 16,007, since other, non-parent respondents could not answer the question of the hours they spend with their children (Table 2).

7.3 Results

7.3.1 Differences Between Countries

First, we checked if there was a significant difference between the variables across countries. Therefore, we tested our variables with a conventional ANOVA test

Table 1 Sample size per country

	Sample	Men	% of men	Fathers	% of fathers	% Female Labor Force
Argentina	1906	1020	53.5	658	34.5	0.47
Chile	7661	3800	49.6	2773	36.2	0.49
Colombia	4070	3484	85.6	2650	65.1	0.58
El Salvador	2888	1375	47.6	913	31.6	0.47
Guatemala	1651	987	59.8	665	47.1	0.41
Mexico	3213	1844	57.4	1243	38.7	0.44
Rep. Dominicana	681	268	39.4	134	19.7	0.53
Total	22,070	12,778	57.9	9036	40.9	**0.49**

Table 2 Reports descriptive statistics for each variable

	Dinner	Playing	Reading	FSSB	Children	Gender	Gender supervisor
Playing	0.74***						
Reading	0.63***	0.76***					
FSSB	0.19***	0.20***	0.15***				
Children	0.02*	−0.03***	0.01	−0.01			
Gender	−0.19***	−0.10***	−0.10***	−0.09***	0.08***		
Gender supervisor	−0.15***	−0.11***	−0.08***	−0.16***	0.03***	0.40***	
% Female Labor Force	−0.26***	−0.26***	−0.20***	−0.10***	−0.03***	0.18***	0.27***

Note. * $p < 0.05$, ** $p < 0.01$, *** $p < 0.001$;

Table 3 ANOVA results for the study variables

	Family Dinner (days/week)	Playing (days/week)	Reading (days/week)	Number of Children	FSSB
Argentina	5.28	4.03	2.22	1.98	5.30
Chile	4.07	3.42	2.50	2.02	5.45
Colombia	2.52	1.95	1.43	1.90	4.59
El Salvador	3.89	3.25	2.66	1.75	5.28
Guatemala	4.89	4.79	4.37	2.31	4.89
Mexico	4.17	3.34	1.82	1.81	5.24
Rep. Dominican	4.42	3.43	2.33	1.95	5.60
Total	3.88	3.15	2.25	1.95	5.18
ANOVA (F)	200.3***	158.92***	135.00***	51.37***	103.05***
Df	6.	6.	6.	6.	6.

Table 4 Average time Men and Women Spend in Positive Engagement Activities

	Family Dinners (days/week)		Playing (days/week)		Reading (days/week)		FSSB	
	Men	Women	Men	Women	Men	Women	Men	Women
Argentina	4.76	5.92	3.89	4.05	2.02	2.43	5.30	5.30
Chile	3.74	4.37	3.43	3.42	2.45	2.61	5.38	5.54
Colombia	2.13	4.78	1.77	3.13	1.27	2.38	4.54	4.83
El Salvador	3.93	3.87	3.28	3.23	2.45	2.84	5.14	5.39
Guatemala	4.76	5.20	4.68	4.85	4.41	4.09	5.03	4.69
Mexico	4.03	4.35	3.45	3.19	1.79	1.88	5.14	5.40
Dominican Republic	4.15	4.52	3.44	3.40	2.14	2.35	5.66	5.58
Total	3.41	4.52	2.92	3.47	2.02	2.58	5.05	5.37

broken down by country. The difference in the country means is significant for all our variables of interest. While Argentina reports the highest levels of family dinners, Colombia reports the lowest. In our variables of playing and reading, Guatemala reports the highest number of hours, while Colombia reports the lowest. A possible explanation for the Colombian case is that it is the country with the longest commute time to work (Statista Research Department 2018). We show results in Table 3.

7.3.2 Differences Between Fathers and Mothers

Next, we checked if there is a difference in the time fathers and mothers spend in positive engagement activities with their children. First, we compared the mean between fathers and mothers. Results are presented in Table 4.

Table 5 Gender and country effect: ICC for each variable

	Family Dinners	Playing	Reading	Number of Children	FSSB
Between-individual variance (%)	82.90	88.01	89.35	96.16	93.90
Between-gender variance (%)	7.02	1.93	2.12	1.35	1.58
Between-country variance (%)	10.08	10.06	8.53	2.49	4.52
ICC (1) gender	0.08	0.02	0.02	0.01	0.02
ICC (2) country	0.11	0.11	0.09	0.03	0.05

Table 6 SEM results

	Family Dinner		Playing		Reading	
	Coef	z	Coef	z	Coef	z
FSSB	0.67***	22.72	0.64***	22.47	0.44***	7.27
Female labor force participation (FLFP)	0.47	1.30	−0.93**	−2.69	−0.89**	2.18
Gender	0.50*	2.22	0.22***	5.59	0.76***	3.15
Gender of the supervisor	−0.05	−0.61	−0.01	−0.12	0.07	2.83
Number of children	0.28***	7.94	0.11***	3.31	0.20***	3.63
FSSB*FLFP	−0.30***	−7.64	−0.30***	−7.82	−0.22***	−3.75

Looking at the average, we can see that there is a difference among countries and between genders. To test which effect is stronger (gender or country), we calculated the Intraclass correlation for each variable. Results are presented in Table 5.

Table 5 shows interesting results. Except for Family Dinners, where the gender effect is higher t, in all other variables the country effect is stronger, showing that the context is very relevant to the time parents spend with their children.

7.3.3 The Manager Effects

To test if the manager and the organizational culture have an impact on the time fathers spend with their children, we ran a Structural Equation Modeling (SEM). Results are presented in Table 6.

Results presented in Table 4 confirm that the manager and his family-friendly behaviors impact the time fathers spend with their children. Also, results show that this influence is moderated by the gender of the parent. This means, that managers will have a greater influence with their behaviors on fathers more than on mothers. In order to see this effect, we present Figs. 1, 2 and 3 to see the moderating role of gender.

The family-friendly behaviors of the manager are positively related to the time parents spend with their children at family dinners, but this effect is stronger in

Small Changes that Make a Great Difference: Reading, Playing and Eating... 259

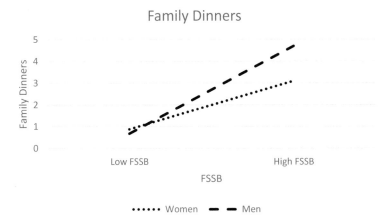

Fig. 2 The moderating role of gender on the relationship between FSSB and the time fathers and mothers spend in Family Dinner

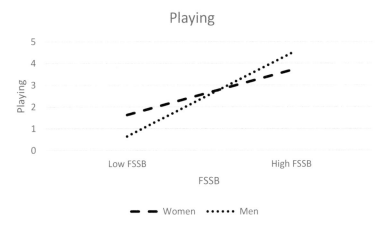

Fig. 3 The moderating role of gender on the relationship between FSSB and the time fathers and mothers spend in Playing

fathers than in mothers. In companies where managers behave with family friendly behaviors fathers spend more time at family dinners.

Additionally, in the case of playing, FSSB has a positive impact on the time parents spend in this positive engagement activity with their children. However, gender has a moderating effect on this relationship. FSSB has a stronger positive on fathers than on mothers (Fig. 4).

Again, our results show that managers who show FSSB have a positive impact on the time parents spend playing with children. Again, gender has a moderating effect on this relationship. In the case of fathers, the positive effect becomes stronger.

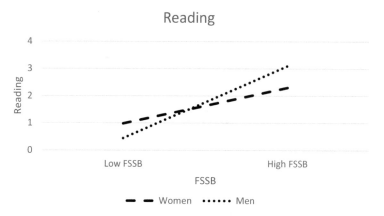

Fig. 4 The moderating role of gender on the relationship between FSSB and the time fathers and mothers spend in Reading

8 Discussion

There is a considerable amount of research that supports the importance of parents participating in positive engagement activities with their children. Moreover, the role of fathers has gained importance. Our study recognizes the importance of fathers in the development of their children, and how organizations, through their managers, promote positive engagement activities. The time fathers spend in family dinners, playing, and reading, will also have an impact on organizations, and the development of employees' children. This influences the talent that the organization will look for in the future. Also, as we explained before, these activities reduce several social problems that affect society and, thus, will help organizations in society.

Many factors influence the decision about parental time distribution, but as fathers spend a substantial amount of time at our jobs, managers play a key role in this decision-making process. They act as both a gatekeeper and a role model and influence the father's decisions. Therefore, it is imperative to recognize this influence and potential outcomes, as organizations can take actions by facilitating and promoting family-friendly behaviors among their managers.

Our study also contributes to the contextual conditions to explain under which context the relationship between FSSBs and the time a father spends in family dinners, playing, and reading takes to unfold. As previous research shows, context matters (Bosch et al. 2018). Our results show that interaction between FSSB and the hours that fathers spend with their children is stronger in fathers than in mothers in Latin American countries. A potential explanation for this influence is that when managers show FSSB, fathers feel that they are also allowed to spend more time in family activities. For example, playing with your children is not confined to only women, and therefore fathers (and mothers) need to achieve work-life balance.

Our life is divided into different roles. How we distribute our time among these roles, impacts not only our welfare but also affects the people we care about. This is especially important in the parent-child relationship, where parents have a direct impact on a child's development. An organization influences these developments. Therefore, it is relevant to continue fostering such positive dynamics to not only impact the family dimension, but also the work dimension and even society.

References

Allen TD, Shockley KM, Poteat LF (2008) Workplace factors associated with family dinner behaviors. J Vocat Behav 73(2):336–342
Amunategui CFA (2006) El Origen de los Poderes del PaterFamilias: El PaterFamilias y la PatriaPotestas. Revista de Estudios Histórico-Jurídicos, XXVIII, pp 37–143
Anderson EA, Spruill JW (1993) The dual-career commuter family: a lifestyle on the move. Marriage Fam Rev 19(1–2):131–147
Barnett RC, Rivers C (1996) She works/he works: how two-income families are happier, healthier, and better-off. Harper, San Francisco
Bosch MJ, Heras ML, Russo M, Rofcanin Y, Grau MG (2018) How context matters: the relationship between family supportive supervisor Behaviours and motivation to work moderated by gender inequality. J Bus Res 82:46–55
Bronfenbrenner U (1994) Ecological models of human development. In: Husen T, Postelthwaite TN (eds) International Encyclopedia or Education. Pergamon Press, Oxford, pp 1642–1647
Buswell L, Zabriskie R, Lundberg N, Hawkins A (2012) The relationship between father involvement in family leisure and family functioning: the importance of daily family leisure. Leis Sci 34 (2):172–190
Cassidy J, Shaver PR (eds) (1999) Handbook of attachment. Theory, research, and clinical applications. The Guilford Press, New York
Chacko A, Fabiano GA, Doctoroff GL, Fortson B (2018) Engaging fathers in effective parenting for preschool children using shared book Reading: a randomized controlled trial. J Clin Child Adolesc Psychol 47(1):79–93
Cho E, Allen TD (2012) Relationship between work interference with family and parent-child interactive behavior: can guilt help? J Vocat Behav 80(2):276–287
Coleman JS (1988) Social Capital in the Creation of human capital. Am J Sociol 94:S95–S120
Duursma E (2014) The effects of Fathers' and Mothers' Reading to their children on language outcomes of children participating on early head starts in the United States. Fathering 12 (3):282–302
Duxbury LE, Higgins CA (1991) Gender differences in work-family conflict. J Appl Psychol 76 (1):60–74
Eisenberg ME, Olson RE, Neumark-Sztainer D, Story M, Bearinger LH (2004) Correlations between family meals and psychosocial Well-being among adolescents. Archives of Pediatric Adolescent Medicine 158(8):792–796
Fischler C (2011) Commensality, society and culture. Soc Sci Inf 50(3–4):528–548
Gillman MW, Rifas-Shiman SL, Lindsay Frazier A, Rockett HRH, Camargo CA Jr, Field AE, Berkey CS, Colditz GA (2000) Family dinner and diet quality among older children and adolescents. Arch Fam Med 9:235–240
Graves LM, Ohlott PJ, Ruderman MN (2007) Commitment to family roles: effects on managers attitudes and performance. J Appl Psychol 92(1):44–56
Greenhaus JH, Powell GN (2006) When work and family are allies: a theory of work-family enrichment. Acad Manag Rev 31(1):72–92
Hammer LB, Kossek EE, Yragui NL, Bodner TE, Hanson GC (2009) Development and validation of a multidimensional measure of family supportive supervisor behaviors (FSSB). J Manag 35 (4):837–856

Heras L, Mireia ST, Escribano PI (2015) How national context moderates the impact of family-supportive supervisory behavior on job performance and turnover intentions. Management Research 13(1):55–82

Hofferth SL, Goldscheider F (2010) Does change in Young Men's employment influence fathering? Fam Relat 59(4):479–493

Hofstede G, Hofstede GJ (2005) Cultures and organizations: software of the mind. McGraw Hill, New York

Hofstede Insights (2019) Hofstede Insight. https://www.hofstede-insights.com/country-comparison/chile/

Kalil A, Rege M (2015) We are family: fathers time with children and the risk of parental relationship dissolution. Soc Forces 94(2):833–862

Kennedy LB, Dunn T, Sonuga-Barke E, Underwood J (2015) Applying Pleck's model of paternal involvement to the study of preschool attachment quality: a proof of concept study. Early Child Development Care 185(4):601–613

Kim J (2018) Workplace flexibility and parent - child interactions among working parents in the U.S. Soc Indic Res. https://doi.org/10.1007/s11205-018-2032-y

Kirchmeyer C (1992) Perceptions of nonwork-to-work spillover: challenging the common view of conflict-ridden domain relationships. Basic Appl Soc Psychol 13(2):231–249

Kossek EE, Pichler S, Bodner T, Hammer LB (2011) Workplace social support and work–family conflict: a meta-analysis clarifying the influence of general and work–family-specific supervisor and organizational support. Pers Psychol 64(2):289–313

Ladge JJ, Humberd BK, Watkins MB, Harrington B (2015) Updating the organization MAN: an examination of involved fathering in the workplace. Acad Manag Perspect 29(1):152–171

Lamb ME (2010) How do fathers influence children's development? Let me count the ways. In: Lamb ME (ed) The role of the father in child development, 5th edn. Wiley, London, pp 1–26

Lamb ME, Tamis-LeMonda CS (2004) Fathers' role in child development. In: Lamb ME (ed) The role of the father in child development. Wiley, New York

Lapierre LM, Li Y, Kwan HK, Greenhaus JH, DiRenzo MS, Shao P (2018) A meta-analysis of the antecedents of work–family enrichment. J Organ Behav 39(4):385–401

Larson N, Neumark-Sztainer D, Hannan PJ, Story M (2007) Family meals during adolescence are associated with higher diet quality and healthful meal patterns during Young adulthood. J Am Diet Assoc 107(9):1502–1510

Maccoby E, Martin J (1983) Socialization in the context of the family: parent- child interaction. In: Hetherington EM (ed) Handbook of child psychology: socialization, personality, and social development, 4th edn. Wiley, New York, pp 1–101

MacWayne C, Downer JT, Campos R, Harris RD (2013) Father involvement during early childhood and its association with Children's early learning: a meta-analysis. Early Educ Dev 24(6):898–922

Mallan KM, Daniels LA, Nothard M, Nicholson JM, Wilson A, Cameron CM, Scuffham PA, Thorpe K (2014) Dads at the dinner table. A cross-sectional study of Australian fathers' child feeding perceptions and practices. Appetite 73(1):40–44

Matthews RA, Mills MJ, Trout RC, English L (2014) Family-supportive supervisor behaviors, work engagement, and subjective Well-being: a contextually dependent mediated process. J Occup Health Psychol 19(2):168–181

McGill B (2014) Navigating new norms of involved fatherhood: employment, fathering, attitudes, and father involvement. J Fam Issues 35(8):1089–1106

Mead GH (1934) Mind, self and society. University of Chicago Press, Chicago

Muse LA, Pichler S (2011) A comparison of types of support for lower-skill workers: evidence for the importance of family supportive supervisors. J Vocat Behav 79(3):653–666

Neumark-Sztainer D, Hannan PJ, Story M, Croll J, Perry C (2003) Family meal patterns: associations with sociodemographic characteristics and improved dietary intake among adolescents. J Am Diet Assoc 103(3):317–322

Pleck JH (2007) Why could father involvement benefit children? Theoretical perspectives. Applied Development Science 11(4):196–202

Pleck JH (2010) Parental involvement: revised conceptualization and theoretical linkages with child outcomes. In: Lamb ME (ed) The role of the father in child development. Wiley, London, pp 67–107

Pleck EH, Pleck JH (1997) Fatherhood ideals in the United States: historical dimensions. In: Lamb ME (ed) The role of the father in child development. Wiley, London, pp 33–48

Roeters A, Van der Hippe T, Kluwer E, Raub W (2012) Parental work characteristics and time with children: the moderating effects of parent, gender and children age. Int Sociol 27(6):1–18

Rofcanin Y, Heras ML, Bosch MJ, Wood G, Farooq Mughal F (2018) A closer look at the positive crossover between supervisors and subordinates: the role of home and work engagement. Hum Relat 72(11):1776–1804

Roy J (1999) Polis and Oikos in classical Athens. Cambridge Core: Greece and Rome 46(1):1–18

Ruderman MN, Ohlott PJ, Panzer K, King SN (2002) Benefits of multiple roles for managerial women. Acad Manag J 45(2):369–386

Sarkadi A, Kristiansson R, Oberklaid F, Bremberg S (2007) Fathers involvement and Children's developmental outcomes: a systematic review of longitudinal studies. Acta Paediatr 97(2):153–158

Shor JJ, Greenhaus JH, Graham KA (2013) Context matters: a model of family-supportive Supervision & Work-Family Conflict. Acad Manag Proc 1:14613

Spector PE, Cooper CL, Poelmans S, Allen TD, O'Driscoll M, Sanchez JI, Siu OL, Dewe P, Hart P, Luo L (2004) A cross-National Comparative Study of work-family stressors, working hours and Well-being: China and Latin America versus the Anglo world. Pers Psychol 57(1):119–142

Statista Research Department (2018) Statista global consumer survey: mobility: duration of daily commute. https://www.statista.com

Tamis-Lemonda CS, Shannon JD, Cabrera NJ, Lamb ME (2004) Fathers and mothers at play with their 2- and 3- year olds: contributions to language and cognitive development. Child Dev 75(6):1806–1820

Taveras EM, Rifas-Shiman SL, Berkey CS, Rockett HRH, Field AE, Lindsay Frazier A, Colditz GA, Gillman MW (2005) Family dinner and adolescent overweight. Obes Res 13(5):900–906

The National Center on Addiction and Substance Abuse at Columbia University (2012) The importance of family dinners VIII. Columbia University, New York. https://www.centeronaddiction.org/addiction-research/reports/importance-of-family-dinners-2011

Thompson CA, Beauvais LL, Lyness KS (1999) When work–family benefits are not enough: the influence of work–family culture on benefit utilization, organizational attachment, and work–family conflict. J Vocat Behav 54(3):392–415

Unterhofer U, Wrohlich K (2017) Fathers, parental leave and gender norms DIW (Deutsches Institut Für Wirtschaftsforschung) discussion paper 1657. German Institute for Economic Research (DIW Berlin), Berlin

Videon TM, Manning CK (2003) Influences on adolescent eating patterns: the importance of family meals. Journal of Adolescence Health 32(5):365–373

Vigoya MV (2001) Contemporary Latin American perspectives on masculinity. Men Masculinities 3(3):237–260

Wallace JE, Young MC (2008) Parenthood and productivity: a study of demands, resources and family-friendly firms. J Vocat Behav 72(1):110–122

Yeung WJ, Sandberg JF, Davis-Kean PE, Hofferth SL (2001) Children's time with fathers in intact families. J Marriage Fam 63(1):136–154

Open Access This chapter is licensed under the terms of the Creative Commons Attribution 4.0 International License (http://creativecommons.org/licenses/by/4.0/), which permits use, sharing, adaptation, distribution and reproduction in any medium or format, as long as you give appropriate credit to the original author(s) and the source, provide a link to the Creative Commons license and indicate if changes were made.

The images or other third party material in this chapter are included in the chapter's Creative Commons license, unless indicated otherwise in a credit line to the material. If material is not included in the chapter's Creative Commons license and your intended use is not permitted by statutory regulation or exceeds the permitted use, you will need to obtain permission directly from the copyright holder.

Fatherhood Among Marginalised Work-Seeking Men in South Africa

Mandisa Malinga and Kopano Ratele

1 Introduction

I love my children. I'm just saying I can uhm...the problem is there is just one thing I am thinking about, you see, in my thoughts, I am thinking I should just pay 'ilobolo' for the children. I should take them to my family home, uhm...I should pay damages for all three of them. -John

Twenty-four year-old John, a father of three, had difficulties getting involved in his children's lives. He said that he would love to spend time with them, but because he was unable to "pay *ilobolo*," he did not have access to them. *Ilobolo* is a Nguni word referring to bride-wealth (sometimes erroneously referred to as bride-price or dowry). In mentioning *ilobolo* John is gesturing to *amasiko* (plural; singular *usiko*) which are cultural rituals and practices performed in many Nguni ethnic communities in South Africa. John is pointing out the fact that his inability to offer *ilobolo* "for the children" to the children's mothers' families – the children had different mothers – so that he can be close to them (and not because he wants to marry the mother) is the reason behind the difficulties he was facing with gaining access to his children. Though he refers to *ilobolo*, unmarried men like John are expected to pay *inhlawulo* (what he also refers to as 'damages') in order to be acknowledged as fathers and gain access to their children.

Similar to many unemployed or precariously employed men, John could not afford to offer *ilobolo* or *inhlawulo* because he "worked" as a day labourer, and, if he

---

M. Malinga (✉)
University of Cape Town, Cape Town, South Africa
e-mail: mandisa.malinga@uct.ac.za

K. Ratele
University of South Africa, Pretoria, South Africa
e-mail: kopano.ratele@mrc.ac.za

did get a job for the day, he was poorly paid. Stable, gainful employment is an essential concern to consider in examining the involvement or lack of involvement of some men in their children's lives.

In this chapter we focus on the stories of men like John, who, due to precarious employment, are inconsistently present or absent in their children's lives. The relationship between unemployment and fathering is particularly important in South Africa which is characterized by high levels of unemployment (Statistics South Africa 2019) and low levels of paternal involvement (Ratele and Nduna 2018). While there are many studies examining precarious work across the world and in different contexts (Devault et al. 2008), these studies often cite unemployment as one of the factors that impact on fatherhood without investigating in detail the ways in which fathers' relationships and engagement with their children is complexly impacted. Furthermore, these studies often draw on forms of precarious work that involve a formal employment contract. The aim of the present study is to explore a different kind of employment precarity, that of day labour workers who engage in seasonal work with no employment contract. According to Blaauw et al. (2006), who conducted a survey on 'day labour' work, there were nearly 1000 day labour sites (roadside hangouts where men go daily to wait for any type of work) in South Africa, with about 45,000 men occupying these sites. These are men (and increasingly women) who wait on the side of the road for any work ranging from construction to domestic work. Given the significance of paid work and the impact of this type of precarious work on constructions of fatherhood and masculinities (see Malinga 2016), examining the views and practices of this particular group of men offers us an in-depth and contextual understanding of the conditions under which some men are expected to father. Additionally, a unique contribution of the chapter is the mediation of the relationship between precarious employment and fathering by cultural practices.

In the next section we sketch the context of our studies on fathers and fatherhood in South Africa, providing a synopsis of work on fathers and fatherhood in the country. We highlight the emergence of the new fatherhood discourse but also the persistence of the traditional fatherhood discourse. And then we turn to the changes in the cultural constructions as well as the socio-political and economic contexts of fatherhood as some of the factors that shape such discourses.

2 Context

2.1 Emergence of the New Fatherhood Discourse, and Persistence of the Traditional Fatherhood Discourse

A set of dynamic relational practices tied to context, fatherhood is a historically and culturally contextual practice. What it means to be a father and the activities associated with it change over time and across places. Fatherhood is shaped by the economic, cultural, political contexts within which men become fathers (Hauari and Hollingworth 2009). At the same time, we also observe that within the same historical-political era, for example South Africa during the apartheid, or the same cultural milieu, for example among the Nguni, meanings attributed to and practices of fatherhood can vary and even clash.

Different forms of fathering are encouraged in different cultures and times. For example, while many scholars cite the emergence of the "new father" who is reportedly more actively involved in the parenting process (Lamb 2000), this form of fathering may be less visible in some contexts. Remarking the persistence of the "traditional breadwinner" discourse, Enderstein and Boonzaier (2015) contend that changes in discourses of fatherhood reflect an *integration* of parenting roles among men (caregiving and financial provision) and not necessarily a shift from provision to caregiving. Evidence from other South African studies show that even though fathers have become more involved, or in some cases desire to do so, their roles remain centred on providing for their children and families' financial needs (Enderstein and Boonzaier 2015; Hunter 2006). Moreover, evidence from South Africa (Hunter 2006) and Germany (Tölke and Diewald 2003) suggest that men's ability to provide for their children and families remains a critical signifier of both culturally exalted masculinity and fatherhood. In South Africa, the relationship between the ability to economically provide for one's children and conceptions of masculinity and fatherhood is complicated by high levels of unemployment.

While the discourse of an *emergent* nurturing father suggests that this kind of fatherhood is uncommon, some authors have pointed out that the active involvement and participation of fathers in children's lives has been part of the way of life for many African societies. Ahadi and Mandy (2007) present an extensive list of responsibilities traditionally assumed by African fathers, including, providing love to their children, building self-esteem, practising non-violence, and taking equal share of housework. Similarly, Lesejane (2006:176) outlines the responsibilities that the position of father carried historically among Africans, extending from father as moral authority, leader, provider, and protector to role model. Mkhize (2006) writes about collective fathering and the importance of kin and community in parenting among African people. What is of especial interest in the work of the latter two authors is in highlighting that the traditional responsibility of the father in some African communities extended beyond one's own children and the children of the extended family members (such as brothers, sisters, and cousins), to other children in the broader community. Among many Black South African communities, men's ability to fulfil these roles is determined by their ability to fulfil certain cultural practices that determine and legitimise their access to their children. We discuss these practices and their implications in the following section.

2.2 Cultural Practices and Constructions of Fatherhood

Whilst South African research and government reports have shown the decreasing rates of marriage, in particular among Black South Africans (Posel et al. 2011), scholars who work on masculinities and fatherhood have remarked the weight of marriage and building a home for one's family in constructions of culturally recognized fatherhood and masculinity (Hunter 2006; Lesejane 2006). Historically – and to a lesser but still significant extent, contemporaneously – marriage did not merely bring two people together but functioned to legitimize a man's position within a cultural world. Marriage earned a man a particular kind of value – cultural credit. But in the enduring contemporary economic climate that characterises South Africa, a situation that has followed a long period of an entrenched, brutalizing system of economic migration tied to colonialism and apartheid economies, marriage has become out of reach for many men. The customary practice of *ilobolo* is one of the reasons for the unaffordability of marriage and, hence, the decline in marriage rates.

Built into a custom like *ilobolo* are important processes that are designed to prepare both women and men for parenting and marriage. These cultural practices have, however, become commercialised and less accessible to men who lack stable employment and live in poverty. There are also implications for unemployed men who are not able to fulfil the costs associated with these rituals. For example, in some ethnic groups in South Africa, when the father does not marry the mother (for reasons such as economic constraint) and fails to offer *inhlawulo* to her family, he loses his right to the child (Lesch and Kelapile 2016). *Inhlawulo* is the offering, usually financial, made by the male's family to a female's family when there is an unplanned pregnancy or where there is no intention of getting married (Lesch and Kelapile 2016). While such rights and access can be negotiated and challenged through the courts, many men who do not pay these "damages" often cannot afford them, but likewise cannot afford the legal process that would help them reclaim their legal rights of access to their children. In such cases it is not only the fathers who are affected, but children too. For example, when a man pays *inhlawulo* to the woman's family and is then recognised as the child's father with access to the child, he also extends his own social and kin networks to the child (Madhavan 2010). Such an extension of networks can be beneficial – immediately, and more so later – for children's cultural existence, broadening their access to cultural capital. For unemployed men who desire to be recognised as fathers to their children, their non-recognition means not only their own exclusion from certain rights and decision-making powers, but also cultural isolation from their children – a phenomenon experienced disproportionately by Black men in South Africa whose lives remain affected by the country's violent and oppressive history.

It is critical for us as critical cultural subjects and fatherhood scholars, to observe that beside finances, culture (and religion) are two key facts to understanding men's actions in those contexts in which culture (or religion) is a salient element of social and personal life. At the same time, to avoid stereotyping African communities, it is necessary to recognize that *amasiko* and rituals and customs such as *ilobolo* and *inhlawulo* are neither universal across Nguni communities nor are they performed by all Africans.

2.3 Socio-Political and Employment Contexts and Fatherhood

While collective fathering remains a part of life in some communities in South Africa (Mkhize 2006), the practice has declined in many other parts. This decline is partly attributable to the fact that Black men and women are experiencing a transitional period of cultural renegotiation, remain economically marginalised, and are disproportionately represented among the unemployed in the country. This decline suggest that fatherhood continues to be shaped by the country's economic and political past of colonialism and apartheid and its continuing legacy. Whilst Black people are in the majority in South Africa, the history of white racism continues to have effect on Black cultures. Therefore, the decline in cultural practices such as collective fathering is in part due to the enduring impact of colonial and apartheid injustices on the lives of many Black South Africans alongside contemporary racialised economic inequalities.

It is important to note that while South Africa has been liberated from a white racist rule, the effects of colonisation and apartheid continue to haunt many Black families. These effects are evidenced in the numbers of children who are growing up without their biological fathers or any father figure at all (Ratele and Nduna 2018), and most critically, the high unemployment rates among particularly the Black population (Statistics South Africa 2019). According to the Quarterly Labour Force Survey published at the end of the second quarter of 2019, 29% of the working age population in South Africa was found to be unemployed. Of these, the previously disadvantaged groups had the highest levels of unemployment: the unemployment amongst Black was 32.7%; Coloured 22.5%; Indian 11.2%; and amongst Whites 7.4% (Statistics South Africa 2019). While unemployment remains higher for women than it is for men (Statistics South Africa 2019), Black men find it harder to find stable jobs in South Africa. In addition to the unemployment rates, there has also been a decrease in the formal sector employment, while the informal sector continues to grow (Statistics South Africa 2019). What this data suggests is that in the absence of formal and stable jobs, and as a result of the desperation that comes with being unemployed, people are more likely to move towards the informal sector as well as informal employment.

3 Methodology

This chapter is based on data collected as part of an ethnographic research study conducted in 2014 with men who spend their days on the side of a road looking for work. The ethnographic study focused on constructions of masculinities and fatherhood among these unemployed/precariously employed men. Data gathering for the study included semi-structured interviews and participant observations. Interviews were conducted with 54 men over a period of 17 weeks in Cape Town, South Africa. We draw from 46 participants who identified as fathers, of whom 15 shared residence with their children. The participants were all indigenous African men who were either born in Cape Town (15) or had migrated from various parts of South Africa (22) or neighbouring countries (8 from Zimbabwe and 1 from Lesotho) to Cape Town in the Western Cape Province of South Africa. The majority of the men went to Cape Town in search for work. One went to complete his high school education (but, due to financial constraints, he never did and ended up seeking work on the side of the road). And one was moved from the Eastern Cape Province through the prison system and was later released around Cape Town where he had no family and had to live on the streets.

Participants were recruited using both purposive and snowball sampling methods that allowed the researcher to approach men who were fathers (self-defined) and were seeking work on the side of the road; as well as to be referred to participants by other men who had already participated. Interviews were conducted using a semi-structured interview guide and took place on quieter parts of the sidewalk further away from where other men gathered. Interviews lasted between 10 and 90 min.

The interviews were audio-recorded and later transcribed verbatim and analysed using grounded theory method of constant comparison which involves a detailed coding process (Charmaz 2006). The first step of analysis was initial coding which allows for line-by-line coding. The second step was focused coding which involved an in-depth exploration of the codes from step 1. Following these first two steps, the data was compared for similarities, differences, and contradictions – a process that was constantly repeated. The codes were then thematically grouped together, resulting in the main themes relating to the meanings and practices of fatherhood discussed below. In line with maintaining anonymity and confidentiality, in reporting and discussing the findings, the participants' real names are replaced with pseudonyms.

Drawing on the ethnographic study, in this chapter we examine the impact of precarious work on constructions and practices of fatherhood. More specifically, we highlight the ways in which precarious "day-labour" work shapes the way men think about fatherhood and its associated practices. Following Hobson and Morgan (2002), we distinguish between the terms father, fatherhood, and fathering. We take father to refer to the adult male who contributes to the conception of the child (biological) and/or to the (emotional and economic) upkeep of the child (social). Fatherhood refers to the meanings attached to fathers including their rights and responsibilities. And fathering refers to the actual 'doing' of fatherhood. In this paper, we dwell on the meanings and practices that men associate with their role as fathers, focusing on the experiences of economically marginalised African men.

In the following sections, we now turn to report and discuss selected findings from the ethnographic study, focusing on two thematic threads. First, we highlight economic provision as a key aspect of fatherhood among men juxtaposing this with some men's recognition that love and presence are necessary in fatherhood. Then we turn to cultural practices as possible impediments to the involvement of men with their biological children.

4 Findings and Discussion

4.1 *To Provide, to Love, and Be There*

Participants in this study were asked what fatherhood meant to them and it was not unexpected that all of them made reference to the responsibilities they thought fathers ought to fulfil. The least surprising in this regard, despite the much touted discourse of the emerging new father, was the view that fathers' main responsibility is to provide for their children's material needs for food, clothing, shelter, and school requirements.

It is clear, on the basis of this finding, that economic provision remains an important aspect of fatherhood among men in men's eyes. This finding is another confirmation of the work of many scholars (e.g., Enderstein and Boonzaier 2015; Hunter 2006). The importance of financial provision is, according to Robert Morrell (2006), more emphasised among men who struggle to fulfil this ideal as a result of poverty and unemployment. This makes obvious sense: men who struggle to fulfil what has been, and may still be, the elementary requirements of manhood and fatherhood, that being to provide for one's children, will perceive the inability to economically provide for one's children as failure. The present study thus confirms that, even though constructions and practices of fatherhood may continue to evolve over time and across cultures, the expectation placed upon men to provide for their children and families' financial needs remains intact.

Many earlier reports and studies on fatherhood maintained a pathologizing view on poor and Black fatherhood (and motherhood, and broadly the Black family), uncritically arguing that these fathers often abandon their children and families. In the context of the U.S., the 1965 Moynihan Report on "The Negro Family" is a notorious exemplar of such a view (e.g., see Blount and Cunningham 2014; Collins 1989; Hunter and Davis 1994). The findings from the present study illustrate that many of the men acknowledged the importance of physical presence, support, and love for their children. However, and as a result of unemployment and labour migration, it was difficult for them to fulfil even the nurturing aspect of their role as fathers. In an attempt to move away from pathologizing constructions of Black fatherhood, we highlight the importance that men placed on nurturing their children and being there for them in many different ways.

As noted earlier, colonialism and apartheid greatly affected the ability of fathers to not only provide for their children and families, but also to be physically present and participate in their children's lives. Of all the men studied, 31 (67%) did not live with their children, mirroring the national picture (Ratele and Nduna 2018). We found that financial provision, the significance of showing one's children love, and being present were important to all men, whether they shared residence with their children or not. Due to poverty, even those men who shared residence with their children spent very little time with them, as they spent most of their time out seeking work. For some, it was the shame and humiliation associated with a lack of financial stability that forced them to spend time outside of their homes. Despite the physical distance, the importance of love was highlighted several times. For example, Sicelo (a Zimbabwean father of one who did not share residence with his child) noted that "the first responsibility of a father is to love the children, be there for the children." Several other participants shared the same sentiments as shown below by Jason, a 37 year-old father of 3 who was one of the 15 who shared residence with their children:

Loving them is the most important thing. Because if you don't wanna give them love, they gonna feel that there's no love. That's why most of the kids turn out...changing their lives to drugs, doing this, doing that, getting into gangs and all that. It is very important for a father to love his kids. -Jason

Jason highlights 'father love' as an important factor in children's emotional and psychological development. He underlines that it is not only physical presence that matters, but also – "the most important thing" – the love children can experience from their fathers. Furthermore, Jason argues that children who do not receive such love may in fact experience negative social, behavioural, and psychological outcomes.

Themba is another example of a poor man who highlighted the love of the father. But, in addition to loving one's children, Themba argues that it is important that fathers fight for and defend their families:

I think maybe as a father it is love, love...just love...like love you see, and also defending your family. To them even if you have nothing, you say 'hey, hey, hey, that's my family!' I have to fight for them, to defend whatsoever. It gives you something to...even if you are going through rough patches in life where you have nothing like money you understand, not much, they look at you and say 'eish that guy you understand has...has love for us and he [inaudible segment: 0:19:27.9] *he knows how to defend his family you understand', yeah I think that the one thing that is important to me is love, being able to protect them as a father.* -Themba

In the extract above, Themba argues that it is important for men to love and defend their families so that even when they are going through financial difficulties and are unable to provide their families can still appreciate them.

Jacob – a father of two who did not live with his children – spoke about his desire to live with and be present for his children.

...And I want them to stay with, with me, I want to stay with my children. I want them to feel that their father is here even when I have even when I don't have. -Jacob

Similar to Themba above, Jacob wants to be there for his children so that even when he is not able to provide for them they can still appreciate his presence. And yet, because they have to seek work on the side of the road, Themba and Jacob are not always able to provide for their families. Even when they do get jobs, the wages do not cover their own living expenses, and they are therefore not always able to send any remittances back home to their families. In the absence of the highly emphasised role of men as economic providers, they want to be present for their children in other ways – such as living with them, protecting them, and showing them love. These are important statements that challenge the arguments that seek to brand poor and unemployed men as "bad fathers."

While it was clear that participants thought it was important for them to share residence with their children, they were also not prepared to just go home (Zimbabwe in Jacob's case, and the Eastern Cape in Themba's case) and stay at home caring for their children while they do not have the means to provide for them. As noted above, financial provision remains a dominant feature of "responsible" masculinity and fatherhood across many cultures. As such, men do not want to risk facing the humiliation that is associated with not meeting the requirements of "successful" masculinity and fatherhood.

The dilemma of love and money was captured by Spikiri. A 27-year old father of one, Spikiri saw financial provision – eating – as the "first" responsibility of a father. For him, it is most important for a father to feed his children, then love can follow.

> *You must first make sure that children eat, [my] sister. You must make sure that you provide them with clothes to wear and [only] then you have to make sure that they get a father's love at all times.* -Spikiri

Roy (2004) reports similar findings which showed that even while nurturing is considered important, financial provision was still the primary role men thought they ought to fulfil. It is clear from the findings of this study that men's views differ on the order of importance of the roles they are expected to play in their children's lives. These differences are shaped by their material conditions and the support they have in providing for their children. The focus on and prioritisation of economic fatherhood, particularly in the context of poverty, is likely the reason studies on fatherhood often do not reveal much about how men "do" fatherhood outside of the economic provider model. What this suggest it that we need more studies that tell us how these men express love and other positive parenting practices, particularly in context of deprivation. As East et al. (2006) argue, existing literature does not articulate the importance of "father love" very well (see also the chapter by Macht in this volume).

In this section we have sought to illustrate that while financial provision remains an important role for fathers, love and physical presence are also valued by men as important in their parenting roles. These findings also show that these men desire to fulfil the nurturing father ideal, however, they are challenged by their socio-economic circumstances. This data suggests then that though desired by most fathers, the nurturing father ideal is not always accessible to all.

4.2 Amasiko *as Impediments to the Involvement of Men with their Biological Children*

As noted earlier, there are certain cultural practices that are essential for some men as they are for women. These rituals and customs vary across ethnicities, with evidence suggesting that some are in fact eroding as a result of many factors, including urbanisation and economic conditions. Most of the participants in this study indicated that these cultural practices applied among their ethnic groups. While the men were expected to fulfil the cultural expectations, they were not in a position to do so as a result of their economic circumstances.

We began with the case of John who indicated his inability to pay *inhlawulo* to his children's mothers' families as the main reason behind the challenges he was facing with gaining access to his children. Another man who spoke on the impact of *amasiko* such as *inhlawulo* was Sthe, a father of two. In the extract below he highlights his desire for marriage. But, he says, he cannot afford to get married because he does not work.

> *I am supposed to be living with them and their mother, but now I am what you call...not married, I have not yet had enough money to get married because of work, I don't work.*
> -Sthe

The extract from the interview with Sthe again indicates joblessness and lack of money as a decisive but unfavourable fact in the lives of many of the men in this study. Because they do not have stable gainful employment, men like Sthe, John, and Spikiri are not seen as legitimate fathers within their communities and families, and as such, have little authority and decision-making power in their children's lives. These men often feel a continued sense of disempowerment and are excluded from the privileges afforded to men who meet the requirements associated with dominant and successful masculinity and fatherhood (Strier et al. 2014).

Similar to John's case, 30 year-old father of one Siseko did not have access to his child. He was not married to the mother although he was still in a relationship with her. He said he could not take the children to live with him as he would like to because he had not paid *inhlawulo*. The mother's family denied him access to the child despite the relationship with the mother – as she still lives with her family who helps her support and raise the child.

Father of three, Demaine, was another man who did not have access to his child. He used legal means to challenge the maternal family for access to his child. He highlights that it was in fact the mother's brother that had denied him access to the child following her (the mother's) death. Highlighted here is the role played by social fathers (uncles, grandfathers, brothers) who take responsibility for the child and play an important role in shaping their life (Morrell 2006).

> *It is a big problem, we went to court with her uncle over these children. The court found that he had no rights to my children. The only person with rights is me, the father. If their mother was around she would have the right to them, but because their mother passed away, the person left is their father, so I am the one who has a right to these children. But they also*

know being where they are, that I am the one who has a right to the children, but I am not taking care of them.- Demaine

While they previously had no legal rights to their children, unmarried men in South Africa now have rights to their children (Morrell 2006). However, in order for these rights to be enforced, these men would need to challenge the maternal families through the Courts, which they often cannot afford. In Demaine's case, even though the courts granted him access to his children, they continued to live with their maternal uncle. Demaine stated that he could not afford to provide for his children and hence continued to let them stay with their uncle. In some cases, this would be viewed as abandonment, but according to him, he was doing what he thinks is best for his children.

Demaine's experience also highlights a point noted earlier– the value of kin networks. According to Datta (2007:102), these networks are consequential as they shield the child, and it is often the maternal grandfathers and uncles who are then expected to "integrate such children into their own lineages thus guaranteeing them social positions as well as ritual, political, rural, and economic rights and responsibilities." It is, however, not only the maternal kin networks that contribute to the child's cultural status. In cases where paternity was acknowledged and the father given access to and the opportunity to live with their child, it is the paternal family that often helps with supporting the children of unemployed men. For example, Spikiri and Mzo below make the point that because they are not able to provide for themselves and their children, they often rely on family for support.

Eish, I am just saying sister that I am receiving some support from my family, I understand that I am struggling on my side but at least I have my family's back-up because they know that I am not working, when I work like this I am not working. So I can talk to my brothers and sisters and say 'I need this and that' because it is the same as not working when you work like this. -Spikiri

No my mother and them try to help me with the 'pay' money…I do try when I get the opportunity…I try so that there is something coming from my side. -Mzo

Spikiri indicates that he has his family's "back-up." Mzo refers to "pay" money – meaning old-age pension grant. In both instances, we have a fascinating and vital aspect of South African Black life, a worldview captured by the notion of *ubuntu*. The word refers to a way of life characterized by values that favour collectivist over an individualist orientation; that well-being emerges from reciprocity, caring for others, and compassion (Lesejane 2006). *Ubuntu* is centred upon the harmonious co-existence and sharing among communities, as captured in the saying "*umuntu ngumuntu ngabantu*". The common saying translates into "a human being (*umuntu*) is human (*ngumuntu*) because of other humans (*ngabantu*). Alternatively, we could render it as "I am because we are." Men like Mzo and Spikiri (and their children) benefit from *ubuntu*; specifically, they benefit from collective fathering where uncles, grandfathers, and brothers all participate in providing for children and other family members (Mkhize 2006). As shown by Mzo above, he also has to make sure that when he does get a job, there is also "something" coming from his side to reciprocate his family's support for him. While clearly important, anecdotal evidence suggests that even the principles of *ubuntu* (the cultural ethic of taking care of each other) are eroding in some parts of the communities, especially in the context of poverty, dispossession, displacement, and the resultant destitution, where people are now constantly in competition with each other over resources.

5 Conclusion

This study showed that the fatherhood practices of unemployed/precariously employed and marginalised men are challenged by their economic circumstances as well as cultural norms. At the same time, these men have a strong desire to not only provide for their children but to also be present in the children's lives and show them love. Fatherhood as understood by the participants in this study, then, involves an integration of fatherhood roles, rather than a shift from one type of fatherhood to another. While clearly acknowledged and accepted by this group of poor and unemployed men, the nurturing father ideal remains somewhat inaccessible to the men as they have to prioritise providing for their children's economic needs over meeting other needs like emotional support and physical presence.

A critical implication of the study is the importance of having a stable, secure job – a major constraint in countries with high levels of joblessness – in shaping men's fathering practices, a finding noted in previous studies. It remains important, however, that we continue to explore the views and experiences of men in various socio-economic positions so as to deepen our understanding of the changing socio-economic, political, and cultural contexts and their impact on fathering (as opposed to rehashing stereotypes). It is noteworthy that the participants in this study saw rituals and customs such as *inhlawulo* as a hindrance to their parenting. Yet the cultural practices associated with the conception or birth of a child (or with marriage) may have favourable outcomes for children and men themselves through the extended kin support networks and social capital they enable, as well as the support unemployed men are able to receive as a result of such networks. However, these cultural practices and rituals need to be continuously examined in the context of the economic circumstances South Africa is confronting.

Acknowledgments This research was funded in part by the 'Engaging South African and Finnish youth towards new traditions of non-violence, equality and social well-being' project funded by the Finnish National Research Council, the Academy of Finland and the National Research Foundation of South Africa.

References

Ahadi H, Mandy L (2007) Fathering and the Afrikan-centred worldview/paradigm. The Black Scholar 37(2):9–13

Blaauw D, Louw H, Schenck R (2006) The unemployment history of day Labourers in South Africa and the income they earn: a case study of day Labourers in Pretoria. S Afr J Econ Manag Sci 9(4):458–471

Blount M, Cunningham G (2014) Representing black men. Routledge, New York

Charmaz K (2006) Constructing grounded theory: a practical guide through qualitative analysis. Sage, Los Angeles

Collins PH (1989) A comparison of two works on black family life. Signs J Women Cult Soc 14(4):875–884

Datta K (2007) 'In the eyes of a child, a father is everything': changing constructions of fatherhood in urban Botswana? Women's Stud Int Forum 30:79–113

Devault A, Milcent M-P, Ouellet F, Laurin I, Juaron M, Lacharité C (2008) Life stories of young fathers in contexts of vulnerability. Fathering 6(3):226–248

East L, Jackson D, O'Brien L (2006) Father absence and adolescent development: a review of literature. J Child Health Care 10(4):283–295

Enderstein AM, Boonzaier F (2015) Narratives of young south African fathers: redefining masculinity through fatherhood. J Gend Stud 24(5):512–527

Hauari H, Hollingworth K (2009) Understanding fatherhood: masculinity, diversity and change. Joseph Rowntree Foundation, York. https://www.jrf.org.uk/report/understanding-fathering-masculinity-diversity-and-change

Hobson B, Morgan D (2002) Introduction. In: Hobson B (ed) Making men into fathers: men masculinities and the social politics of fatherhood. Cambridge University Press, Cambridge, pp 1–2

Hunter M (2006) Fathers without *amandla*: Zulu-speaking men and fatherhood. In: Richter L, Morell R (eds) Baba: Men and Fatherhood in South Africa. HSRC Press, Cape Town, pp 99–107

Hunter AG, Davis JE (1994) Hidden voices of black men: the meaning, structure, and complexity of manhood. J Black Stud 25(1):20–40

Lamb ME (2000) The history of research on father involvement: an overview. Marriage Fam Rev 29(2–3):23–42

Lesch E, Kelapile C (2016) 'In my dream she finds me...and she wants me as I am': fatherhood experiences of unmarried men in South Africa. Men Masculinities 19(5):503–523

Lesejane D (2006) Fatherhood from an African cultural perspective. In: Richter L, Morell R (eds) Baba: men and fatherhood in South Africa. HSRC Press, Cape Town, pp 173–182

Madhavan S (2010) Early childbearing and kin connectivity in rural South Africa. Int J Sociol Fam 36(2):139–157

Malinga M (2016) Precarious employment and fathering practices among African men. University of South Africa. http://uir.unisa.ac.za/handle/10500/20283. Accessed 13 Sept 2019

Mkhize N (2006) African tradition and the social, economic and moral dimensions of fatherhood. In: Richter L, Morell R (eds) Baba: men and fatherhood in South Africa. HSRC Press, Cape Town, pp 187–193

Morrell R (2006) Fathers, fatherhood and masculinity in South Africa. In: Richter L, Morell R (eds) Baba: men and fatherhood in South Africa. HSRC Press, Cape Town, pp 13–25

Posel D, Rudwick S, Casale D (2011) Is marriage a dying institution in South Africa? Exploring changes in marriage in the context of *ilobolo* payments. Agenda 25(1):102–111

Ratele K, Nduna M (2018) An Overview of Fatherhood in South Africa. In: Van den Berg W, Makusha T (eds) State of South Africa's Fathers 2018. Sonke Gender Justice & Human Sciences Research Council, Cape Town, pp 29–46

Roy KM (2004) You can't eat love: constructing provider role expectations for low-income and working-class fathers. Fathering 2(3):1–21

Statistics South Africa (2019) Quarterly Labour Force Survey: Quarter 2 of 2019. http://www.statssa.gov.za/publications/P0211/P02112ndQuarter2019.pdf. Accessed 13 Sept 2019

Strier R, Sigad L, Eisikovits Z, Buchbinder E (2014) Masculinity, poverty and work: the multiple constructions of work among working poor men. J Soc Policy 43(2):331–349

Tölke A, Diewald M (2003) Insecurities in employment and occupational careers and their impact on the transition to fatherhood in Western Germany. Demogr Res 9:41–68

Open Access This chapter is licensed under the terms of the Creative Commons Attribution 4.0 International License (http://creativecommons.org/licenses/by/4.0/), which permits use, sharing, adaptation, distribution and reproduction in any medium or format, as long as you give appropriate credit to the original author(s) and the source, provide a link to the Creative Commons license and indicate if changes were made.

The images or other third party material in this chapter are included in the chapter's Creative Commons license, unless indicated otherwise in a credit line to the material. If material is not included in the chapter's Creative Commons license and your intended use is not permitted by statutory regulation or exceeds the permitted use, you will need to obtain permission directly from the copyright holder.

The Role of Love and Children's Agency in Improving Fathers' Wellbeing

Alexandra Macht

1 Introduction

> "...love is also the very reason why we are ready to exploit ourselves in the process of achieving the resources and means to give the best to our beloved intimates." (Seebach 2017:199–200)

Love might indeed entice family members to self-sacrifice as Swen Seebach's quote above reminds, but in this book chapter I argue for a different perspective, one that proposes a definition of paternal love as a source of energy and motivation, one which is influencing diverse spheres of life (such as men's engagement in paid work). Previously, and in earlier chapters of this volume, it has been shown that the close and nurturing bond that can develop in time, between involved fathers and their children, helps fathers maintain and increase their wellbeing and as such, fathers have reported becoming better at work (Ranson 2012).

In this chapter, I support this positive perspective, and rather than focusing on the fathers' relationship to their partners, I highlight the child's significant role and the emotions which support the child-father relationship. The aims of this chapter are the following: a) to bring attention to children's agency in relation to father's wellbeing, and b) to highlight the important role that emotions play in men's wellbeing in intimate contexts. To illustrate these arguments, my analysis centres on findings from a piece of research with two groups of European of fathers: Romanian and Scottish fathers, usually overlooked by the literature. By focusing on overlooked populations new insights can be gained as to the cultural variation of love, fathering, and children's agency. In the conclusion of this chapter, I also briefly reflect on how academic research on involved fathering and emotions can inform changes in family policies.

A. Macht (✉)
Independent Researcher, Bucharest, Romania
e-mail: macht.alexandra.georgiana.pfa@gmail.com

© The Author(s) 2022
M. Grau Grau et al. (eds.), *Engaged Fatherhood for Men, Families and Gender Equality*, Contributions to Management Science,
https://doi.org/10.1007/978-3-030-75645-1_16

1.1 Theoretical Background

In accurately analysing fathers, any discussion of the role of the father needs to begin with the delineation between the terms *fathers* (the biological or social parent), *fathering* (the everyday practices of caring for a child enacted by fathers) and *fatherhood* (the *public meaning of fathering,* the social discourse and cultural beliefs regarding fathers) (Featherstone 2009; Morgan 2011). However, some argue that fathering refers to the process by which a man becomes a father (be it biological or social) and includes aspects related to the care of a child which do not necessarily happen in the presence of the child (Smith-Koslowski 2008). In this chapter, I focus specifically on "involved fathering," considered in the literature as a socio-psychological concept which refers to a father's participation in his child's life through four characteristics: accessibility (whether physically close or proximate), engagement, responsibility, and the more recently added dimension of "warmth" (Lamb 2010). The dimension of "warmth" is usually studied by sociologists as affection or even love, and thereby my focus fell on fathers' overlooked experiences of love in their families. At the moment, there are no extensive sociological studies on paternal love, and mine is the first. Therefore, I was keen to understand men's emotional experiences of fathering, as these were theoretically interpreted as being linked to the achievement of equal work and care arrangements in family life (Hooks 2004).

Considering that both *affective* practices and *social* practices feed into fathers' personal biographies (Jamieson 1998), it is time that social policymakers take this often-neglected aspect into account. But why focus on father's love? One reason for this is because amongst many emotions, love is perhaps one of the most powerful ones connected to the role of a parent, and it outlines usually one of the increasingly few long-lasting relationships that people experience across their life-span (Beck and Beck-Gernsheim 2014). Advances in the study of emotions, allow sociologists to interpret the micro-social landscape of relationships in new ways. One such perspective is offered by the *aesthetic theory of emotion* (Burkitt 2014). Applied to the topic of fatherhood and love, Ian Burkitt's framework considers fathering as part of everyday situations and as a deeply relational creation, embedded in family life in a complex network of relationships: to themselves, their own parents and family of origin, their romantic partner and their children. Seen from this lens, fathers are not just individual family members, but part of an interdependent network of support, as they are emotionally and relationally linked to their close family members. Therefore, if their children are affected by life circumstances, their fathers' wellbeing is also affected. Because of this theoretical understanding, I challenge in my qualitative research the pervasive idea that men's lives are governed solely by autonomy and individuality (Gilmore 1990).

At the moment in the literature on fathering there are two main models: the persistent *breadwinner/provider* model which relies on men's adherence to traditional masculinity, emotional stoicism, and focus on work and authority (Jansz 2000; Larossa 1997) and the *nurturant father's* model (Johansson and Klinth 2008;

Marsiglio and Roy 2012) reliant on caring forms of masculinity (Elliott 2015) and supporting a more progressive view of masculinity, which focuses on affective engagement in childrearing. However, there is a growing awareness that contemporary fathers experience tensions between new ideals of "good fathering" which equate it with love and nurturance, and "successful masculinity" which is still assessed based on toughness and emotional control. If such tensions are left unsolved, they could potentially affect men's health, as research into Scottish masculinity has shown (O'Brien et al. 2007; O'Brien et al. 2009). However, rather than understanding masculinity and fathering as separate and contradictory roles, one way to move beyond this simple dichotomy is considering the multi-dimensionality of men's emotions through a term I called *"emotional bordering."* This term emerged from the grounded data I collected while interviewing a speficic sample of European men on their emotional experiences of fathering (Macht 2019b). Results show that, contrary to the understanding that men have fixed emotional responses, men as fathers can express more diversified and complex emotions; as they are fathering they are also *shifting* emotionally between love and detachment, and between intimacy and stoicism in what they do and say in their everyday lives; this means that their emotional responses shift according to their social relationships, creating different 'emotional boundaries' between themselves and their loved ones. In this way, emotional bordering describes the process through which men experience more flexible emotional roles as fathers. The term also attempts to define masculinities in a more fluid manner and from an emotional perspective.

1.2 Presentation of Data and Findings

This study compared the fathering and emotional narratives of involved Scottish and Romanian fathers living in Edinburgh and Bucharest. Fathers self-identified as "involved" and were acknowledged as such by the people who helped me recruit them for the study through snowball sampling. Being involved meant that they were actively engaged in hands-on-care for their children, emotionally accessible to them, and made changes in their work life to adapt to their children's needs (Lamb 2010). The study explored whether the idea of "the involved father" was an equally relevant discourse in what are the Eastern and the Western parts of Europe, and whether these cultural variations influenced fathers' emotions (Johansson and Klinth 2008). A key aim of the research was to understand what fathers' love for their children means to them, if fathers value love, and how they feel that they can or cannot express it (Padilla et al. 2007). The core findings that have emerged from this qualitative investigation, and have appeared in a research report (see Macht 2017), are:

- Involved fathers experience love as something they "do," as a verb and in this process, they exercise *emotional bordering*.

- Loving their children took time to develop; even if it was deemed a very strong initial feeling.
- Ways of displaying love varied with cultural background.
- Maintaining a loving relationship with the child required emotional effort.
- Fathers prioritised their unconditional love for their children over a certain conditional love for their partner and own parents.
- Children had a positive influence on involved fathers' health and engagement with work.

The data presented in this chapter is focused on the last finding listed above, because I have expanded upon the other findings in previous publications. To briefly sketch the theoretical and methodological background: it is worth mentioning that the socio-constructionist study design involved Ian Burkitt's (2014) theory of emotions as social relations and Kathy Charmaz's (2013) improved version of grounded theory. This adapted version of the grounded theory methodology was used in designing the research, through a pilot phase carried out with the purpose of sensitizing the interview guide. This consisted of seven initial and open-ended interviews which for reasons of time and funding, took place in Scotland. Based on the feedback received from the participants, questions were tested and re-tested. As fathers provided content, I generated preliminary concepts and then compared these with available concepts from the literature. This process continuously refined the interview guide by rearranging the order of questions or thinking through where the participants needed only gentle prompting. The analysis proceeded in the following way: paragraphs were given a code, N-vivo codes were selected, then, in a process of distilling the most often occurring and meaningful codes, categories were created. Afterwards, memos were written to define each novel category. Themes appeared and these were then re-checked alongside relevant quotes in the process of constructing arguments. The analysis was done by hand using pen and paper, to become familiar with the data and immerse myself in the research, after which the transcriptions were uploaded to the program NVivo and were queried by doing common word searches and mapping out concepts. Case-studies for each participant were compiled by incorporating field-notes with relevant quotes from the interviews.[1] The grounded theory approach was chosen to keep as close to the participants' interpretations as possible and explore their discourses on love and intimate relating in their families, as they viewed this process themselves.

In addition, a diverse sample was prioritized to ensure that a range of views was represented. This was because I was aware that fathers from the same culture and profession might describe love in a similar way. The final sample included qualitative interviews with 47 fathers from two different cultures: they were aged between 28 and 56 years old, of which 27 were Scottish fathers and 20 were Romanian fathers; 5 were self-identified carers (3 were full-time, 1 was a part-time dad and 1 was on extended sick leave) and from the remainder of the fathers, 41 were full-

---

[1] For an in-depth description of how I employed Charmaz's grounded theory and the challenges I faced, see Macht (2018a, 2019a).

time working fathers and only 1 worked part-time. Almost all were married or co-partnered, and only 2 were undergoing separations. Interviews were carried out during 2014 and 2015, in offices, homes, and public cafes. Six situations permitted for spontaneous observations of direct interactions between fathers and their children, as their children were also present during our interviews.

2 Emotional Bordering and Family to Work Transitions

In this section, I explore the first aim of this book chapter which is to highlight the important role that emotions play in men's wellbeing in family contexts. It is important to underline that almost all involved fathers in my sample were also working fathers. In relation to employment, Gillian Ranson (2012:742) conceptualizes working fathers as "(...) men who do take advantage of the workplace initiatives most commonly used by mothers and who in other ways explicitly organize their working lives around the family responsibilities they are committed or obliged to assume." However, in what continues to be, for the majority of workplaces, a masculinist career culture, sharing family responsibilities is seen as weakening not only a man's work performance, but his identity as a breadwinner. Not only that, but fathers who want to be more involved incur work-place penalties, even if this happens to a lesser degree than the penalties incurred by working mothers (Haas and Hwang 2019). However, and again according to Ranson, working fathers are at the forefront of change, as they mediate the transition from the public sphere into the private one (for example, with couples deciding to share caregiving) and the other way around, as working environments adapt to parental demands (i.e., flexible parental leave, extended day-care services etc.).

In my own research, I uncovered that for fathers, spending time with their children at home, although sometimes hard to come by, also had the meaning of re-energizing them for engagement in work the next day. Fathers reported being more engaged at work if they had time to talk, play, and help children after the working day. However, fathers struggled with making time for their children, as their work responsibilities increased, and some of them would also bring their work home with them; they also felt that they had to raise an 'emotional border' and be more stoic in the workplace, due to the persisting traditional gender regimes of the workplace. Upon arriving home, some of the fathers felt that they could lower or relax their emotional border, and be more nurturing in how they expressed their feelings to their children. In addition, and as I describe at length in my book (Macht 2019b), fathers also bordered emotionally according to the ways in which they understood themselves in relation to their own fathers, and what kind of parent they aimed to be (not only in their provider's role but also in their intimate, nurturing role). Providing data in support of this view, the fathers in my study described how they externalized and internalized their emotions, in rather flexible ways, and according to their social contexts and to the degree of familiarity and intimacy they had with someone. In this respect, three strategies emerged from their narratives, organised for clarity on an imaginary emotional spectrum that waddled between stoicism and intimacy:

(a) *Some involved fathers set lower emotional borders* in building their masculine emotional identity, resorting to increased *warmth* and *intimacy* (these were situated at the intimate end of an imagined emotional spectrum)
(b) *Some were ambivalently placed in the middle, preferring a balanced approach* (these were situated in the middle of the emotional spectrum because they combined stoicism with nurturance)
(c) *Other involved fathers set higher borders by employing more emotional control and detachment* (theses were placed at the stoic end of the emotional spectrum)

According to the fathers I interviewed, the above strategies were employed through every day *emotional revisions* in the process of relating to their children, as they cared for them and spent time with them. The types of places and spaces they were in, their child's birth-order and age (not gender), and who else happened to be around (parents, partners, friends or co-workers) also influenced how much fathers raised or lowered their emotional borders in expressing love to their children. Emotional bordering is significant because it reminds sociologists of the "emotional costs" of parenting and not only of its material aspects (Zelizer 1994). Moreover, the concept describes how men resolve tensions created by their gendered identity in combination with their fathering discourses. Therefore, the basis of these role tensions might not simply be a "crisis of masculinity" (de Boise and Hearn 2017), but it could be enhanced by the emotional revisions which are necessary to maintain good fathering in relation to changing masculine norms. It could be more succinctly said that emotional bordering explains the process of creating a father's role in relation to masculinity.[2] The discussion around emotional borders and whether these could be 'raised' or 'lowered' depended therefore on fathers' close relationships, everyday circumstances, and how they understood their role in their family lives. For example, I focus below on just some of the many quotes from my research, and I focus here on those in relation to fathers' wellbeing to illustrate the rather tense connections between the satisfactions of loving their children and not having enough time to do so because of work. Nonetheless, when they had some time to spend with them, some fathers reported being re-energised by their children:

Daniel (Romanian, 38, Engineer[3]) explains how he can't wait to come home and see his son, no matter what mood the child might be in:

> "I don't even know how to express it, love. It's something I feel for him. Simply put, I just can't wait to see him! Even if he's angry, when I come home from work. I never know if he's angry or happy. If he wants to hug me or he's been upset with his mom. But I just can't wait to come home and see him. And yeah, it really charges me up for the next day at work."

---

[2] For a lengthier discussion of this concept in relation to the commodification of parenting and emotions, see Macht (2018b); also for how fathers maintained love during family separations, see Macht (2019d).

[3] To help contextualize the quotes, demographic information on each participant concerning their culture, age and occupation is provided in brackets.

Mihai (Romanian, 43, Computer Specialist) describes that work takes too much of his time to be as involved as he would like, and therefore he experiences guilt in relation to his fathering:

"I'm not really happy with what I've done and how much I've done [in terms of parenting]. For example, a lot of my time is taken up with work. Now, I can't say I'm a hero or something, because this is not the case, the reality is that I can't do more. If I can't do my work, then I won't be here anymore [his workplace]. And if I'm no longer here, then our problems become worse."

In addition, Malcolm (Scottish, 42, Investment Professional) reflects on how loving his children means that he wants to spend more time with them:

"Coming back to your question of 'Do you feel you love her more or less at some times?'... No, it doesn't really matter. I want more time with her because I love her. I don't love her because I get time with her, if that makes sense."

The last two fathers whose quotes I present, describe how they carry-over private images or fragments of talk into their public professional role, with different effects. For Petre (Romanian, 28, pilot) looking at clips of his son on his phone works to soothe the stress he experiences in his high-stake occupation:

"When I'm at work he sometimes appears almost in front of my eyes so to say. And then a big smile appears on my face without even noticing. When there are slow moments at work I sit and go through pictures and clips of him on my phone, because, thanks to technology nowadays, we film him quite a lot, and as I look at his clips he brings me such great joy."

While for Nicholas (Scottish, 38, Engineer) talking about his daughter at work, must be done in a sarcastic way to express his emotions in what continues to be a highly-masculinized work environment, that of engineering:

"I work in an entirely male industry. There's no women in engineering (...) So, you can't gush too much, if you're in a coffee room and there's somebody else whose got a child you might afford yourself a couple of minutes of being loving about your children. But for the main part, you have to be sarcastic. If I'm asked 'How's your daughter?' 'She's alright, but she's very selfish' I would say. You still have to hide. You wouldn't gush. It's different in the way women and men describe their children [at work]."

The themes of needing more time with their children, of benefiting from seeing them and relating to them and yet having to conceal their loving and positive emotions at work, emerge from these quotes. These could be interpreted as denoting the inherent pressures for contemporary fathers to reconcile their ideal worker role to that of caring fathering; this happens despite disagreeing with the idea that "love is a chore." Building upon these quotes, Andrea Doucet (2013) reminds us that men speaking in a language of care might provoke social and political anxieties in a system created by their fathers, as modern men might want to do things differently. This attitude certainly relies on father's agency as some decided to be different than their own fathers, where these elderly fathers were deemed stoic or emotionally closed off. However, such a progressive intimate attitude encounters conflict where there is a continuous and fixed male work-norm, one that does not allow for flexible adjustments in workplace environments and blocks men from exercising a public form of emotional pleasure and engagement in childrearing. In this way, caring forms of fathering that are hidden and concealed should become public, in order for workplace attitudes to visibly change. If men continue to be associated with the public realm, then as they are transforming a traditional form of masculine identity into a more loving, intimate and respectful one to their children, this transformation needs to become visible and publicly supported.

From this perspective, it emerges that fathers' emotions and strategies for handling them, are integrative parts of their wellbeing both at work and at home. For example, it has been shown that emotions influence male embodiment. One study found that there are correlations between experiencing discrimination and enacting stoicism (or the more popular term "taking it like a man") which increases men's likelihood to develop depression (Hammond 2012). Additionally, anger was found to be linked to higher rates of substance abuse, and mistrust plays a part in mediating men's relationship to social institutions and their subsequent health outcomes (Hammond et al. 2016). It is therefore important to remain aware that both caring fathering and breadwinning are *emotional identities* as well as social roles. In the next section, I present selective excerpts from the main data analysis, that specifically focus on father-child wellbeing.

3 Towards a Child-Led Understanding of Paternal Wellbeing

In this section, I focus on the second aim of the chapter which is to bring attention to children's agency in relation to father's wellbeing. In this manner, new theoretical insights can appear, if researchers interested in father's wellbeing shift their attention from the parent to the child's role in the family.

A child is increasingly seen as a person with agency and human rights,[4] particularly in nations of the North-Western part of the world. In the UK, this is due to the rising strength of the judicial protection of children's rights.[5] For example Tisdall (2012) defines children's agency as: "Children are to be seen as agents and not passive objects of concern nor empty vessels to be filled with adult wisdom. (...) If children were agents and worthy of respect, then their human rights – and particularly their civil and political rights – gain a foothold." Moreover, discourses of intensive parenting construct the child as affection- and protection-needy (Lupton 2013). However, it is not always true that children are disempowered and vulnerable (Valentine 1997), as they manage to have an important influence and often guide parental behaviour. In line with this, the quotes below illustrate that having children

---

[4]It's important to keep in mind that conceptualizing children and their roles remains culturally dependent. There are cultures who continue to use physical and verbal violence to discipline their children since this is considered a core practice of the "good parent" role (Selin 2013).

[5]Children and Young People Scotland Act, 2014. Available at: http://www.legislation.gov.uk/asp/2014/8/pdfs/asp_20140008_en.pdf [Accessed 03/02/2020]

played an important role in getting fathers to stop bad habits, such as smoking, reckless driving and the consumption of drugs. To this end, it appears that children, through their mere presence, were engaging fathers in ceasing drug-use, losing weight, or driving more carefully. Some fathers explained that these changes happened as they became fathers and realized that they had to remain healthy and present in their children's lives for longer. For example, Stephen (Scottish, 35, Part-time dad[6]) talks about how having his daughter changed his life, by helping him get motivated to let go of drugs:

> "She changed my whole life around. I was on drugs and other stuff and now because of her I'm not on drugs. And that's 'cause of myself realistically because I chose not to be anymore. I'm quite strong-minded that way when it comes to my daughter [...] you want her to look up to you, and say 'That's my daddy!'"

Mark (Scottish, 36, Team leader) as well, describes how becoming a father made him aware that he had to be 'available' for the long-term and therefore he cut back on his smoking:

> "That probably scares me quite a lot as well, that I don't particularly look after myself [...] I think I'd be devastated that what I did to myself meant he didn't have me around. So that's something I need to change as well and I am gradually. But it's a good thing. He has helped me cut down smoking a lot."

And lastly, Emil (Romanian, 37, Executive director) reflects on how having two daughters made him aware of needing to lose weight to maintain his health, as well as driving more carefully:

> "Since I had the girls, I became very careful with myself. I started losing weight. I realise that they need me long-term, and I have to behave in such a way so as not to endanger myself. Up until they were born, I used to drive around like a mad man. Now I'm more careful behind the wheel, I drive slowly and not only when I'm in the car with them, also when I'm by myself. I think because I'm aware now that I have to remain available for a longer time."

Another interesting finding that emerged is that children of both genders could energize and empower their parents, but they could also conflict with them. Children were far removed from the image of *intimate subordinates* to their parents' socialization practices. What this means is that instead of seeing children merely as dependent on their fathers and mothers for love, children could also play a central role in how love was perceived in the family and sustained. In my study, for most fathers, love for their children was described as a powerful emotion, one that could energize them to deal with the obstacles encountered in their everyday life. This is because love was understood as *an emotional complex* as Ian Burkitt (2014) described it in the literature; so love as a complex, contingently included other emotions such as worry. [*Editors' Note*: see also chapters by Kotelchuck in this volume for more on the reciprocal relationship between the emotional health of father and child.]

---

[6]The participant specifically filled in the demographic form I offered him on the day of our interview in this way; this is not my own classification.

Worry[7] in fathers' narratives appeared linked to wellbeing and played an important part in enacting control and protection in how fathers related to their children. However, there were some cultural nuances: Scottish fathers overall were worried about external dangers in the environment that might harm their children, while Romanian fathers were preponderantly more worried about their child's agency in getting sick and putting him—/her-self at risk unnecessarily. Worry was the energizing and emotional engaged component of the good father's role, even if some fathers struggled with describing this vulnerable side of their fathering. The conclusion of this section, as illustrated by the data, is that even if fathers have the overall responsibility for their children's wellbeing, they were also influenced by the child's own agency in how they emotionally self-regulated. Loving their children and being engaged in their lives gained an everyday distinctive meaning for fathers; this was connected to a reshaping of their identity as *healthy or better men*. In this way, being involved signified not only being a "good father" but also improving as a man.

4 Dependable and Inter-Dependent Men?

The literature on fatherhood has consistently addressed issues of father's employment (Ranson 2012), their responsibility and levels of involvement (Lamb 2010), adjustments to fatherhood and fathering practices (Shirani 2013), but in the quest for gender equality it has reached a certain impasse, whereby fathers are just being continuously redefined according to the same categories of analysis, that is *when* emotions are not taken into consideration. On a more pragmatic level, it is not only that focusing academically on the social significance of understanding fathers as emotional beings might be important, but also seeing intimate fathers as such in *social policies* makes a difference for their inclusion in hospital rooms, parenting classes and playgrounds, and might help reduce discrimination and stigma. It is conceivably odd and ilogical that caring men continue to be socially stigmatized for showing emotions in public, and especially when these are positive ones.

The employment conditions and structural support that fathers receive is important *alongside* the emotional characteristics of their professed involvement in childrearing. Social policies aimed at sustaining the work-family balance must consider that men do not only *acquire* a fathering role but they also *embody* and *feel it*, which could have potential consequences for their long-term health. In addition, as women take on increasing work responsibilities, having support from their partners at home becomes quintessential for gender equal opportunities. It is not a question of reshaping only the public sphere to include women, but also the private sphere to allow more men to participate in what was traditionally considered a

---

[7]For an in-depth analysis of how worry is part of love as an emotional and relational complex, see Macht (2019b, 2019d).

"feminized" domain. And much like women are given options to tackle the world of work according to a variety of options and increasingly flexibile schedules, so should men be allowed to practice nurturing/caring/intimate forms of masculinity according to their own choices. 'One-size fit all' models should be decisively avoided in both women's career advancement and men's participation in child-care.

It has been argued before that the workplace needs to be considered a family-friendly environment (O'Brien et al. 2007), much as the home has become more recently, a place of extended work through digital and technological accessibility. Fluid interactions between the two are usually mediated by both parents, although continuous unequal, systemic arrangements usually over-burden working mothers. On the path towards establishing long-term and realistic gender equal opportunities for both men and women as parents, states must get involved to support their working families and their intimate lives. One such avenue of opportunity is to equate "manhood" with everyday acts of care and nurturance in public and visible social images of support (Schrock and Schwalbe 2009) and to dissolve the exclusive association of acts of caring and love with the mother's role. Promoting caring forms of masculinity (Elliott 2015) means no longer thinking of loving as something to hide, to be ashamed of or as "un-manly", but rather seeing love in both the public and the private sphere as a core characteristic of a progressive, intelligent and respectful man.

5 Conclusion

In this chapter, I argued that involved fatherhood offers the opportunity to resist risk-taking practices which are intrinsically linked to traditional images of what it means to be a (tough) man, images which are also harmful to men's wellbeing. Incipient data was presented to illustrate how children were re-energising fathers for work and helping them let go of negative health habits (smoking, consuming drugs, reckless driving). In turn, fathers adopted a future-oriented and emotionally-engaged perspective with the aim of spending more time with their children, which was essential in the transformation of their daily habits. In this process fathers of both cultures had to border emotionally to appease the tensions they experienced as they were balancing work with personal life and their masculinity with their good father's role. Children could therefore play a key role in counteracting toxic masculinities, as they could help fathers shift from sustained emotional stoicism (which can be harmful to health due to consistent emotional repression), to increased nurturance and intimacy (which can increase the well-being of both family members through emotional attunement).

However, a father's desire to be involved in childcare and his need to show and receive love from his family members, remains incomplete without state-supported measures that can foster more progressive gender regimes in the workplace and the legal right for paid parental leave. Men with children need social and governmental support to practice nurturing fathering, and this needs to be done in a serious manner, rather than just by supplying men with a symbolic couple of weeks of paid paternal leave and in some cases only just some days of unpaid leave.

At present, the available provisions of paternity leave of 2 weeks in Scotland and 5–15 days in Romania, are insufficient towards fostering involved fathering (Koslowski et al. 2019). It is obvious that in the world's population not all men are fathers, and not all fathers are involved. And yet fatherhood emerges as a key stage in the life-course transition of men (Draper 2002). The literature has certainly evolved from portrayals of fatherhood as either "good" or "bad" (Furstenberg Jr 1988) to depictions of fathers as "struggling" with their "complex" and "problematic" role (Johansson and Klinth 2008). This is because becoming a father is considered to have the potential to contest hegemonic masculinity, as evidence suggests that this life-transition can emotionally and relationally transform men's identities. Some consider fatherhood to be especially important for men who are looking to embody more nurturing masculine roles, especially as ideals of "new" and "nurturant" fatherhood entail *both* providing and active, engaged parenting. For example, Andrea Doucet (2013) who investigated the important role of men's emotional responsibility for their children, showed that fathers enact masculinity in practices of both "holding on" and "letting go.", which bring to mind the similar emotional process I indentifed in my own research, that of employing emotional bordering to shift flexibly between stoicism and intimacy.

Dissenting voices have argued that fatherhood continues to be peripheral in the construction of adulthood for men, since successful masculinity is not usually tied into the achievement of fatherhood (Connell 2002). It's important however, to underline that in some situations, men's dominant social role can be reinforced through fathering, as this new position adds to a man's social capital without interfering with other social privileges which are not so easily granted to women as mothers. It is therefore arguable whether becoming a father leads to more caring masculinities (Elliott 2015), as it could be just re-asserting masculine dominance in more subtle ways. To ascertain the extent of such practices, social-policy makers should base their decisions on research grounded on data depicting fathers' practical experiences of care and everyday involvement in their families' lives. Investigating men's subjective and emotional understandings of fathering and how they are fathering *in practice* remain equally important for future sociological analyses. And it needs to be underlined that children play an important, if often neglected role, in counteracting the toxic aspects of traditional forms of masculinity.

5.1 Future Research

Some argue that men's fixed emotional models, stem from a traditional understanding of masculinity which continues to block gender equality efforts, preserve a tense work-life imbalance, and affect men's long-term intimacy and personal relationships (Macht 2019c). Studies have shown that where there are marked gendered differences in parenting there are also increased tensions and dissatisfactions, while dual sharing strategies and de-gendering parenting has the effect of lessening conflict and tensions between family members (Hochschild 2001; Ranson 2010). On a different note, it could be that researchers are struggling to resolve tensions between fathering and masculinity because they are recruiting participants for their studies from similar cultural backgrounds; so diversifying recruitment and opting for heterogeneity instead of homogeneity in sampling, might be a solution forward in fathering research.

What stands out in the current fatherhood research is the fact that knowledge-production overwhelmingly represents Anglo-American perspectives, limiting thereby the representation of other cultural groups (usually deemed "marginal"). This continues to be a curious development of knowledge, since evidence is pointing towards a panoply of cultural variations in fathering (Inhorn et al. 2014). Views "from the margin" of Western-focused research have the potential to challenge the prevailing values of individualism, stoicism, and autonomy, by shedding light on how different models of masculinity and fathering roles exist in relation to distinct values and emotional rules. More research is needed with non-white populations and also from outside the European perimeter, as well as comparing working class with middle-class, and elite masculinities, in the effort to represent neglected samples of working and involved fathers. Researching overlooked populations remains important since it is also part of the decolonizing process (Connell 2018). In this way researchers, who mainly stem from Anglo-Saxon, North-American, and Scandinavian cultures in the Global North can avoid over-generalizing from their specific populations and thereby reduce the application of policies and creation of research designs that are culturally insensitive to diverse families in other parts of the globe (such as marginalized populations from Eastern-Europe and the Balkans and from countries in the Global South).

5.2 Policy Suggestions

Lastly, there needs to be a consideration that both men and women are emotionally attached to their families. Seen from this perspective, analyses could focus more on how both parents are influenced by worry, motivation to engage in work (or lack thereof) and the spaces within which they work (as some are increasingly moving to nomadic or home-based forms of economic activity), and capacity to express love, not only to provide; the material and emotional levels should be considered in non-gendered ways. As future citizens of any country, children benefit from the emotional involvement, physical presence *and* material resources that their parents or parental figures provide. As such nation-states need to support flexible parenting practices and father's agency in moving beyond the unidimensional role of the breadwinner. Considering the data presented in this chapter and the subsequent reflections throughout this edited volume, it could be that the best manner to *elevate* contemporary fatherhood is to include, in pragmatic and policy-focused ways, the relational and emotional interactions between fathers and their children into programmes that foster father-child wellbeing in family lives. These programmes could have educational and preventive goals, but they need to be aimed at the general population of working fathers and not solely designed for at-risk groups of fathers (Waller and Swisher 2006).

Some further suggestions for policymakers would be granting fathers the same amount of leave as mothers, or providing choices, such as a set of benefits and flexible times which parents can adapt to their individual circumstances. In establishing a work and life balance families must be supported by states; they simply cannot achieve this balance by themselves. Moreover, nation-states need to move away from a "one size fits all" approach in family policy-making by taking into account the diversity of family forms which exist in societies (from blended and mixed-race families, to surrogate, one-parent and adoptive families, to foster- and young-carers, to LGBTQ parenting, to name just a few). This would mean creating a set of family policies which refrain from gendering the role of the caregiver but describe its role, responsibilities and benefits according to skill-sets rather than biology; state-supported leave policies should let the parents decide whether they choose to gender their intimate relationships, as the leave provision should be focused on pragmatic aspects that take into account the type of occupation, time spent away and with the child, and emotional effects on each parent's and child's wellbeing that an assigned leave can have. As my research has shown, love is a form of activity which develops as the caregiver does things together with the child, and by getting to know the child. Therefore time and adequate resources are needed to support families as they balance their emotional, relational, mental, and material wellbeing.

Furthermore, fathers themselves need to be brave enough to care and love, and to be willing to take risks in the workplace to defend their fathering role. Perhaps the new measure for masculine 'heroism' can be to show how men persevere in tackling a social system that does not allow them the right to a well-paid paternity leave and limits their chances of becoming everyday "superdads" (Kaufman 2013). The time has come for feminist men to encourage and educate other men in their environment to take gender equal leaps of faith at work and in their private lives. Since feminist women's work has achieved as much as it could (Deutsch 2007), it currently needs men supporting other men to complete the unfinished gender revolution. This is because, caring for future generations is a collective responsibility rather than a "female" one. In order to help societies thrive, governments must provide flexible and inclusive family policies that benefit as many people as possible, rather than merely a select few. To conclude, I leave social policymakers with the following pragmatic questions:

- How are children helping their fathers increase their health and wellbeing in everyday situations?
- What are the positive health consequences of involved fatherhood *both* for fathers and their children?
- How can father involvement be fostered to resolve men's identity tensions in the shift from work to home and in the transition to fatherhood?

Acknowledgments Thank you very much to Dr. Marc Grau Grau and Dr. Hannah Riley Bowles for inviting me to the interdisciplinary seminar at the Women and Public Policy Program at the Harvard Kennedy School in 2017 which led to the creation of this edited volume. The research I discuss in this chapter was completed at the University of Edinburgh and was funded with grant number ES/J500136/1 from the UK's Economic and Social Research Council (ESRC)].

References

Beck U, Beck-Gernsheim E (2014) Distant love: personal life in the global age. Polity Press, Cambridge
de Boise S, Hearn J (2017) Are men getting more emotional? Critical sociological perspectives on men, masculinities and emotions. Sociol Rev 65(4):779–796
Burkitt I (2014) Emotions and social relations. Sage, London
Charmaz K (2013) Constructing grounded theory. Sage, London
Connell RW (2002) Studying men and masculinity. Resources for Feminist Research 29 (1/2):43–55
Connell R (2018) Decolonizing sociology. Contemp Sociol 47(4):399–407
Deutsch FM (2007) Undoing Gender. Gend Soc 21(1):106–127
Doucet A (2013) A 'Choreography of Becoming': fathering, embodied care, and new materialisms. Can Rev Sociol 50(3):284–305
Draper J (2002) Fatherhood as transition: the contemporary relevance of transition theory. In: Horrocks C, Milnes K, Roberts B, Robinson D (eds) Narrative, memory and life transitions. University of Huddersfield Press, Huddersfield, pp 85–94
Elliott K (2015) Caring masculinities: theorizing an emerging concept. Men Masculinities 19 (3):240–259
Featherstone B (2009) Contemporary fathering: theory, policy and practice. Policy Press, Bristol
Furstenberg FF Jr (1988) Good dads-Bad dads: the two faces of fatherhood. In: Cherlin AJ (ed) The changing American family and public policy. Urban Institute Press, Washington, DC, pp 193–218
Gilmore DD (1990) Manhood in the making: cultural concepts of masculinity. Yale University, New Haven
Haas L, Hwang PC (2019) Company support and European fathers' use of state policies promoting shared childcare. Community Work Fam 22(1):1–22
Hammond WP (2012) Taking it like a man: masculine role norms as moderators of the racial discrimination-depressive symptoms association among African American men. Am J Public Health 102(suppl2):232–241
Hammond WP, Adams LB, Cole-Lewis Y, Agyemang A, Upton RD (2016) Masculinity and race-related factors as barriers to health help-seeking among African American men. Behav Med 42 (3):150–163
Hochschild AR (2001) The time bind: when work becomes home and home becomes work. Henry Holt, New York
Hooks B (2004) The will to change: men, masculinity, and love. Washington Square Press, Washington
Inhorn MC, Chavkin W, Navarro J-A (2014) Globalized fatherhood. Berghan Books, Oxford, New York
Jamieson L (1998) Intimacy: personal relationships in modern societies. Polity Press, Cambridge
Jansz J (2000) Masculine identity and restrictive emotionality. In: Fischer AH (ed) Gender and emotion: social psychological perspective. Cambridge University Press, Cambridge, pp 166–186

Johansson T, Klinth R (2008) Caring fathers: the ideology of gender equality and masculine positions. Men Masculinities 11(1):42–62

Kaufman G (2013) Superdads: how fathers balance work and care in the 21st century. New York University Press, New York

Koslowski A, Blum S, Dobrotić I, Macht A, Moss P (2019) 15th International review of leave policies and related research 2019. https://www.leavenetwork.org/annual-review-reports/review-2019/

Lamb ME (ed) (2010) The role of the father in child development, 5th edn. Wiley, London

Larossa R (1997) The modernization of fatherhood: a social and political history. University of Chicago Press, Chicago

Lupton D (2013) Infant embodiment and interembodiment: a review of sociocultural perspectives. Childhood 20(1):37–50

Macht A (2017) Love, fatherhood and possibilities for social change. CRFR Briefing 90. https://www.era.lib.ed.ac.uk/handle/1842/25691

Macht A (2018a) Grounding reflexivity in a qualitative study on love with fathers. SAGE Research Methods Cases. https://doi.org/10.4135/9781526439376

Macht A (2018b) Resisting the commodification of intimate life? Paternal love, emotional bordering and narratives of ambivalent family consumerism from Scottish and Romanian fathers. Families, Relationships and Societies doi:10.1332/204674318X15384702551202

Macht A (2019a) Shifting perspectives: becoming a feminist researcher while studying fatherhood and love. Vitae Scholasticae 35(2):101

Macht A (2019b) Fatherhood and love: the social construction of masculine emotions. Palgrave Macmillan, Basingstoke

Macht A (2019c) Doing Gender. In: Spillman L (ed) Oxford bibliographies in sociology. Oxford University Press, New York. https://doi.org/10.1093/OBO/9780199756384-0229

Macht A (2019d) Travelling feelings: narratives of sustaining love in two comparative cultural case studies of fathering during family separations. In: Murray L, Ferreira N, McDonnell L, Hinton-Smith T, Walsh K (eds) Families in motion: space, time, materials and emotion. Emerald Group, Bingley

Marsiglio W, Roy K (2012) Nurturing Dads: Social Initiatives For Contemporary Fatherhood. Russell Sage Foundation, New York

Morgan DHJ (2011) Rethinking family practices. Palgrave Macmillan, Basingstoke

O'Brien R, Hart G, Hunt K (2007) 'Standing Out from the Herd': men renegotiating masculinity in relation to experiences of illness. Int J Men Health 6(3):178–200

O'Brien M, Brandth B, Kvande E (2007) Fathers, Work and Family life. Community Work Fam 10(4):375–386

O'Brien R, Hunt G, Hart K (2009) The average Scottish man has a cigarette hanging out of his mouth, lying there with a portion of Chips': prospects for change in Scottish Men's constructions of masculinity and their health-related beliefs and Behaviours. Crit Public Health 19(3–4):363–381

Padilla MB, Hirsch JS, Munoz-Laboy M, Sember R, Parker RG (eds) (2007) Love and globalization: transformations of intimacy in the contemporary world. Vanderbilt University Press, Nashville

Ranson G (2010) Against The Grain: Couples, Gender, and the Reframing of Parenting. University of Toronto Press, Toronto

Ranson G (2012) Men, Paid Employment and Family Responsibilities: Conceptualizing the 'Working Father'. Gender, Work & Organization 19(6):741–761

Schrock D, Schwalbe M (2009) Men, masculinities and manhood acts. Annu Rev Sociol 35:277–295

Seebach S (2017) Love and society: special social forms and the master emotion. Routledge, London

Selin H (2013) Parenting across cultures: childrearing, motherhood and fatherhood in non-Western cultures. Springer, The Netherlands

Shirani F (2013) The spectre of the wheezy dad: masculinity, fatherhood and ageing. Sociology 47(6):1104–1119

Smith-Koslowski A (2008) Who cares? European fathers and the time they spend looking after children. VDM, Saarbrücken

Tisdall EKM (2012) The challenge and challenging of childhood studies? Learning from disability studies and research with disabled children. Child Soc 26(3):181–191

Valentine G (1997) My Son's a bit dizzy, my Wife's a bit soft: gender, children and cultures of parenting. Gend Place Cult 4(1):37–62

Waller M, Swisher R (2006) Fathers' risk factors in fragile families: implications for "healthy" relationships and father involvement. Soc Probl 53(3):392–420

Zelizer VA (1994) Pricing the priceless child: the changing social value of children. Princeton University Press, Princeton

Open Access This chapter is licensed under the terms of the Creative Commons Attribution 4.0 International License (http://creativecommons.org/licenses/by/4.0/), which permits use, sharing, adaptation, distribution and reproduction in any medium or format, as long as you give appropriate credit to the original author(s) and the source, provide a link to the Creative Commons license and indicate if changes were made.

The images or other third party material in this chapter are included in the chapter's Creative Commons license, unless indicated otherwise in a credit line to the material. If material is not included in the chapter's Creative Commons license and your intended use is not permitted by statutory regulation or exceeds the permitted use, you will need to obtain permission directly from the copyright holder.

Part IV
Conclusion and Principles for Promoting Gender Equity

Reducing Barriers to Engaged Fatherhood: Three Principles for Promoting Gender Equity in Parenting

Hannah Riley Bowles, Milton Kotelchuck, and Marc Grau Grau

1 Purpose

It has been our collective endeavor through this volume to motivate broader and more coordinated action to reduce the barriers to engaged fatherhood. The diverse contributors to this book came together out of a shared recognition that important work on fatherhood was being done largely in parallel in our respective fields with only modest cross-fertilization. Most of the scholarly leaders on fatherhood engagement through social policy have been in Europe at the cutting edge of progressive family leave (cf. Petts et al. 2020). Many of the frontrunning medical scientists advocating for fatherhood engagement, particularly in Maternal Child Health (MCH) and Pediatrics, have been leading their charge from Australia, Great Britain, and the United States. Organizational scholars who study working fathers are thinly scattered around the globe and have only recently begun to shape mainstream scholarship on gender, work, and organizations. This book makes a valuable contribution by providing readers with a cross-national and cross-disciplinary

---

H. R. Bowles (✉)
Harvard Kennedy School (HKS) and HKS Women and Public Policy Program, Cambridge, MA, USA
e-mail: hannah_bowles@hks.harvard.edu

M. Kotelchuck
Harvard Medical School and Massachusetts General Hospital Fatherhood Project, Boston, MA, USA

M. G. Grau
Women and Public Policy Program, Harvard Kennedy School, Cambridge, MA, USA

Joaquim Molins Figueras Childcare and Family Policies Chair, Universitat Internacional de Catalunya, Barcelona, Spain
e-mail: mgraug@uic.cat

© The Author(s) 2022
M. Grau Grau et al. (eds.), *Engaged Fatherhood for Men, Families and Gender Equality*, Contributions to Management Science,
https://doi.org/10.1007/978-3-030-75645-1_17

perspective on fatherhood, which, in compilation, produces a richer picture and deeper insights than could be gained from the disconnected sum of its parts. We hope that readers share our experience of seeing the landscape of fatherhood engagement anew from this novel vantage point.

Our aim in this concluding chapter is to illuminate three working principles that emerged from insights gained at the Experts Meeting on Fatherhood and that became more crystalized in the editing of this volume. As we will elaborate, our three working principles relate to (1) creating individual, non-transferable parenting resources explicitly for fathers, (2) reducing economic conflicts between breadwinning and caregiving, and (3) building supportive social networks for engaged fatherhood. We offer these working principles as a preliminary framework for transcending and empowering efforts to support and promote engaged fatherhood within and across the social policy, organizational work, and healthcare fields. We then propose next steps in this work agenda to expand our scope and community of collaborators.

2 Why Promote Engaged Fatherhood?

In our cross-disciplinary conversations, three distinct, if complementary, arguments arose for promoting engaged fatherhood. By "engaged fatherhood," we are referring to involved parenting by biological and/or socially identified "fathers" in terms of direct caregiving ("engagement"), availability to a child ("accessibility"), and "responsibility" for meeting a child's needs (Lamb et al. 1985). The first argument is based on straightforward advocacy for the wellbeing of men. Gendered cultural norms and institutionalized practices of work and healthcare constrain fathers from participating in the human developmental benefits and joys of being an engaged parent. This is a central theme in the chapter by Kotelchuck on the "Impact of Fatherhood on Men's Health and Development" and the inspiration for the chapter by Macht on the "Role of Love and Children's Agency in Improving Fathers' Wellbeing."

A second argument stems from an interest in the welfare of families and the demonstrable advantages to children of a parent-rich start to life (O'Brien 2009). As explained in the opening chapters of this volume by Yogman and Eppel and by Kotelchuck, there is now overwhelming evidence showing that engaged fatherhood has meaningful implications for the health and welfare of families, including for mothers', fathers', and children's physical, mental, and relational wellbeing. From a child development perspective, fatherhood engagement is associated with a breadth of important outcomes—ranging from decreased infant mortality to heightened parental attachment, reductions in child abuse and behavior problems, and increased cognitive test scores (see also, Guterman et al. 2009; Huerta et al. 2013; Nandi et al. 2018; Nepomnyaschy and Waldfogel 2007; Paxson and Waldfogel 1999; Petts et al. 2020).

Finally, overcoming the barriers to engaged fatherhood is fundamental to achieving gender equality. The industrial revolution reified the public and private spheres of human labor by institutionalizing the separation of work for pay from care of home and family (Goldscheider et al. 2015). Efforts to promote gender equality have largely focused on increasing women's access to and status in the male-dominated public sphere. Over the past 50 years, a "quiet revolution" has occurred in women's expectations of and participation in paid labor (Goldin 2006). However, this gender revolution is widely perceived to be stalled (England 2010), primarily because women's occupational and earning potential remain anchored down by the challenges of integrating labor in the public and private realms and by the intransigent archetypes of men as "breadwinners" and women as "caregivers" (Brighouse and Wright 2008; Goldin 2014; Morgan 2002; Ridgeway 2011).

2.1 Stalled Revolution

The gendered division of labor in the United States is illustrative of this one-sided progress. Even among married-couple families with children, a majority now have mothers who work for pay (69% in 2019) (U.S. Department of Labor, Bureau of Labor Statistics 2020). In one of three married or cohabiting couples in the United States, women bring in half or more of household earnings—a three-fold increase between 1980 and 2017 (Parker and Stepler 2017). In spite of the fact that comparable proportions of U.S. fathers (48%) and mothers (52%) of children under 18 report that they would rather stay home with their kids if they did not need to work for pay (Parker and Wang 2013; see also Harrington's chapter), fewer than 1 in 15 dads are "stay-at-home" parents as compared to more than 1 in 4 moms (Livingston 2018). Fathers' propensity to work full time tends to be unaffected by the age of their children, whereas mothers' likelihood of working full time declines with the arrival of infants and increases gradually once children reach school age (e.g., U.S. Department of Labor, Bureau of Labor Statistics 2020) (see also, Bianchi 2011; Bianchi et al. 2006; Goldin and Mitchell 2017).

Increasing women's access to higher levels of pay and authority in the public realm is necessary, but insufficient, to achieve gender equality. As Goldscheider et al. (2015) have argued, the "second half of the gender revolution" is about *both* "strengthening countries' economies, as women join their skills and energies to men's in the marketplace" *and* "strengthening families, as men increasingly take on important roles in the home" (p. 231). Toward these dual aspirations of strengthening economic and familial welfare, we advocate for overcoming barriers to engaged fatherhood, as well as for loosening the practical and perceived incompatibility of labor in the public and private realms.

We consciously argue for promoting "gender equity" as opposed to "gender equality" in parenting because we believe that, at this point in history, gender-differential interventions are required (i.e., "equity") to make progress toward the ideal of "equality"—that is, the point at which all people would be free to define and pursue their work aspirations and "caregiving ambitions" (Bear 2019) unconstrained by gender bias (Pavlic et al. 2000). It is also sensible to consider the differential needs and contributions of fathers and mothers because the perinatal period (i.e., immediately preceding and following the birth of a child) is a time of life in which distinctions of biological sex and socially constructed gender are maximally heightened (Doucet 2009). In the healthcare system, the perinatal period is commonly exclusively dedicated to maternal and infant care (see chapters by Kotelchuck, Levy and Kotelchuck, and Simon and Garfield in this volume). As explained by Koslowski and O'Brien in this volume, family leave policies were also originally conceived as exclusive protections for female workers before and after childbirth. More than a half century passed between the International Labor Organization's standard-setting Maternity Protection Convention in 1919 and Sweden's pathbreaking decision in 1974 to give fathers access to parental leave. In 1993, Norway was the first country to introduce a period of parental leave specifically dedicated to fathers, with the objective, as Kvande explains in her chapter, "to send a strong signal to parents as well as employers that men as well as women are parents with obligations and rights as caregivers" (insert page).

In sum, men's engagement in fatherhood is core to the gender revolution. The march toward gender equality will not progress without transforming the gender segregation of household labor and mitigating the incompatibilities between paid labor and familial care. "Gender equality" and "family values" are mantras commonly pitted against one another, but they are actually mutually reinforcing—particularly if one conceives of "gender" and "family" in inclusive terms. Engaged fatherhood is a strategy for gender equality that is good for the welfare of men, their children, and familial partners.

3 Unresolved Tensions in Fathers' Roles as "Breadwinners" and "Caregivers"

Over the past 30 years, the message that "fathers are caregivers" has continued to spread and take root in cultures worldwide, though broad variation persists in practice, in terms of time invested and types of involvement (Altintas and Sullivan 2017; Coleman, Garfield, and Committee on Psychosocial Aspects of Child and Family Health 2004; Jeong et al. 2016). Within this book, some of this variation is illustrated by Bosch and Las Heras's chapter on fathers' participation in family life across Latin America and by the "traditional," "conflicted," and "egalitarian" types of fathers that emerged from surveys of U.S. managers and professionals reported on in Harrington's chapter. There is a wealth of vivid quotes from fathers in Kvande's chapter on the case of Norway; in Bueno and Oh's comparative analysis of the perspectives of working fathers in Korea, Spain, and the United States; in Borgkvist's exploration of masculinity and fatherhood in Australia; in Tanquerel's conversations with French professional and working-class fathers; and in Macht's accounts of fatherly love in Scotland and Romania. In the text box, the selected quotes from these chapters illustrate varying degrees of tension between "father as breadwinner" and "father as caregiver."

> **Selected Quotes from Fathers across Cultures**
> *Norway (Kvande)*
> "If you want to be a good parent, or a good father, then you have to take the daddy leave."
> *Spain (Bueno and Oh)*
> "If I could afford [part-time unpaid parental leave], I would not mind at all. Of course! But, [my work] is not very flexible..., not even with women. I can't even imagine how they would be with men."
> *United States (Bueno and Oh)*
> "A man taking time [family leave]—I don't know... I have never known anybody that has."
> *Scotland (Macht)*
> "I work in an entirely male industry... So, you can't gush too much... about your children. ... You still have to hide... It's different in the way women and men describe their children [at work]."
> *Australia (Borgvist)*
> I have never asked for flexible work arrangements for childcare because I do not "want to be seen as someone who tries to get out of doing work."
> *Korea (Bueno and Oh)*
> "It is natural to focus on working when you become a father. I will be working harder for my family, for my child, as head of the family."
> *South Africa (Malinga and Ratele).*
> "I am supposed to be living with [my children] and their mother, but ... I have not yet had enough money to get married because of work; I don't work."

The chapters in this volume depict how men's engaged participation in fatherhood is taken for granted in some socioeconomic contexts, constrained by conflicting masculine breadwinner ideals in others, and sometimes even directly obstructed if the men are not strong enough economic providers. A compelling illustration of breadwinning as an obstacle to caregiving is found in Malinga and Ratele's accounts of day laborers in South Africa who have lost their privileges to a relationship with their children for lack of stable employment. As discussed in Kotelchuck's chapter on the "Impact of Fatherhood on Men's Health and Development," the exclusion of low-income men from engaged fatherhood is also evident in historic U.S. Welfare and Medicaid laws that incentivized mothers to live separately from fathers who could not provide sufficient economic support. In this concluding chapter, we aim to invite cross-sectoral collaboration in the development and implementation of evidence-based strategies for reinforcing fathers' self-identity and participation as familial caregivers, taking into account cultural and socioeconomic constraints on men's parenting engagement.

4 Proposed Working Principles for Reducing Barriers to Engaged Fatherhood

In the following sections, we explain our three working principles for overcoming barriers to engaged fatherhood: (1) create individual, non-transferable parenting resources explicitly for fathers, (2) reduce economic conflicts between breadwinning and caregiving, and (3) build supportive social networks for engaged fatherhood. We discuss evidence motivating each working principle and suggest ways in which each could be applied to promote engaged fatherhood in social policy, work practices, and the healthcare system. We offer these working principles as a common point of departure for problem-solving within and across sectors to support and promote engaged fatherhood through institutional and behavioral change.

4.1 Working Principle #1. Create Individual, Non-Transferable Parenting Resources Explicitly for Fathers

We start with our boldest principle: that promoting gender equity in parenting requires, at this point in history, the creation of individual, non-transferable parenting resources explicitly for fathers. We use the term "parenting resources" to refer to any forms of economic, educational, and organized social support that enhance mothers' and fathers' capacity to effectively care for their child(ren) and be available and responsible for meeting their child(ren)'s needs (as above, following Lamb et al. 1985). Parenting resources include provisions, such as access to family-friendly social or work policies (e.g., paid paternity, maternity, or parental leave; flexible work), parental training and educational materials, parental guidance from medical and developmental experts, or parental support groups.

It might seem more reasonable to start in reverse order with our third working principle—build supportive social networks for engaged fatherhood—so as to enhance men's sense of belonging and inclusion on the parenting journey. However, one of the most important insights we have gained from the work in this volume is that, at this point in time, welcoming fathers to be engaged parents is insufficient to make most men feel entitled to or capable of being fully engaged parents in the absence of individual, non-transferable paternal parenting resources. Fathers are commonly perceived—and perceive themselves—to be taking up space that belongs to mothers when they seek to play a larger role in their infants' and children's care (Allen and Hawkins 1999). For normative and practical reasons, men are expected to devote the bulk of their time and energies to the public sphere in order to collect and contribute resources (e.g., food, money, status) that will protect and sustain their families' private realm (Morgan 2002; Pleck 2010). Absent specifically designated parenting resources for fathers, the default assumption tends to be that parenting resources are intended for mothers, and fathers are left ill equipped to play larger parenting roles.

4.1.1 Social Policy

This principle is well supported by research on the conditions that increase men's utilization of their statutory rights to parental leave. In recent decades, natalist social policies, such as exclusive or extended maternal leave, have come to be recognized as "impeding" gender equality (Brighouse and Wright 2008) because they fuse the caregiving of young children with motherhood and contribute to a perceived and actual distancing of women from paid labor (Gangl and Ziefle 2009; Mandel and Semyonov 2005). However, even when lawmakers have tried to "enable" greater gender equality (Brighouse and Wright 2008) by introducing policies such as paid "parental" as opposed to "maternal" leave, they tend to observe little effect because mothers are the perceived targets and primary users of resources intended to reduce conflicts between paid work and childcare (Mandel and Semyonov 2005; Moran and Koslowski 2019). As explained in the chapters by Koslowski and O'Brien and by Kvande, what has made a difference in "promoting" gender equality in early parenting (Brighouse and Wright 2008) has been the creation of parental leave policies that provide an individual, non-transferable entitlement specifically for fathers to participate in infant care (see also, Bartel et al. 2018; Brandth and Kvande 2018; Castro-García and Pazos-Moran 2016; Dearing 2016; Patnaik 2019).

As recounted by Kvande, in 1978, Norway introduced a paid parental leave policy that parents could share. However, few fathers made claim to a portion of this leave. In 1993, Norway introduced a transformational innovation that became known as the "father's quota," a period—initially four weeks long and extended over time—of non-transferable, generously paid parental leave earmarked for fathers. As explained by Kvande, today more than 90 percent of fathers use some or all of their specifically designated leave, while mothers still utilize most of the leave eligible to be shared between parents.

In order to encourage women's workforce participation and to promote gender equity in infant care, many other countries have followed suit (International Network on Leave Policies and Research 2019). Germany, for example, has reduced generous maternal leave policies, introduced parental leave, and created added incentives for fathers' use of leave policies (e.g., two additional months of benefits if utilized by the father) (Erler 2009; Geisler and Kreyenfeld 2019; Reimer et al. 2019). As explained in the chapter by Koslowski and O'Brien, parental leave policies targeting fathers (e.g., "paternity" leave, "daddy month," "father's quota") have spread rapidly around the globe in order to reinforce in principle and practice that men have a role in children's care.

Importantly, evidence suggests that there are more than temporary benefits from policies that boost fathers' participation in early parenting (Patnaik 2019). Cross-national evidence indicates that men's participation in parental leave—particularly longer and more independent participation—contributes in lasting ways to fathers' involvement in caregiving and other forms of household labor (Bünning 2015; Huerta et al. 2014; Nepomnyaschy and Waldfogel 2007; O'Brien and Wall 2017; Patnaik 2019; Petts et al. 2020; Pragg and Knoester 2017; Rehel 2014). In sum, social policy research strongly suggests that individual, non-transferable resources explicitly designated for fathers is a way to "promote" gender equity in parenting, particularly when simply "enabling" fatherhood engagement is not effective (Brighouse and Wright 2008).

4.1.2 Work Practices

In a place like the United States, access to family leave or flexible work arrangements depends overwhelmingly on workplace practices (Kaufman 2020; Koslowski et al. 2019; Petts et al. 2020). But, even when employers offer family-friendly work policies, they are often not utilized by employees—sometimes because they are unaware of them and sometimes because they are hesitant to use them (Beauregard and Henry 2009). As illustrated by the quotes in the textbox, some fathers experience a sense of incongruence between taking family leave and fulfilling their primary responsibilities as breadwinners. Even when fathers would like to be more engaged caregivers, many forego family-friendly work benefits to avoid being stigmatized as a less productive (Leslie et al. 2012), less promising (Bear and Glick 2017), or less committed worker (Petts et al. 2020). In the Nordic countries, one reason why men do not use the shared portion of statutory parental leave is that they are concerned about how they will be viewed by their employers if they negotiate for more than the "father's quota" (Brandth and Kvande 2016; Närvi and Salmi 2019).

In reviewing literature on family-friendly workplace practices (as opposed to social policies), we uncovered no systematic studies of how variation in the design of parental leave policies offered by private employers affects their utilization, particularly by fathers. However, one recent survey experiment based on a U.S. private employment scenario showed that fathers who took "paternity" leave were perceived as more committed workers than fathers who took "parental" leave (Petts et al. 2020). More broadly, evidence from opinion surveys suggests that American men feel more ambivalent about fathers taking a share of parental leave to which mothers would otherwise be eligible than they do about men taking advantage of individual, father-specific (e.g., "paternity") leave policies (Petts et al. 2020) and that men strongly support employers offering paid paternity leave (Harrington et al. 2014).

Anecdotal evidence suggests other ways in which employers can offer individual, non-transferable parenting resources specifically for fathers. For instance, AB Volvo created a program for fathers to come together in a safe space to discuss work and family issues (Greenberg and Ladge 2019). American Express established a "fatherhood breakfast series" (Lindzon 2015). Other organizations have created employee resource groups for fathers or in which fathers are explicitly included (e.g., see Dowling 2018 for suggestions). These types of programs recognize fathers' work-family concerns as legitimate and worthy of problem solving. They also create opportunities for informal information sharing and sensemaking in the formation of new norms, the importance of which we discuss in relation to our third working principle about building supportive social networks for fatherhood engagement.

We should acknowledge that the evidence is mixed on whether offering family-friendly work practices or other types of parental resources enhances work performance. However, the variation in research findings tends to range between showing no and positive effects (as opposed detrimental implications) on productivity and employee engagement (Beauregard and Henry 2009). A challenge in demonstrating effects of work-life practices on productivity is that they tend to co-exist with better overall management practices (Bloom and Van Reenen 2006). This might help to explain why one study showed that the announcement of work-life initiatives by Fortune 500 firms was associated with increased shareholder returns (Arthur 2003). There is clearer evidence that offering work-life balance practices enhances employee recruitment (Beauregard and Henry 2009). Supporting working fathers is a way for companies to signal to prospective talent their commitment to gender equality and family values.

4.1.3 Healthcare

Whether or not mothers and fathers have access to statutory leave or family-friendly work practices, they are likely to interact with the healthcare system as they travel along their parenting journey (National Academies of Sciences, Engineering and Medicine, Board on Children, Youth, and Families, Division of Behavioral and Social Sciences and Education, and National Academies of Sciences, Engineering, and Medicine 2016; World Health Organization 2007, 2020). As emphasized in the healthcare chapters in this volume, obstetric, pediatric, and even primary care providers have important roles to play in encouraging or discouraging engaged fatherhood—from preconception health and reproductive knowledge, attitudes, and behavior (KAB) (Garfield et al. 2016) to perinatal care (Fisher et al. 2018; Garfield 2015) through child development (Yogman, Garfield, and Committee on Psychosocial Aspects of Child and Family Health 2016).

Similar to the way that fathers' taking a portion of shared parental leave is often perceived as an encroachment on mothers' time with children, medical attention to men's health and parental roles, especially during the perinatal period, is commonly perceived as sapping precious time and resources from mother and infant. However, as emphasized in the chapters by Yogman and Eppel and by Kotelchuck, this type of zero-sum logic is misguided because there is now overwhelming evidence that positive paternal engagement—and, conversely, the prevention of paternal disengagement—enhances the mental and physical welfare of mothers, the healthy development of children, and the mental and physical welfare of fathers themselves. In other words, paternal inclusion in Maternal Child Health (MCH) and Pediatrics is a win-win, as opposed to zero-sum, proposition.

One compelling example of this is the treatment of paternal depression. There is clear evidence that paternal depression is harmful to children's development (Garfield 2015; Garfield and Fletcher 2011; Ramchandani et al. 2011), both directly (e.g., in terms of less reading and more spanking, Davis et al. 2011) and indirectly (i.e., in terms of the toll it takes on the mother and couple's relationship, Gutierrez-Galve et al. 2015). Most pediatricians in the United States recognize the importance of tracking and treating maternal depression for children's welfare (e.g., Heneghan et al. 2007), but attention to paternal depression is much less widespread (Davis et al. 2011; Garfield and Fletcher 2011). Given that the overwhelming majority of U.S. fathers participate at some point in their children's acute-care or well-child pediatric visits (Garfield and Fletcher 2011; Garfield and Isacco 2006), pediatricians have both motive and opportunity to screen fathers specifically for depression and to help them get the services they need—but too few do (Garfield and Fletcher 2011).

Leading health advocates for engaged fatherhood offer numerous suggestions of individual, non-transferable resources that healthcare practices could provide specifically for fathers. These include inserting father-specific items or themes on clinical checklists that involve collecting health, welfare, and medical information from fathers (e.g., depression, family planning, obesity, use of health services) and then sharing with patients the significance of that information for reproductive, family, and child health (see Levy and Kotelchuck in this volume; Yogman et al. 2016). Obstetric practices could go further to develop services specifically for fathers, such as a paternal preconception visit or paternal prenatal consult, but many argue they are not trained to do so (see chapters by Kotelchuck and by Levy and Kotelchuck). Pediatricians and other health professionals can and do offer fathers parental training and education to help them recognize and feel competent in their parenting roles (National Academies of Sciences, Engineering and Medicine, Board on Children, Youth, and Families, Division of Behavioral and Social Sciences and Education, and National Academies of Sciences, Engineering, and Medicine 2016), such as bathing or providing skin-to-skin care to a newborn infant (Yogman et al. 2016) or encouraging language development and curiosity and being a role model as children grow (Garfield and Mesman 2016; World Health Organization 2007).

As advocated in the chapters by Levy and Kotelchuck and by Simon and Garfield, more research is required to motivate and inform the development and provision of parenting resources specifically for fathers. There is also a need to develop educational materials and trainings for healthcare service providers—doctors, nurses, and midwives—to help them recognize and advocate for the importance of father involvement during pregnancy, in the perinatal period, and throughout children's development (e.g., see Association of Maternal and Child Health Programs 2009; Fletcher et al. 2008, 2016; Garfield 2015; Garfield et al. 2016; Yogman et al. 2016).

In sum, exclusive associations of perinatal healthcare with mothers and infants, as well as the broader socio-cultural fusing of childcare with mothering, obscure fathers' roles, needs, and potential contributions to maternal and child health and family welfare (Association of Maternal and Child Health Programs 2009; Garfield 2015; Lu et al. 2010; UNICEF 2017; Yogman et al. 2016). To bring fathers out of the margins and into the center of family healthcare and to genuinely "promote"—as opposed to passively "enable" or "impede"—gender equality (Brighouse and Wright

2008), sustained efforts are required to explicitly and specifically include fathers in MCH, obstetric, and pediatric practices.

4.2 Working Principle #2. Reduce Economic Conflicts Between Breadwinning and Caregiving

As discussed in numerous chapters in this book, the traditional and primary normative prescription of fatherhood is to be the family provider. Across socioeconomic and cultural divides, there is a central tension between "cash" and "care" for contemporary fathers (Morgan 2002). The point of this working principle is to highlight that, even if men are provided individual, non-transferable parenting resources explicitly for fathers, they may not be utilized if they are economically out of reach or if grasping for those opportunities undermines or risks their families' economic welfare.

4.2.1 Social Policy

There are at least three ways in which economic factors influence men's experience of social policies aimed at fatherhood engagement. The first is eligibility and access. For instance, state-sponsored parenting-related leaves are typically designed for people who are formally and stably employed (Boll et al. 2014; Huerta et al. 2014). This leaves many economically underprivileged workers, such as the precariously employed or underemployed, with little or no access to parenting-related leave benefits (Koslowski and Kadar-Satat 2019; O'Brien 2009).

A second way is in terms of the relative financial benefits or costs of accessing the policy. As discussed by O'Brien and Koslowski in this volume, paid family leave that approximates wage replacement increases uptake by all parents, but by fathers especially. Cross-national comparative studies indicate that men are significantly more likely to utilize statutory parenting-related leave benefits when there is a combination of a "father's quota" (following Working Principle #1) and a high level of wage replacement benefit (Boll et al. 2014; Karu and Tremblay 2018).

Policies that increase the perceived costs of fatherhood engagement are potentially demotivating. For instance, the U.S. government has sponsored programs, such as Parents' Fair Share (PFS), that target low-income fathers in custodial arrears. The aim had been to increase men's economic contributions to their families by providing them with employment services and skills training. Program evaluations of PFS revealed income and parental engagement gains among the most needy cases (i.e., those with the greatest employment barriers and lowest levels of parental involvement). However, evidence suggests that the program's focus on capturing child support payments alienated many men and encouraged avoidance of formal employment (Knox et al. 2011).

A third economic consideration is mothers' and fathers' relative contributions to household income. Evidence suggests that men's utilization of parental leave hinges in part on the relative income of their domestic partners, such that greater income parity between domestic partners increases paternal leave taking (Moss et al. 2019; Reich 2010). Bueno and Oh's discussion of the case of fathers in Spain is illustrative. They explain that, in contrast to Korea or the United States, many Spanish couples tend toward a more gender-egalitarian division of childcare, but for economic as opposed to ideological reasons: labor market conditions require dual incomes to sustainably support most families.

In this volume, the social policy discussion has focused primarily on parenting-related leaves as a particularly robust area of research on how to support fatherhood engagement. There are obviously other ways in which social policy makers could support fatherhood engagement, such as by expanding healthcare access for fathers or by sponsoring programming to support fatherhood engagement (e.g., father support groups, discussed below). While constricted in scope, the generalizable insights from this research are transparent: any policy intervention designed to support fatherhood engagement needs to take into account its economic feasibility and attractiveness for fathers and their families, including how economic constraints might impede access or effectiveness.

4.2.2 Work Practices

Economic factors also influence men's access to and participation in father-friendly employment policies. In the absence of state-sponsored parental benefits—as is the case in much of the United States (Engeman et al. 2019), a minority of workers have access to paid family leave from their employers (Kaiser Family Foundation 2020; U.S. Department of Labor, Bureau of Labor Statistics 2019). Within the United States, the privileged few fathers who do have access to paid paternity leave through their employers tend to hold more prestigious and higher paid occupations (e.g., professionals, executives) (Nepomnyaschy and Waldfogel 2007; Petts et al. 2020) or benefit from union representation (Budd and Brey 2003).

As compared to social policy research, there is less data on how employer leave benefits are remunerated and the effects thereof. Our review of the literature on work and organizations uncovered no systematic studies of the relationship between the economic generosity of employers' family-friendly work policies and their utilization by fathers. One survey of working fathers found that 86 percent of the men reported that they would not take paid family leave offered by their employer unless it covered at least 70% of their salary (Harrington et al. 2014; see also Harrington chapter).

Another economic consideration for working fathers—as well as mothers—is whether accessing family-friendly employment policies could undermine their long-term earning potential. As noted earlier, there is evidence that workers who utilize flexible work practices to resolve work-family conflicts are vulnerable to being stigmatized as less than "ideal workers" (Acker 1990; Bear and Glick 2017; Ladge et al. 2015; Leslie et al. 2012; Perrigino et al. 2018). One U.S. survey found that hourly workers who lacked union representation were three times more likely than salaried employees to fear losing their jobs and twice as likely to worry about losing seniority if they took family leave (Budd and Brey 2003). Longitudinal studies show that men who take longer paid leaves or time off from paid labor for family reasons tend to have reduced long-term earnings (Coltrane et al. 2013; Rege and Solli 2013), as do women (e.g., Bertrand et al. 2010).

In some professions, such as in law, business, or finance, there are nonlinear, upward sloping payoffs for extreme work devotion (e.g., long hours, high travel, constant availability) (Goldin 2014). In such work contexts, employees must effectively forego income growth if they want more flexible or predictable work arrangements to manage work-family or other work-life conflicts (Goldin and Katz 2011). In her Presidential Address to the American Economic Association, Goldin (2014) argued that what is needed to achieve gender equality in the labor market is a restructuring of jobs and how they are compensated to enhance temporal flexibility:

> "What the last [historical] chapter must contain for [the attainment of] gender equality is not a zero-sum game in which women gain and men lose. This matter is not just a woman's issue. Many workers will benefit from greater flexibility... The rapidly growing sectors of the economy and newer industries and occupations, such as those in health and information technologies, appear to be moving in the direction of more flexibility and greater linearity of earnings with respect to time worked. The last chapter needs other sectors to follow their lead" (p. 1118).

To be inclusive of engaged parents, workplaces need to find integrative solutions to the actual and perceived trade-offs between participating in family-friendly work practices and maintaining one's productivity and earning potential. The most promising research along this vein suggests moving away from work-family "accommodation" toward problem-solving around "work redesign," such as using technology-enabled coordination, teaming, or "results only" evaluations to give workers more predictability and control in their schedules (Goldin and Katz 2016; Perlow and Kelly 2014). As discussed in relation to our third working principle (i.e., build supportive social networks for engaged fathers), there are complementary steps that organizational leaders can take to create work cultures that reduce the perceived incongruity between being an engaged father and an "ideal worker" (Humberd et al. 2015).

In sum, the economic factors that influence fathers' access to and utilization of family-friendly workplace policies appear similar to those we discussed in relation to social policies. Economically privileged fathers (i.e., more skilled, higher income, fully employed) are more likely to have access to family-friendly work policies. Fathers, in general, report less willingness to utilize policies, such as paternity leave, that would substantially reduce their earnings even for short amounts of time. At work, fathers, as well as mothers, also have to consider whether using family-friendly policies could reduce their longer-term earning potential, if doing so might lead them to be perceived as less committed or productive employees. Employers who are serious about promoting gender equality and family values should consider both the immediate economic costs and longer-run career implications of their employment practices (i.e., how work is structured and who gets promoted, as well as benefits packages) and their work culture (i.e., norms and biases) for working fathers, as well as mothers.

4.2.3 Healthcare

The healthcare sector also has to take economic considerations into account. As discussed in the two chapters by Kotelchuck, socioeconomic factors influence men's mental and physical health, as well as their access to and participation in the healthcare system (Braveman et al. 2011; Marmot et al. 2012). Particularly in healthcare systems that do not provide universal access, such as the United States, reproductive health services are typically only covered for mothers. Thus, any co-participation by fathers in reproductive health services or utilization of fatherhood-related medical or mental health services would not typically be covered by healthcare insurance and, as a result, are economically out of reach for most fathers.

In countries that lack universal healthcare, the inability to cover the costs of father-specific services also constrains healthcare providers. The absence of insurance coverage or other reimbursement for services, such as preconception care or depression testing for fathers, is a disincentive for service providers to address men's health in perinatal care. The data presented in Levy and Kotelchuck's chapter gives voice to men—a majority in their sample—who seek much more involvement in obstetric prenatal care than practitioners typically provide.

Finally, if men accompany their partners for reproductive health services (including delivery) or later pediatric services, they commonly must either take time off from work and forgo pay or utilize sick leave or vacation time—all of which are financial disincentives for fathers' involvement in childcare. Healthcare practices can accommodate working parents by offering flexible or extended office hours (Coleman et al. 2004), providing telehealth options, or posting online resources (Fletcher et al. 2008; Yogman et al. 2016). Service providers can also help address families' economic burdens by ensuring parents are aware of their eligibility for health, social welfare, and work programs and financial (e.g., tax) benefits.

In sum, the direct and indirect economic costs of fatherhood engagement in perinatal and pediatric care create barriers for healthcare providers, as well as fathers. In the absence of institutional mechanisms to pay or reimburse fatherhood-related health services or to support family-related employment absences, men's fatherhood engagement becomes dependent on their current financial abilities to absorb those costs. This leaves healthcare services for fathers primarily within reach of those who have the economic means to access and utilize them, even though those fathers who are less financially able often have some of the greatest needs (see chapter on "Impact of Fatherhood on Men's Health and Development" by Kotelchuck).

4.3 Working Principle #3: Build Supportive Social Networks for Engaged Fatherhood

In order to challenge default assumptions that childcare is about mothering, our first working principle was aimed at creating individual, non-transferable parental resources explicitly for fathers. Our second principle recognizes that, even if fathers are granted specifically designated parenting resources, they require the current economic resources and income potential to take advantage of such opportunities. We now turn to our third working principle: to build supportive social networks for engaged fatherhood. This principle stems from evidence on the influence of interpersonal relationships on fathers' propensity to take opportunities for engaged parenting.

We have put this principle last, even though being inclusive and encouraging of fatherhood engagement would seem to many like the obvious starting point. A critical insight we gained from the research reviewed for this volume is that the marginal value of additional social support is much greater once our first two working principles have been met than before. Starting with social support risks falling into the trap of "enabling" gender equality in parenting without actually "promoting" it (Brighouse and Wright 2008). It also contributes to the common misunderstanding that men are not interested in being engaged fathers if they do not participate when welcomed. Welcoming men to be engaged fathers is less meaningful if men feel ill equipped to participate as parents (Working Principle #1) or, if doing so, would come at an unacceptable economic cost for themselves or their families (Working Principle #2). However, as discussed in this section, once fathers have the resources and economic capacity, social support is critical to helping them overcome cultural barriers to embracing their caregiver roles.

4.3.1 Social Policy

A study of middle-class immigrant fathers in Norway illustrates how a lack of social support from friends and family can inhibit fathers from accessing even well-compensated father-specific statutory leave benefits. Kvande and Brandth (2017) interviewed immigrant men in professional positions about their experience with Norway's "father's quota." In one illustrative case, an Italian father living in Norway recounted the teasing he received when describing to his home-country peers his plans to take paid leave after the birth of his child:

> "It was a bit like I felt bullied by friends... It was like absurd that I was taking leave. In Italian it is called *maternita* [maternity leave], so it was like 'Ha, ha, ha, are you taking *maternita*?' ... Not really serious bullying, but it felt a little bit like it" (p. 29).

He continued on to explain how older family members watched him with amusement when he participated in childcare (e.g., changing diapers). Kvande and Brandth (2017) explored how some immigrant men struggled to reconcile parenting attitudes within their home-country social networks with the more progressive Norwegian norms.

Conversely, another Norwegian study by a team of economists demonstrated how peer effects contributed to the growth in men's participation in parenting-related leaves after the government introduced a full month of paid paternity leave in 1993. Dahl et al. (2014) showed that having either an eligible brother or a co-worker take paternity leave significantly increased new fathers' take-up of the newly introduced paternity leave policy. These "peer effects" were even stronger in less secure employment contexts (e.g., weaker unionization, private vs. public sector, higher turnover) and for senior managers from whom extra work devotion is typically expected.

Another illustration of this principle is the formation of father support groups. For example, the Supporting Father Involvement study, a government-sponsored randomized control trial to foster responsible fatherhood among low-income families in agricultural centers of the United States, demonstrated significant and lasting positive effects of peer support groups for fathers and of co-parenting support groups for couples on fathers' involvement with their children and on children's subsequent avoidance of problem behaviors. Fathers in the couples group also reported decreased relational stress with mothers and more stable partnerships over time (compared to peer-support or control groups) (Knox et al. 2011).

As argued by Dahl et al. (2014), close workplace and family networks are important social spaces for information sharing and sensemaking and may be especially influential in relation to gender-role adaptions. Social policy makers would be well advised to consider how patterns of social interaction and, potentially, other sources of role modeling (e.g., by public figures) could influence fatherhood engagement. As emphasized in the chapters by Simon and Garfield and by Levy and Kotelchuck, the fact that fathers are rarely even surveyed for their perspectives is evidence of missing links in social networks that could support fatherhood engagement and of lost opportunities for policy makers to learn from and influence fathers' behavior and perspectives.

In sum, social policy makers could enhance the effectiveness of their programming if they were able to build social support networks that encourage fathers' participation, particularly among close peers and family members. Moreover, the creation and tracking of social support networks for fathers is likely to be a valuable channel for information exchange, both to keep fathers informed and educated and to collect data for program evaluation, policy design, and knowledge development.

4.3.2 Work Practices

Workplaces are among the most influential social environments shaping men's perceptions of and capacity for fatherhood engagement. As discussed by Ladge and Humberd in this volume, "ideal workers" are commonly cast from a masculine stereotypic mold of employees whose primary responsibility is paid labor (Acker 1990)—the archetypal "organization man" (Ladge et al. 2015). In the United States, where there is no statutory right to paid leave, studies suggest that men who are open about balancing their work and family devotions are vulnerable to "not man enough" harassment and other forms of social backlash for their failure to conform to traditional gender norms (Berdahl and Moon 2013; Rudman and Mescher 2013; Thébaud and Pedulla 2016; Vandello et al. 2013). As discussed by Koslowski and O'Brien, fathers in countries with statutory rights to remunerated leave commonly report a sense of unease about being perceived as putting caregiving ahead of paid work even for short amounts of time and especially when they are in senior management roles (Brandth and Kvande 2002; Koslowski and Kadar-Satat 2019; Moran and Koslowski 2019; Närvi and Salmi 2019; Tanquerel and Grau-Grau 2020).

As discussed above, more elite workers tend to have more economic security, as well as employment privileges, to balance work-family conflicts. However, they often suffer a paradoxical tension between having a wealth of resources to manage work-family conflicts and constrained ability to deploy those resources if they want to maintain their elite status (Allard et al. 2007; Kelly et al. 2010; Shows and Gerstel 2009; Williams 2010). This dynamic is explored in the chapter by Tanquerel for which she interviewed French working-class and professional fathers. Professional men in her sample tended to characterize family issues as a "private matter" about which, one of her interviewees explained, "nobody cared, nobody wanted to hear" (insert page). In contrast, the working-class men Tanquerel interviewed reported more open discussions with their managers about taking statutory paternity leave or managing other work-family conflicts (cf. Williams 2010 on class and working fatherhood in the United States).

As discussed in the chapter by Bueno and Oh, it is not only cultural conceptions of gender, but also the culture of work, that influences men's choices to be engaged fathers. For instance, in Korea or Japan, the gendered division of household labor (i.e., women as caregivers and men as breadwinners) is reinforced by national work cultures that demand extreme work devotion (e.g., long and inflexible work hours). Being an engaged parent is unreconcilable with being a devoted employee, for women as well as men (Brinton and Mun 2016; Brinton and Oh 2019). Demanding work structures and cultures rely on the segregation of "cash-making" and "caregiving" (Goldin 2014; Padavic et al. 2020; Slaughter 2015).

A growing body of evidence suggests that the propensity of working dads to invest time and energy in engaged fatherhood is significantly influenced by the perceived supportiveness of their work environment, particularly their supervising managers (Humberd et al. 2015; Moran and Koslowski 2019; Petts et al. 2020; Stropnik et al. 2019; Tanquerel and Grau-Grau 2020). Within this volume, Bosch and Las Heras report evidence that Latin American fathers' propensity to participate in family life (e.g., eat dinner at home) depends on the extent to which they benefit from Family Supportive Supervisor Behaviors (FSSBs) (e.g., managers who role model work-family balance). Other investigations of how men navigate fathering identities at work have similarly concluded that direct managers play a key role in encouraging and enabling working fathers' involvement in their children's lives (Humberd et al. 2015; Ladge et al. 2015).

The provision of family-friendly work policies in itself is insufficient if workers lack information or social support within their workplaces to utilize them (Beauregard and Henry 2009; Kelly and Kalev 2006). Policies to promote gender equality and work-family integration are more likely to be effective if organizational leaders and managers act as role models and partners in information sharing and problem-solving around potential work-family conflicts. For example, Accenture, a large professional services firm, reported a three-fold increase in men's participation in paid parental leave between 2016 and 2019. Consistent with our first two working principles, this achievement followed the introduction of a fully paid parental leave policy for "all permanent full-time and part-time employees of all gender identities." However, professionals in the firm also credited "seeing other dads"—including senior leaders in the firm—as an important factor in normalizing utilization of the new leave policy (Women's Agenda 2020). As suggested above for policy makers, organizational leaders should consider how interpersonal support networks within their organizations shape fathers' perceptions and use of opportunities for work-family integration.

4.3.3 Healthcare

New parents especially look to healthcare providers for guidance and affirmation, and medical service providers should be aware that how they interact with fathers may tacitly convey a message—intended or not—about their positive or negative perceptions of fathers' status as parents. As suggested in the chapter by Levy and Kotelchuck, there are meaningful social gestures that medical professionals and staff can make to be inclusive of fathers from the beginning of pregnancy—or, alternatively, to reinforce traditionally gendered parenting roles. To reinforce men's parental status, they can make a habit of addressing fathers directly and welcoming them explicitly into the process of prenatal, perinatal, and postnatal care—traditionally maternal-only spheres of health services. Healthcare providers can enhance fathers' sense of belonging by displaying inclusive imagery of fathers in their offices, on websites, and in other communications.

Active outreach to fathers by healthcare professionals is especially important for potentially marginalized fathers and their families (World Health Organization 2007; Yogman et al. 2016). For instance, Moore and Kotelchuck (2004) found Black urban fathers in the United States were more likely to feel uncomfortable participating in pediatric visits and less likely to do so when their families had no health insurance (a traditional fatherhood responsibility). Fathers suffering socioeconomic strains may be among those whose families would benefit most from trusting, supportive relationships with healthcare providers.

Pediatricians have a distinctive role to play in overcoming the perpetuation of stereotypes of fathers as incompetent caregivers (Garfield and Isacco 2006), which demotivate fathers themselves and thinly justify gendered gatekeeping between the public realm of paid labor and private realm of familial care (Allen and Hawkins 1999; Doucet 2009; Zvara et al. 2013). The overwhelming majority of fathers participate at some point in their children's well visits or critical care (Garfield and Fletcher 2011; Garfield and Isacco 2006). These touchpoints give pediatricians opportunities to help fathers develop their sense of confidence and identity as engaged parents. For instance, they can emphasize to fathers and their parenting partners the importance of giving fathers time with primary responsibility for infant care (Yogman et al. 2016; see also chapters on "The Role of Fathers in Child and Family Health" and "Impact of Fatherhood on Men's Health and Development" by Yogman and Eppel and by Kotelchuck, respectively) or highlight their important roles in adolescent development (Lucey and Garfield 2019).

Some pediatricians have created new father support groups that help men to collectively recognize their common experiences and concerns and be a locus for new practical skill development and enhanced paternal confidence (Spain 2018). Other healthcare professionals and community groups have designed fatherhood support programs, such as The Healthy Start Program or The Fatherhood Project, that similarly help men support one another, gain new skills and knowledge, and strengthen their sense of paternal identity, including overcoming traditionalist prejudices as well as addressing practical, psychosocial, and economic barriers to becoming more engaged fathers (Harris and Brott 2018; Levy et al. 2012). The success of these programs and others, such as the Supporting Father Involvement study (referenced above), suggest that fatherhood support groups may be an underutilized resource, especially for improving the health and welfare of families burdened by challenging socioeconomic circumstances (Baumgartner et al. 2020; Lu et al. 2010; see also Kotelchuck chapter on "Impact of Fatherhood on Men's Health and Development").

In sum, healthcare professionals have enormous potential to be influential contributors to the social support networks for engaged fatherhood, particularly for first-time parents. They should recognize that their interpersonal interactions are influential opportunities to share information and shape perceptions about engaged fatherhood. Beyond interactions within the healthcare system itself, healthcare providers have a role to play in creating and sustaining spaces for fathers to develop supportive relationships with peers to sympathize, encourage, and problem-solve with one another.

5 Closing

In this concluding chapter, we have proposed three working principles that would not have been transparent without the insights we gained from our collaboration on the Experts Meeting and this edited volume. Our first two principles—(1) create individual, non-transferable parenting resources explicitly for fathers and (2) reduce economic conflicts between breadwinning and caregiving—reflect core findings in social policy. The cross-disciplinary and cross-national sharing of ideas and perspectives at the conference and the subsequent editing of the volume helped us to recognize the central relevance of these principles for workplace and healthcare practices.

Our third principle—(3) build supportive social networks for engaged fatherhood—is the first we all espoused. However, it was only through deeper reflection that we realized its limitations absent attention to the preceding principles. Moreover, we came to see that the importance of social support comes more sharply into focus when one recognizes that our first two principles are necessary, but still insufficient, if men perceive those close to them as dismissive of or resistant to their fatherhood engagement. We offer these working principles as a preliminary basis for analyzing the barriers to engaged fatherhood and for generating policies and behavioral interventions to promote gender equity in parenting.

We hope that the evidence presented in this book has made a compelling case for reducing the barriers to engaged fatherhood—for men, for families, and for gender equality. We offer this summary of evidence and our working principles at a time in history when many believe the revolution toward gender equality is in need of a push forward (England 2010) *and* when a growing number of people are recognizing that deepening men's engagement in care and women's in paid labor would strengthen both our families and our economies. The motivation for this work has been to put our shoulders to the wheel in support of these dual purposes.

5.1 *Looking Forward*

We started with a conversation among fatherhood experts from the social policy, work and organization, and health fields. Unclear exactly what we would grasp from one another, we were nonetheless highly curious about what novel insights might be gained and transferable across the sectors. We were uniformly delighted with how much we had to learn by sharing our distinctive vantage points on fatherhood engagement. Indeed, this collaboration has left us more hungry than satisfied by our potential for cross-disciplinary and cross-national collaboration. As we close this chapter, we are eager to pursue new research informed by this endeavor and to bring more viewpoints into the conversation.

In future rounds of this conversation, we aspire to invite more direct conversation with policy makers and organizational leaders. We would also like to invite more of our colleagues from professional schools (e.g., graduate schools of education) and from the social sciences, particularly political science, psychology, and sociology, in order to fill out missing perspectives and to refine and elaborate our working principles for collaborative action. Completing this volume, we are aware that we have barely scratched the surface of how important factors, such as socioeconomic status, moderate the barriers to fatherhood engagement. We have not delved into the implications of systemic racism, mass incarceration, or other forms of social and economic marginalization. We have focused primarily on the benefits of constructive and gender-equitable parenting engagement and recognize the need to shine more light on the darker margins of abusive fatherhood, patriarchal forms of fatherhood identity, and toxic masculinities. While we have tried to define fathers in inclusive terms, we have written this book from a predominately heteronormative perspective. Any expansion of this conversation should more explicitly consider a diversity of family structures and the limits and extensions of the work to people with queer, non-binary, or transgender identities. Finally, we are writing the final pages of this book in a period of potentially historic transformations at the intersections of work and family due to the Covid-19 pandemic, and we are all impatient to learn about how families are coping and what will be the lasting implications for work and gender equality.

In sum, we are closing this book with a deep sense of gratitude for all we have learned from our fellow contributors and with enthusiasm to join more companions in the work to promote fatherhood engagement for the welfare of men and for the strengthening of families and economic productivity through increased gender equality.

Acknowledgements We are enormously grateful to Alison Koslowski, Craig Garfield, Jamie Ladge, and Richard Petts for their insightful feedback and constructive suggestions on this chapter.

References

Acker J (1990) Hierarchies, jobs, bodies: a theory of gendered organizations. Gend Soc 4 (2):139–158
Allard K, Haas L, Hwang CP (2007) Exploring the Paradoxs: experiences of flexible working arrangements and work–family conflict among managerial fathers in Sweden. Community Work Fam 10(4):475–493
Allen SM, Hawkins AJ (1999) Maternal gatekeeping: mothers' beliefs and behaviors that inhibit greater father involvement in family work. J Marriage Fam 61(1):199–212
Altintas E, Sullivan O (2017) Trends in fathers' contribution to housework and childcare under different welfare policy regimes. Soc Polit Int Stud Gender, State Soc 24(1):81–108
Arthur MM (2003) Share Price reactions to work-family initiatives: an institutional perspective. Acad Manag J 46(4):497–505
Association of Maternal & Child Health Programs (2009) AMCHP Fact Sheet Father Involvement in MCH Programs
Bartel AP, Rossin-Slater M, Ruhm CJ, Stearns J, Waldfogel J (2018) Paid family leave, fathers' leave-taking, and leave-sharing in dual-earner households. J Policy Anal Manage 37(1):10–37
Baumgartner S, Friend D, Holcomb P, Clary E, Zaveri H, Overcash A (2020) Pathways-to-outcomes: how responsible fatherhood program activities may lead to intended outcomes. OPRE report #2020-58. U.S. Department of Health and Human Services, Administration for Children and Families, Office of Planning, Research, and Evaluation, Washington, DC
Bear JB (2019) The caregiving ambition framework. Acad Manag Rev 44(1):99–125
Bear JB, Glick P (2017) Breadwinner Bonus and caregiver penalty in workplace rewards for men and women. Soc Psychol Personal Sci 8(7):780–788
Beauregard TA, Henry LC (2009) Making the link between work-life balance practices and organizational performance. Hum Resour Manag Rev 19(1):9–22
Berdahl JL, Moon SH (2013) Workplace mistreatment of middle class workers based on sex, parenthood, and caregiving. J Soc Issues 69(2):341–366

Bertrand M, Goldin C, Katz LF (2010) Dynamics of the gender gap for young professionals in the financial and corporate sectors. Am Econ J Appl Econ 2(3):228–255

Bianchi SM (2011) Family change and time allocation in American families. Ann Am Acad Pol Soc Sci 638(1):21–44

Bianchi SM, Robinson JP, Milkie MA (2006) The changing rhythms of American family life. Russell Sage Foundation, New York

Bloom N, Van Reenen J (2006) Management practices, work-life balance, and productivity: a review of some recent evidence. Oxf Rev Econ Policy 22(4):457–482

Boll C, Leppin J, Reich N (2014) Paternal childcare and parental leave policies: evidence from industrialized countries. Rev Econ Househ 12(1):129–158

Brandth B, Kvande E (2002) Reflexive fathers: negotiating parental leave and working life. Gender, Work & Organization 9(2):186–203

Brandth B, Kvande E (2016) Fathers and flexible parental leave. Work Employ Soc 30(2):275–290

Brandth B, Kvande E (2018) Enabling or promoting gender equality though parental leave policies. Revista Española de Sociología 27(3 Suplemento):107–120

Braveman P, Egerter S, Williams DR (2011) The social determinants of health: coming of age. Annu Rev Public Health 32(1):381–398

Brighouse H, Wright EO (2008) Strong Gender Egalitarianism. Polit Soc 36(3):360–372

Brinton MC, Mun E (2016) Between state and family: managers' implementation and evaluation of parental leave policies in Japan. Soc Econ Rev 14(2):257–281

Brinton MC, Oh E (2019) Babies, work, or both? Highly educated Women's employment and fertility in East Asia. Am J Sociol 125(1):105–140

Budd JW, Brey AM (2003) Unions and family leave: early experience under the family and medical leave act. Labor Stud J 28(3):85–105

Bünning M (2015) What happens after the 'daddy months'? Fathers' involvement in paid work, childcare, and housework after taking parental leave in Germany. Eur Sociol Rev 31(6):738–748

Castro-García C, Pazos-Moran M (2016) Parental leave policy and gender equality in Europe. Fem Econ 22(3):51–73

Coleman WL, Garfield C, Committee on Psychosocial Aspects of Child and Family Health (2004) Fathers and pediatricians: enhancing Men's roles in the care and development of their children. Pediatrics 113(5):1406–1411

Coltrane S, Miller EC, DeHaan T, Stewart L (2013) Fathers and the flexibility stigma. J Soc Issues 69(2):279–302

Dahl GB, Løken KV, Mogstad M (2014) Peer effects in program participation. Am Econ Rev 104(7):2049–2074

Davis RN, Davis MM, Freed GL, Clark SJ (2011) Fathers' depression related to positive and negative parenting behaviors with 1-year-old children. Pediatrics 127(4):612–618

Dearing H (2016) Gender equality in the division of work: how to assess European leave policies regarding their compliance with an ideal leave model. J Eur Soc Policy 26(3):234–247

Doucet A (2009) Dad and baby in the first year: gendered responsibilities and embodiment. Ann Am Acad Pol Soc Sci 624(1):78–98

Dowling DW (2018) How to launch a working parents' support Group in Your Organization. Harv Bus Rev

Engeman C, Petts RJ, Gabel SG, Kaufman G (2019) United States country note. In: Koslowski A, Blum S, Dobrotić I, Macht A, Moss P (eds) International review of leave policies and research 2019

England P (2010) The gender revolution: uneven and stalled. Gend Soc 24(2):149–166

Erler D (2009) Germany: taking a Nordic turn? In: Kamerman SB, Moss P (eds) The politics of parental leave policies: children, parenting, gender and the labour market. Bristol University Press, Bristol, pp 119–134

Fisher D, Khashu M, Adama EA, Feeley N, Garfield CF, Ireland J, Koliouli F, Lindberg B, Nørgaard B, Provenzi L, Thomson-Salo F, van Teijlingen E (2018) Fathers in neonatal units:

improving infant health by supporting the baby-father Bond and mother-father Coparenting. J Neonatal Nurs 24(6):306–312

Fletcher R, May C, Wroe J, Hall P, Cooke D, Rawlinson C, Redfern J, Kelly B (2016) Development of a set of Mobile phone text messages designed for new fathers. J Reprod Infant Psychol 34 (5):525–534

Fletcher R, Vimpani G, Russell G, Keatinge D (2008) The evaluation of tailored and web-based information for new fathers. Child Care Health Dev 34(4):439–446

Gangl M, Ziefle A (2009) Motherhood, labor force behavior, and Women's careers: an empirical assessment of the wage penalty for motherhood in Britain, Germany, and the United States. Demography 46(2):341–369

Garfield CF (2015) Supporting fatherhood before and after it happens. Pediatrics 135(2):e528–e530

Garfield CF, Duncan G, Peters S, Rutsohn J, McDade TW, Adam EK, Coley RL, Chase-Lansdale PL (2016) Adolescent reproductive knowledge, attitudes, and beliefs and future fatherhood. J Adolesc Health 58(5):497–503

Garfield CF, Fletcher R (2011) Sad dads: a challenge for pediatrics. Pediatrics 127(4):781–782

Garfield CF, Isacco A (2006) Fathers and the well-child visit. Pediatrics 117(4):e637–e645

Garfield CF, Mesman J (2016) Time and money: extending fathers' role in economically challenging contexts. Pediatrics 138(4):e20162456–e20162456

Geisler E, Kreyenfeld M (2019) Policy reform and fathers' use of parental leave in Germany: the role of education and workplace characteristics. J Eur Soc Policy 29(2):273–291

Goldin C (2006) The quiet revolution that transformed Women's employment, education, and family. Am Econ Rev 96(2):1–21

Goldin C (2014) A grand gender convergence: its last chapter. Am Econ Rev 104(4):1091–1119

Goldin C, Katz LF (2011) The cost of workplace flexibility for high-powered professionals. In: Christensen K, Schneider B (eds) The ANNALS of the American Academy of Political and Social Science 638(1): 45–67

Goldin C, Katz LF (2016) A Most egalitarian profession: pharmacy and the evolution of a family-friendly occupation. J Labor Econ 34(3):705–746

Goldin C, Mitchell J (2017) The new life cycle of Women's employment: disappearing humps, sagging middles, expanding tops. J Econ Perspect 31(1):161–182

Goldscheider F, Bernhardt E, Lappegård T (2015) The gender revolution: a framework for understanding changing family and demographic behavior. Popul Dev Rev 41(2):207–239

Greenberg D, Ladge JJ (2019) Maternal optimism: forging positive paths through work and motherhood. Oxford University Press, Oxford

Guterman NB, Lee Y, Lee SJ, Waldfogel J, Rathouz PJ (2009) Fathers and maternal risk for physical child abuse. Child Maltreat 14(3):277–290

Gutierrez-Galve L, Stein A, Hanington L, Heron J, Ramchandani P (2015) Paternal depression in the postnatal period and child development: mediators and moderators. Pediatrics 135(2):e339–e347

Harrington B, Van Deusen F, Fraone JS, Eddy S, Haas L (2014) The new dad: take your leave. Boston College Center for Work & Family, Chestnut Hill

Harris K, Brott A (2018) NHSA healthy start fathers – real life, real dads. National Healthy Start Association. http://www.nationalhealthystart.org/what_we_do/male_involvement/nhsa_healthy_start_fathers_real_life_real_dads. Accessed 31 Aug 2020

Heneghan AM, Morton S, DeLeone NL (2007) Paediatricians' attitudes about discussing maternal depression during a Paediatric primary care visit. Child Care Health Dev 33(3):333–339

Huerta M d C, Adema W, Baxter J, Han W-J, Lausten M, Lee RH, Waldfogel J (2013) Fathers' Leave, Fathers' involvement and child development: are they related? evidence from four OECD countries, OECD Social, Employment and Migration Working Paper No. 140. OECD, Paris

Huerta MC, Adema W, Baxter J, Han W-J, Lausten M, Lee R, Waldfogel J (2014) Fathers' leave and fathers' involvement: evidence from four OECD countries. Eur J Soc Secur 16(4):308–346

Humberd B, Ladge JJ, Harrington B (2015) The 'new' dad: navigating fathering identity within organizational contexts. J Bus Psychol 30(2):249–266

International Network on Leave Policies and Research (2019) 15th International Review of Leave Policies and Related Research

Jeong J, McCoy DC, Yousafzai AK, Salhi C, Fink G (2016) Paternal stimulation and early child development in low- and middle-income countries. Pediatrics 138(4):e20161357

Kaiser Family Foundation (2020) Paid Family and Sick Leave in the U.S. https://www.kff.org/womens-health-policy/fact-sheet/paid-family-leave-and-sick-days-in-the-u-s/#. Accessed 31 Aug 2020

Karu M, Tremblay D-G (2018) Fathers on parental leave: an analysis of rights and take-up in 29 countries. Community Work Fam 21(3):344–362

Kaufman G (2020) Fixing parental leave: the six month solution. NYU Press, New York

Kelly EL, Ammons SK, Chermack K, Moen P (2010) Gendered challenge, gendered response: confronting the ideal worker norm in a white-collar organization. Gend Soc 24(3):281–303

Kelly EL, Kalev A (2006) Managing flexible work arrangements in US organizations: formalized discretion or 'a Right to Ask'. Soc Econ Rev 4:379–416

Knox V, Cowan PA, Cowan CP, Bildner E (2011) Policies that strengthen fatherhood and family relationships: what do we know and what do we need to know? Ann Am Acad Pol Soc Sci 635(1):216–239

Koslowski A, Blum S, Dobrotić I, Macht A, Moss P (2019) International review of leave policies and research 2019

Koslowski A, Kadar-Satat G (2019) Fathers at work: explaining the gaps between entitlement to leave policies and uptake. Community Work Fam 22(2):129–145

Kvande E, Brandth B (2017) Individualized, non-transferable parental leave for European fathers: migrant perspectives. Community Work Fam 20(1):19–34

Ladge JJ, Humberd BK, Watkins MB, Harrington B (2015) Updating the organization MAN: an examination of involved fathering in the workplace. Acad Manag Perspect 29(1):152–171

Lamb ME, Pleck JH, Charnov EL, Levine JA (1985) Paternal behavior in humans. Am Zool 25(3):883–894

Leslie LM, Manchester CF, Park T-Y, Ahn Mehng SI (2012) Flexible work practices: a source of career premiums or penalties? Acad Manag J 55(6):1407–1428

Levy RA, Badalament J, Kotelchuck M (2012) The fatherhood project: connecting fathers and children. The Fatherhood Project. https://www.thefatherhoodproject.org/. Accessed 31 Aug 2020

Lindzon J (2015) Top 50 best places to work for new dads. Fast Company. https://www.fastcompany.com/3045664/top-50-best-places-to-work-for-new-dads. Accessed 31 Aug 2020

Livingston G (2018) Stay-at-home moms and dads account. Pew Research Center, FactTank News in Numbers. https://www.pewresearch.org/fact-tank/2018/09/24/stay-at-home-moms-and-dads-account-for-about-one-in-five-u-s-parents/. Accessed 1 June 2020

Lu MC, Jones L, Bond MJ, Wright K, Pumpuang M, Maidenberg M, Jones D, Garfield C, Rowley DL (2010) Where Is the F in MCH? Father Involvement in African American Families. Ethnicity Dis 20:S2-49-S2-61

Lucey K, Garfield CF (2019) Fathers' engagement in their sons' sexual and reproductive health. Pediatrics 143(1):e20182595

Mandel H, Semyonov M (2005) Family policies, wage structures, and gender gaps: sources of earnings inequality in 20 countries. Am Sociol Rev 70(6):949–967

Marmot M, Allen J, Bell R, Bloomer E, Goldblatt P (2012) WHO European review of social determinants of health and the health divide. Lancet 380(9846):1011–1029

Moore T, Kotelchuck M (2004) Predictors of urban fathers' involvement in their Child's health care. Pediatrics 113(3):574–580

Moran J, Koslowski A (2019) Making use of work–family balance entitlements: how to support fathers with combining employment and caregiving. Community Work Fam 22(1):111–128

Morgan D (2002) In: Hobson B (ed) Making men into fathers: men, masculinities, and the social politics of fatherhood. Cambridge University Press, Cambridge

Moss P, Duvander A-Z, Koslowski A (eds) (2019) Parental leave and beyond: recent international developments, current issues and future directions. Policy Press, Chicago

Nandi A, Jahagirdar D, Dimitris MC, Labrecque JA, Strumpf EC, Kaufman JS, Vincent I, Atabay E, Harper S, Earle A (2018) The impact of parental and medical leave policies on socioeconomic and health outcomes in OECD countries: a systematic review of the empirical literature. Milbank Q 96(3):434–471

Närvi J, Salmi M (2019) Quite an encumbrance? Work-related obstacles to Finnish fathers' take-up of parental leave. Community Work Fam 22(1):23–42

National Academies of Sciences, Engineering and Medicine, Board on Children, Youth, and Families, Division of Behavioral and Social Sciences and Education, National Academies of Sciences, Engineering, and Medicine (2016) In: Gadsden VL, Ford M, Breiner H (eds) Parenting matters: supporting parents of children ages 0–8. National Academies Press, Washington, DC

Nepomnyaschy L, Waldfogel J (2007) Paternity leave and fathers' involvement with their young children. Community Work Fam 10(4):427–453

O'Brien M (2009) Fathers, parental leave policies, and infant quality of life: international perspectives and policy impact. Ann Am Acad Pol Soc Sci 624(1):190–213

O'Brien M, Wall K (eds) (2017) Comparative perspectives on work-life balance and gender equality: fathers on leave alone, vol 6. Springer, London

Padavic I, Ely RJ, Reid EM (2020) Explaining the persistence of gender inequality: the work–family narrative as a social defense against the 24/7 work culture. Adm Sci Q 65(1):61–111

Parker, Kim, and Renee Stepler. 2017. "Americans see men as the financial providers, even as Women's contributions grow." Pew Research Center, FactTank News in the Numbers. https://www.pewresearch.org/fact-tank/2017/09/20/americans-see-men-as-the-financial-providers-even-as-womens-contributions-grow/. Accessed 1 July 2020

Parker K, Wang W (2013) Modern parenthood: roles of moms and dads converge as they balance work and family. Pew Research Center, Washington, DC

Patnaik A (2019) Reserving time for daddy: the consequences of fathers' quotas. J Labor Econ 37 (4):1009–1059

Pavlic B, Ruprecht L, Sam-Vargas S (2000) Gender equality and equity: a summary review of UNESCO's accomplishments since the fourth world conference on women (Beijing 1995). Unit for the Promotion of the Status of Women and Gender Equality. UNESCO, New York

Paxson C, Waldfogel J (1999) Parental resources and child abuse and neglect. Am Econ Rev 89 (2):239–244

Perlow LA, Kelly EL (2014) Toward a model of work redesign for better work and better life. Work Occup 41(1):111–134

Perrigino MB, Dunford BB, Wilson KS (2018) Work–family backlash: the 'dark side' of work–life balance (WLB) policies. Acad Manag Ann 12(2):600–630

Petts RJ, Knoester C, Li Q (2020) Paid paternity leave-taking in the United States. Community Work Fam 23(2):162–183

Petts RJ, Knoester C, Waldfogel J (2020) Fathers' paternity leave-taking and Children's perceptions of father-child relationships in the United States. Sex Roles 82(3):173–188

Petts RJ, Mize TD, Kaufman G (2020) Attenuating the commitment penalty: the effects of organizational policies and workplace culture on perceptions of workers who take parental leave. Harper, San Francisco

Pleck JH (2010) Fatherhood and masculinity. In: Lamb ME (ed) The role of the father in child development. Wiley, Hoboken, NJ, pp 27–57

Pragg B, Knoester C (2017) Parental leave use among disadvantaged fathers. J Fam Issues 38 (8):1157–1185

Ramchandani PG, Psychogiou L, Vlachos H, Iles J, Sethna V, Netsi E, Lodder A (2011) Paternal depression: an examination of its links with father, child and family functioning in the postnatal period. Depress Anxiety 28(6):471–477

Rege M, Solli IF (2013) The impact of paternity leave on fathers' future earnings. Demography 50 (6):2255–2277

Rehel EM (2014) When dad stays home too: paternity leave, gender, and parenting. Gend Soc 28 (1):110–132

Reich N (2010) Who cares? Determinants of the Fathers' use of parental leave in Germany. Working Paper No. 5491. National Bureau of Economic Research, Cambridge

Reimer T, Erier D, Schober P, Blum S (2019) Germany Country Note. In: Koslowski A, Blum S, Dobrotić I, Macht A, Moss P (eds) International review of leave policies and research 2019

Ridgeway CL (2011) Framed by gender: how gender inequality persists in the modern world. Oxford University Press, Oxford

Rudman LA, Mescher K (2013) Penalizing men who request a family leave: is flexibility stigma a femininity stigma? J Soc Issues 69(2):322–340

Shows C, Gerstel N (2009) Fathering, class, and gender: a comparison of physicians and emergency medical technicians. Gend Soc 23(2):161–187

Slaughter A-M (2015) Unfinished business: women men work family. Random House, New York

Spain E (2018) Modern-day fatherhood and the health of dads with Craig Garfield, MD. Breakthroughs, Northwestern University Feinberg School of Medicine. https://www.feinberg.northwestern.edu/research/news/podcast/modern-day-fatherhood.html. Accessed on 31 Aug 2020

Stropnik N, Humer Ž, Mrčela AK, Štebe J (2019) The problem is in practice: policy support and employer support for fathers' participation in childcare in Slovenia. Community Work Fam 22 (1):77–95

Tanquerel S, Grau-Grau M (2020). Unmasking work-family balance barriers and strategies among working fathers in the workplace. Organization 27(5):680–700

Thébaud S, Pedulla DS (2016) Masculinity and the stalled revolution: how gender ideologies and norms shape young Men's responses to work–family policies. Gend Soc 30(4):590–617

U.S. Department of Labor, Bureau of Labor Statistics (2019) Access to paid and unpaid family leave in 2018. TED: The Economics Daily. https://www.bls.gov/opub/ted/2019/access-to-paid-and-unpaid-family-leave-in-2018.htm. Accessed on 31 Aug 2020

U.S. Department of Labor, Bureau of Labor Statistics (2020) Employment Characteristics of Families—2019. USDL-20-0670. Washington, DC

UNICEF (2017) Super dads: new UNICEF campaign spotlights fathers' critical role in Children's early development. UN News. https://news.un.org/en/story/2017/06/558912-super-dads-new-unicef-campaign-spotlights-fathers-critical-role-childrens-early. Accessed 11 June 2020

Vandello JA, Hettinger VE, Bosson JK, Siddiqi J (2013) When equal Isn't really equal: the masculine dilemma of seeking work flexibility. J Soc Issues 69(2):303–321

Williams JC (2010) Reshaping the work-family debate: why men and class matter. Harvard University Press, Cambridge

Women's Agenda (2020) Now offering 18 weeks of paid parental leave, Accenture sees massive increase in dads taking it. Women's Agenda. https://womensagenda.com.au/life/jugglehood/now-offering-18-weeks-of-paid-parental-leave-accenture-sees-330-increase-in-dads-taking-it/. Accessed on 25 July 2020

World Health Organization (2007) Fatherhood and health outcomes in Europe. World Health Organization, Copenhagen

World Health Organization (2020) World health statistics 2020: monitoring health for the SDGs, sustainable development goals. World Health Organization, Geneva

Yogman M, Garfield CF, Committee on Psychosocial Aspects of Child and Family Health (2016) Fathers' roles in the care and development of their children: the role of pediatricians. Pediatrics 138(1)

Zvara BJ, Schoppe-Sullivan SJ, Dush CK (2013) Fathers' involvement in child health care: associations with prenatal involvement, parents' beliefs, and maternal gatekeeping. Fam Relat 62(4):649–661

Open Access This chapter is licensed under the terms of the Creative Commons Attribution 4.0 International License (http://creativecommons.org/licenses/by/4.0/), which permits use, sharing, adaptation, distribution and reproduction in any medium or format, as long as you give appropriate credit to the original author(s) and the source, provide a link to the Creative Commons license and indicate if changes were made.

The images or other third party material in this chapter are included in the chapter's Creative Commons license, unless indicated otherwise in a credit line to the material. If material is not included in the chapter's Creative Commons license and your intended use is not permitted by statutory regulation or exceeds the permitted use, you will need to obtain permission directly from the copyright holder.

Printed in the United States
by Baker & Taylor Publisher Services